D0812734

0008908

(

PAU PRAE 99

Property Rights and
Eminent Domain

Property Rights and Eminent Domain

ELLEN FRANKEL PAUL

Transaction Books
New Brunswick (U.S.A.) and Oxford (U.K.)

Library of Congress Catalog Number: 86-16106
ISBN: 0-88738-094-8
Printed in the United States of America

Library of Congress Cataloging in Publication Data

Paul, Ellen Frankel.
  Property rights and eminent domain.

  Includes index.
  1. Right of property. 2. Right of property—
United States. 3. Eminent domain—United States.
I. Title.
JC605.P38   1986   323.4′6   86-16106
ISBN 0-88738-904-8

To the memory of my father
Edward Marvin Frankel
who inspired my interest in the law.

Contents

Acknowledgments

This book could not have been written except for the opportunity provided to me by the Hoover Institution. During the 1980-81 academic year, I served as a National Fellow at Hoover, where I greatly profited from the stimulating atmosphere and the chance to devote my full energies to research. I owe a profound debt of gratitude to W. Glenn Campbell, director of the Hoover Institution, and also to Dennis Bark.

Many individuals read and suggested improvements for earlier versions of the manuscript, and my appreciation of their efforts is heartfelt. They include James Buchanan of the Center for Study of Public Choice at George Mason University, Richard Epstein of the University of Chicago Law School, Thomas Moore and Robert Hessen of the Hoover Institution, and Fred Miller of the Social Philosophy and Policy Center at Bowling Green State University. John Gray of Oxford University and Howard Dickman deserve special thanks for their editorial suggestions for improving the final manuscript. Richard O'Reilly of the *Los Angeles Times* and Kati Corsaut of the California Coastal Commission were particularly helpful in tracking down some loose ends regarding the Sea Ranch case. Kathy Treimann, Chris Morton, Gene Humphreys, and Kory Tilgner provided valuable research assistance.

The Social Philosophy and Policy Center, which I joined as research director in the fall of 1981, provided a congenial atmosphere in which to work. Lori Morlock and Terrie Kelly, the center's indefatigable secretaries, deserve special appreciation for the prompt and accurate typing of the manuscript.

Introduction

That august political philosopher of the seventeenth century, John Locke, insisted that governments are constructed by men for one reason only, and that is to protect their property rights. He believed that the right to acquire, possess, and enjoy property is the fundamental liberty upon which all other inherent rights of life and liberty depend. The American founding fathers were deeply imbued with these Lockean notions. They, too, cherished property and the opportunity for personal development it represented. They embraced the idea that government exists to protect people's inalienable rights and should be tolerated only so long as it acts as a rights protector. In recent years these tenets have been much battered by legislative encroachments and castigated by philosophers more favorable toward state power. Still, average Americans, landowners or not, would probably endorse some variant of these Lockean principles as their own. They would entertain the conviction that when they owned a portion of this earth, they thereby possessed the right, absolutely, to exclude all others from encroaching upon it, so that they could use it, enjoy it, or dispose of it as they alone choose.

Yet, despite these beliefs of Locke and our average Americans, governments today do exercise considerable powers over how any of us can use our property. We enjoy our plots of land only so long as we pay our real estate taxes. We have come to accept zoning regulations. Sometimes we stand by helplessly while the government condemns our property and takes it for public purposes, or even gives it to other private individuals. Principally, governments in the United States exercise control over property by employing three powers: the taxing power, the police power, and the power of eminent domain.

In this book we will exclude taxation and discuss only the latter two powers, for they result in regulations and takings that fall disproportionately on certain unlucky property owners. If, for example, Jones received a property tax bill for $5,000 and Smith a bill for $1,000 even though they both owned farms assessed at the same value, everyone, including our courts, would acknowledge the inequity and a correction

3

would be made. However, if a state legislature were to invoke the police power and suddenly prohibited Brown from developing his property without the permission of several state commissions (a permission these commissions are increasingly less likely to grant), there would be no universal perception of injustice, nor would Brown be assured a sympathetic hearing by many of our courts. Similarly, if Freemont's ranch house happened to stand upon land that the city of Oxnard required for a new municipal parking garage, and the city proceeded to condemn it, no enraged citizenry would arise to defend Freemont's rights, nor would the courts come to his aid. Thus, the police power and the power of eminent domain cry out for examination, precisely because they are so uncritically accepted by citizens and jurists alike.

Those few philosophers, judges, and commentators who even recognize the need to defend the power of eminent domain generally argue that government would be inconceivable without it, that it is an "inherent" attribute of government. Most writers on eminent domain consider the power so obviously justified that even this flimsy explanation is absent from their discussions. Surely such a sweeping power—the power to confiscate a person's hard-earned property, or property that has passed to an owner through generations of labor by forebears—deserves a more compelling defense than the unabashed assertion that it constitutes an inherent attribute of sovereignty.

The power of eminent domain is nowhere expressly granted to the federal government in the Constitution, nor to the states in most state constitutions. Rather, it is circumscribed in our federal Constitution (and by similar language in state constitutions) by a portion of the Fifth Amendment that reads: "nor shall private property be taken for public use, without just compensation." These restrictions—that property can be taken only for "public use" and that all takings must be accompanied by "just compensation"—limit a power that, according to conventional wisdom, would otherwise remain boundless. As we shall discover shortly, however, the eminent domain power is hardly as innocuous as the near-universal acceptance of it would lead one to believe. Property owners dispossessed of their holdings often fail to perceive the justification for the supposed "public use" to which their property will be put by government. Others recoil at the prospect of receiving a "just compensation" that fails to compensate them for all the ancillary losses accompanying a forced sale.

As for the police power, it has become in our time the most expansible and adaptable tool by which governments of all sizes and varieties seek to control private property, property still nominally residing in the name of its owner. The police power is, yet again, considered by most theoreticians to be an "inherent" component of any state. It is the power to regulate private property for the "health, safety, morals," and, more recently, "general welfare" of the public. Particularly with the inclusion of this "general welfare" category, the police power has greatly expanded its purview. Economic rights have taken a back seat to the police power when judges have found them in conflict. Under our system of government, it is the states that possess the police power. The federal government is an institution of delegated powers and is usually not considered to possess the police power. Nevertheless, the federal government regulates property in a similar manner. It does so under its expressly granted powers: the powers to regulate interstate commerce, to provide for the general welfare, to defend the nation, and so on. The states, then, are the principal engines of police-power legislation, together with municipalities that derive their powers from the states. Usury laws, minimum wage and maximum hour legislation, zoning, no-growth policies, and statewide land-use restrictions have all been justified by invoking this nebulous police power. As we come to explore the justifications for this power and the uses to which it has been put in recent years, some alarming trends will emerge. Property rights cannot long survive legislatures that are willing to divest owners of virtually all beneficial uses of their property, certainly not if courts are willing to uphold such excesses, and legal commentators encourage them. Some police power enthusiasts have even encouraged city councils and state legislatures to expand the police power to its constitutional limit, that is, to the point where it trenches upon the Fifth Amendment's prohibition on the taking of property without payment of just compensation. Of course, I do not want to leave the false impression that the police power is a wholly unjustifiable exercise of state power. In its proper place—as a tool for prohibiting criminal activity and setting punishments for transgressions—it is eminently justifiable.

Scholarly articles on the police power and eminent domain are numerous, yet practically all of them focus upon the problem to which I have just alluded. The "taking issue," as our contemporary commentators perceive it, constitutes the heart of what is interesting about these two powers. The crucial question in the debate is when does a police power regulation become so onerous that its purpose could be constitutionally accomplished only by the exercise of the eminent domain power. For the police power, in contrast to eminent domain, requires no compensation for its proper exercise. Police power and eminent domain are pictured as though they were on a continuum. If a police power regulation goes too far in the direction of eminent domain, by depriving an owner of too much control over the property owned, it is unconstitutional.

This whole debate, I will argue, is misconceived. Rather than focusing upon this secondary issue, attention ought to focus upon the natures of the two powers themselves. Where do they come from? Can they be justified? What are their proper limitations? These lead us to even more fundamental questions. What is the nature of property? Are property rights defensible? What limitations ought to be placed on individual appropriation? Before the narrowly conceived takings issue can be resolved, all of these fundamental questions need answers.

The first chapter will examine the arguments of environmentalists in support of land-use legislation, and explore a few particularly troubling examples of the exercise of eminent domain and police powers. The rise of the environmental movement in the 1970s has had an enormous impact upon the rights of ordinary property owners, and not just the conduct of business enterprises. While the latter connection has been well documented, the former has not. Environmentalist philosophers have greatly influenced the way we can use and dispose of our land. Chapter 2 will trace the philosophical arguments for the two powers as well as their tortuous judicial history. The third chapter, in some ways the heart of the book, will examine the meaning of property rights, investigate how previous thinkers have defended these rights, and suggest a more adequate defense for them. We will see that the "takings issue" is essentially insoluble as it is now conceived. What we need to do to work ourselves out of the current morass is fundamentally to rethink the basic issues. *Ad hoc*, pragmatic decision making by the courts simply has not worked. In the concluding portion of the book, the very legitimacy of eminent domain will be questioned. The police power will emerge as a partially justifiable power, but one not sufficient for accomplishing the objectives of those who favor rigorous land-use regulation. Finally, I will offer recommendations that will move our real world closer to the ideal of pure theory.

1

Environmentalism and Property Rights

The Land-Use Battleground

Imagine that you are a skilled watch repairer who owns a small shop in a lower-middle-class, ethnically heterogeneous neighborhood in downtown Cincinnati, Ohio. You are far from wealthy, yet your modest business affords you many satisfactions, not the least of which is a long association with your customers, some of whom recall the days when your father, and even your grandfather, fixed their watches and exchanged pleasantries in this very same store. Then one day you hear disturbing rumors. The city council, which wishes to revitalize the downtown area, is contemplating a proposal from a group of out-of-state developers to construct several luxury hotels, condominiums, and office buildings. To attract this development, the city will have to offer a convenient downtown location, parking facilities, and various public services. Lamentably, the block upon which your shop now stands lies precisely at the spot where the projected redevelopment will occur. Several months later you receive a condemnation notice: your property will be taken from you. You are to receive "fair market value" and relocation costs, but no recompense for such psychic detriments as loss of business goodwill, possible loss of income due to the dismemberment of the community from which you drew your customers, and the incalculable losses associated with leaving a business you loved.[1] *This is eminent domain.*

Now imagine that you are a retired salesperson who, through hard work and thrift, has amassed enough money to purchase a lot in an attractive development along the northern coast of California. Your dream is to build a small hideaway where you can spend your declining years close to nature and free from the smog and congestion of metropolitan life. Attaining building permits for your dream house from the county does not prove insurmountable, but a seemingly insuperable obstacle lies ahead. Something relatively new, the California Coastal Commission, has different plans for your town, plans that include the provision of public beaches and public accessways. These accessways, as things turn out, must be carved out

7

of your lot. Unfortunately, your lot lies within a planned development, and you, as an individual lot owner, are subject to a deed restriction by which the homeowners' association forbids any further subdivision of your land. You are unable to accommodate the demands of the Coastal Commission for accessways across your property. Other homeowners who already have constructed homes on their lots are not at all disturbed by your predicament because the commission's moratorium on new construction does not adversely affect them. Indeed, it enhances the value of their holdings. Naturally, they are unwilling to alter the deed restrictions affecting your property. You are powerless to comply with the demands of the commission for public access, but you are prohibited from building until you do comply. You are now owner of a nearly worthless lot upon which you must continue to pay property taxes to the state of California, the very agency that rendered your property useless.[2] *This is the police power.*

These are not hyperbolic examples. Property owners throughout the United States increasingly hold their land tenuously, as "stewards" for the "public interest" rather than as absolute owners free to determine how their land shall be used, disposed of, or developed. If you own a marsh and wish to dredge and fill it to construct condominiums, you may find that state law prohibits any modification to the marsh that alters its natural state. If such filling were permitted but your land happened to fall within a state coastal zone, you would be confronted with a myriad of bureaucratic stumbling blocks. These might include local zoning commission permits, or state permits if your project had more than local impact, or forced dedication of public accessways to the ocean, or height and density restrictions to preserve scenic vistas, or possibly a requirement to construct "affordable" units for low-income people, or the entire project might be vetoed. Property owners face uncertainties, costly delays, and outright prohibitions against the development and use of "their" land. Undeniably, government has arrogated a substantial portion of what has traditionally been considered by Americans to be the prerogatives of property owners. Rather than confining its role to the protection of owners in the enjoyment of their land—that is, the role assigned to it by John Locke—government now sees its function in more interventionist if not feudal terms.

Since the mid-1960s governments in the United States have moved away from the Lockean individualism that infused the thought of our founding fathers and their earlier successors. They have enacted land-use regulations the spirit of which reflects feudal more than Lockean conceptions of land ownership. For the Englishman, John Locke, property belonged to an individual not because a king granted it to him, but because he "mixed his labor" with it and thereby transformed it into something separate and distinct from the common, unowned land in the state of nature. This view contrasts markedly with the feudal notion of property as a system of privileges imposed from the top rather than generated by individual initiative.

It is ironic that today many environmentalists explicitly reject these Lockean notions of land as an absolute dominion in favor of a nostalgic vision of duties, obligations, and a sense of community supposedly exemplified by the feudal land tenure system, that is, the system of conquerors and not of free men.[3] Environmentalists think of themselves as progressives, yet some of them feel an affinity for a reactionary system; this is puzzling. E.F. Roberts, to cite just one example, enthusiastically embraces a return to a more feudalistic conception of landholding. In "The Demise of Property Law," he writes:

> We may yet choose a new praxis. Zoning and local government devices demonstrably have not worked very well to control haphazard development and urban sprawl. . . . that is, we might choose to socialize land, at least on the urban fringes, and then either keep it in public ownership, leasing it back to private use, or sell it back to private use at a subsidized price after stamping it with covenants locking it into regional master plans. . . . within the traditions of property law, moreover, there is nothing particularly radical in visualizing land being owned by the sovereign and being channelled out again to persons who would hold it only as long as they performed the requisite duties which went with the land. In this instance, of course, instead of knighthood service, the landholder would have to hold and use his parcel according to the purposes set forth in the regional or statewide master plan.[4]

Thomas Jefferson presumably would be aggrieved at our calm acceptance of a slide back toward a feudal notion of the state as ultimate authority over the use and disposition of land. As a shaper of the Northwest Ordinance and the Virginia Constitution, Jefferson vigorously contended for the abolition of all remnants of the feudal landholding system. He argued in favor of allodial ownership instead, ownership in which estates would be held in absolute dominion free of any feudalistic obligations to one's lord or the state. Such feudal remnants as primogeniture and entail were anathema to him as badges of serfdom imposed upon free Saxons after the Norman Conquest. It was precisely this conception of property as the prerogative of the state, to be dispensed at the discretion and pleasure of William the Conqueror and his successors, whether kings or states, that Jefferson abhorred.[5] If the state held ultimate ownership of all land, then it could at any time reduce any man to penury, or worse, to serfdom, as William had dealt with the vanquished Saxon freeholders after the Battle of Hastings. Then, surely, no man could long remain secure in his freedom.

Most proponents of an expanded state role in determining land use do not see themselves as embracing a return to feudalism. Rather, they focus upon the supposed waste and environmental degradation foisted upon society by rapacious developers who are concerned only with profits and care nothing for the welfare of future generations. To replace these individual market decisions, they advocate some form of state or national land-use policy that will collectivize decision making while leaving the ownership of property in private hands. To go further than this and urge outright land nationalization would, of course, be nearly suicidal as a political strategy, given the American hostility toward anything that overtly smacks of socialism. However, it is possible to imagine that the current process may one day lead to the same result. First, property owners are denied portions of their decision-making powers through such devices as local zoning or state planning in areas of critical environmental concern. Gradually even that amount of control seems insufficient, and property owners suddenly find their land declared a scenic treasure, which they may never develop. Eventually, the rights of property ownership may become so eviscerated that explicit land nationalization will seem politically acceptable.

To recognize the credibility of such a scenario one need only examine the land-use legislation passed by the federal government in recent years, all of which extends governmental control over decisions previously left to individuals. Should the market provide housing or should the state intervene? With a whole series of legislative acts—from the Housing Act of 1949, to the Demonstration Cities and Metropolitan Development Act of 1966, to the Fair Housing Act of 1968, to the Urban Growth and New Community Development Act of 1970, to the Housing and Community Development Act of 1974—the federal government has become a direct provider of housing.[6] It also subsidized nearly all new apartment complexes, encourages the destruction of old neighborhoods via urban renewal and, later block grants to localities,[7] and mandates standards of racial impartiality in the rental and sale of housing. Is the quality of our environment a private, local, or state concern, or is it a federal problem? Again, the policies pursued in the past fifteen years have resoundingly shifted the balance in the direction of federal involvement. A few of the most conspicuous federal efforts are the Clean Air Acts of 1963 and 1970, the National Environmental Policy Act of 1969, the establishment of the Environmental Protection Agency in 1970 and the Council on Environmental Quality in 1969, the Water Quality Act of 1965 (which created the federal Water Pollution Control Administration), the far more rigorous federal Water Pollution Control Act Amendments of 1972 (which mandated the eradication of all pollution in navigable waters by 1985), and the Solid Waste Disposal Act of 1968. Should landowners control the use of their marshes, beaches, bogs, and coastal land or should the federal government? Again, recent policy decisions have shifted the locus of control from individuals and local government to Washington. The Federal Coastal Zone Management Act of 1972 called for statewide planning for coastal conservation, with the federal government paying 80 percent of the planning bill.[8]

As this sampling of federal legislative initiatives indicates, the early 1970s spawned an elaborate apparatus of controls over the use of land, water, and air. Even more notable than the successes of those who favor greater control over land use was their one conspicuous legislative failure: the attempt to enact a national land-use policy. A pronouncement by President Richard Nixon in 1970 illustrates the sentiment behind that attempt:

> Today we are coming to realize that our land is finite, while our population is growing. The uses to which our generation puts the land can either expand or severely limit the choices our children will have. The time has come when we must accept the idea that none of us has a right to abuse the land, and that on the contrary society as a whole has a legitimate interest in proper land use. There is a national interest in effective land use planning across the nation.[9]

From 1971 to 1975 the Nixon administration's bill competed with another one introduced in the Senate by Henry Jackson and in the House by Morris Udall. The intent of the two proposals was roughly similar. Both bills envisioned federal funding on a modest scale ($800 million over eight years in Jackson-Udall; $100 million over five years in the administration bill). The money would be used to promote or mandate (depending on which version of the two bills one inspects) state land-use planning, with the federal government ultimately judging the adequacy of the state plans. Under the Nixon proposal, states that did not qualify for the planning grants would be penalized by reductions in their federal grants for highways, airports, and recreational facilities. Both proposals justified national land-use planning on the ground that areas of critical environmental concern needed immediate protection. The Jackson bill passed the Senate in 1972, but failed in the House. In 1974 a version of the same bill died in the House on a 211 to 204 vote.[10]

It is difficult to suppose that if these plans had been adopted matters would have ended there. As Bernard Siegan observed, the penchant for regulation, once appeased, takes on a driving force of its own.

> Few, if any of the benefits that better planning and more regulation are supposed to bring about will actually occur. . . . The expectations created by the rhetoric will remain just expectations. The usual pattern emerges anew. The existing legislation will be condemned as inadequate, and new and more restrictive legislation will be sought and probably obtained. A greater federal role will continue to evolve as each new legislative version fails again to meet the expectations of the rhetoric. The same people will find that the landscape and the buildings are still not beautiful and that housing problems still re-

main. The chronology of local zoning will be repeated; the failure of existing land use controls leads down the Parkinsonian path to more, or more severe, controls, not less, or less stringent, ones.[11]

We were prevented from taking the first step down this path by a handful of votes in the House of Representatives.

But the environmentalist activism of the past few years has not been limited to shifting the locus of control over land use to the federal government. Of equal or even greater impact has been the veritable flood of state land-use programs. These seek to supersede local zoning authorities and regulate land that falls into the nebulous category of land involving "state-wide concern." The earliest and most comprehensive of these efforts began in Hawaii in 1961, when all property was subjected to statewide zoning in an attempt to preserve the state's agricultural land. All land within the state was assigned to one of three, later four, categories: conservation, agriculture, urban, and rural. Any developers seeking a change in the status of their land were required to seek a variance from the State Land Commission. Not surprisingly, land and housing costs have escalated dramatically in Hawaii. Although other factors such as population growth undoubtedly contributed to the increase, extensive land-use regulation played a significant role.

Other states, including Colorado, Florida, Minnesota, Nevada, Oregon, Wyoming, and Vermont have enacted comprehensive statewide mechanisms for regulating so-called critical areas. Vermont presents a particularly interesting case. In 1970 the legislature passed the Vermont Environmental Control Act (Act 250), which mandated state oversight of large-scale developments (over ten units). It established environmental standards and created regional commissions to administer a permit system. In addition, a plan for what amounted to statewide land classification was initiated. As a further indicant of the strength of antidevelopment sentiment in the state, the legislature in 1973 enacted a special capital gains tax on land speculation. The final stage of Act 250 was supposed to be a state land-use plan designating permissible densities on all land. A map was published that showed how each landowner's holdings were to be regulated, with 80 percent of the land designated for construction of no more than one dwelling per twenty-five to one hundred acres. An uproar ensued, and the legislature failed to enact the plan. This experience has led some environmental activists to warn against such foolhardy explicitness, and to advise keeping landowners in the dark until they are confronted with a *fait accompli*.[12]

Various states have pursued regulatory policies directed at particularly sensitive areas. New York designated the Adirondack Park area in 1971 as an environmentally sensitive area. Massachusetts regulates land use on Martha's Vineyard. California established the San Francisco Bay Area Conservation and Development Commission. Nevada and California jointly administer the Tahoe Regional Planning Agency. Underlying all of these regional programs is a conviction that local zoning has not functioned adequately, and that the state must supersede local control where it does exist, or create new controls (such as in rural areas like the Adirondack Park) where little if any governmental supervision previously operated.[13]

If one were an uninformed observer and simply contemplated the volume of federal and state legislative initiatives that have extended government regulation over land since the late 1960s, one might suspect that virtually nothing had been done in the past on the local level to control land use: that, in effect, a truly free market operated in land; that one could use one's land, develop it, or even destroy its value with utter abandon. Given the picture of the voracious developer, oblivious to social concerns that many environmentalists embrace, one might conclude that the land-use campaign of recent vintage was operating *de novo*. But this conclusion would be wrong. In fact, local control over the use of land has been a decisive force in shaping our land-use patterns since the early twentieth century. If we have unsightly strips of garish neon lighting, if we have cities congested by high-rise office buildings, if we have suburban sprawl and neighborhoods in which it is impossible to do your shopping without hopping into your car—all phenomena castigated by environmentalists—then zoning can take its fair share of the blame.

But local control over land has not been limited to zoning. Municipalities regulate or prohibit the erection of billboards, either on the basis of public health or safety, or more recently on purely aesthetic grounds. They have declared certain districts as historic, prohibiting future alterations in their appearance, usually under a theory that the police power is broad enough to cover the maintenance of endangered architectural treasures. More recently cities such as Boca Raton, Florida, have enacted growth moratoria in an attempt to squelch the influx of outsiders into their attractive neighborhoods and relieve the strain on public services. They also wish to preserve the natural amenities that attracted those already admitted. Other cities have declared wide swatches of their vacant land as "open space," and have prohibited all uses except agricultural ones.

Although the focus of this study is upon the twin governmental powers of eminent domain and police, on the legitimacy of both, and the demarcation between them, our gaze must be broader than this. To comprehend fully the influences on judges and legislators, one must examine the environmentalists' arguments. Environmentalists have been very successful in dramatizing their cause, and their influence upon legal writers dealing with the police power and its proper limits is in no small part responsible for the wave of environmental legislation and for the generally sympathetic review of it by the courts. Land-use regulation of one sort or another is of ancient vintage, and zoning has been practiced in the United States since the early years of this century. But what makes the arguments of the environmentalists so important is that they have argued for far more drastic solutions than conventional zoning. Although the full, radical implications of some of their proposals have not been realized, they have greatly influenced public debate and the minds of judges.

Environmentalism: The Battle over Who Should Control the Land

> Air and water can be cleaned up and recycled, even if at great cost to society, but once prime agricultural land is paved, estuaries filled, or wetlands drained, little can be done to undo the results. Moreover, the pattern of land use in this country contributes to the loss of valuable open space and to the wasteful consumption of energy.
>
> Problems arise because land use decisions are generally determined by the unrestricted forces of the market.[14]

This pronouncement by Morris Udall, made during the early 1970s when his plan for a national land-use policy remained a live issue, succinctly captures the suppositions shared by most environmental activists: that man's artifacts and civilization threaten the environment; that our limited "spaceship earth's" finite resources are being eroded; that pollution threatens life on earth and must be eradicated at great cost; and that the root cause of all these impending disasters lies in the "unrestricted forces of the market." Others sound equally alarming themes. A human population explosion threatens the earth and lower forms of life as it multiplies, wildly out of control.[15] The conclusion is that individual free choice must be supplanted by "mutual control, mutually agreed upon," to paraphrase Garrett Hardin's formulation in his famous article, "The Tragedy of the Commons." Property, too, must be redefined, so that the pollution engendered by a combination of the free enterprise system and a burgeoning population does not succeed in befouling "our nest."[16] In other words, even in the most private of decisions, whether to reproduce, the state ought to intervene. Why? What disaster impends if we ignore the warnings of the neo-Malthusians?

The Club of Rome attracted considerable media attention in 1972 when it employed computer modeling techniques to project current trends into the twenty-first century. The result was a purportedly scientific prediction of doomsday.[17] Founded in 1968 by a wealthy Italian industrialist, this international group of experts in diverse fields shared a common belief, namely, that the world was on the brink of a disaster of immense proportions. The harbingers of this disaster were such worldwide problems as "poverty in the midst of plenty, degradation of the environment, loss of faith in institutions, uncontrolled urban spread, insecurity of employment, alienation of youth, rejection of traditional values, and inflation and other monetary disorders."[18] Employing a "world model" devised by Professor Jay W. Forrester of the Massachusetts Institute of Technology, the group extended five trends to their ineluctable conclusions: accelerating industrialization, rapid population growth, widespread malnutrition, depletion of unrenewable resources, and deterioration of the environment. As each trend was plotted, the noose tightened. Even when seemingly hopeful developments, such as the green revolution in agriculture or future technological innovations, were factored in, they only delayed or even exacerbated the final collapse. The green revolution would produce even more uncontrollable population growth, for example, and technological inventions would increase pollution, thus causing a calamitous fall in population. If, on the other hand, pollution were controlled, then collapse would occur as a result of food shortage. Each glimmer of hope that one could imagine was systematically expunged.

Still, the club's members did not close out all possibility of avoiding disaster. They concluded that although "the basic behavior mode of the world system is exponential growth of population and capital, followed by collapse," there remained a scintilla of hope. Collapse might be avoided through the establishment of supernational economic controls. National planning alone would be fruitless. Only through a worldwide effort could a "state of global equilibrium" be designed that would provide the basic material needs to each person on earth and secure to each an "equal opportunity to realize his individual human potential."[19] The policies that they recommended to avoid collapse consisted of a panoply of controls over individuals. Population would have to be stabilized, as would the amount of industrial capital. Resource consumption would be limited to one-fourth of its level in 1970. Economic preferences would be shifted to services rather than factory-produced goods. Pollution would be reduced to one-quarter of its level in 1970. Developed countries would have to decelerate their growth and assist developing nations. The club did not specify how these goals were to be achieved, but such policies clearly would require the superannuation of national sovereignty and the control of everyone's life by omnipotent world designers.

Critics vigorously objected to the computer modeling techniques employed by the Club of Rome. "Garbage in, garbage out" was a frequently repeated complaint. The report relied heavily on quotations from John Stuart Mill on his halcyon vision of a future "stationary state" (the same state much dreaded by Ricardo and Malthus) where people, undiverted by the distractions of wealth production and lust after profits, would be free to seek higher aesthetic and moral goals. Had not the club done nothing more than provide graphs and computer printouts, mere window dressing on the doomsday prophecies of the British classical economists of the nineteenth century? David Ricardo and, of course, Robert Malthus projected imminent stultification for the capitalist system. Obviously, they erred, for they mistook the beginnings of the capitalist revolution in production for its final state of collapse. But unlike their contemporary counterparts of the Club of Rome, they did not follow these predictions with calls for a regulated, collectivized world order.[20] In fact, they argued that such measures would only hasten and exacerbate the misery of the stationary state. That the human condition could somehow be improved by controlling human enterprise and decision making was an idea repugnant to the original Malthusians.

Considering today's examples of controlled societies, the Soviet Union and its satellites (with their perpetual shortages of food due to "bad weather" and their bread lines and rationing), one suspects that regulation on a global scale might accelerate the approach of any cataclysm that lies in the future. One need only reflect upon the effects of the recent deregulation of oil in the United States to see the error of the doomsdayers' remedies. Suddenly, oil gushed from the most unlikely places; Wyoming's desolate landscape sprouted oil derricks, and dirt farmers in Louisiana reaped windfalls from oil leases. If the policies advocated by the Club of Rome had been instituted by the Malthusians of the last century we might well be living in a "stationary state" of unremitting child labor, pestilence and disease, and mass starvation. The evidence of history contradicts the club's assertion that "historically mankind's long record of new inventions has resulted in crowding, deterioration of the environment, and greater social inequality." Perhaps we are but at the beginning of a new technological age that will transform and improve life for humankind even more than the industrial revolution did for our forebears. The remarkable advances in computer technology, robotics, and genetic engineering make this a real possibility. One fears that if society adopts the recommendations of the authors of the Club of Rome report this creative leap will be forestalled.[21]

The economist Julian L. Simon, to mention just one critic, in his book *The Ultimate Resource*, has presented a compelling critique of the doomsayers' presuppositions and predictions.[22] He denies that a burgeoning population threatens worldwide starvation. Rather, he argues, that as industrialization progresses, the birthrate declines because children become a net economic liability. Even if this were not the case, increased numbers, rather than simply dividing a preordained pie of commodities into even smaller morsels, can produce more goods. More people can augment the stock of human knowledge, thus enhancing everyone's well-being. As regards the popular view that resources are limited and non-renewable and, consequently, that disaster looms if we refuse to contract our wasteful consumption patterns, Simon argues that, on the contrary, resources are discovered as they are needed. He cites projections from the early 1900s that purveyed similar warnings about imminent resource depletion. Historically, technological innovations have lowered the cost of mineral extraction, and Simon sees no reason to doubt that such will be the case in the future. Likewise, he finds the "spaceship-earth" analogy misleading; he points to the immense amount of matter constituting the earth, and notes that we still know very little about the earth's contents.[23]

The ecological nightmare—as represented in the Club of Rome report and in the "Global 2000 Report" published by the United States government in 1980—predicted by environmentalists has been contested by many scientists and economists, yet these views still carry great weight. For this reason the philosophical assumptions of the movement and their implication for land-use policy still need to be examined. Fundamental to the views of those on the more extreme fringe of the environmentalist movement is a rejection of many fundamental Western values. Both Christianity and the Greek tradition emanating from Aristotle placed the human race at the focus of moral concern and atop the hierarchy of earthly beings. Environmentalist thinkers such as the lawyer Lawrence Tribe and the philosopher Peter Singer reject this "homeocentric" perspective.[24] Singer contends that such "specieism" ought to be as repugnant to us as white racism or sexism, and that any creature that experiences pleasure and pain (and has an interest in seeking the former and avoiding the latter) ought to count for something in our moral calculus. The notion of the supremacy of our species should be replaced by a "humility of species," to quote Lynn White's phrase. Western man, no longer the focus of moral concern, ought to learn from the Zen Buddhists, Asian mystics, and ancient pagans who knew how to live in harmony with nature and nature's laws. We should bridge the dualism of the human race and nature foisted upon us by Christianity and Aristotelianism. Atomistic individualism also must be rejected. It should be replaced by a holism that acknowledges our interrelationship with the rest of the natural order. Kenneth Goodpaster writes in his "From Egoism to Environmentalism":

> The oft-repeated plea by some ecologists and environmentalists that our thinking needs to be less atomistic and more "holistic" translates in the

present context into a plea for a more embracing object of moral considera-tion. In a sense it represents a plea to return to a richer Greek conception of man by nature social and not intelligibly removable from his social and political context though it goes beyond the Greek conception in emphasizing that societies too need to be understood in a context, an ecological context, and that it is this larger whole that is the "bearer of value."[25]

This effort to expunge anthropomorphism has its price, as some ecolo-gical advocates frankly admit, but they seem sanguine enough about this price that will have to be paid in the form of a lower standard of living. "For my part," Christopher Stone concedes, "I would prefer a frank avowal that even making adjustments for esthetic improvements, what I am proposing is going to cost us, i.e., reduce our standard of living as measured in terms of our present values."[26] This animus against Western civilization, its mate-rial abundance, its artifacts, and its technology, has prompted some, like J. Baird Callicott, to favor a return to a more "tribal ethic":

This means. . . the reappraisal of the comparatively recent values and con-cerns of "civilized" *Homo sapiens* in terms of our "savage" ancestors. . . . The land ethic requires a shrinkage, if at all possible, of the domestic sphere; it rejoices in a recrudescence of wilderness and a renaissance of tribal cultural experience.[27]

As a corollary to this holistic, antihomeocentric view, the extreme en-vironmentalists abhor the products of the mind, technological abilities that enable the human race to overmaster nature and mold nature to its vision. Technology, rather than being the vehicle for the ascent from savagery, is the bane of all life on earth. Lynn White illustrates the tone of this con-tempt for the artifacts of reason when he writes: "With the population explosion, the carcinoma of planless urbanism, the new geological deposits of sewage and garbage, surely no creature other than man has ever man-aged to foul its nest in such short order."[28]

The values shared by such hard-core environmentalists—holism and a condemnation of individualism, rejection of the view that humanity stands at the pinnacle of nature, denial of the dualism of man and nature, and hostility to technological progress—amounts to a repudiation of the values that inspired the founders of our nation. In their scorn for the faith in progress born of the European Enlightenment,[29] they condemn people, particularly those still living in poverty, to an even more degraded status in the future. It is no wonder, then, that critics of this atavistic worldview have attacked it as elitist and antihumanitarian, as the musings of upper-middle-class intellectuals who are more concerned for rocks and trees than for the inhabitants of Harlem or Watts.[30] These charges are particularly compelling in the face of certain remarks by Garrett Hardin, a respected figure among environmentalists. Society should not rescue a beleaguered wilderness adventurer, Hardin maintains, because the world has an abundance of people. Polluting the wilderness through helicopter rescue flights would constitute a greater loss than the death of one more supererogatory person. Starving nations, he adds, ought not be aided for the same reason: overpopulation.[31]

To categorize these philosophical tenets as anti-Western does not refute them, but an examination of the arguments of several leading environmentalists will illustrate some of the internal problems with their value system. Whether their arguments emerge from a belief in rights or from a utilitarian foundation, their extension of moral status to beings and objects other than persons leads to contradictions. To attempt to apply their values to real-world policy decisions would be chaotic.

Aldo Leopold and the Radicals

The most radical wing of the environmentalist philosophers takes its inspiration from Aldo Leopold and his "land ethic," which he enunciated in 1949 in his *A Sand County Almanac*.[32] These thinkers wish to extend value or rights to nonconscious entities, thus extending the purview of moral consideration beyond humans and animals to include plants, rocks, streams, oceans, and the atmosphere. Although it would be wrong to suppose that all environmentalists fall into this category, the radicals do in a sense set the agenda. By establishing the far reaches of the environmentalists' stance, they make less extreme positions appear moderate.

Leopold's "land ethic," assertedly an "evolutionary possibility and an ecological necessity," was designed to release "land," meaning all of nature, from its shackles as mankind's "slave-girl" and raise it to equal moral status. His system emphasizes our obligations to nature rather than our privilege to rule over it as mere property. His conception of an interdependent "biotic community" was definitely not human-centered. Consequently, he disparaged the efforts of others who pursued the conservation of nature motivated by an ethic based principally upon human or economic concerns. He argued that all members of the "biotic community" ought to be preserved as ends in themselves rather than as means to fulfill human needs. Species with no discernible economic value should continue undisturbed as a matter of pure "biotic right." Leopold sounded a note destined to be repeated by his intellectual heirs when he wrote: "It is clear without further discussion that mass-use involves a direct dilution of the opportunity for solitude; that when we speak of roads, campgrounds, trails, and toilets as 'development' of recreational resources, we speak falsely . . . such accommodations for the crowd are not developing (in the sense of adding or creating) anything. On the contrary, they are merely water poured into the already-thin soup."[33] Elitism and contempt for middle-class pleasures, as mere recreation of the masses, seem to be clear implications of Leopold's position. What is even more indicative of future environmentalistic argumentation is a seemingly irresolvable contradiction: how are we to combine the rights of biotic creatures and entities with the undeniable need of humans to use nature for their own ends, the most conspicuous being the need for food? Leopold, himself an avid hunter, seems to have impaled himself upon the horn of a dilemma of his own making.[34]

Typical of the quest for a true "environmental ethic" among Aldo Leopold's heirs, are the writings of Tom Regan, particularly his article "The Nature and Possibility of an Environmental Ethic." Regan categorically rejects what he calls the "human interest principle": "Whenever human beings can benefit more from overriding the preservation principle than if they observe it, the preservation principle ought to be overridden."[35] For Regan, the preservation principle, which is not clearly defined, ought to take precedence over humans' needs and objectives. He sees the "human interest principle" as a distortion of the inherent goodness of the "preservation principle." Instead, he attempts to extirpate all human valuation from environmental ethics. This new ethic, he argues, must postulate that nonconscious natural objects can have value in their own right, independent of human interests. From this undefended postulate, Regan attempts to demonstrate that all conscious beings, and *some* nonconscious beings must be held to possess "moral standing." It is precisely at this juncture that Regan's chain of reasoning falls apart; for how can one distinguish nonconscious entities that have "moral standing" from those that do not, once Regan removes the human evaluator from his central role in ethics?

Let us examine Regan's attempt to surmount this difficulty. He contends that certain natural entities possess "inherent goodness" because they partake of an "inherent value," a value independent of any awareness, interest, or appreciation of it on the part of any conscious being.[36] They lay claim to such value, Regan insists, because of the properties they exhibit. Their "inherent value" is an objective property: "Certain stretches of the Colorado River, for example, are free not subjectively, but objectively. The freedom expressed by (or in) the river is an objective fact . . . *the value of the river's being free* also is an objective property of the river."[37] How ought people to react to natural objects that have "inherent value"? With, Regan thinks, "admiring respect," a respect that leads inexorably to the "preservation principle." This principle states that one ought not interfere with, destroy, or meddle with such natural objects. "One must realize that its being valuable is not contingent on one's happening to value it, so that to treat it *merely* as a means to human ends is to mistreat it."

However, to make any sense at all out of his position, Regan resorts, in the final analysis, to employing precisely the standard of human valuation that he earlier banished from the realm of environmental ethics: "Thus, if *I regard* wild stretches of the Colorado River as inherently valuable and *regard* these sections with admiring respect, *I also think* it wrong to destroy these sections of the river. *I think* one ought not to meddle in the river's affairs, as it were" (emphasis added).[38] Notice what has transpired here. Suddenly the human valuer is "regarding" and "thinking," that is, passing value judgments of precisely the sort that Regan had previously excluded. Perhaps such an illicit borrowing was unavoidable, given Regan's admission that he has not answered the crucial questions, namely, how do we know that anything is inherently good, and what in general makes something inherently good? Nevertheless, such an obvious employment of concepts borrowed from the anthropocentric position that he is attempting to disprove seriously damages his own position. And is it not peculiar to speak of rivers having "affairs"? Does not this concept make sense only when applied to conscious beings who possess the faculty of rational choice, who can make decisions and implement them, who are not merely driven by natural forces over which they have no control and cannot even comprehend because they lack the faculty of awareness? Has not Regan infused natural objects with human characteristics in his vain attempt to remove human valuation from its pivotal role in ethics? Has he not anthropomorphized rocks and rivers while dehumanizing man?

In Christopher Stone's influential piece, "Should Trees Have Standing?—Towards Legal Rights for Natural Objects," we can discern what may be one motive behind arguments such as these. He proposes to grant legal rights to forests, oceans, rivers, and other natural objects in the environment, and "indeed, to the natural environment as a whole." While conceding that such rights might seem anomalous, at least initially, he points to earlier bequests of rights to inanimate entities that seemed strange in their time: to corporations, and to trusts. Stone finds the state of the common law in respect to natural objects defective, and he offers the following example as an illustration. In deciding whether an upper riparian (a riparian owner owns land adjacent to a river) should compensate a lower riparian for pollution damage, courts weigh the economic hardship this would inflict upon the upper riparian against the cost of the continued pollution to the lower riparian. Yet the courts never take into account the damage to the stream, or fish, or turtles; because these entities have no legal standing, they are never awarded damages to repair themselves.

Because turtles are patently incapable of pleading their case at bar, what recourse should they be granted? Just as human incompetents are assigned guardians by the courts to speak for their interests, so natural objects, according to Stone, ought to be granted guardians upon the request of environmental groups. Stone writes:

> If for example, the Environmental Defense Fund should have reason to believe that some company's strip mining operations might be irreparably destroying the ecological balance of large tracts of land, it could, under this procedure, apply to the court in which the land were situated to be appointed guardian. As guardian, it might be given rights of inspection (or visitation) to determine and bring to the court's attention a fuller finding on the land's condition. If there were indications that under the substantive law some redress might be available on the land's behalf, then the guardian would be entitled to raise the land's rights in the land's name, i.e., without having to make the roundabout and often unavailing demonstration . . . that the "rights" of the club's members were being invaded.[39]

Clearly, the traditional rights of property owners would be rendered precarious if not entirely vitiated by any such extension of legal guardianship over natural objects to environmentalists. Can I build a house upon "my" land, can I fill or dredge "my" wetland, can I mine "my" coal? All such previously private decisions could be held hostage to appeals by environmentalists to the courts, raising such "injuries not presently cognizable as the death of eagles and inedible crabs, the suffering of sea lions, the loss from the face of the earth of species of commercially valueless birds. . . ."[40] Property rights would be threatened for the sake of values that cannot even be measured, and for values irrelevant to human welfare: "inedible crabs" and "commercially valueless birds."

Stone's attempt to resolve the problems of (1) the extent of rights that should be granted to natural objects, and (2) how to weigh the value of transgressions against these rights takes a bizarre turn. He begins soberly enough, by noting that granting rights to trees does not imply that people can never fell trees. He admits that not all entities in the environment should have the same rights, and he offers a rather nebulous solution to these problems of determining the extent of rights and the proper recompense for transgression against them. What he aims at is clear enough—he wants polluters to pay, not only for the homeocentric costs of their lapses but also for the "costs to the environment *per se*." After interjecting the remark that, of course, the latter costs are "priceless," he proposes a second-best solution, which would equal the cost of making the environment whole again. Factored in, additionally, would be a monetary value attached to the suffering of displaced or exterminated sentient creatures. So, damages would be assessed upon the polluter and, in cases where the social need for a polluting activity was high enough to overbalance all homeocentric and environmental costs, the polluter might be allowed to continue the activity but would have to pay damages to a trust fund for the environment. The bizarre element slips in when Stone suggests that the environment itself might bear liability for its own misdeeds, paying recompense out of its trust fund for floods, say, or earthquakes.

This cost-benefit solution to evaluating transgressions is problematic enough, but it also fails to resolve the far more difficult question of what rights natural objects hold against human transgressors. Particularly unhelpful is his suggestion that National Environmental Protection Act-type environmental impact statements should be required of corporations whose actions might impinge upon nature, and that all corporations should be required by law to appoint, at their own expense, a vice president for ecological affairs. No guidance is provided as regards the substantive rights enjoyed by sea lions or estuaries. The closest that Stone comes to providing such a standard is his admonition that in instances in which irreparable damage would be inflicted upon the environment no cost-benefit or balancing test should be employed. Instead, such activities should be absolutely proscribed. For all other cases, courts would be given the discretion to apply their balancing test, a rather imprecise and arbitrary method. To instruct judges to render the components of their calculus explicit, as Stone does, still fails to provide judges with a standard by which to determine the extent of a tree's rights as against a logger's. Just as judges now choose to protect certain rights of humans as "preferred rights," Stone wishes them to devise a list of "preferred objects." Would this not result in the trivialization of the concept of the rule of law?

Stone completes his attempt to enshrine legal rights for natural objects with a refrain typical of the extreme environmentalists. He states that humans must desist from their wasteful ways by suppressing their standard of living and by stabilizing their numbers, the latter to be achieved by individuals relinquishing their right to produce as many offspring as they like. Humankind must be controlled, even in the most private of human domains, that of giving life to children.

Trees No, Animals Yes: The Animal Liberationists

While the "land-ethic" advocates hold down the extreme wing of the environmentalist movement, another, sightly less globalistic group, has received equal if not greater attention. These thinkers share some of the basic attitudes of their more radical compatriots—denial of an anthropocentric ethic, loathing of technology, and so on—yet they do not wish to extend our ethical purview beyond sentient beings. For them it is enough to demonstrate that animals have rights without extending the argument to trees and rocks. These "animal liberationists," whether they present a utilitarian or rights defense, all concur in the belief that animals have either rights or, some say, interests that should be taken into account by human beings in their moral calculations.[41] If animals do have rights, then this fact places bounds upon human action, the most conspicuous one being the proscription against the consumption of animal flesh. Animal liberationists are avowed vegetarians.

Peter Singer espouses a utility-based animal-liberationist ethic, one that grants moral consideration to all creatures that have the capacity to suffer and to feel pain. This capacity for consciousness eliminates such things as trees, and probably insects, crustaceans, mollusks, and vegetables from moral relevance. To all other beings that have consciousness and at least one interest—specifically an interest in experiencing pleasure and avoiding pain—this interest entitles them to a certain amount of consideration in any utilitarian calculus. But does this entail that all beings possessed of an interest should count equally? Singer thinks not:

> Giving equal consideration to the interests of two different beings does not mean treating them alike or holding their lives to be of equal value. We may recognize that the interests of one being are greater than those of another, and equal consideration will then lead us to sacrifice the being with lesser interests, if one or the other must be sacrificed.[42]

Singer offers an example of a situation in which one is forced to choose between saving a man or saving a dog when both cannot be rescued. He argues that one ought to save the man because having greater awareness he would suffer more before dying than would the dog. Moreover his family would suffer, and he has greater potential for future happiness. However, things can get messy if certain assumptions are altered: "In a different situation—say, if the human were grossly mentally defective and without family or anyone else who would grieve for it—the balance of interests might favor the nonhuman."[43]

Singer's moral arithmetic encounters some of the same problems that have driven many philosophers to abandon utilitarianism. First, how do you quantify pleasure and pain? That is, how do you place a value upon Adolphe's enjoyment of apple pie or his pain upon stubbing his big toe? Second, how do you make interpersonal comparisons of utility among humans, let alone between animals and humans? Singer admits this "difficulty of comparison," yet all he offers us as guidance are very rough rules of thumb, such as that the killing of nonhuman animals is not as significant as the killing of normal humans. A hypothetical example will illustrate the problem with Singer's scheme. Imagine a scenario in which one human would have to be sacrificed to preserve the lives of twenty-five buffaloes (let us say the human is an Indian hunter who will slay the buffaloes if not killed himself). The inadequacy of the utilitarian apparatus is apparent. How many "utiles" does a buffalo's life represent? What if buffaloes are an endangered species, does their value as represented by "utiles" increase? And how do we value the life of the Indian? Such a system might conceivably condone the murder of the Indian to save the buffaloes, a rather unsettling deduction from an ethical system. Even worse, every philosopher employing this utilitarian calculus would arrive at different valuations for buffalo and human lives. Their judgments would depend upon their own personal preferences. In other words, the utilitarian apparatus appears to be unworkable.

Those who argue for animal liberation from a rights foundation fare no better. Typically, such an argument proceeds by ascribing rights to animals, the proponent having failed to discover any attribute or faculty that so distinguishes people from animals that people would have rights while animals would not. Here, again, a problem arises when the animal's rights would have to be overridden, perhaps to prevent a much greater harm to other animals or to people. It is not clear whose rights ought to take precedence, the animal's or the human's, and under what circumstances. However, a more fundamental problem confronts the rights-based animal liberationist. How can humans share an ethical standing on equal terms with animals when animals lack the understanding necessary to obey ethical precepts? Does a shark evaluate the weights of competing rights considerations before it attacks and bites off an approaching surfer's foot? Does a grizzly bear consider the harm to itself of forsaking dinner versus the harm inflicted on campers by being eaten; does it consider whether its right overrides theirs before proceeding to attack? These examples illustrate the fundamental problem with entering into a rights nexus with beings who do not have the capacity to respect the rights of others. While it is undoubtedly true that not all humans strongly adhere to a moral precept that recognizes the right to life of all other humans—indeed, there are murderers and even cannibals among the human race—yet all human beings, with the exception of the cretinous or the vegetative, have the *potential* of respecting the rights of others. Thus, humans can be given the benefit of the doubt (until shown to be transgresssors) in a way that a shark, a grizzly bear, or a coyote cannot.[44] Thus, if a rights position were defensible, it would make good sense to limit rights to those beings who have the capacity to respect the rights of others. Rights would be limited to humankind, and perhaps to extraterrestrial beings who might someday be encountered and who share our capacity to promulgate, understand, and observe moral rules.

A Dwindling Band of Moderate Ecologists

To complete our survey of environmentalist philosophies, we must mention another position, probably the least favored by activists but the most influential with the general public. This position might be called the "right wing" of the ecological movement. These thinkers, relatively few in number, reject the Weltanschauung of their more radical colleagues and seek to preserve endangered species or threatened biosystems from an avowedly anthropocentric standpoint.[45] They view other species and nature itself through a human prism. Other entities have value only because they are currently valued by people or because they may hold some future use for humankind. Although they reject the two more extreme versions of environmentalism—which both necessitate the sacrifice of human betterment in deference to the well-being of nonhuman entities—they nevertheless do not repair to a laissez-faire position as regards humans' use of the earth and its creatures. Rather, they endorse environmental legislation that seeks to control people's discretion over the use of their property. Government, according to them, has a legitimate role to play as arbiter, to determine exactly which natural objects and species ought to be preserved for their future utility to humankind. Although more reasonable than other environmental philosophies, this position still grants to government decision-making power in an area where personal values decree the result rather than hard, scientific evidence. How are officials to determine the value of a wetlands, for example, when no market competition informs their decision, and they must rely upon their personal understanding of the "public interest"?[46]

The Environmentalists' Influence

These environmentalist ideas have played a seminal part in influencing legislators, judges, and legal theorists. Through judicial decisions environmentalist ideas have eroded property rights. This connection between ecological thought and the law can be seen most clearly in a study by the Task Force on Land and Urban Growth published in 1972 by the Citizens' Advisory Committee on Urban Growth, a body established by presidential order in 1969. The study, *The Use of Land: A Citizen's Policy Guide to Urban Growth*, was sponsored by the Rockefeller Brothers Fund and the task force chairman was Laurance Rockefeller. It began with a phrase out of Aldo Leopold:

> It is time to change the view that land is little more than a commodity to be exploited and traded. We need a *land ethic* that regards land as a resource which, improperly used, can have the same ill effects as the pollution of air and water, and which therefore warrants similar protection.[Emphasis added.][47]

The study proceeded to paint a dire picture of "unrestrained, piecemeal urbanization" that has produced "too many dreary environmentally destructive suburbs of a single life style." As a solution the task force recommended a sweeping national land-use policy that would place government at the center of future development. The federal government would become the recipient of "open-space" land through mandatory exactions on developers, donations, and grants in lieu of federal estate taxes. A national lands trust would be established and noncompensatory greenbelt plans (like those enacted in Britain) would further extend government regulation. Local zoning would be made more discretionary, to be constrained only by conflict-of-interest laws and citizens' suits in the "public interest." New communities would be encouraged in preference to private, piecemeal development. Environmental impact statements would be required of all substantial private development. With no apparent unease, the report went on to praise New York's Governor Nelson Rockefeller for establishing a state agency, the New York State Urban Development Corporation, to assist and encourage large-scale development. Areas of environmental, aesthetic, historic, or cultural merit should be preserved, not by purchase but by tough "police-power" restrictions. What the task force envisioned was a changed attitude toward land that would make all of this possible. Ownership of land should be separated from development rights. Development rights would be created and allocated to the land by society: by government. In the words of the task force: "Historically, Americans have thought of urbanization rights as coming from the land-itself, 'up from the bottom' like minerals or crops. It is equally possible to view them as coming 'down from the top,' as being created by society and allocated by it to each land parcel."[48] Under such a scheme, if you wanted to build a house on your lot you would need to purchase "development rights" from the state.

The task force conceded that tough, uncompensated restrictions would need to be placed upon the use of land to protect open space, historical treasures, and environmentally sensitive areas. But how will courts look upon such encroachments? Will they see them as tantamount to a takings under the Fifth Amendment or, rather, will they view them as constitutionally harmless exercises of the police power? This is the crucial issue, for as the task force recognized, its program rests heavily upon land-use regulation without the necessity of compensation. When such things as precedents might get in the way of the achievement of its design, the task force handled the problem by arguing that these precedents are anachronistic. If land were to be considered as a social resource requiring public guidance and control, then decisions based upon traditional property-rights theories would be outmoded. It urged legislators to keep passing stringent regulations (despite their dubious constitutionality) to create a climate of opinion that would force judges to regard stringent regulatory measures as legitimate exercises of governmental power.[49] In the same spirit, the report urged environmentalists, in jurisdictions where courts have not upheld stringent, uncompensated regulations, to fight for the passage of such legislation anyway. This would serve the purpose of keeping developers tied up in the courts, delaying development until a more hospitable judicial climate develops.

The task force admired various British experiments with stringent land-use regulations. These regulations were designed to capture all "betterment" profits for the state, and give government the responsibility for all "positive planning." The British experience has been chaotic, as we shall see, and so it is somewhat surprising that the task force embraced it.

This report is an excellent example of the use of environmentalist ideas to shape policy prescriptions. These policies would alter our traditional notions of property rights while disregarding the constitutional protection afforded owners by the Fifth Amendment's takings clause. In fact, the report urges courts to adopt a position on government regulation of land that would hold that a loss in land value will *never* serve as justification for invalidating a regulation. The task force's stated objective—to give a balanced evaluation of the need for development versus the need for protection of the environment—ends up as a plea for stringent governmental regulation.

The Eminent Domain Power: How Innocuous Is It?

The power of eminent domain may seem innocuous to some, but its use can cause serious psychological and economic damage to property owners. Perhaps, the reason that most citizens unaffected by its use find it noncontroversial is that for most of its history it was used in a very limited way. Few people would quibble over a power used to provide land for post offices or even highways. Today, however, its reach has been greatly extended, and many landowners have been severely affected. This damage has become worse in recent times as courts have emasculated one of the principal constraints upon the exercise of eminent domain: the "public use" proviso, which used to mean that property could not be taken merely to transfer it to another private owner. Eminent domain—the "power of the sovereign to take property for public use without the owner's consent"[50]—is a potentially tyrannical power if it is released from the bounds of strict accountability. One such limiting notion is provided by the requirement that courts examine the necessity for any taking. But with the Supreme Court's sanction for the taking of a nondilapidated building that happened to lie within a blighted area destined for urban renewal (in *Berman v. Parker* in 1954[51]), courts throughout the country have been encouraged to find a public use in a variety of imaginative takings by the states. These takings have only a tenuous connection to public necessity or public purpose, and they often simply transfer property from one private owner to another.

Even when an eminent domain taking does not fall into this gray area where it is difficult to draw the line between a legitimate taking for a public use and an illegitimate one, the power is not unproblematic. Another important protection of the takings clause is the compensation requirement. The usual rationale for compensating victims for takings is that a person should be made whole again. Without such reimbursement, the burden of public improvements, carried out for the "public good," would fall disproportionately and unjustly upon a few unlucky landowners. More fundamentally, the compensation requirement provides another guarantee against tyrannical government. It cautions government that it must match its desire for public works with its treasury, and that it cannot confiscate property. But one problem has arisen with the growth of uncompensated police power regulations over the use of property. Even severe regulations under the police power require no compensation. Another problem arises because compensation very often leaves former owners far from whole. Is the person who loses a small shoe store to urban renewal made whole again when paid fair market value for the store but when payment does not include such factors as court costs, legal fees, appraisal costs, and loss of business goodwill? All these costs to the owner are usually not considered a part of "just compensation." Although recent federal legislation mandates the payment of moving expenses in federal takings cases,[52] compensation often falls below true costs. This requirement does not apply to the more prevalent instances of takings by states, localities, and public utilities.

Furthermore, the fair-market-value standard of compensation employed in eminent domain cases seems quixotic when there is no market relationship, no free bargaining process, between seller and buyer. Rather, in eminent domain there is a coerced seller forced to deliver up property to one buyer, the state. This brings into doubt whether the "just compensation" paid is "fair" or "market" value. Undeniably, fair market value is better than receiving nothing, than having one's property simply expropriated and nationalized as happens in some other countries, yet it still carries coercive implications. This is particularly true when the taking is resisted by the owner.

Two recent instances of the exercise of the power of eminent domain— one by the federal government for the construction of the Tellico Dam and the other by the city of Detroit over Hamtramck—illustrate some of these problems with eminent domain. Even with the Fifth Amendment in place, government takings can have devastating effects on property owners.

Playing Politics with Someone Else's Property in the Tellico Valley

On September 25, 1979 President Carter signed a public works bill accompanied by an amendment exempting the Tellico Dam from all federal legislation, including the Endangered Species Act. This action disappointed environmentalists, landowners, and Cherokee Indians who had counted on Carter's stated opposition to completion of the dam. A controversy that began in 1939 in the heyday of the Tennessee Valley Authority was finally settled. For proponents of the dam, most conspicuously Howard Baker of Tennessee (the minority leader of the Senate) and Representative John Duncan, it was undoubtedly a day of immense satisfaction. These two men had spearheaded the legislative horse-trading that finally succeeded in salvaging the project.

Proponents of the dam had offered visions of opportunities to be derived from the lake to be formed by the damming of the Little Tennessee River: recreation, increased industrial development, a veritable bonanza of new jobs for a depressed area, and additional capacity for the production of hydroelectric power. Despite the roadblocks thrown up in their path, despite the snail darters, the claims of desecration of Indian sacred burial grounds, the change of heart by the TVA itself, the supporters of the dam persisted in their enthusiasm. For local developers, unions, and politicians, the project promised to be a long-hoped-for panecea. Some looked forward to huge profits to be reaped from speculation in shorefront lands along the soon-to-be created lake.

Baker was the most enthusiastic of the supporters, remaining undeterrable through the years despite numerous obstacles. Having shepherded a bill through Congress to establish a cabinet-level Endangered Species Committee with the power to exempt federal projects from the strictures of the Endangered Species Act of 1973, he remained undaunted when his own creation voted unanimously against completing the dam. It gave as a reason the economic infeasibility of the project: proponents failed to demonstrate any sizable benefits of the dam over those of the free-flowing river. But eventually Baker succeeded in appending an obscure amendment to a $10.8 billion public-works appropriation bill, and this accomplished what years of court battles had failed to do. With Supreme Court dismissal of the Cherokee Indians' claims of a violation of their First Amendment right to religious freedom, the last act of the long drama drew to a close and the dam was finally completed.

Although public attention was drawn to the Tellico Dam dispute because of the apparent incongruity of stalling the completion of a $145 million dam for the convenience of a three-inch variety of perch, the much-maligned snail darter, the interests of property owners divested of their lands via eminent domain received scant notice. The snail darter was only one ploy in a drawn-out battle between local farmers and the TVA with its power of eminent domain. What the local property owners found so appalling was that the TVA had seen fit to condemn not merely the 16,500 acres necessary for the dam's reservoir but a total of 38,000 acres of rich farmland. Some of the homesteaders were the descendants of pioneers who settled the valley in the early 1830s after the Cherokee were herded off to Oklahoma or up into the nearby mountains. The land had been passed from generation to generation of poor but industrious farmers. Many of these 341 families deeply resented the forced expulsion from their land to make way not only for the unwanted dam but also for recreational and industrial development by private companies and individuals who would reap profits from the use of *their* land. They attempted a whole series of desperate legal strategies to stop the dam. In 1971 they succeeded in halting construction by showing that the project failed to meet newly enacted environmental impact statement standards of the National Environmental Policy Act of 1969. This barrier was soon surmounted and construction resumed. Then in 1977 they persuaded a federal court to halt construction again by arguing that flooding from the dam would destroy the only habitat of the newly discovered, and now endangered, snail darter.

Neither the owners of the land nor the descendants of the dispossessed Cherokee could stop the dam by asserting their property rights. Rather, they had to resort to shaky side issues to delay construction, making arguments so transparently hollow that they ultimately led to public ridicule of their position, and to defeat. Given public acceptance and judicial deference to governments' use of the power of eminent domain for almost any purpose, no matter how shakily "public," it is little wonder that these property owners were forced to rest their futures upon such a feeble hope as the snail darter.

Public debate over the desirability of completing the Tellico Dam was, undeniably, trivialized by the injection of the snail darter issue. However, had the landowners directly attacked the necessity or expediency of the taking in judicial proceedings, the likelihood of success would have been even less. One reason for this is the Supreme Court's often-stated rule of deference to legislative decisions unless they are so outrageous as to "involve an impossibility."[53] For example, had the farmers challenged the legitimacy of the public use involved in the taking of an extra 22,000 acres to be resold by the TVA to private developers, their chance of success in the courts would have been bleak, as the failure of the Poletown Neighborhood Association, in our next example, will amply attest. Thus the owners of land within the valley were left virtually defenseless. Unable to confront the true issue of property rights versus the power of the state to take property, they were forced to resort to makeshift devices. What it came to in the end were two hardy holdouts—one a seventy-five-year-old widow, Nellie McCall—being driven from their farms by United States marshals. Thomas Moser, the other recalcitrant, said it was "like wanting to die," and Mrs. McCall sobbed uncontrollably as they burned her home, little consoled by the $86,000 in "just compensation," and embittered over the fact that only 2 acres of her 90 acre farm were actually needed for the reservoir. Indeed, she had offered these 2 acres gratis to the TVA if only it would have allowed her to keep her homestead. Two years after the dam flooded the valley, no recreational opportunities had been created, no new industrial developments had arisen, no new jobs had materialized, and some of the dispossessed farmers still came back to picnic on land that once had been theirs.[54]

The Tellico Dam controversy became something more dramatic than the run-of-the-mill eminent domain case, yet it is hardly exceptional. Throughout the country landowners have confronted similar, yet not nearly as well-publicized, problems. In Grimes County, Texas, for another example, local ranchers formed an alliance to fight a $580 million steam electricity-generating plant and strip-mining project that called for the flooding of 5,000 acres of their land. To proceed with the project, the Texas Municipal Power Agency was granted the status of a municipality replete with the power of eminent domain. What outraged the local ranchers was the fact that the electricity from the project would benefit residents of cities far from Grimes County but the ranchers would suffer all the losses, including the uncompensable psychological loss of their land, to which they had formed deep and abiding attachments.[55]

The Extinction of a Community: Poletown

Even more troubling than the fate that befell the landowners of the Tellico Valley was the taking by the city of Detroit for a General Motors plant. The citizens of Hamtramck, known colloquially as Poletown for its largely Polish, lower-middle-class population, were the unhappy victims. Detroit, battered by the slump in automobile sales and the ripple effect on suppliers, was experiencing a rapid escalation in unemployment when, in the spring of 1980, the General Motors Corporation delivered another blow to the city in the form of a virtual ultimatum. By 1983 the Detroit Cadillac and Fisher Body plants would be shut down unless the city could meet certain conditions. If not, GM would proceed to construct a new Cadillac plant in a more hospitable Sunbelt locale. What GM wanted from the city was the presentation by May 1, 1981 of clean title to a 450-to-500 acre site of rectangular shape with access to long-haul railroad connections and the freeway system. Only then would GM consent to erect its new Cadillac plant within the boundaries of the city.

After investigating nine potential sites, the city settled upon one encompassing a deserted Dodge plant and, in addition, a healthy chunk of Poletown. Thirteen hundred sixty-two homeowners would have to be removed, along with their businesses and churches, at a cost of $200 million, some of it to be contributed by an accommodating Carter administration. Mayor Coleman Young and the supporters of the project claimed in its defense that slightly over 6,000 jobs would be saved for the city, while the plant would eventually generate $15 million a year in new property taxes. However, the plant would enjoy a tax abatement for a period of twelve years. Skeptics pointed to GM's heavy-handedness. For example, Michigan Supreme Court Justice Ryan, who dissented from the opinion of his peers upholding the actions of the city and its Economic Development Corporation in a case brought by ten disgruntled Poletowners (*Poletown v. Neighborhood Council City of Detroit*), had this to say:

> The evidence then is that what General Motors wanted, General Motors got. The corporation conceived the project, determined the cost, allocated the financial burden, selected the site, established the mode of financing, imposed specific deadlines for clearance of the property and taking title, and even demanded 12 years of tax concessions.[56]

Indeed, General Motors would pay a pittance for the land acquired by the city at a cost of $200 million—a mere $8 million.

As the majority of the Michigan Supreme Court viewed the issues in the case it came down to this: does the use of eminent domain, here, constitute a taking of private property *for private use*, thereby contravening the Michigan Constitution, which, like that of the United States, bars taking property "for public use without just compensation"? The state legislature, in its Economic Development Corporations Act of 1974, had granted to municipalities the use of the eminent domain power to provide industrial and commerical sites. The stated reason for the grant was to assist "industrial and commerical enterprise in locating, purchasing, constructing, reconstructing, modernizing, improving, maintaining, repairing, furnishing, equipping, and expanding in this state and its municipalities," so as to prevent and alleviate conditions of unemployment. The act declared that these objectives constitute an essential "public purpose," but the Michigan Supreme Court would question this assertion of "public purpose." Is it legitimate for a municipality, under this act, to condemn private property to be transferred to another private party to build a plant that would add jobs and taxes to the economy? it asked.

What the Poletowners objected to was not the declaration by the legislature that programs to alleviate unemployment and promote industry
constitute essential "public purposes" but, rather, the constitutionality of
using the power of eminent domain to condemn one person's property in
order to convey it to another private entity. They contended that there is a
distinction in the law between "public use" and mere "public purpose."
The former is a much more limited notion, restricting the exercise of
eminent domain to instances in which there will be a direct public use of
the property taken, or at the very least a sense in which the public is the
direct beneficiary of the taking. In this instance, they argued, there was
only an incidental benefit to the public from the taking. The principal
beneficiary was none other than General Motors in its profit-making capacity: a decidedly private use.

In fact, the law has been none too clear about exactly what constitutes a
public use in satisfaction of the Fifth Amendment stricture. Indeed, even in
colonial days colonies enacted mill acts that permitted lower riparians to
contruct mills across their portions of rivers, thus taking the land of upper
riparians by flooding. Later, states considered the encouragement of industrial development to be a sufficient public benefit to constitute a public use,
and the courts usually concurred, provided that just compensation was
paid. Eminent domain was often granted to landlocked owners, who used
it to construct private roads. Later in the nineteenth century, private railroads were given the power of eminent domain. But even the railroad
example differs markedly from that of General Motors. The grant of condemnation power to the railroads was most often justified on the ground
that they were businesses heavily regulated first by state governments and
later by the federal government, so although they had this extraordinary
power, they were less free than other purely private businesses. Government controlled their rates: they were businesses "affected with a public
interest." Thus, even before the 1954 *Berman v. Parker* decision upholding
takings for urban renewal purposes, the courts had not limited "public
use" simply to possession by an arm of government. But as the commentators frequently note, whether the courts invoke the stricter notion of
"public use" or the more malleable one of "public purpose," they agree
that eminent domain cannot be used for the purpose of transferring property from one private individual to another for principally private, profit-
making purposes.[57] In Nichols's authoritative treatise, *The Law of Eminent
Domain*, it is stated that even if a plan for a large factory would be of great
benefit to a whole community and it was being blocked by a selfish owner,
"the public mind would instinctively revolt at any attempt to take such
land by eminent domain."[58] As with most elements of the law on takings,
the definition of what is and what is not a "public use" is left in limbo, to be

determined on the basis of an *ad hoc*, case-by-case "gradual process of judicial exclusion and inclusion."[59] Such a process is fraught with dangers, as we shall see in the next chapter.

As we return to *Poletown v. City of Detroit*, after our brief digression into the state of legal interpretations of the "public-use" proviso, we find Detroit and its Economic Development Corporation disputing the Poletowners' contention that the GM taking did not constitute a constitutionally legitimate public use. Rather, the city pled, the taking of this land to create an industrial site that would be used to combat unemployment and fiscal distress, constituted a "controlling public purpose." The fact that the land once acquired would be transferred to a private manufacturer did not defeat the predominant "public purpose" embodied in the taking.

In its *per curiam* decision the Michigan Supreme Court summarily dismissed the argument of the Poletowners that a legal distinction exists between "public use" and "public purpose." The terms, the court concluded, were used interchangeably, and as synonyms for "public benefit." Therefore, the sole issue was whether the condemnation amounted to a taking for private use; that would be constitutionally prohibited. Or rather, was it primarily for public benefit and only incidentally, or secondarily for private profit, and thus constitutionally permissible? In other words, was the condemnation primarily for public or private use?

Here we see an effect of the "deference-to-legislative-judgments" doctrine in economic and property rights issues so often invoked by the courts since the U.S. Supreme Court repudiated substantive due process in its 1934 *Nebbia*[60] decision. The Michigan court's majority argued that the legislature had determined that government actions of this type serve a public purpose, and that, therefore, the "Court's role after such a determination is made is limited." The determination of what "public purpose" encompasses is a legislative function, subject to judicial review but usually not reversible "except in instances where such determination is palpable and manifestly arbitrary and incorrect." As has become customary in these cases, the Michigan court invoked the Supreme Court's decision in *Berman v. Parker*. There the Supreme Court stipulated that when the legislature speaks the public interest has been declared in terms "well-nigh conclusive."

The Michigan court concluded that in this case clear benefits would accrue to the municipality in the form of alleviating unemployment and revitalizing the city, while a private benefit would accrue to GM only as an "incident thereto." The court's decision closed with a homily to *ad hoc* decision making, as it cautioned that its decision might not necessarily be the same in other cases where the public benefit might not be so clear and significant.

Two justices dissented from the decision of their five colleagues. They balked at the city's seizure of land from some owners to transfer it to others. Justice Fitzgerald pierced the veil of the "legislative-deference" doctrine with this remark: "If a legislative declaration on the question of public use were conclusive, citizens could be subjected to the most outrageous confiscation of property for the benefit of other private interests without redress." Although not willing to go so far as to jettison the "legislative-deference" doctrine, he admonished his colleagues to be more vigilant about their duty to exercise ultimate judicial judgment on the validity of legislative determinations. This case, Fitzgerald contended, differed from previous ones, such as those concerning urban renewal. The transfer to private parties of the property taken was only an incidental occurrence in the other cases; in this one the transfer to GM was the motive force behind the entire chain of events. Here the economic benefits to the community were merely incidental to GM's private use of the property. Thus, he concluded that the present case amounted to the taking of private property for private use, and he sounded an ominous warning:

> Now that we have authorized local legislative bodies to decide that a different commercial or industrial use of property will produce greater public benefits than its present use, no homeowner's, merchant's or manufacturer's property, however productive or valuable to its owners, is immune from condemnation for the benefit of other private interests that will put it to a "higher" use.[61]

Justice Ryan, appending his own lengthy dissent, disparaged the notion that the determination of "public use" ought to reside almost conclusively with the legislature. He saw it as fundamentally a judicial question, not to be sidestepped by the minimal standard of review invoked by the majority. Furthermore, he argued, the GM taking did not fall into any of the recognized exceptions to the rule proscribing the private use of eminent domain; specifically, it did not fall under any of the "instrumentality of commerce exceptions" (e.g. highways, railroads, canals). With these exceptions went stringent protections for the public, namely, (1) that the public necessity be of the most extreme sort, (2) that there be a continuing accountability to the public, and (3) that the land would be selected according to facts of independent public significance. Ryan found all three criteria violated in this case. Thus, he considered it particularly distressing that a powerful and influential company could use an attribute of sovereignty—that is, the power of eminent domain—in furtherance of its own financial gain. More important, he denounced the ease with which both the city and the court were led by the "frenzy of perceived economic crisis" to "disregard the rights of the few in allegiance to the always disastrous philosophy that the end justifies the means."[62]

The two dissenters offered compelling arguments that we dismiss at our peril.[63] Should other companies, powerful and arguably vital to the communities, be permitted to assemble plant sites in a similar fashion? Should they then be permitted to "purchase" those sites at below-market prices? The Michigan court's decision certainly provides inspiration to any who might care to try. And what of the rights of property owners, of those destined for the same fate as the Poletowners?

The Police Power Run Amuck

Courts and commentators have repeatedly asserted that the state's supposedly inherent police power is undefinable, illimitable, and almost infinitely malleable, to be shaped by courts and legislators as changing societal needs dictate.[64] Thus, over time, it is not surprising that this broad and expansible power of the states to regulate private behavior and the use of private property has been used, often inventively, to control a wide variety of disfavored activities. If government frowns upon the consumption of alcoholic beverages, then their production should be banned, for the police power is certainly extensive enough to accomplish such a prohibition. If billboards offend the aesthetic tastes of city council members, then they, too, should be banished under the police power. If brickyards in residential neighborhoods depress property values and offend the sensibilities of politically influential residents, then the police power should be invoked to shut down the offending business. If your old neighborhood is being threatened by the wrecking ball of a developer, why, then get it declared a historic district under the police power and prevent anyone from altering the architectural heirlooms, even if the developer happens to "own" the buildings.[65] If a wealthy suburban neighborhood would be offended by the erection of apartment buildings in its midst, then use the police power to zone the whole area for single-family residential housing, perhaps with a one-acre minimum lot size for good measure.

It is precisely this latter power, zoning, that has proven so unsettling to traditional conceptions of property rights. Whether in its older guise as a local preserve delegated to the municipalities by the state governments, or in its newer variation as a direct exercise of statewide land-use control, zoning strikes at the heart of the individual's right to control the use of personally owned property. Old-style zoning has fallen into increasing disfavor. It was enacted in all the states under direction provided by the United States Department of Commerce with its Model Standard State Enabling Act in the early 1920s, and endorsed by the Supreme Court in its landmark decision in *Village of Euclid v. Ambler Realty* in 1926. It has been variously assaulted by both ardent defenders of property rights (who see it as violative of those rights, disruptive of free-market exchanges of property, and inefficient) *and* equally adamant environmentalists (who view it as corrupt and subject to manipulation by developers). The recent trend, inspired in no small part by the latter forces, has been to erode local control over zoning by having the states reassert their control over land use. The American Law Institute's Model Land Development Code, a project commenced in 1965 under a grant from the Ford Foundation, has been influential in promoting this trend. The American Law Institute urged the creation of statewide agencies to promulgate regulations for the preservation of land having "critical state" or "regional impact" and to oversee developments of "more than local concern." In fact, the Florida Environmental Land and Water Management Act of 1972 was directly inspired by the ALI model code. Contributing to the widespread disillusionment with local zoning, in addition to the familiar charges of favoritism and corruption, is the awareness of minority groups, the NAACP most conspicuously, that zoning has served an exclusionary purpose. Zoning has made it easy and respectable for white suburbanites to protect themselves from the poor and Blacks under the cloak of a mere zoning regulation that prices the disadvantaged out of suburban communities.

Bernard Siegan, a respected opponent of zoning, has remarked upon one of the recurring oddities in the arguments of the environmentalist critics of zoning. While these critics denounce, often eloquently and perceptively, the failures of local zoning, they then go on not to condemn the very idea of zoning as mistaken but, rather, to urge the adoption of more extensive regulatory programs, at ever more encompassing levels of government. The past inequities suffered by property owners and excluded would-be homeowners become the pretext for an even more heavily regulated system. Siegan writes:

> In my view, most of these proposals are essentially a replay of what has occurred in zoning since its inception: more and greater controls over land use designed to cure the failures of prior controls which were likewise supposed to have cured the defects of a previous set of controls, et cetera, *ad nauseam*. The dogma persists that if zoning doesn't work, try more of it.[66]

Land Use in California: 1972-1982

California, always at the forefront of cultural and political trends, was an early entrant into the movement to supplant local zoning with a vigorous statewide effort to control land use. Not all land in the state would fall under state supervision, only that portion within an environmentally sensitive and purportedly endangered section adjoining the Pacific Ocean.

Even before adoption of the sweeping California Coastal Zone Conservation Act (Proposition 20) by the voters in 1972, the state had not been backward in its environmental enthusiasm. The Williamson Act of 1965 aimed at the preservation of prime agricultural land by offering farmers the carrot of tax reductions in exchange for an agreement to keep the land in an undeveloped state for ten years. In 1969 the Porter-Cologne Water Quality Act gave the State Water Control Board power to veto any development that threatened water-quality standards. The California Environmental Quality Act of 1970 mirrored its federal counterpart in mandating environmental impact statements for state projects, soon to be extended by an environmentally activist state Supreme Court to private developments as well. This latter development proved to be a virtual Pandora's box for environmentalists, who filed hundreds of cases against developers in an attempt to delay or stop growth.[67]

On the regional level, too, California had been innovative. The state adopted an ambitious control system for San Francisco Bay in 1965. The act would eventually serve as the model for the California Coastal Act of 1972, for both plans relied on an interim permit system that would run concurrently with the development of an overall plan. The San Francisco Bay Conservation and Development Commission was given permanence by the legislature in 1969. Interstate planning, also, was no stranger to pre-Proposition 20 California. In 1969 California joined with Nevada in the regulation of the Lake Tahoe scenic area under federal legislative sanction. And many California municipalities were just beginning to shift from encouragement of development in their zoning and permit practices to slow-growth policies. Cities such as Petaluma, located north of San Francisco, led the wave by invoking an annual quota for new homes by placing a limit on building permits. Such practices,[68] inspired by the desire of homeowners to preserve their amenities, which they saw threatened by hordes of new arrivals, would spread to many cities in California as the decade of the 1970s unfolded.[69]

Between 1968 and 1972 environmental groups in California concentrated their energies upon the state legislature, fighting unsuccessfully, as it turned out, to pass coastal legislation. Their efforts were stymied repeatedly by a balky Senate. In 1971 these disparate groups coalesced to form the California Coastal Alliance, having concluded that past failures may have been attributable to divisiveness among the competing activist groups.[70] Marshaling its forces in unison—107 organizations comprising 27,000 members[71]—and altering its strategy from the doomed legislative route to that of a public referendum, the environmentalist lobby proved to be a relentless and ultimately successful adversary. It was successful in portraying its business, union, and developer opponents as selfish enemies of the people's access to the beaches. The "Save Our Coast" campaign, adroitly managed by the Coastal Alliance, handily vanquished the opposition at the polls on November 7, 1972. Proposition 20 became law, heavily indebted for its victory to highly educated, urban, and upper-middle-class voters.[72]

Given the distribution of population in California, with 85 percent of its 20 million people living within an hour's drive or less of the coast, and the burgeoning growth of the state's population during the last few decades, voters in sufficient numbers responded to the call for protectionism and preservation. They embarked on an uncharted course that would eventually lead the state to dizzily escalating housing prices, resulting in a much-ballyhooed "housing crisis," with some people reaping unearned rewards and others suffering costly inconveniences or large losses. As Robert Ellickson, a persistent critic of the coastal plan, would later conclude, the benefits and losses would not be distributed equally among the populace. Rather, some groups would greatly profit—such as members of planning professions, attorneys for environmental groups, the economic and intellectual elite, and current homeowners—while other less fortunate groups would bear the burden. Average taxpayers, young couples seeking entry into the housing market, coastal tenants and landlords, and the poor would be the losers.[73]

This sweeping regulatory scheme would serve until 1976 as the vehicle for controlling development until a permanent plan could be devised by the State Coastal Commission and, then, enacted by the legislature. Its objectives were vaguely stated, and consequently the discretion given to its commissioners was very broad. Its basic ethical assumptions were curious, given the country's long-standing commitment to individual, not collective, property rights. In the words of the opening policy pronouncement of the Coastal Act:

> The people of the State of California hereby find and declare that the California Coastal zone is a distinct and valuable national resource belonging to all the people and existing in a delicately balanced ecosystem . . . . that in order to promote the public safety, public health, and welfare, and to protect public and private property, wildlife, marine fisheries, and other ocean resources, and the natural environment, it is necessary to preserve the ecological balance of the coastal zone and prevent its further deterioration and destruction; that it is the policy of the state to preserve, protect, and where possible, to restore the resources of the coastal zone for the enjoyment of the current and succeeding generations.[74]

Although anyone who has spent any time touring California's coast along the scenic and often treacherous Highway 1, would undoubtedly agree with the "people of the state" that the coastal zone forms a "distinct and valuable national resource," one might justifiably balk at the further, unsupported allegation that this coast belongs "to all the people." One might also wince at the conspicuously contrived "police power" language—"to promote the public safety, health, and welfare"—wondering how such uncompensated regulatory power could cohabit with the protection of "private property."

The Coastal Act of 1972 was a temporary measure designed to circumvent a recalcitrant legislature and initiate an ongoing process that would lead to a permanent regulatory scheme by 1976. In the interim period six regional commissions, composed of six to eight representatives of the public (appointed by the governor, the Senate Rules Committee, and the speaker of the Assembly) and a varying number of elected officials, city council members, supervisors, and regional officials would oversee all development in their regions. They would parcel out building permits to those who ran the gauntlet of public hearings and majority commission approval, or two-thirds approval in cases involving the developing or filling of marshy areas, or reducing the size of beaches, or adversely affecting water quality, or interfering with the motorists' view of the sea. The statewide Coastal Commission, likewise composed of public and governmental representatives but, as it turned out, somewhat more skewed to the former, would serve as an appeals agency from the decisions of the regional commissions. Concurrently with this review function, the Coastal Commission would prepare a plan by December 1, 1975 to establish both "ecological planning principles" for assessing future development, and specific plans for (1) land use, (2) transportation, (3) conservation of natural and scenic resources, (4) public access to maximize physical and visual use of the coast, (5) recreation, and (6) the siting of public services, facilities, and power plants in "the least environmental destructive manner." Also, the commission would produce projections for an ocean mineral-and-living-resources element, a population element to establish "maximum desirable population densities," and an educational or scientific use element.[75]

Enthusiasts of the California approach point to this combination of an ongoing permit-granting function with the ultimate objective of designing a permanent plan, as exemplifying an optimum solution. While the commissioners would gain hands-on experience by reviewing a variety of types of permit cases, they would use this experience to generate a richer, more personalized, more informed plan. Critics, on the other hand, chafed at the wide discretion ceded by the legislature to a commission guided only by vaguely defined objectives. Such critics of the commission as Professors Hagman and Kanner would point to the "circus-like atmosphere of the Coastal Zone Conservation Commission which has been positively berserk in its arbitrary and inconsistent treatment of land use applicants, and whose proceedings consistently act out a grotesque parody of procedural due process."[76] The plan put forth by the Coastal Commission would cover the coastal zone, defined for that purpose as extending seaward to the outer limit of the state's jurisdiction and inland to the highest elevation of the nearest coastal range or five miles. Its permit authority would be more restricted, covering only one thousand yards landward.

Certain features of the 1972 act bear most conspicuously the imprint of their environmentalist authors. For example, the burden of proof in all cases was placed upon the permit seeker. Builders had to demonstrate that their developments would not "have any, substantial adverse environmental or ecological effect," and that they would be consistent with the objectives of the as-yet-undevised coastal zone plan, i.e. that it would not interfere with

> a) The maintenance, restoration, and enhancement of the overall quality of the coastal zone environment, including but not limited to, its amenities and aesthetic values.
>
> b) The continued existence of optimum populations of all species of living organisms.
>
> c) The orderly, balanced utilization and preservation, consistent with sound conservation principles, of all living and nonliving coastal zone resources.
>
> d) Avoidance of irreversible and irretrievable commitments of coastal zone resources.[77]

Furthermore, all permits would be subject to "reasonable terms," which might include forced dedication of beach accessways, reservation of public recreation areas and wildlife preserves, provision of waste treatment facilities, and assurance that minimum damage would be done to "scenic resources." Another feature of the act that was destined to vex property owners was the wide "standing" provision that enabled any concerned citizen, irrespective of whether the citizen enjoyed any direct property interest in the granting of a given permit, to appear before a regional commission and then to appeal an adverse decision to the state commission and ultimately the courts. Any person could also appeal to the courts for declaratory and equitable relief to restrain violations of the act. In addition, any citizen who prevailed in an action would receive court and attorney costs.

Defenders of the coastal commissions point to the high rate of approval of permits during the 1972-76 enforcement period; some say it was as high as 97 percent for the approximately 25,000 cases.[78] They do concede that a high proportion of these permits involved significant design alterations or conditions, and that the number of would-be builders who were discouraged from entry because of the process is incalculable. It is revealing that no new major development was approved during the interim permit period for the entire regulated zone extending down the 1,072-mile coast of California.

Applicants who shared the aims of the commission, for example in promoting beach access by conditioning permits upon the dedication of accessways, were often disappointed by the failure of these dedications actually to result in the opening of new pathways to the ocean. Journalist Richard O'Reilly, in a series on the effects of the act in the *Los Angeles Times*,[79] related the story of landowner Phylis Wayne of Malibu, who supported the access policy and, indeed, had purchased her oceanfront lot in full awareness of the access condition. She dedicated a six-foot-wide strip of her land for such a public accessway, provided only that a public or private agency would assume maintenance of it and construct suitable gates and walkways. Her neighbors, leery of the prospect of transients invading their luxury neighborhood, sued both Wayne and the Coastal Commission to prevent the imposition of the access conditions. Eventually, the neighbors lost their suit and the accessway was dedicated, but only after Wayne suffered a $38,000 loss in defending herself against the lawsuit and a 25 percent increase in building costs attributable to the delay. When interviewed by O'Reilly, Wayne made several interesting observations about her experience. "But now that I've been here a while," she remarked, "I see that the people who sued me are probably right." She reached this conclusion after observing that access was of little value when the sandy part of the beach remained as private property and, more significantly, that her particular accessway was of no use to anyone because the Los Angeles Board of Supervisors, claiming paucity of funds, had not opened the strip to the public. As of mid-1981, as O'Reilly pointed out, only thirty-nine new accessways to the beaches had been opened to the public throughout the state, and this despite the upwards of one thousand coastal permits that had been conditioned upon ceding public access.

Oceanfront property owners, too, have been forced to yield lateral strips of beach to the government for public use, or face denial of their permits. But as of 1981 only 6.5 miles of new beaches had been opened to the public through this extraction process. What resulted, often, was a crazy-quilt pattern of swatches of disconnected beaches of little use to anyone being turned over to the state. Beach access, it will be recalled, was one of the prime selling points of the Coastal Act, despite the fact that 39 percent of the coast was already in governmental hands before the inception of the act.

In December of 1975 the Coastal Commission delivered to the legislature its Coastal Plan. It is a prodigious document of nearly 450 pages, composed of no less than 160 policy pronouncements. The commission's vision was nearly limitless, extending to water quality, agriculture, forestry, air quality, mineral resources, preservation of scenic communities, energy, transportation, recreation, scientific education, and so on. Cities were quick to observe that providing housing in the coastal zone received the lowest priority, to be countenanced only when it fit in with such slow-growth goals as limiting future development of already heavily developed areas and avoiding suburban sprawl. Of paramount concern were such objectives as protecting, enhancing, and restoring the resources of the coast, preserving special communities and neighborhoods, giving priority to coastal-dependent development, and maximizing access to the coast for people of all incomes, but consonant with protecting the coast itself.[80] In the page and a half of type devoted to "Rights of Property Owners," the plan seems somewhat disingenuous. Although it declared that "the Coastal Plan cannot violate these constitutional mandates" against the taking of private property without compensation, it was quick to point out that "the property rights of a landowner are not absolute" and can change over time. In a rather contrived formulation, the plan states that property owners' rights would not be violated by the plan but that their expectations of financial gain might be disappointed. (This assumes that financial "expectations" form no legitimate part of property rights.) And the planners went on to minimize the burdens to be placed upon would-be home builders. They stated that if an owner had no reasonable use for a lot other than the construction of a single-family home, the owner would be allowed to build, and only "in a slightly different manner from what he might otherwise like to do."[81] But when coupled with the 162 policy pronouncements (which include assigning priority to public access and tourism over private housing in suitable coastal areas;[82] placing the burden for demonstrating compliance with the plan upon those proposing development;[83] advocating novel taxes, including a land-gains tax on land-sale profits; endorsing subsidies and loan programs to prevent agricultural land from being developed;[84] and attempting to limit future development to already developed urban areas[85]), the claim that property will not be taken or property rights violated appears hollow.

Particularly revealing of the ideological commitments of the architects of the plan are two pronouncements: one on the protection of coastal views; the other on preserving the aesthetics of rural coastal villages. Both of these disdain middle-class values and pleasures. On protection of coastal views, the plan states:

> Pre-set architectural styles (e.g., pseudo-Spanish mission and standard fast-food restaurant designs) should be avoided.

On coastal villages it proclaims:

> Motels in rural coastal villages, for example, shall be unpretentious in appearance (stereotyped motel-chain architecture should be prohibited) and shall feature some small separate structures rather than large bulky facilities so as to complement the detached homes and small commercial buildings that characterize most such villages.[86]

The *reductio ad absurdum* of this kind of thinking is apparent in a story that appeared in the *San Francisco Sunday Examiner and Chronicle*.[87] The state commended a development—winner of a Special Mention Award by the National Association of Home Builders and *Better Homes and Gardens*—as a model for good resource conservation. Portola Valley Ranch, perched upon 453 acres in the foothills bordering Stanford University, was praised for exemplifying careful land planning and the preservation of hundreds of acres of wilderness and scenic open space. The 205 homes that eventually will complete the development sell in the $359,000 to $600,000 price range. While this example cannot be directly attributed to the Coastal Commission or its plan because Portola Valley does not lie in the Coastal Zone, this governmental thinking was certainly encouraged by such Coastal Plan pronouncements as those that disparaged middle-class lifestyles and suburban and single-family land-use patterns. Certainly, for anyone affluent enough to afford the $600,000 price tag, Portola Valley Ranch sounds ideal.

The 1976 Coastal Plan departed in one crucial respect from the 1972 act. Local governments, purposefully spurned by the environmentalist alliance that drafted the 1972 Coastal Act (because they were viewed as prodevelopment and hence as obstacles to coastal preservation), were given a piece of the regulatory action by the new Coastal Plan. Aware of strong sentiment against the continued exclusion of local participation, and politically astute enough to realize that a continuation of the 1972 division of power might jeopardize the adoption of the plan by the legislature, the commission abandoned its initial draft, which called for the continuation of both the regional commissions and the state commission. The final plan envisioned the termination of the regional commissions upon the submission of coastal plans by localities and counties, with the state commission permanently surviving in its role as reviewer of local permit decisions. It was this final version that won approval by the state legislature in 1976. But even with the plan's having conceded this point to its adversaries in advance, it did not glide through the legislature. It cleared the Senate Natural Resources Committee by one vote; it failed by one vote in the Senate Finance Committee. Only after a backup bill, which limited the permit area from five miles to 1,000 yards, was substituted, did it pass.[88]

The 1976 act, while more sympathetic to development than its predecessor, and more cognizant of violations of property rights, still preserves the spirit of governmental regulation. Coastal-dependent development is still granted priority over other development near the shoreline. New residential, commercial, and industrial developments will be directed toward already populated areas. And now the Coastal Commission's policy of encouraging low-cost visitor facilities and housing opportunities near the coast is enshrined in law. On June 30, 1981, the six regional commissions expired after having served for eight years, in which time they processed over 50,000 permits. At least for the short term this added to the chores assigned to the State Coastal Commission. It was burdened with hearing initial permit requests because only three of sixty-seven coastal cities and counties had submitted acceptable plans to the commission.[89]

Several years after the adoption of the Coastal Act by the legislature, opposition had not completely faded. In San Mateo County, for example, a group of disgruntled owners of farmland filed suit in Superior Court to bar the county from enforcing its newly approved coastal plan, which establishes stringent growth limits on a huge swatch of oceanside land. They contested the legality of the county's plan on the grounds that it amounts to a violation of their civil rights. They claimed that the plan imposed "ludicrous land use restrictions that virtually destroy the use and value of property holdings throughout the San Mateo County Coastside."[90] The San Mateo plan placed a population ceiling on the county of an additional 10,000 people in the next twenty years, imposed strict density limits, and employed various devices to preserve open space and public access to beaches.

Others argue for more extreme measures. Gerald Gray and his California Coastal Council want to abolish the Coastal Commission. Senator Jim Ellis attempted to shepherd a bill through the State Senate to repeal the Coastal Act, an attempt that stalled in the Natural Resources Committee. In late April 1981 the committee heard testimony from a number of supporters and opponents of the commission.[91] The witnesses included two former members of regional commissions who claimed that the commission was "one of the scariest agencies I have ever witnessed," out of control, and "stepping on people" out of "malice." Carolyn Higland, a property owner in Shelter Cove in Humboldt County, told a harrowing tale of her unsuccessful attempt to get approval from the Coastal Commission to build a home for herself on a one-fifth-acre oceanfront site. She spent $12,000 and three years in her fruitless quest. She cannot build and her undevelopable lot is unmarketable. "They have in fact stolen our property for public use" she lamented.

Higland represents only the tip of the iceberg, for there are many other Californians equally frustrated and financially devastated as a result of Coastal Commission decisions. Many hold title to land at the scenic but politically disfavored Sea Ranch development in northern Sonoma County. Herein lies an astonishing tale—of commission discretion run amuck, judicial acquiescence, legislative intervention, and property owners driven to distraction by mercurial decision makers.[92]

In 1964 Oceanic California, Inc., purchased 5,200 acres along a ten-mile stretch of beach adjacent to scenic Highway 1 at the Sonoma-Mendocino boundary. Its intention was to develop the property as a planned unit development. It would offer condominiums, cluster homes, and sub-divided lots prepared for single-family home construction subject to design controls by the community. Beginning in 1964, well before the Coastal Plan could have been anticipated, the Sea Ranch development proceeded to apply for planned community zoning under the then-existing county zoning regulations. The initial plans for 1,800 acres were approved by the county planning commission and the board of supervisors after submission of a detailed evaluation by the developer of soil conditions, vegetation patterns, weather and precipitation factors, and forest management. The developer agreed to a stipulation that all improvements made by Oceanic California would preserve the environment. Development proceeded. In 1968 Oceanic applied for and received zoning approval on the remaining 3,400 acres. Beach access became an issue in the county, and in 1969 the developer agreed with the board of supervisors to dedicate a 150-acre parcel at the northern end of the property to the county for use as a regional park, in lieu of any additional access corridors through Sea Ranch. Finally, in 1972 the county approved a specific plan for Sea Ranch. This was an additional planning requirement necessitated by a state law passed in 1971. As of 1971, 1,770 lots had been sold and over 550 homes had been built. The developer had built a lodge, store, recreational facilities, and other improvements, obtained permits to build three waste treatment plants, two of which were actually built, and had expended prior to November 8, 1972 (the date of the inception of the Coastal Act), more than $26,900,000.

Despite the considerable sum spent by the developer, the numerous design awards won by the community for its voluntary environmental controls, and the record of successful compliance with all previous county and state zoning requirements, Sea Ranch fell afoul of the Coastal Commission and then of state and federal courts. The battle would rage on for years. Margaret Azavedo, a member of the North Central Coast Regional Commission who supported the majority in its decision in 1974 to hold up building permits at Sea Ranch on "legally subdivided lots" until five more public accessways were dedicated to public use, subsequently lamented her decision. "Seven years later," she wrote in 1981, "there is still no access, the state has spent hundreds of thousands of dollars in administrative review, public hearings and litigations, and a lot of Sea Ranch people are fed up. What was an innocent intention has become a monument to governmental ineptitude."[93] She came to recognize that the commission's strategy of holding the owners of the 1,391 vacant lots "hostage" was "wrong, and obviously was futile." Her recollections of how the commission adopted this strategy are disconcerting. A tired group of commissioners accepted a staff report at the end of an exhausting night's work. They instituted a novel program of "mandatory overall conditions" to be applied to developments that had been subdivided prior to the Coastal Act. These conditions could be applied to individual applicants for permits even though their lots could not meet the requirements imposed on the entire development. This policy created the "hostage" situation at Sea Ranch. Lot owners desirous of building new homes had their permits granted, but conditional upon the ceding of pubic accessways that were the common property of the Sea Ranch Association of homeowners. Thus, it was not within the power of single property owners to comply. In April of 1974 the State Coastal Commission heard an appeal from Sea Ranch permit seekers, and modified North Central's strictures. It allowed lot owners to pay $1,500 into an "environmental fund" that would supposedly purchase accessways. Some Sea Ranchers paid this "tribute money," as they called it, until the practice was discontinued four years later. As of 1981 nearly one hundred permit holders were unable to build because the commission's conditions had not been met. Others did not bother to seek permits simply because building costs had doubled between 1974 and 1981.

That Sea Ranch lot owners were "fed up" is undeniable. They were caught in a catch-22 situation. As individuals they were powerless to comply with access requirements. The Homeowners Association was caught in the middle with most of the present owners indifferent to the plight of the lot owners because they preferred not having an additional 1,200 homes built to partake of the splendor of their coast. In February of 1981 a referendum of lot owners was held in which 83 percent voted; 71 percent said they preferred awaiting the outcome of a court case (in which they were contending that access conditions of their permits amounted to an unconstitutional taking of property without just compensation) rather than accept a compromise fashioned by the state legislature (the Bane Bill) that would have paid Sea Ranch $500,000 for the accessways and allow building to proceed. The suit ultimately was lost.[94]

In December 1977 the California Senate's Select Committee held hearings on implementation of the Coastal Act of 1976 and Sea Ranchers formed an impassioned contingent at these hearings. They contributed their tales of bureaucratic frustrations, power plays by commissioners, and violations of what they took to be their property rights.[95] One of these frustrated lot owners was Fred W. Trumbull, who testified:

> I will soon be 68 years old. For the past nine months all permits to build at The Sea Ranch have been "frozen." My wife and I have been living in a 25 foot trailer waiting to build a retirement home on our Sea Ranch lot purchased 10 years ago for this sole purpose. To obtain our permit we traveled over 7,000 miles attending 15 Regional and State hearings, from Long Beach to Sacramento, Los Angeles to Monterey. We spent hundreds of hours traveling, writing letters, presenting our case to the Commissions, transcribing recordings made of these incredible and seemingly endless bureaucratic sessions. Our costs for travel, motels, meals, etc. are well over $1,000.

Despite the fact that his proposed home would obstruct no coastal views, despite his compliance with septic tank requirements of the commission and all other conditions within his power, his permit was withheld while the cost of his proposed home increased by ten thousand dollars. Finally, Trumbull received a permit, but only after agreeing to pay $1,500 into an "environmental fund." What enraged Trumbull, in addition to the loss of over $12,000 of his retirement income, was the wide-open discretion given to the commission under the vaguely worded statute:

> Because the Act is unclear as to what is legally required of us, it is difficult for the Commissioners to determine their rights and responsibilities. When we asked of the Commissioners what right they had to withhold our permit under the terms of the Act, we received no answers but instead were referred to their staff. When we asked the same question of their staff we received evasive answers and finally a response that "there is no answer." When we asked the same question of members of the Attorney General's office in San Francisco who are advising the Commission we learned that there had been *no written research* done on this insofar as the new Coastal Legislation is concerned. They stated merely that "this is new law—we *think* we have the right to do this."

An attorney in the attorney general's office proffered a remark that stuck in Trumbull's mind, having seen the same attitude reflected by some of the regional commissioners: "We don't care who we get access from as long as we get it."

Another Sea Ranch resident, Donald Jacobs (chairman of the Sea Ranch Design Committee), a practicing architect who had represented clients before the commission, related his experiences. He found the commission to be capricious, ill informed, supercilious, and disdainful of the architectural awards and of the detailed environmental planning and architectural controls enforced by Sea Ranch itself. The commission staff would impose site, height, and bulk requirements, ignoring those enforced by the Sea Ranch architects, and this despite the lack of architectural credentials of the staff. Numerous times Jacobs had to construct plywood mock-ups on his clients' land in order to convince the commissioners that their guidelines were not applicable, at needless expense to the clients. Clients also were forced to apply for county permits at considerable cost for the preparation of construction blueprints, without any idea whether the shifting winds at the commission would swing their way and deliver the elusive permit. Galling, too, was the frequent absence of commission members at hearings. Because each absent vote counted as a negative one, this placed applicants at a serious disadvantage.

Nancy McKnight, another Sea Ranch homeowner, bemoaned the injustice of Sea Ranch's having been singled out as a test case, with the attendant inequities experienced by individual property owners. She expressed sentiments shared by other disillusioned property owners who have falled afoul of the Coastal Commission:

> Individual responsibility for one's own destiny must be respected. There is honor in enjoying one's freedom to earn pleasures, and the government must cease destroying the incentive to work for certain privileges. The people at Sea Ranch are people who have worked hard to earn the privilege to live in and maintain their property and be a part of the basic concept that the Sea Ranch represents . . . . No one is excluded who works for and earns the privilege of owning a piece of property . . . . It is not a "gift" to the wealthy, but rather a reward to those who have contributed to the work force of our society.

The attempt by Sea Ranchers and their environmentalist opponents to seek justice through the court system has produced a tangled web of suits and countersuits, and a legion of decisions, all of which through 1981 have been decided against the homeowners and in favor of the Coastal Commission. In a 1981 decision, a three-judge panel of the United States District Court for the Northern District of California once again dashed the hopes of the Sea Ranch lot owners. The Sea Ranch controversy was certainly not new to the court, which had previously resolved in 1976 to abstain from deciding on the merits of the appellants' case, deferring instead to the California state courts.[96] When the California Appeals Court finally reached its decision, it ruled against the Sea Ranchers. In that case Oceanic California, the developer of Sea Ranch, had sought an exemption from the permit requirements of the Coastal Act, on the theory that it had acquired a vested right by virtue of having attained subdivision approval and performed substantial construction prior to the inception of the Coastal Act.[97]

The court of appeals concluded that no vested right to develop inhered in Oceanic as a result of prior county zoning approval. It stated, "It is beyond question that a landowner has no vested right in existing or anticipated zoning." Oceanic, therefore, failed in its effort to have itself and its lot purchasers freed from the purview of the Coastal Commission.

When the U.S. District Court again heard from the Sea Ranch Association, it could no longer sidestep the constitutional issues.[98] Plantiffs argued that the Coastal Act as applied to them was unconstitutional in that it took their property for public use without just compensation and denied them due process and equal protection. The takings contention revolved about two conditions imposed upon thirty-two permit seekers that required public access and view easements. They saw a takings in the fact that no individual lot owner was able singly to comply with the requirements, and that the conditions were imposed without regard to the relationship between a particular application and the conditions imposed. The court rejected both theories. In a condensation of U.S. Supreme Court decisions on takings, the court succinctly captured the current state of the law, which places a nearly insurmountable hurdle before the aggrieved landowner:

> The United States Supreme Court has held that property may be regulated to a certain extent, but if that regulation goes too far it will be recognized as a taking . . . . Land use regulations, however, have been upheld as a proper exercise of the police power if they are reasonable and a presumption of reasonableness lies with the state or agency action . . . . The reasonableness of each regulation must be evaluated on the specific facts of each case.[99]

Given the California constitutional provision that directs that no person owning frontage on a navigable water may exclude the public's right of way to the water when required for a public purpose, and the Coastal Act's mandate to promote maximum access to the beaches, the court concluded that the commission would have been remiss in its duties had it not imposed access conditions. "Absent imposition of these or similar condition," the court reasoned, "ten miles of the California coastline would become a private beach with many portions of it cut off from the public's view."

The crux of the dispute, as the court saw it, was the contention by the Sea Ranchers that the commission's conditions were invalid because none of the lot owners as individuals had the power to comply. This argument, too, was rejected by the court. Because plaintiffs knowingly bought land subject to Sea Ranch Association control, they cannot charge a taking when the Coastal Commission attempts to deal with them through the association. The court lectured the plaintiffs that they might be more successful in building their homes if they stopped fighting the commission and, instead, lobbied their neighbors in the association to approve the conditions. But was the court not slightly disingenuous when it claimed that the "plaintiffs knew, or should have known, at the time they purchased their lots that certain of their actions would be subject to Association approval or action"? What they bargained for when most of them bought their lots was association control over such things as garbage collection and architectural style. They did not knowingly place themselves at the mercy of the Coastal Commission, which did not even exist at the time some of them purchased their land. Such factors did not dissuade the court from its ultimate conclusion:

> In short, neither the conditions nor the method the Coastal Commission has chosen to enforce them are impermissible. The conditions are a necessary and reasonable way for the Coastal Commission to deal with the problems of preserving public views and access to the coastline while allowing building and growth at the Sea Ranch, now and in the future.[100]

The judicial wranglings did not end there. The U.S. Supreme court remanded the case to the district court for consideration of the effects of the Bane Bill. And environmentalists sued over the bill.[101]

Judicial acquiescence to commission actions and to the Coastal Act itself is not unique to this case. Both the California courts and the federal courts displayed an almost total deference to the act and to the commission. Property owners won suits only on technical matters pertaining to the vested rights portion of Proposition 20. Courts found it relatively easy to deny plaintiffs' claims of takings. They relied in their earlier, precedent-setting decisions on the notion that the 1972 Coastal Act was only a temporary measure and what might amount to a taking if permanently prohibited would not constitute a taking if only applied for a few years.

The California real estate market has experienced a galloping inflation during the hegemony of the Coastal Act, a price spiral that has effectively stifled the dreams of home ownership for young couples and first-time potential purchasers. During the early 1980s California newspapers, particularly their Sunday home sections, scarcely missed a weekend without a scare story about a "housing crisis" or the danger of massive defaults on homes saddled with second, third, and even fourth mortgages and other artifacts of "creative financing." While definitive studies of the effects of the Coastal Act and its permit system upon this phenomenon are few, some indication of the effects can be surmised by monitoring the price differentials and the extent of inflation in the rest of the country compared to that in California. As a further factor complicating any precise comparisons, one need recall only that many California cities that lie ouside the coastal zone adopted their own restrictive, no-growth policies during the 1970s. It would be safe to conclude that when all of these factors are taken into account, California represents the most highly regulated real estate market of all the states. A study by Kenneth Rosen and Lawrence Katz, published by the Center for Real Estate and Urban Economics at the University of California, Berkeley concluded that "land use regulations and growth controls may be environmentally sound but they have negative effects in some cities by pricing many potential first-time homebuyers out of the housing market."[102] Local land-use regulations, they found, contributed an 18 to 28 percent increase to the cost of housing. Development restrictions also served to skew the market to higher-income customers. Developers realized that with the additional risks of regulation, only higher-priced homes held out the promise of a reasonable profit. Rosen and Katz discovered that in California between 1976 and 1979 construction costs on a new home rose by 52.2 percent; lot costs, an astonishing 88.5 percent. The latter figure was more than double the increase in other growth sectors of the country such as Texas, and quadruple that experienced in Florida.

No one ought to be greatly surprised at these results. The following chart lists prices as of February 1981 for comparable homes in Sunbelt cities that, like California, have experienced surges in population.[103] The columns represent three levels of housing from modest to more luxurious.

San Francisco	$202,500	$247,500	$299,475
San Diego	139,500	170,500	206,303
Palo Alto	153,000	187,000	226,270
Los Angeles	144,000	176,000	212,960
Riverside	81,000	99,000	119,790
Houston	81,000	99,000	119,790
Dallas	121,500	148,500	179,685
Atlanta	82,800	101,200	122,452

These figures tell an intriguing story. Palo Alto, well inland and beyond the reach of the Coastal Commission, lies squarely within the burgeoning "Silicon Valley." This area is the focus of the computer chip industry, genetic engineering, and other high-technology industries that have attracted people in record numbers. Palo Alto met the influx with regulations designed to slow growth by, for instance, designating the only available unbuilt land in the foothills as an "open space" preserve. By winter of 1980 the Palo Alto Planning Commission and City Council recognized that the 1976 Comprehensive Plan, which was supposed to last until 1990, had been devastated and needed revision, primarily due to a "jobs-housing imbalance." Still enamored of planning solutions rather than market ones, the council decided to pursue a policy of "limiting employment intensification" through zoning revisions and possibly new taxes on business.[104] High-tech businesses, not coincidentally, have responded to the housing crisis and the inhospitable political climate by channeling plant expansions to places like Texas, and some have even considered removing their corporate headquarters from the peninsula. During all of 1980 only 8,000 new homes were built in Santa Clara county, the heart of "Silicon Valley," while four times as many jobs were created in the northern part of the county alone.

Riverside's relatively inexpensive housing prices can be attributed to its location well away from the coast. In fact, Californians have been retreating into the heartland, fleeing the historically more attractive coastal cities in pursuit of an affordable lifestyle.[105] The *Wall Street Journal* reported in October of 1981 that businesses in California were beginning to build their own housing for employees, having found it difficult to attract new workers because of the outrageous cost of housing coupled with interest rates on mortgages in the 17 to 20 percent range. A city like Houston, a hotbed of population and industrial growth, has not experienced a housing price spiral of nearly the same proportion as California cities. This may have something to do with Houston's unique status as the only major city in the country without a zoning law. Will California some day soon suffer the same fate as Frost Belt cities, economically depressed and with shrinking population due not to their intemperate climates but, rather, to the heavy hand of governmental regulatory and tax policies? The jury is still out.

Is Britain the Wave of the Future?

As with most affairs human, matters could be a lot worse, as indeed they are in Great Britain. British land-use controls since their inception in 1947 under a Labour government might be considered the *reductio ad absurdum* of police power regulation over land.[106] In ensuing years British landowners were condemned to the vicissitudes of changing governmental policy. When Conservatives took power they repealed Labour's controls. When Labour ascended they instigated another ambitious new policy, triggering another turn of the cycle. What impelled Labour's persistent efforts was the sentiment, inspired by such nineteenth-century advocates of land nationalization and reform as Henry George and John Stuart Mill, that landowners reaped unjust rewards when their property just happened to lie in the path of development. David Ricardo, the early classical economist, may have contributed something to this belief with his notion that landlords receive unmerited windfalls as land becomes an ever more scarce commodity. These unearned windfalls penalize other productive segments of the population. Whatever the source, this distaste for property ownership apparently ran pretty deep in the Labour party.

The Town and Country Planning Act of 1947 was undeniably ambitious, amounting to a nationalization of all development rights in land.[107] Also, the act attempted to recoup the development value of land by levying an equivalent tax upon the sale of land.[108] As of July 1, 1948, all land values in Britain were frozen and all development rights taken by the government with a £ 300 million fund established to pay owners for the loss of their land's development value. As things turned out this compensation was never paid. No development could take place without the permission of a central land board, and developers had to pay a 100 percent development tax when permission was granted. When government took land by what we call eminent domain, the owner would receive only the equivalent of present use value as compensation, rather than fair market value, because the government already had expropriated the land's development value. The results were predictable: massive distortions in the real estate market, with shrinking supplies of land offered for development; and inflation in both the price of land and the cost to the ultimate consumer. The Conservatives promised to abolish the law. In 1953 when they again attained power they repealed those portions of the law that assessed development charges and denationalized development rights.

Once again when the Labour party came to power it reinstituted elaborate land use controls. First with the Finance Act of 1965, which imposed a 30 percent capital gains tax on increases in existing use value, and then with the Land Commission Act of 1967, which inaugurated a "betterment levy" (of between 40 and 50 percent) to be paid by the seller. The Land Commission was empowered to purchase land, either by compulsion or by agreement, once planning permission had been given with payment on a standard of existing use value. This "land bank" would provide planners with land so that they could engage in "positive" planning, rather than simply responding to the initiative of the market. When the Conservatives returned to power in 1970, history repeated itself and the act was repealed, after having produced the same kind of market dislocations as its predecessor. During its tenure the Land Commission had purchased 2,500 acres and collected £ 100 million in "betterment levy." The Conservatives, too, proved themselves vulnerable to public wrath against speculators and developers. In 1974 they proposed instituting a 30 percent tax on land granted planning permission. Before their plan could be enacted, they were swept from office and the Labour party went them one better.

Labour enacted new corporation taxes and income taxes on land development gains that put the Conservatives' 30 percent tax to shame. Labourites came back with renewed vigor in 1975 to try for the third time to alter radically land ownership, its rights, and perquisites. In November they enacted the Community Land Act designed to, once more, attack the perceived problem of speculative windfalls. It gave planners the initiative in development: the tools to engage in "positive urban planning."[109] A good indication of the motivation behind the act can be gleaned from a Labour Government White Paper published in 1974. After contending that government needs the power to initiate planning, rather than just responding to private proposals, the White Paper stated:

> Side by side with the need to secure positive planning, the nation has to deal with another problem, that of land prices and betterment. "The growth in value, more especially of urban sites, is due to no expenditure of capital or thought on the part of the ground owner, but entirely owing to the energy and enterprise of the community . . . . It is undoubtedly one of the worst evils of our present system of land tenure that instead of reaping the benefit of the common endeavour of its citizens a community has always to pay a heavy penalty to its ground landlords for putting up the value of their land." (Rt. Hon. David Lloyd George—Official Report 29th April 1909, vol. IV, Col. 532) The public ownership of development land will secure these increments for the community that has created them.[110]

Instead of nationalizing land, Labour chose this time to municipalize it, with local governments eventually acquiring all land for development and either leasing it or selling it back to developers or engaging in construction themselves. The act projected a two-stage progression. In the first, a development gains tax of 80 percent was imposed by the prior Finance Act of 1974. Local authorities were placed under a general duty to acquire land for development, with all owners obligated to inform local authorities of their desire to dispose of their land. The city would decide whether to purchase the land or not. The second phase projected a permanent scheme in which local authorities would be placed under an obligation to acquire all land designated for development, with compensation fixed at current use value. No land could be developed without first passing through the hands of a local government. Owners would be deprived of the right to a public hearing on the merits of community acquisition, and the state would be freed from any requirement to state the purpose to which the land would be put. Land would be sold at fair market value. As with its predecessors, the Community Land Act succeeded only in inhibiting the supply of land available for development. The act proceeded under the usual cloud of a Conservative party promise to repeal the legislation once it again acquired power, a promise that was brought to fruition in 1980.

Remarkably, this chaotic and inefficient "system" of governmental interference with the land market that has characterized Britain since 1947 has its American admirers. The late Donald Hagman, among others, argued for a "windfalls-for-wipeouts" scheme that takes its inspiration directly from the British quest for a way to recoup "betterment" values for the government. He wrote, "Society *feels* somewhat more strongly these days that windfall profits from speculation in land is [*sic*] wrong and that something should be done about it."[111] Thus, he advocated transferable development rights (a scheme for establishing a market for government privileges to develop land in excess of zoning restrictions[112]) or a system in which those who benefit from zoning pay those who lose via the mechanism of special assessments. Notably, Hagman adverted in eulogistic terms to the British experience. The presidential commission sponsored by the Rockefeller Brothers Fund in its report, *The Use of Land*, which we discussed previously, also praises the British model when it urges the establishment of a National Lands Trust and, ultimately, a scheme in which all development rights would be sold by government.[113]

The excesses of eminent domain suffered by farmers in the Tellico Valley and the Polish residents of Hamtramck, the use of the police power to harass residents of Sea Ranch, and the mercurial British land use system should give us pause. Perhaps something is amiss in our calm acceptance of these two supposedly inherent governmental powers. When homeowners, normal everyday people like the rest of us, neither wealthy nor big corporations nor "evil" speculators, can have their lives disrupted and their life's savings dissipated by governmental actions, then it is time to examine the history and legitimacy of such sweeping powers. Americans started out with the idea that eminent domain and police power were necessary powers of government. Equally necessary, however, were strong constitutional safeguards to protect the liberty to own and use property. Yet over time we have reached the stage where these safeguards have been sorely tested. How has this happened? This is the question that chapter 2 addresses.

Notes

1. This example is loosely based upon an actual incident that occurred in Cincinnati, Ohio. See "Shop Keepers Find Some Happiness in Dislocation," CINCINNATI ENQUIRER, May 4, 1979.
2. This example is not a figment of the imagination but, rather, is based upon the experience of numerous landowners in California, particularly those who purchased lots in a development called Sea Ranch in Sonoma County. More of these hapless landowners subsequently.
3. Eugene Hargrove, certainly not an extremist on environmental issues, expresses the fairly widespread sentiments of his colleagues when he writes:
   The worst result of Locke's property theories is the amoral or asocial attitude which has evolved out of it. Locke's arguments have encouraged landowners to behave in an antisocial manner and to claim that they have no moral obligation to the land itself, or even to other people in the com-

munity who may be affected by what they do with their land . . . . This transfer [from the absolute right of kings to Locke's grant of ultimate rights to each property owner] has been a moral disaster in large part because the King's rights involved moral elements which did not carry over to the new rights of the private landowner . . . . The standard which landowners adopted to guide their actions was a purely selfish and egotistical one.

See Eugene C. Hargrove, *Anglo-American Land Use Attitudes*, 2 ENVIRON-MENTAL ETHICS 121, 145 (1980).

4. E. F. Roberts, *The Demise of Property Law*, 57 CORNELL L. REV. 1, 43 (1971). This resemblance of much of the environmentalist agenda concerning land to feudalism has not gone unremarked by critics. For example, Congressman Steve Symms wrote (Minority view, House Committee on Interior and Insular Affairs, *Land Use Planning Act of 1974*, H. Rept. 10294, 93d Cong., 2d sess. (1974), 104, in opposition to Morris Udall's bill advancing a national land use scheme:

The most basic of [private property] rights is the right to use and enjoy. [Under national land-use controls] this right will now be regulated in the interests of society as a whole. The right to exchange will be destroyed as the right to use and enjoy is circumscribed . . . . The duke and baron of old will be replaced by the state, supposedly acting in the name of "the people". Today's independent landowner will become the serf of tomorrow's New Feudalism.

5. For an incisive discussion of Jefferson's views on land reform, and his indebtedness to the Saxon heritage, see Hargrove, *Anglo-American Land Use Attitudes*.

6. With passage of the Housing and Community Development Act of 1974, the federal role has become more indirect. Rather than directly supervising urban renewal projects, the federal role was limited to disseminating "block grants" to localities for projects of their own determination.

7. See William Murray, *New Communities: In Search of Cibola—Some Legislative Trails*, 12 URBAN LAW ANNUAL 177 (1976), in which the author documents the difficulties experienced by the New Community Development Corporation within HUD. Financial disasters plagued most of the new communities, in addition to problems engendered by poor planning and management, and maladministration of the program by HUD, all of which left most of the communities faced with the possibility of imminent foreclosure.

8. The act was amended in 1976 to authorize the Office of Coastal Zone Management to spend an additional $1.6 billion over ten years for grants, loans, and loan guarantees to the states. The amendment was prompted by the acceleration of the federal outer continental shelf leasing program, and the resulting sentiment that the states should repair any environmental damages generated by the program.

9. Richard Nixon, Introduction, Council on Environmental Quality, FIRST ANNUAL REPORT (1970), xii-xiii.

10. For details of the intricacies of these bills, see *Hearings, National Land Use Planning, Before the Subcommittee on the Environment of the House Committee on Interior and Insular Affairs*, 92d Cong., 1st sess. (1971); *Hearings on S. 268, Land Use Policy Assistance Act, Before the Senate Committee on Interior and Insular Affairs*, 93d Cong., 1st sess. (1973); *Land Use Policy and Planning Assistance Act, Report of the Committee on Interior and Insular Affairs,*

United States Senate, to Accompany S. 268, Rept. 93-197 (1973); *Hearings on HR 4562, National Land Use Planning Act of 1973, Before the Subcommittee on the Environment of the House Committee on Interior and Insular Affairs*, 93d Cong., 1st sess. (1973); *Hearings on HR 10294, Land Use Planning Act of 1974, Before the Subcommittee on the Environment of the House Committee on Interior and Insular Affairs*, 93d Cong., 1st sess. (1974).

11. Bernard H. Siegan, LAND USE WITHOUT ZONING (Lexington, Mass.: Lexington Books, 1972), 166. See also M. Bruce Johnson, *Land Use Planning and Control by the Federal Government*, in NO LAND IS AN ISLAND (San Francisco: Institute for Contemporary Studies, 1975), 78, who argued that the Udall bill could not end in halfway measures but would lead inevitably to state command.

12. See McClaughry, John, *The New Feudalism*, 5 ENVT'L L. 675 (1975).

13. For useful discussion of state and regional land use policies in the 1970s, see Robert G. Healy, LAND USE AND THE STATES (Baltimore: Johns Hopkins University Press for Resources for the Future, 1976); Thomas C. Pelham, *Regulating Areas of Critical State Concern: Florida and the Model Code*, 18 URBAN LAW ANNUAL 3 (1980); Note, *Preserving Scenic Areas: The Adirondack Land Use Program*, 84 YALE L. J. 1705 (1975); Sylvia Lewis, *New York's Adirondacks: Tug of War in the Wilderness*, 42 PLANNING 9 (September 1976); Note, *Saving San Francisco Bay: A Case Study in Environmental Legislation*, 23 STAN. L. REV. (1971); Suzanne Dean, *How to Kill a Land-Use Bill*, 42 PLANNING 22 (January 1976), in which the author contends that Utah's land-use bill was defeated by blue-collar voters while "blueblood Republican areas" supported it.

14. Morris K. Udall, *Land Use: Why We Need Federal Legislation*, in NO LAND IS AN ISLAND, 59.

15. See F. Fraser Darling, *Man's Responsibility for the Environment*, in BIOLOGY AND ETHICS (Proceedings of a Symposium held at the Royal Geographical Society, London, on 26–27 September 1968), 119; Garrett Hardin, *The Tragedy of the Commons*, 162 SCIENCE 1243 (1968), reprinted in ECONOMIC FOUNDATIONS OF PROPERTY LAW, ed. Bruce Ackerman, (Boston: Little, Brown, 1975). The whole panoply of the environmentalists' agenda is captured in the "Environmental Bill of Rights," endorsed by leading environmental groups (see 3 ENVT'L ETHICS 95 (1981):

> The People have a right to a healthful and productive environment. Such right includes, but is not limited to, the benefits and enjoyment of:
> 1. Clean air in urban centers, industrial and agricultural work places, and elsewhere throughout the State;
> 2. Adequate amounts of water, unpolluted by toxic wastes or excessive sediments, in streams, rivers, lakes, underground basins, and coastal areas;
> 3. Renewable, non-polluting, and non-wasteful energy systems;
> 4. Freedom from involuntary exposure to chemicals, minerals, radioactive substances and energy forms that are hazardous to health;
> 5. Liveable urban and rural environments, with productive employment, affordable housing, efficient transportation, and freedom from excessive noise;
> 6. Accessible parks, recreational areas, and open spaces;
> 7. Agricultural lands protected from urban or suburban sprawl;
> 8. Unique and scenic resources, including wilderness and coastal areas, free-

flowing rivers, lakes, mountains, deserts, historic structures and arch-
eological sites;
9. Fish and wildlife populations, rare and endangered flora and fauna, and
other native plant and animal life, protected and enhanced where possible;
10. A population level compatible with a good standard of living.

The people have a "right" to this agenda, but provided by whom?
16. Hardin, *Tragedy of the Commons* at 5.
17. Donella H. Meadows et al., THE LIMITS OF GROWTH: A REPORT FOR
THE CLUB OF ROME'S PROJECT ON THE PREDICAMENT OF MAN-
KIND (New York: Universe Books, 1972).
18. *Id.* at 10.
19. *Id.* at 23-24.
20. This statement is not a strictly accurate representation of John Stuart Mill's
views, for he underwent several transformations in his life in which he was at
some times more attracted to socialism than at others. Yet, he expected that
such a socialist state could be attained only in the far distant future, awaiting
the improvement of the human stock. For the foreseeable future, then, he
remained an advocate of the laissez-faire principle, but, again, not without
substantial reservations. See his PRINCIPLES OF POLITICAL ECONOMY,
the first edition of which was published in 1848, particularly Bk. 5, ch. 11.
Also see his posthumously published *Chapters on Socialism*, FORT-
NIGHTLY REVIEW, January-June 1879, n. s. 25, o. s. 31, 217-37, 373-82,
513-30.
21. There abound in the ecological literature calls for revolution. Just a few will
suffice to give a taste of the rest. Barry Commoner writes in *The Closing
Circle-II*, NEW YORKER, October 2, 1971, 99-101:

> My own judgment, based on the evidence now at hand, is that the present
> course of environmental degradation, at least in industrialized countries,
> represents such a serious challenge to essential ecological systems that if it is
> continued it will destroy the ability of the environment to support a reason-
> ably civilized human society . . . . The world is being carried to the brink of
> ecological disaster not by a single fault, which some clever scheme could
> correct, but by a phalanx of powerful economic, technological, and social
> forces. What is required is nothing less than a change in the course of
> history.

And J. Baird Callicott writes in *Animal Liberation: A Triangular Affair*, 2
ENVT'L ETHICS 311, 338 (1980):

> Implementation of the land ethic would require discipline, sacrifice, re-
> trendment, and massive economic reform, tantamount to a virtual revolu-
> tion in prevailing attitudes and lifestyles.

And Charles A. Reich writes in THE GREENING OF AMERICA (New York:
Random House, 1970), 4:

> There is a revolution coming. It will not be like revolutions of the past. It
> will originate with the individual and with culture, and it will change the
> political structure only as its final act. It will not require violence to succeed,
> and it cannot be successfully resisted by violence. It is now spreading with
> amazing rapidity, and already our laws, institutions and social structure are
> changing in consequence. It promises a higher reason, a more human com-
> munity, and a new liberated individual. Its ultimate creation will be a new

and enduring wholeness and beauty—a renewed relationship of man to himself, to other men, to society, to nature, and to the land.

22. Julian L. Simon, THE ULTIMATE RESOURCE (Princeton: Princeton University Press, 1981).

23. Others have written books sounding similar themes throughout the 1970s. See John Maddox, THE DOOMSDAY SYNDROME (New York: McGraw-Hill, 1974); William Brown and Herman Kahn, THE NEXT 200 YEARS (New York: Morrow, 1976); and the spirit of the Club of Rome report still persists, as evidenced by the U.S. government's "Global 2000 Report" issued in 1980 (New York: Paragon Reprint Corp.).

24. Lawrence Tribe, *Ways Not to Think About Plastic Trees: New Foundations for Environmental Law*, 83 YALE L. J. 1315 (1974); Peter Singer, *Not for Humans Only: The Place of Nonhumans in Ethics*, in ETHICS AND PROBLEMS OF THE 21st CENTURY, ed. K. E. Goodpaster and K. M. Sayre (Notre Dame: University of Notre Dame Press, 1979). Lynn J. White, Jr., *The Historical Roots of Our Ecological Crisis*, 155 SCIENCE 1203 (1967), argues in a similar vein, namely, that we ought to reject the Christian axiom "that nature has no reason for existence save to serve man" (1207). Rather, we ought to embrace a "humility of species," born of such philosophical antecedents as Zen Buddhism, Francis of Assisi, and the latter-day beatniks.

25. Kenneth Goodpaster, *From Egoism to Environmentalism*, in ETHICS AND PROBLEMS OF THE 21ST CENTURY, 30.

26. Christopher D. Stone, *Should Trees Have Standing? —Towards Legal Rights for Natural Objects*, 45 S.CAL. L. REV. 450, 491 (1972).

27. Callicott, *Animal Liberation* at 334.

28. White, Jr., *The Historical Roots of Our Ecological Crisis* at 1204.

29. For a thorough, scholarly analysis of the environmentalists' repudiation of Western values, see John Passmore, MAN'S RESPONSIBILITY FOR NATURE: ECOLOGICAL PROBLEMS AND WESTERN TRADITIONS (New York: Scribner's; London: Duckworth, 1974).

30. See A. Lawrence Chickering, *Land Use Controls and Low Income Groups: Why Are There No Poor People in the Sierra Club*, in NO LAND IS AN ISLAND, 87, who cites the fact that members of the Sierra Club are drawn from economic classes populating the Social Register; and Benjamin F. Bobo, *The Effects of Land Use Controls on Low Income and Minority Groups: Court Actions and Economic Implications*, in NO LAND IS AN ISLAND, 93, who writes that land-use controls have served as a pretext by the rich to exclude the poor from proximity to their neighborhoods. Also B. Bruce-Briggs, *Land Use and the Environment*, in NO LAND IS AN ISLAND, 9, who makes the same point about class interests. He presents in addition a devastating critique of environmentalists' scare stories about the shrinkage of agricultural land and the supposed nightmare caused by unplanned land use. Population growth he sees as a nonissue, given the thousand acres per person in the United States (the United States comprises 3.5 billion square miles of land). Although the environmentalists cite the figure that 70 percent of our people live on 2 percent of the land, this works out to three to four persons per acre, and population is actually declining in the most congested cities. Suburban sprawl, rather than a devastation, he views as a blessing, allowing more people to enjoy a better and much-desired standard of living. Environmentalists love to cite the figure that 5 million acres are absorbed by urban growth each decade; this

represents only one-fourth of 1 percent of total land area. The loss of agricultural land is not a problem, either, for he contends that with existing technology a 50 percent increase in population could be comfortably fed on present agricultural land. After all, 1 billion acres are currently devoted to agriculture, so the 1 million acres converted to other uses each year represents an insignificant factor.

31. Garrett Hardin, *The Economics of Wilderness*, 78 NATURAL HISTORY 173 (1969); *Living on a Lifeboat*, 24 BIOSCIENCE 561 (1974).

32. Aldo Leopold, A SAND COUNTY ALMANAC (New York: Oxford University Press, 1949). I would include in this category, in addition to Leopold, such thinkers as Stone, *Should Trees Have Standing?*; Paul W. Taylor, *The Ethics of Respect for Nature*, 3 ENVT'L ETHICS 197 (1981); Tom Regan, *The Nature and Possibility of an Environmental Ethic*, 3 ENVT'L ETHICS 19 (1981): Callicott, *Animal Liberation*.

33. Leopold, A SAND COUNTY ALMANAC, 172.

34. Some critics have attempted to reconcile this putative inconsistency in Leopold's position. J. Baird Callicott, for one, argues that for Leopold what mattered was preserving the ecological system as an entity—"land the collective organism"—and toward that end supererogatory individual animals could be removed by hunting. See *Animal Liberation*.

35. Regan, *The Nature and Possibility of an Environmental Ethic* at 33.

36. *Id.* at 30.

37. *Id.* at 31.

38. *Id.* at 31-32.

39. Stone, *Should Trees Have Standing?* at 466.

40. *Id.* at 475.

41. For articles advocating the animal liberationist position see Singer, *Not for Humans Only*; Tom Regan, *Animal Rights, Human Wrongs*, 2 ENVT'L ETHICS 99 (1980). Regan argues here for the animal liberationist position based upon the postulation of animal rights.

42. Singer, *Not for Humans Only* at 195-96.

43. *Id.* at 196.

44. For arguments upholding various distinctions between people and animals that would preclude animals from having rights, see Passmore, MAN'S RESPONSIBILITY FOR NATURE; L. P. Francis and R. Norman, *Some Animals Are More Equal than Others*, 53 PHILOSOPHY 507 (1978); Michael Fox, *Animal Liberation: A Critique*, 88 ETHICS 106 (1978).

45. See Gene Spittler, *Sensible Environmental Principles for the Future*, ENVT'L ETHICS 339 (1980). Spittler, an assistant secretary of the Standard Oil Company of California and a former manager of environmental planning for Chevron, USA, is typical of this breed. This position reflects the older tradition of the "conservationists" rather than the newer position of the "preservationists," in that it is explicitly people centered.

46. M. Bruce Johnson ably makes this point; see his *Land Use Planning and Control by the Federal Government*, 82.

47. William K. Reily, ed., THE USE OF LAND: A CITIZEN'S POLICY GUIDE TO URBAN GROWTH, A Task Force Report Sponsored by the Rockefeller Brothers Fund (New York: Thomas Y. Crowell, 1973), 7.

48. *Id.* at 22.

49. *Id.* at 24.

50. Philip Nichols, THE LAW OF EMINENT DOMAIN, 3d ed. by Julius L. Sackman (New York: Matthew Bender, 1980), 1.11.
51. *Berman v. Parker*, 348 U.S. 26 (1954).
52. The Uniform Relocation Assistance and Real Property Acquisition Policies Act of 1970, 42 U.S.C. § 4624 (1970).
53. *United States v. Gettysburg Electric Railway Company*, 160 U.S. 668 (1896).
54. For more details of the involved history of the Tellico dispute, both legislative and judicial, see Peter Matthiessen, *How to Kill a Valley*, NEW YORK REVIEW OF BOOKS, February 7, 1980; *Snail Darter vs. Dam: Pork Barrelers Win*, 116 SCIENCE NEWS 230 (October 6, 1979); *Tellico Dam Battle—It's Not Just Snail Darter*, U.S. NEWS & WORLD REPORT, September 17, 1979; *TVA's Bitter Victory*, NEWSWEEK, November 26, 1979; Robert A. Liroff, *NEPA—Where Have We Been and Where Are We Going*, APA JOURNAL 154 (1980); Robert Cahn, *The Triumph of Wrong*, 81 AUDUBON 5 (November 1979).
55. For a discussion of this issue, see Don Gardner, *Rural Texans Fight Utility to Save Their Wide Open Spaces*, PLANNING 11 (March 1978).
56. *Poletown Neighborhood Council v. City of Detroit*, 304 N.W. 2d 455, 470 (Mich., 1981), Justice Ryan dissent.
57. For examples, see William B. Stoebuck, *A General Theory of Eminent Domain*, 47 WASH. L. REV. 553, 595-96 (1972); the authoritative treatise by Nichols, EMINENT DOMAIN, sec. 7.61.
58. Nichols, EMINENT DOMAIN at sec. 7.61. But Nichols notes that Judge Colley's rule, enunciated in 1870—it is illegitimate for a legislature to assist one private enterprise at the expense of another—is subject to numerous exceptions based upon local conditions. Such "private uses" as irrigation, drainage, reclamation of wetlands, mills, mines, lumbering, private roads, and clearing a doubtful title have all served as exceptions and sometimes have been accorded aid by the invocation of eminent domain (sec. 7.62). Nichols writes that even on the modern, broad view of "public use" by the federal courts certain restrictions apply: (1) that the use affects the community as distinguished from an individual, (2) that the law control the use to be made of the property, (3) that the title so taken be not invested in a person or corporation as private property to be used and controlled as private property, and (4) that the public reap the benefit of public possession and use, and that no one exercise control except the public (sec. 7.2). The Poletown case seems to violate, arguably, all four of these restrictions.
59. *Id.* at sec. 7.212.
60. *Nebbia v. New York*, 291 U.S. 502 (1934). In *Nebbia* the Supreme Court by a 5-4 decision upheld an attempt by New York State to support sagging milk prices by fixing the price at an artificially high level. The Court rejected Nebbia's contention that such price fixing constituted a violation of the due process and equal protection clauses of the Fourteenth Amendment. Justice Roberts, writing for the majority, concluded that legislative interferences with prices would violate due process only if they were unreasonable or arbitrary, and bore no substantial relation to the objectives sought. This test proved much more amenable to governmental interference with the economy than that invoked by the "Old" Court, the champion of economic due process. The worm completely turned by 1937, when in *West Coast Hotel Co. v. Parrish*, 300 U.S. 379, the Court, again by a 5-4 division, upheld a Washington State

law enacting minimum wages for women and minors, thus repudiating the "Old" Court's rejection of minimum wage laws (*Adkins v. Children's Hospital* 261 U.S. 525 (1923)). See chapter 2's sections on the police power and the due process and equal protection clauses.

61. *Poletown v. City of Detroit*, Fitzgerald dissent at 464.

62. *Id.* at 465, Ryan dissent.

63. In fact, prior to the *Poletown* decision there have been others from different states reaching similar conclusions: *Yonkers Community Development Agency v. Morris*, 335 N.E. 2d 327 (N.Y., 1975), where the Otis Elevator Company was unable to buy land for expansion from a neighboring landowner, and the city intervened and took the land by eminent domain, subsequently reselling it to Otis at a fraction of its cost of acquisition. For a critique of this case, see S. Mohlo and G. Kanner, *Urban Renewal: Laissez-Faire for the Poor, Welfare for the Rich*, 8 PAC. L. J. 627 (1977). The court upheld this action as constitutional. Justice Fitzgerald in his dissent in *Poletown* cites two other cases in a similar vein: *Prince George's County v. Collington Crossroads, Inc.*, 275 Md. 171, 339 A 2d 278 (1975) (where the county condemned land for an industrial park along a highway); and *City of Minneapolis v. Wurtele*, 291 N.W. 2d 386 (Minn., 1980) (where the city condemned development district and chose the developer). Fitzgerald also cites four cases in which courts declared such activities unconstitutional as exceeding the power of government to take private property: *City of Owensboro v. McCormick*, 581 S.W. 2d 3 (Ky., 1979); *Opinion of the Justices*, 152 Me. 440, 131 A 2d 904 (1957); *Karesh v. City Council of the City of Charleston*, 274 S.C. 339, 247 S.E. 2d 342 (1978); *Hogue v. Port of Seattle*, 54 Wash. 2d 799, 341 P. 2d 171 (1959).

64. E.g. William A. McClain, *Modern Concepts of Police Power and Eminent Domain*, in PROCEEDINGS OF THE NINTH INSTITUTE OF EMINENT DOMAIN, The Southwestern Legal Foundation, Dallas, Texas, 1968 (New York: Matthew Bender, 1969), 167-68:

> The police power is dynamic, not static. Subjects encompassed by it are not limited by precedent based upon conditions in the past. The scope of the police power expands with the growing needs and complexities of modern civilization. It is frequently said that police power is as broad as the public needs, subject only to constitutional limitations. The extent of police power is frequently expressed by the well known maxim, "Salus populi supreme lex est."
>
> The police power is not susceptible of exact definition and there should be no specific definition of it. The power knows no definite limitations, since in its widest sense it is the power "to govern men and things" and includes all legislation and almost every function of civil government.

65. A particularly apt example of this was the declaration of a 125-block swatch of Miami Beach as a historic district by the National Register of Historic Places. Denounced by developers as "this Art Deco scam," preservationists have succeeded in delaying demolition of these buildings under a county ordinance requiring developers to submit their plans to a historic preservation board with the power to delay demolition for up to six months. See Joe Thomas, *Miami Beach Conflict Pits Developers Against Lovers of Art Deco*, NEW YORK TIMES, Feb. 26, 1981; William Safire, *What Government Is For*, NEW YORK TIMES, March 2, 1981.

66. Siegan, LAND USE WITHOUT ZONING, 149. A good example of this kind of thinking that Siegan condemns is exhibited by Lindell Marsh (among many others who could be cited), *Innovative Programs and Proposals for the Reconciliation of Private and Public Interest in California*, 10 NAT. RESOURCE LAW 257, 263 (1977): "Zoning schemes . . . have proven to be inadequate to deal with the problems of increasing urbanization and have generally supported the private development and use of land." This failure, he argues, should be remedied by resorting to higher levels of government and more coordinated regulation, such as that exemplified by the California Coastal Act.

67. For a fuller discussion of these acts and decisions, and a thorough study of the impact of no-growth or slow-growth policies on several California cities, see Bernard J. Frieden, THE ENVIRONMENTAL PROTECTION HUSTLE (Cambridge: MIT Press, 1979).

68. *Id.* at 5. Frieden enumerates some of the ploys used by the no-growth advocates:

    Their tactics included putting land into agricultural preserves, declaring moratoria on new water and sewer connections, setting explicit growth quotas, establishing service boundaries beyond which there would be no extensions of utility lines, charging thousands of dollars in "hook-up" fees for each new house as a price for local public services, and creating a climate of hostility that encouraged all opposition groups to bring pressure against proposed new developments.

69. Bernard Frieden, professor of urban studies and planning at MIT and former director of the MIT-Harvard Joint Center for Urban Studies, is particularly perceptive in analyzing the motivation of those who sought to exclude others from invading their stretch of California paradise. His book abounds with observations concerning the connection between elitism and the quest for protectionism, of the haves excluding the have-nots under the cloak of protecting the environment.

    A closer look at how the growth control and environmental coalition operates in local controversies shows that its effects are far less benign. It has made a clear and substantial contribution to the escalation of new home prices; yet its success in discouraging homebuilding has failed to produce important environmental benefits for the public at large. Instead it has protected the environmental, social, and economic advantages of established suburban residents who live near land that could be used for new housing [p. 4].

    Frieden goes on to cite a survey of Sierra Club members that showed that two-thirds of the principal wage earners in member households were doctors, lawyers, dentists, or other professionals (college teachers, managers, executives, engineers). Over half had some postgraduate education. Thus, Frieden sees environmentalists who oppose homebuilding as acting out of self-interest (p. 130).

70. Stanley Scott, GOVERNING CALIFORNIA'S COAST (Berkeley: University of California, Berkeley, Institute of Governmental Studies, 1975), 5. Scott documents this period of splintered activity by the environmentalists by pointing to the bevy of bills submitted before the inception of the California Coastal Alliance, numbering 1,100.

71. Tom Gorton, *The Debate Rages Over California's Coastal Law*, PLANNING 31 (April/May 1977).
72. See Healy, LAND USE AND THE STATES. Healy is certainly a sympathetic observer of state land-use schemes, yet he concluded that the 55 percent who approved of Proposition 20 were by and large the well-off: "An analysis of the vote found that Proposition 20 did best in counties with a high proportion of college graduates and a high degree of urbanization. The yes vote was negatively correlated with location along the coast, location in Southern California, median income, and the percentage of families living in poverty (p. 73)."
73. Robert C. Ellickson, *Ticket to Thermidor: A Commentary on the Proposed California Coastal Plan*, 49 S. CALIF. L. REV. 715, 733 (1976), is an analysis of the 1975 Plan proposed by the Coastal Commission.
74. California Coastal Zone Conservation Act of 1972, CALIFORNIA PUB. RES. CODE, §§ 27000-27650 at § 27001.
75. *Id.* at sec. 27304.
76. Hagman and Kanner, amicus curiae brief in support of petitioner at 36, in *H.F.H. Ltd. v. Superior Court*, 15 Cal. 3d 508 (1975), as quoted in Donald W. Pach, *The Coastal Plan and the Property Owner*, in THE CALIFORNIA COASTAL PLAN: A CRITIQUE, ed. Eugene Bardach, et al. (San Francisco: Institute for Contemporary Studies, 1976), 139.
77. CALIFORNIA PUB. RES. CODE, § 27302.
78. Robert G. Healy, ed., PROTECTING THE GOLDEN SHORE (Washington, D.C.: Conservation Foundation, 1978), 21-23. Healy also observes that the rate of regional commission denials increased when the number of people appearing to testify against a permit increased.
79. Richard O'Reilly, *State Landowners Pitted in Beach Access*, LOS ANGELES TIMES, May 12, 1981.
80. CALIFORNIA COASTAL PLAN, California Coastal Zone Conservation Commissions, December 1975, 75.
81. *Id.* at 19-21.
82. *Id.* at 22.
83. *Id.* at 24.
84. *Id.* at 55.
85. *Id.* at 79.
86. *Id.* at 73, 78. In fact, the plan endorses virtually the whole range of environmentalist assumptions also, as evidenced by the following general pronouncements:

> The choice for California in 1976 is this: shall the Coast be abused, degraded, its remaining splendor eroded, or shall it be used intelligently with its majesty and productivity protected for future generations [p. 3].

As though only government planners can use resources "intelligently," and with foresight.

> Nobody can know all the answers, of course, but there is much we do know: that natural resources are limited; that inflation is in part caused by wasteful use of land and other finite resources; that increasing costs of energy and raw materials can only cause major changes in the lives of Californians—and that the irreplaceable agricultural lands needed to feed the world's growing population should not be squandered on developments that can be built elsewhere [p. 4].

Inflation: caused by wasteful use of land and resources? Now the Federal Reserve Board can stop wasting trees by printing up tons of dollars. And it is difficult to see how world hunger can be significantly ameliorated by preserving California agricultural land that produces such Third World staples as artichokes, strawberries, avocadoes, and so on.

87. *$359,000 and up in Portola*, SAN FRANCISCO SUNDAY EXAMINER & CHRONICLE, Feb. 15, 1981, 10.

88. For a detailed treatment of the passage of the 1976 bill, see Healy, PROTECTING THE GOLDEN SHORE, 43-56; Jonathan M. Davidson, *Coastal Zone Management in California: Strategies for Balancing Conservation and Development*, 15 URBAN LAW ANNUAL 253, 274-77 (1978). The bill is the California Coastal Act of 1976, CALIFORNIA PUB. RES. CODE, §§ 30000-30900.

89. *New Coastal Management*, SAN FRANCISCO CHRONICLE, Aug. 1, 1981.

90. *Landowners Fight the Coastal Plan*, SAN FRANCISCO CHRONICLE, Jan. 1, 1981.

91. *Coastal Commission Safe—This Year,* SAN FRANCISCO EXAMINER, April 29, 1981. Senator Ellis conducted two public hearings on his bill, SB 260; unfortunately no transcripts of these hearings were made. (Correspondence with Senator Jim Ellis, Nov. 3, 1981.)

92. For an overview of the facts on the development of the Sea Ranch, see *Oceanic California, Inc. v. North Central Coast Regional Commission*, 63 Cal. App. 3d 57, 133 Cal. Rptr. 664 (1976); Margaret Azavedo, *A Change of Heart on the Sea Ranch Decision*, SAN FRANCISCO CHRONICLE, Feb. 8, 1981. Healy, PROTECTING THE GOLDEN SHORE, 26-27; O'Reilly, *State Landowners Pitted on Beach Access*, LOS ANGELES TIMES, May 12, 1981.

93. Azavedo, *A Change of Heart* at 10.

94. Correspondence from Kati Corsaut, public information officer, California Coastal Commission, Dec. 8, 1981.

95. California Senate Select Committee on Land Use Management, hearings held in San Diego, Dec. 19, 1977, and in San Francisco, December 1, 1977.

96. See *Sea Ranch Association v. California Coastal Zone Conservation Commissions*, 396 F. Supp. 533, aff'd, 537 F. 2d 1058 (9th Cir. 1976). The plaintiffs had challenged the constitutionality of the permit system and the vested rights exemption system under the 1972 Coastal Act.

97. The Coastal Act provided for such vested right exemptions (CALIFORNIA PUB. RES. CODE, § 27404) but this provision proved controversial, generating a host of court cases.

98. *Sea Ranch Association v. The California Coastal Commission, et al.*, 527 F. Supp. 390 (N. Cal. 1981).

99. *Id.* at 392. The cases referred to in each of the quoted sentences are *Pennsylvania Coal Co. v. Mahon*, 260 U.S. 393 (1922); *Goldblatt v. Hempstead*, 369 U.S. 590 (1962); *Kaiser Aetna v. United States*, 444 U.S. 164, 175 (1979).

100. *Sea Ranch Association v. California Coastal Commission* at 397.

101. 701 L. ED. 2d (1981). In fact, the judicial web is even more intricate than indicated in the text. There was another case instigated by the Natural Resources Defense Council (*Natural Resources Defense Council v. California Coastal Zone Conservation Commission*, 57 Cal. App. 3d 76; 129 Cal. Rptr. 57 (1976)) that challenged a commission decision granting permits for the construction of fifteen homes at Sea Ranch. The environmental group con-

tended that the commission should have evaluated the environmental effects of the entire Sea Ranch project if completed, not just the effect of the fifteen homes. The court upheld the commission's grant of the conditional permits.

102. Lawrence Katz and Kenneth T. Rosen, THE EFFECT OF LAND USE CONTROLS ON HOUSING PRICES, Working Paper 80-13, (Berkeley: University of California, Berkeley, Center for Real Estate and Urban Economics, 1981).

103. *Housing Costs Here vs. Nation*, SAN FRANCISCO SUNDAY EXAMINER & CHRONICLE, Feb. 15, 1981.

104. Don Kazak, *Council Opts for Jobs Curb*, PALO ALTO WEEKLY, Oct. 2, 1980; *A Gradualist City Approach on Housing and Palo Alto's Future*, PALO ALTO WEEKLY, Sept. 18, 1980.

105. *How People Are Shifting Inland as Housing Prices Are Climbing*, SAN FRANCISCO SUNDAY EXAMINER & CHRONICLE, May 17, 1981.

106. Government regulation over land is nothing new to Britain; land-use and building regulation antedate Britain's industrial revolution. As Fred Bosselman points out (Fred Bosselman, David Callies, and John Banta, THE TAKINGS ISSUE: AN ANALYSIS OF THE CONSTITUTIONAL LIMITS OF LAND USE CONTROL [Washington, D.C.: Council on Environmental Quality, 1973], 65-69), regulatory schemes abounded in the sixteenth and seventeenth centuries: (1) in 1532 a statute of sewers was passed, authorizing commissioners to control the sewers and seawalls, (2) in 1580 Queen Elizabeth forbade the construction of any new houses within three miles of London, (3) in 1588 an act of Parliament mandated zoning, restricting buildings to one per four acres, (4) again in 1592 a parliamentary act prohibited new dwellings within three miles of London and put restraints upon the conversion of existing houses to multifamily use, (5) in 1607 and 1620 royal building regulations were promulgated, specifying types of material to be used and number of windows, and (6) after the London fire of 1666 extensive building codes for London were enacted. Herbert Spencer, in an essay in MAN VERSUS THE STATE, is particularly amusing on the extent of regulation in the precapitalist era.

107. Town and Country Planning Act of 1947, 10 & 11 Geo. 6, c. 51. As Donald Hagman pointed out, the 1947 act was not the first one in modern times to attempt to deal with the recoupment by government of the increase in the value of land. A 1909 Town Planning Act contained provisions for government recapture of the increase in value resulting from zoning, and another act in 1910 sought to gain for the state the unearned increment flowing to land through no effort to its owner. See Hagman, *English Planning and Environmental Law and Administration*, APA JOURNAL 162 (1980). On early precursors, see also Christopher J. Durksen, *England's Community Land Act: A Yankee's View*, 12 URB. L. ANN. 49, 55-57 (1976). He states that early planning acts required the payment of compensation to those injured by any provisions of a planning scheme except provisions imposed for the health or "amenity" of an area. The "betterment" recoupment schemes of the 1909 and 1932 acts never generated any revenue for the government. See also Roger W. Suddards, *The Individual and His Property in the 1980s: The Political and Legislative Outlook: David and Goliath*, J. PLAN. & ENVT'L L. 5 (1980).

108. For a more detailed treatment of the 1947 act, see Malcolm Grant, *The Community Land Act: An Overview; 1 the Planning Framework*, J. PLAN. & ENVT'L. 614 (1976); Hagman, *English Planning and Environmental Law*

and Administration; Jan Krasnowiecki and Ann Louise Strong, *Compensable Regulations for Open Space*; Durksen, *England's Community Land Act*; Lawrence Berger, *A Policy Analysis of the Taking Problem*, 49 N.Y.U. L. REV. 165, 203-4 (1974). For background on English property law, see Vincent Smith-Powell, REAL PROPERTY (London: Butterworth's, 1969); Frederick Pollock and Frederic William Maitland, HISTORY OF ENGLISH LAW (Cambridge: Cambridge University Press, 2d ed., 1899); Thomas P.H. Taswell-Langmead, ENGLISH CONSTITUTIONAL HISTORY (Boston: Houghton Mifflin, 10th ed. rev. by F.T. Plucknett, 1946).

109. On the Community Land Act, see Malcolm Grant, *Community Land?* J. PLAN & ENVT'L L. 669 (1978); Victor Moore, *The Community Land Bill*, 1 and 2, J. PLAN & ENVT'L L. 250 and 319 (1975); Grant, *The Community Land Act*; Frederick Corfield and Robert Carnwath, *The Community Land Bill: An Assessment*, J. PLAN & ENVT'L L. 385 (1975); Durksen, *England's Community Land Act*.

110. LAND WHITE PAPER, LAND, CMND. No.5730 (1974), 1.

111. Donald G. Hagman, *A New Deal: Trading Windfalls for Wipeouts*, in NO LAND IS AN ISLAND, 172.

112. On transferable development rights, see Frank Schnidman, *Transferable Development Rights: An Idea in Search of Implementation*, 11 LAND AND WATER L. REV. 339 (1976).

113. Reily, THE USE OF LAND, 135-42. Another greatly influential work on the takings issue also praises the British system and urges us to try it here. See Bosselman et al., THE TAKINGS ISSUE, 327. Others who argue for some system of recoupment of benefits by government include Charles Haar and Barbara Hering, *The Determination of Benefits in Land Acquisition*, 51 CAL. L. REV. 833 (1963); Wexler, *Betterment Recovery: A Financial Proposal for Sounder Land Use Planning*, 3 YALE REV. L. & SOC. ACTION 197 (1973).

2

The Genesis and Development of the Eminent Domain and Police Powers

The well-known science fiction writer, Robert Heinlein, tells a story of a time traveler sequentially entering alternative axes of reality.[1] In one of the character's time-jumps she lands in New York's Times Square, but she enters the time frame backwards, so that everyone else's past is her future. She flees in terror as people around her run backwards and the famous sign above the square prints its messages backwards also. Upon her return, her mentor remarks that it was fortunate that she escaped in time because in all probability the human mind could not long sustain such dissonance.

One feels much the same cognitive disarray when forced to examine the tortuous judicial history of the Fifth Amendment's takings clause. Whether a property owner recovers damages for losses sustained at the hands of the government is more often than not fortuitous. It depends less on the justice of the owner's claim than on the historical accident that the particular loss has been subsumed under one category rather than another. Thus, seemingly similar economic losses in dollar amount or even in physical kind, can result in wildly divergent treatment by the courts: either full compensation or no compensation at all. Commentators, legions of them, have also failed in their efforts to reconcile these disparate decisions. Nearly everyone of them has despaired at the incongruity of the judicial record.[2] The "takings mess" is so deep that even Supreme Court justices have been known to confuse matters utterly. They end up talking of government condemnation proceedings under eminent domain as though they were adjudicating an instance of the use of the police power.[3] Certain classes of cases have been treated in such an illogical fashion—cases dealing with the servitude of the federal government over navigable rivers for example—that they have carried the phrase "a distinction without a difference" to its limit.

To map this choppy terrain is the mission of this chapter. Understanding both the history and the current application of eminent domain and police power adjudication should convincingly demonstrate the impracticality of

71

pragmatic, *ad hoc* decision making. We will discover that even the original conception of these powers was flawed. They were defended with the flimsiest of arguments. First, let us turn to an examination of the origins of the state's eminent domain power, and the early justifications for it in the works of both legal philosophers and jurists.

The Sovereign's Power of Eminent Domain

> . . . it is evident, that the right of acquiring and possessing property, and having it protected, is one of the natural, inherent and inalienable rights of man. Men have a sense of property: property is necessary to their subsistence, and correspondent to their natural wants and desires; its security was one of the objects that induced them to unite in society. No man could become a member of a community, in which he could not enjoy the fruits of his honest labor and industry. The preservation of property, then, is a primary object of the social compact.[4]

The right to own private property has been long cherished in the Anglo-American tradition, but it has been always qualified by two conditions that make it less than absolute: first, that one not use one's property in such a way as to impair one's neighbor's equal right to enjoy his or her property; second, that one bow to the superior right of the sovereign when called upon to surrender one's property to public exigency. However, in England this latter proviso began to be hedged with protections to the property owner even in early feudal times. In 1215 the Magna Charta proclaimed: "No Freeman shall be taken, or imprisoned, or be disseized of his Freehold . . . but by lawful Judgement of his Peers, or by the Law of the Land."[5] This declaration did not explicitly grant "just compensation" to those ousted from possession of their land, but such gradually became the acknowledged practice. By tradition, then, land could be taken only by a parliamentary act accompanied by the payment of compensation.[6] To do otherwise, it was surely believed, would constitute something less than the notion of fairness embodied in the concept of "law of the land." By the time of the American Revolution, English condemnation practice was well established. No longer could the king by prerogative encroach with impunity upon private property to erect defenses or seize provisions for his household. Rather, property taken had to be paid for, although property merely damaged at the sovereign's hand enjoyed no such protection, nor was the state hampered by any "public use" constraint.[7]

The right of the state to take property by eminent domain was well established in the American colonies. Eminent domain was used principally for the provision of such public improvements as highways, though in some cases it was delegated to private parties for such tasks as the drainage of lowlands, the construction of private roads, and the erection of private mills. The payment of compensation by government was customary by late colonial times,[8] even though in earlier years unimproved land had been taken for roads without any recompense, land of that sort having been abundant and cheap. The various mill acts enacted by the New England and several southern colonies are interesting because they afford an early example of the delegation of sovereign "taking" authority to private businesses. They were justified by the public advantage that would flow from the encouragement of certain nascent industries. For those upper riparian landowners damaged by the overflow of waters caused by the mill dams, remedies in law were provided, and they could recover for their losses.[9]

Thus, by the time of the ratification of the federal Constitution the power of governments to take property was well enshrined. Although the Constitution does not explicitly grant to the national government this power, it might be implied by such provisions as clauses 7 and 17 of Article 1, Section 8, which give Congress the authority to establish post offices and post roads, and to exercise exclusive legislative authority over all places purchased for the erection of forts, magazines, arsenals, dockyards, and other needful buildings. Significantly, the latter grant appeared to limit federal takings to an indirect course, one that would require the "Consent of the Legislature of the State" in which the property lies. And indeed, not until 1875, in *Kohl v. United States*, did the Supreme Court allow the federal government the ability to directly take property in its own name.[10] In this case, Justice Strong deduced a federal power to condemn in its own name both from the very nature of sovereignty and, more concretely, from the Fifth Amendment's takings clause, which reads: "nor shall private property be taken for public use, without just compensation." The latter inference was, undoubtedly, inventive. The requirement that the government must pay compensation when it takes was construed to imply a power to take in the first place. This clause, as virtually all commentators agree, is a restriction on government's powers, not a concession. To get a clearer fix on why the Fifth Amendment appears to qualify a power that the body of the Constitution nowhere expressly grants to the national government, will require a bit of explanation, both historical and philosophical.

The takings clause of the Fifth Amendment had an interesting provenance. Prior to the adoption of the federal Constitution only two states, Vermont and Massachusetts, had constitutional provisions requiring the payment of compensation for exercises of eminent domain. However, a majority of the early state constitutions did incorporate a protection of fundamental rights, the phrasing of which took its inspiration from Chapter 29 of the Magna Charta, something to the effect that "no freeman ought to be taken, or imprisoned, or disseized of his freehold, liberties, or privileges, or outlawed, or exiled, or in any manner destroyed, or deprived of his life, liberty, or property, but by the judgment of his peers, or by the law of the land."[11] It is, once again, important to note that these constitutional provisions were restrictions upon the hegemony of the states rather than entitlements ceded to the states. In none of these constitutions was the power of eminent domain explicitly granted to the states. Instead, their presumed authority was curtailed. Why the drafters of these constitutions, the legislatures, and the courts made such a presumption presents an intriguing puzzle in the history of ideas.

Before we attempt to unravel that puzzle, something ought to be mentioned about the genesis of the Fifth Amendment takings clause itself. Curiously, of the over two hundred proposals for amendments to the Constitution that emanated from the state ratifying conventions, none called for a circumscription of federal power in the manner of the eventually enacted takings clause. Four states did, however, offer proposals similar to the Magna Charta's stricture against depriving a person of life, liberty, or property except by "the law of the land," or "the judgment of his peers" or alternatively, by "due process of law."[12] The takings clause as we know it owes its origination to James Madison, who first introduced a version of it that required compensation for property taken, in a draft of June 8, 1789.[13] Given the dearth of firsthand evidence concerning Madison's intentions, and the lack of congressional debate targeted specifically at this clause, commentators can only speculate as to his motivation for including such a proviso. But given both the nation's colonial experience at the hands of the British and its own tawdry treatment of property rights during the Revolutionary War period—which included the confiscation of the property of Loyalists, the cancellation of debts owed to British subjects by the tobacco states, and the repudiations, inflation, and worthless bills of credit finagled by the states and the Continental Congress—it is not surprising that Madison would have favored an additional provision restricting governmental high-handedness and insuring the security of the individual's property rights.[14] Also, it is likely that Madison was influenced by various seventeenth- and eighteenth-century theoreticians of the natural law. Men like Grotius, Pufendorf, Vattel, Bynkershoek, and Montesquieu from the Continent and Blackstone from England were all well known in the United States and extremely influential. They all spoke of such an eminent domain power of the state, and all hedged it in with constraints of either a compensatory or public exigency variety. Grotius, for example, wrote:

> The property of subjects is under the eminent domain of the state, so that the state or he who acts for it may use and even alienate and destroy such

property, not only in the case of extreme necessity, in which even private persons have a right over the property of others, but for ends of *public utility*, to which ends those who founded civil society must be supposed to have intended that private ends should give way. But it is to be added that when this is done *the state is bound to make good the loss* to those who lose their property.[15]

Similarly, Pufendorf wrote:

The third right is Eminent Domain, which consists in this, that *when public necessity demands it*, the goods of any subject which are very *urgentlly needed* at the time, may be seized and *used for public purposes*, although they may be more valuable than the allotted share which he is supposed to give for the welfare of the republic. On this account, the excess value should, insofar as possible, be refunded to the citizen in question, either from the public funds, or from a contribution of the other citizens. [Emphasis added.][16]

Throughout the writings of the natural law philosophers the same refrains are sounded. These themes were destined to rebound through our two hundred years of constitutional history: that compensation must be paid by the government when property is taken; that property can be taken only when "public necessity" or "public utility" requires it, or when it is "urgently needed" (Pufendorf's language is a bit more restrictive of governmental takings, here, than is Grotius's); and that property taken must be used for a "public purpose." Pufendorf, incidentally, provides a rationale for compensation that has not yet been significantly improved upon by either judges or commentatotrs, i.e., that no one should be compelled to pay more than his fair share for public improvements, and if such a sacrifice is required the burden should be redistributed to others so that those called upon to make excessive sacrifices can be recompensed.

Although all of these thinkers acknowledged the duty of government to pay for abridgments of owners' property rights, and there is little to distinguish between them on this count, each thinker, nevertheless, offered slightly different justifications for the source of the state's eminent domain power. Grotius, for example, derived the power from the presumption that those who consented to join civil society, by affixing their names to the social contract, thereby intended that private claims should give way to those of "public utility." Precisely why such a presumption should be inherent in the social contract, Grotius did not say. That a polity might be conceivable that lacked the power to dispossess private owners did not occur to Grotius and his contemporaries.

These natural law theorists were enormously influential in the United States at the time Madison drafted the takings clause of the Fifth Amendment, and so it is unsurprising that he found it useful to include such a

provision as simply one more protection against the potentially overweening state.[17] It is clear, then, why Madison and the draftees of state constitutions wanted to circumscribe the eminent domain power. However, what
still remains shrouded in doubt is why they thought, in the first place, that
government possessed such a power irrespective of any explicit grants of it
by the people to their governments in their various constitutions. Given the
natural law tradition that permeated the thought of our forbears, it is
somewhat surprising that such a power was conceded with such alacrity,
for, according to contract theorists of the natural law school, people had
natural rights antecedent to government. Government was merely the
creature of human consent, established through the mechanism of a universally agreed upon social compact. If people in the state of nature that
preceded government did not have the right to take the property of another,
how could they, then, transfer this power to government? As John Locke
wrote of the supreme legislative power:

> It is *not*, nor can possibly be absolutely *Arbitrary* over the Lives and Fortunes
> of the People. For it being but the joynt power of every Member of the Society
> given up to that Person, or Assembly, which is Legislator, it can be no more
> than those persons had in a State of Nature before they enter'd into Society,
> and gave up to the Community. For no Body can transfer to another more
> power than he has in himself, and no Body has an absolute Arbitrary Power
> over himself, or over any other, to destroy his own Life, or take away the Life
> or Property of another. A Man, as has been proved, cannot subject himself to
> the Arbitrary Power of another; and having in the State of Nature no Arbitr-
> ary Power over the Life, Liberty, or Possession of another, but only so much
> as the Law of Nature gave him for the preservation of himself, and the rest of
> mankind; this is all he doth, or can give up to the Common-Wealth, and by it
> to the *Legislative Power*, so that the Legislative can have no more than this.[18]

Even Grotius, who acknowledged a right of a starving man to the superfluities of another, did not argue that such may be taken by a pure act of
theft; rather, it becomes a debt that must be repaid by the indigent person
when his fortunes rebound. This doctrine of Grotius presents little support
for governmental confiscation, because few takings perpetrated by the state
fall within these extreme boundaries of utter desperation. But even if a
takings justification could be extended from such a slender reed, Grotius
himself did not make the case.

Yet, despite this philosophical difficulty—of individuals lacking the
power to take from others somehow granting more power to the state than
they originally possessed—natural law theorists committed this logical
leap. Why? The answer seems to be that they found eminent domain to
form so much a part of the nature of government that government would
be inconceivable without it. Bynkershoek declared, if the eminent domain

power were destroyed, "no state could survive . . . that the sovereign has this authority, no man of sense questions." In other words, the power of eminent domain was presumed to be indubitable. They seemed also to assume without question that the "public good" should prevail over the private interests of recalcitrant landowners.

None of these arguments for the putative right of the state to take property—whether it be (1) the inherent attribute of sovereignty claim, or (2) the "public good" contention, or (3) the attempt to extract an implied consent to takings from the initial agreement to join civil society—flow inexorably from the natural law position. Indeed, the power of eminent domain seems to fit better with a feudal conception of property. But this was precisely the adversary that Locke and his later natural law followers like Blackstone attempted to banish. By the lights of feudal law, if William the Conqueror owns all estates and deigns to grant them to his favorites, while retaining ultimate ownership, there is no reason that he should not be able to reclaim them when "public necessity" requires. However, in a Lockean theory of property rights, in which property flows not from the state but from individual labor, and the state is nothing more than a device for the protection of preexisting, individual property, the power of eminent domain is not self-evident.

It is worth repeating that Madison, with his Fifth Amendment takings clause, succeeded only in limiting a power that everyone assumed the government had. Judges and commentators to this day have not really improved upon these sketchy justifications for eminent domain. They tend to echo the sentiments of the natural law theorists.[19] The natural law theorists passionately wished to protect individual liberty, but they simply failed to follow through consistently on their principles. They were great originators, and so their few oversights should not blind us to their achievements. For them, economic rights were of tremendous importance. Thus it is something of an historical irony that their casual acceptance of eminent domain has set the stage for our current situation in which property rights are often but ill protected by our institutions.

Suffice it to say, then, that the Constitution of the United States as amended by the Fifth Amendment came to limit a power—of eminent domain—that is nowhere expressly granted to the government. Why this peculiar state of affairs proved unperplexing to legal theorists and judges can be explained, as we have seen, by the fact that everyone acquiesced in the presumption that the state possessed such a power. The natural law theorists, both Continental and English, concurred in the existence of eminent domain. English parliamentary history confirmed the exercise of the power. In short, eminent domain was uncontroversial, requiring no elaborate justification.

After the adoption of the federal Constitution's Fifth Amendment takings constraint, similar restrictions were fairly rapidly adopted by the states, either by constitutional provision, or by judicial inference from natural law.[20] Thus, property owners enjoyed a certain protection from the confiscatory proclivities of government. That is, while they could not prevent the seizure itself, except in a very few exceptional cases,[21] they would receive the "just compensation" required by either constitutional or judicial construction.

The universal adoption by the states of Fifth Amendment-style restrictions on their taking powers was particularly significant. Virtually all eminent domain disputes were heard in state courts, the Supreme Court under Chief Justice Marshall having decreed very early in the game, in 1833 in *Barron v. Baltimore*, that the federal takings clause was applicable only to the national government and not to the states.[22] Before adoption of the Fourteenth Amendment and its due process clause, which eventually became the vehicle for the Supreme Court's application on a case-by-case basis of nearly all of the Bill of Rights to the States, Marshall's decision blocked eminent domain cases from appeal beyond the state courts. Only one case managed to breach this barricade. In *West River Bridge v. Dix* (1848)[23] the Supreme Court agreed to decide a state case on its merits, but only because the plaintiffs raised not a Fifth Amendment takings objection but, rather, one based on Article I, Section 10 of the Constitution, that is, the provision barring the states from impairing the obligation of contracts. The state of Vermont had granted to West River Bridge an exclusive franchise to operate a bridge for one hundred years. While the Court agreed with the plaintiff that such a charter constituted a contract between the state and the company, it denied that the taking of such a contract breached the impairment of contracts prohibition. Rather, Justice Daniel contended for the majority, the state's power of eminent domain is "paramount to all private rights vested under the government, and these last are by necessary implication, held in subordination to this power, and must yield in every instance to its proper exercise."[24] Thus, all contracts, including those entered into by the legislature, and upon which a company had relied, could be taken by eminent domain, should the public good require. Seemingly, a rather odd conclusion, one among many that served to eviscerate the contract clause, while strengthening the states' power to take all kinds of interests in property.[25]

It was only in 1897 that the high court read the Fifth Amendment's takings clause into the due process clause of the Fourteenth Amendment. The latter amendment, adopted in 1868 to secure equal rights of citizenship to the manumitted black slaves, mirrors the Fifth Amendment's liberty and property protections, except for the omission of the takings clause. While the Fifth Amendment reads in part; "No person shall be . . .

deprived of life, liberty, or property, without due process of law; nor shall private property be taken for public use, without just compensation," the Fourteenth Amendment replaces the takings clause with another, one guaranteeing to all individuals equal rights under the law. Thus, the first section of the Fourteenth Amendment concludes; "nor shall any state deprive any person of life, liberty, or property without due process of law; nor deny any person within its jurisdiction the equal protection of the law." What the Court discerned in *Chicago Burlington and Quincy Railroad Company v. Chicago* (1897)[26] was that the payment of just compensation for property taken formed such an essential right of ownership that any derogation of that right, any taking without recompense, violated "due process of law." The notion of "due process of law," of course, captures the insight that not everything that legislatures might enact, or officials procedurally interpret, would meet constitutional standards. In other words, there exists a higher concept of law against which legislative acts and procedural rules must be measured.

The decision in *Chicago Burlington* was significant because it opened the way for Supreme Court review of state court decisions on eminent domain. Now it would be possible for aggrieved landowners to contend that federal review of their cases was legitimate, because their due process rights under the Fourteenth Amendment had been violated when their property was taken without payment of just compensation.

Winning the jurisdictional battle in this particular case, however, did the appellant railroad no good. The company had argued that when the city of Chicago opened a public street on its land with compensation of one dollar, it had been deprived of property without due process of law. Although Justice Harlan concluded for the majority of the Court that due process requires compensation for property taken, he argued it was improper for the Court to reexamine the final judgment of a state court on a matter of fact, that is, the state court's determination that no significant property right had been taken. The Seventh Amendment explicitly bars federal courts from reexamining facts settled by state tribunals. On the question of whether the trial court erred in prescribing a rule of law to the jury, which is reviewable, the Supreme Court would rule that no such error had transpired. First of all, the Court found nothing objectionable in the city's claim and in state law that if the railroad was not prevented from using the land for railroad purposes, it was not taken. Second, no error of law occurred when the trial court excluded from testimony evidence of the railroad's costs in erecting a gateway to make the street-crossing safe. "Such expenses must be regarded as incidental to the exercise of the police powers of the State," the Court reasoned.[27] In other words, such losses were not recoverable, and must be borne by the landowner.

Justice Brewer, in a rather heated dissent, found his colleagues' decision outrageous, calling it monstrous to deprive the railroad of its property without just compensation. Even though the company's present activities were not substantially interfered with, it was nevertheless deprived of potential uses of its land and should be recompensed for that loss.

Such perplexing decisions as this one in *Chicago Burlington* are more the rule than the exception in this area of the law. Courts frequently proclaim, as the majority did here, strong support for property rights. The Court stated that the taking of property from one to give to another would constitute a violation of due process.[28] But then it left the landowner without compensation. This is not an isolated occurrence.

"Property," "Just Compensation," and "Public Use"

Property and Just Compensation. Ever since *Chicago Burlington*, as the Supreme Court has involved itself with eminent domain cases, it has helped shape condemnation law in respect to the three essential concepts that constitute the takings clause: "property," "just compensation," and "public use." The term *property* has been successively broadened to include all types of interests in land, stretching beyond fee title to include leaseholds, future interests, materialman's liens,[29] contracts[30]—in other words, all rights to use, dispose of, and enjoy dominion over property. In *United States v. General Motors* (1945), for example, the high court declared that the term *property* is not used in the

> vulgar and untechnical sense of the physical thing with respect to which the citizen exercises rights recognized by law. [Rather it] . . . denote[s] the group of rights inhering in the citizen's relation to the physical thing. . . . The constitutional provision is addressed to every sort of interest the citizen may possess.[31]

Although the protections for property owners, built up by both federal and state courts, are extensive, they are not complete, for many losses termed "incidental" escape the protective net. Thus, one can be certain that if the government officially condemns one's land or a property interest one will be compensated. Also, if an actual physical invasion of one's property is perpetrated by the government or its agent, compensation should be recoverable. One can entertain no such certainty when it comes to such losses as the depletion of business goodwill when a company is forced to relocate,[32] or business relocation costs, or a drop in market value of one's home as a result of the construction of a new highway or sewage plant. Such "incidental" or "consequential" damages, unless explicitly covered by legislative provisions allocating compensation, fall between the cracks of judicial notice: they are considered *damnum absque injuria*.[33]

The term *just compensation* as fleshed out by the courts has come to mean "fair market value." But given the nature of the act—that the government is seizing your property, and that you have not voluntarily consented to the exchange, and thus that no "market" transaction could conceivably be involved—courts have done about as well as could be expected. Thus, for those categories of losses that the courts are willing to recognize, former owners can be fairly confident that they will get decent treatment, if not from the condemning agency itself, then upon appeal to the courts. It is a settled judicial practice that the determination of "just compensation" is considered a "judicial question," hence reviewable by the courts. Now, what exactly do the courts mean by "fair market value"? Normally, it is taken to be an approximation of what a willing buyer would pay in cash to a willing seller. The result should place the former owner in the same position monetarily as theretofore. The former owner should neither suffer a detriment nor reap a windfall profit.[34] Government condemners should not take unfair advantage when taking property whose value has depreciated as a result of the anticipated public condemnation, nor should they, on the other hand, reward owners whose land has appreciated through an anticipation of government plans.[35] Courts frequently have represented "fair market value" as equivalent to the "highest and best use" likely for the parcel as that prospect influences market value.[36] As in nearly all things judicial, a not inconsiderable fudge factor has been built into the concept of "fair market value." The high court frequently reiterates that this is not an "absolute standard." Sometimes, in fact, fair market value can mean that an owner is forced to sell property at a government-decreed ceiling price, even though that price represents considerably less than what a market price would be, and much less than the owner originally paid to acquire the property.[37]

While the general framework of "fair market value" seems pretty reasonable in theory, the abuses in practice are legion. Opportunistic speculators avail themselves of political connections to buy up at bargain-basement prices properties that lie in the future path of yet-unannounced public projects. They eventually reap substantial profits in the form of "fair market value." But the blame for these kinds of dealings cannot be placed at the feet of judges; rather, the fault lies with the extent of eminent domain takings. Vast urban renewal projects, intercontinental highways, to say nothing of Cadillac plants, involve takings much beyond those post offices and post roads anticipated by the founding fathers.

Yet there have been improvements in the courts' handling of eminent domain cases. The most significant advance in protection for property owners has occurred in the category of cases falling under the rubric "consequential damages." In such cases owners whose property or property rights have been impaired by a governmental project go to court to recover damages, claiming that what has befallen the property is tantamount to a takings and should be recompensed. These kinds of claims, known as "inverse condemnations," are really the result of historical accident. Because of the doctrine of sovereign immunity, governments at all levels were historically shielded from any suits by individual property owners injured by governmental actions. Thus, owners who could sue other private individuals who might have inflicted the same kinds of injuries as a government had—under nuisance or trespass theories—were barred from bringing those claims against governments. In recent years such barriers have crumbled, and governments are now subject to a wide range of suits. Unfortunately for the sake of legal clarity, such developments came too late. The legal landscape had already been confused as generations of aggrieved property owners had sought the only remedy then available; i.e., a claim of "inverse condemnation," a takings equivalent to eminent domain as a result of the government's infliction of a "consequential injury."

If we return for a moment to nineteenth-century adjudication, we will see that even this remedy was, with few exceptions, denied to adversely affected owners. Despite the efforts of Chancellor Kent of New York in *Gardner v. Newburgh*[38] in 1816 to open the door to recovery for consequential damages, the contrary view prevailed. Landowners were left with no remedy. A leading case from Massachusetts, *Callendar v. Marsh*[39] in 1823, set the judicial course for the next fifty years, when it denied compensation to a homeowner whose house was damaged by the construction of a street. The court reasoned that because street construction fell within the legitimate bounds of the government's police power, and no actual physical taking of the fee to the property had occurred, no compensation was necessary for the consequential damages suffered as a result of the road construction.

Now, back in the early part of the past century governments at all levels were not particularly active in promoting public improvements. When they were, there was still so much empty land, and the country was so sparsely populated, that no critical mass of offended landowners existed to protest these types of decisions. However, as the country developed, population burgeoned in cities, and governments became more active in the erection of infrastructure to promote industrial development. Gradually, enough homeowners saw their houses collapse when street grades were altered or above-ground train tracks were constructed, and enough others empathized with their plight that the law changed in many states. Sometimes this transformation was accomplished by court decisions, but more often it was the result of constitutional changes wrought at the behest of outraged property owners at state constitutional conventions. Illinois got the ball rolling in the early 1870s, and soon half of the state constitutions had eminent domain provisions allowing, now, for recovery when property was "taken or damaged." But even in these states, the courts made it clear soon enough that the public treasury would not be raided for every trivial injury. Rather, the "damage" would have to be significant, peculiar to the offended property, and different in kind from that suffered by the general public. Courts were generally chary of promulgating any rule that would encourage a flood of spurious suits or work to discourage local governments from undertaking needed public improvements.[40]

Recovery for consequential damages first received Supreme Court approval in 1871 in *Pumpelly v. Green Bay Co.*[41] Pumpelly brought an action for trespass on the case against Green Bay Company for flooding 640 acres of his land. The flooding was a result of the company's construction of a dam authorized by a Wisconsin statute. The defendant cited numerous cases holding that consequential damages should be denied to those owning land along navigable rivers, on the ground that states have a superior right to regulate and improve navigation. Nevertheless, the Court found for Pumpelly. The Court argued that such decisions denying recovery, while valid in their proper application, have "gone to the utmost limit of sound judicial construction . . . and, in some cases, beyond it."[42] In this case, where an almost complete destruction of the value of the land occurred as a result of continuous flooding, the Court found a taking, irrespective of the fact that the company had not taken title to the land. A similar result would be reached, the Court indicated, if property were invaded by earth, sand, or other materials, or by having artificial structures placed upon it, which effectively destroyed or impaired the usefulness of the property. To rule otherwise, Justice Miller contended, would constitute a

> very curious and unsatisfactory result, if in construing a provision of constitutional law, always understood to have been adopted for protection and security to the rights of the individual as against the government . . . it shall be held that if the government refrains from the absolute conversion of real property to the uses of the public it can destroy its value entirely, can inflict irreparable and permanent injury to any extent, can, in effect subject it to total destruction without making any compensation, because, in the narrowest sense of that word, it is not *taken* for the public use. Such a construction would pervert the constitutional provision into a restriction upon the rights of the citizen, as those rights stood at the common law, instead of the government, and make it an authority for invasion of private right under the pretext of the public good, which has no warrant in the laws or practices of our ancestors.[43]

When the Court eventually came, in *United States v. Lynah* (1903),[44] to decide a similar case under the Fifth Amendment, and not as in *Pumpelly* under an almost identical provision of the Wisconsin Bill of Rights, it reached the same conclusion. In *Lynah*, the United States government had caused the owner's rice plantation to be converted into an "irreclaimable bog," deprived of all value, due to the erection of a dam across a navigable waterway. The court found that the government must compensate Lynah for his losses. However, three justices dissented from the majority's decision, arguing that because a large segment of Lynah's plantation fell below the high-water mark, and thus was forever dependent for its drainage upon the continuance of low tides, to which he had no right, the loss of drainage should remain uncompensable. As the Supreme Court would come to hear more and more cases of riparian owners suffering injury at the hands of governmental improvements, this issue of low and high tides, which apparently seemed irrelevant to the *Lynah* majority, would take on immense importance to injured owners. And so would the issue of whether affected land bordered on navigable or nonnavigable streams.

To see how these two technicalities took on such awesome dimensions, a little legal background is in order. Under English common law, navigable waterways were considered ones in which the tides ebbed and flowed. The crown was held to be the owner of the beds of all such waterways. U.S. circumstances differed from the English because many rivers that were suitable for navigation were not subject to tides. What developed out of this difference was a new rule regarding the government's "navigable servitude." First of all, a stream, river, or lake was defined as navigable if it could be used for the purpose of navigation, or if it could be rendered suitable for such use by the application of "reasonable improvements."[45] Land bordering upon the ocean is privately owned in most states only to the mean high-tide line, and the shore between that line and the low-tide line is generally considered as held in trust for the people of the state. In regard to navigable rivers and streams, in most states the beds of such waters are claimed by the state, the cutoff point being either the high- or low-water mark. Along nonnavigable streams, adjacent (riparian) owners hold the bed of the streams as their property up to the middle of the waterway, or the entire breadth if they own the land on both banks. Now, the federal government gets into the act by way of its constitutional power to regulate commerce, which includes the power to improve navigation. The states share a piece of the action through their power to improve navigable waters in ways not limited by federal authority.

To see how the plot thickened, let us examine a case decided in 1904, *Bedford v. United States*.[46] The Court bent logic to distinguish the facts of this case from either *Pumpelly* or *Lynah*. *Bedford* concerned damages to land by flooding that resulted from the construction by the federal government of revetments along the banks of the Mississippi River. The revetments were designed to prevent erosion. What the Court, speaking through Justice McKenna, wished to conclude was that such damages were "strictly consequential," and hence were not deserving of compensation. To reach this conclusion, however, either the two earlier cases would have had to be overruled, because they allowed recovery for injuries certainly consequential in nature, or some distinction had to be made between *Bedford* and its forebears. The former course is always distasteful to the Court (after all, what body wants to admit having made a mistake); the second course was the one chosen. What the Court concluded, in effect, was that some consequential injuries are less consequential than others. Justice McKenna drew the distinction that while in *Pumpelly* and *Lynah* there occurred an actual invasion and appropriation—by flooding, let us recall—here the erosion was the result of the river's action over a period of years. The government's action was merely a reaction to natural causes in the interest of preventing further erosion. Some significance was also discerned in the fact that in *Lynah* the obstructing work was placed in the bed of the river, while in *Bedford* the government had placed sandbags only on the banks of the river. A rather strained distinction, especially when it resulted in an uncompensable loss to Bedford of over $3,000.[47] These seemingly trivial technical details, which served to discriminate *Bedford* from its two predecessors, led to wildly different results: Pumpelly and Lynah secured full redress for their grievances in the form of "just compensation," and Bedford was left to suffer his wounds without any relief whatsoever.

As matters progressed, the rules in general became more rather than less confused. However, over some situations the rules became clearer.[48] For example, if an owner suffered losses from denial of access to a navigable river due to a governmental action to improve navigation, no compensation would be recoverable. Similarly, if a riparian owner's wharves or piers on a navigable river were destroyed as a result of a government's construction project in the river, the loss would fall entirely upon the owner. Also, the Court would afix no responsibility upon the government to recompense riparian owners who objected to the construction of navigational aids or railroad tracks built below the high-water mark. Thus, it became a fairly settled rule that property owners abutting navigable rivers could erect improvements below high-water mark only at their own risk. For governmental actions disruptive of business operations—such as those caused by the loss of a head of water, or the fall or rise in the water table affecting an electrical power plant—no recovery would be allowed in the absence of an explicit legislative grant. The government would have to show that its activity proceeded from a desire to improve navigation, broadly construed, and, then, the Court would defer to the legislature in the determination of which activities served to improve navigation.

The reasoning of Justice Jackson in *United States v. Willow River Power Co.* (1945)[49] is particularly revealing. Here, Willow River Power, the owner of a dam and hydroelectric plant near the confluence of a navigable stream and a nonnavigable stream, claimed a right to compensation under the Fifth Amendment when the government raised the level of the navigable stream above the ordinary high-water mark, thereby diminishing the plant's generating capacity. Despite an award of $25,000 from the court of claims for the loss of power, the Supreme Court held otherwise, declaring that no compensable injury had occurred. Justice Jackson, straying far from the judicial concerns of an earlier day for protecting property, contended:

> The Fifth Amendment, which requires just compensation where private property is taken for public use, undertakes to redistribute certain economic losses inflicted by public improvements so that they will fall upon the public rather than wholly upon those who happen to fall in the path of the project. It does not undertake, however, to socialize all losses, but those only which result from a taking of property. . . . It is clear, of course, that a head of water has value and that the company has an economic interest. . . . But not all economic interests are "property rights"; only those economic advantages are "rights" which have the law back of them, and only when they are so recognized may courts compel others to forbear from interfering with them or to compensate for their invasion.[50]

Justice Jackson's reasoning stands in marked contrast to Justice Millers' concern in *Pumpelly* to protect owners from consequential damages. What is disturbing about this line of reasoning is that it places at the discretion of courts and legislatures what they choose to protect under the rubric "property rights." Is it not all too easy, then, one fears, for a future court to come along and declare that many other kinds of holdings are not truly "property" and, therefore, do not deserve compensation because they cannot be "taken" under the Fifth Amendment when the government destroys their value? What the Court said in this case was this: Yes, you have an economic interest, and a "right" with respect to other property owners, but no "property right when confronted by the government; therefore, you have no "right protected by law" when the government depreciates your economic interest. "Where these interests conflict," as between a riparian owner and the government, "they are not to be reconciled as between equals, but the private interest must give way to a superior right, or perhaps it would be more accurate to say that as against the Government such private interest is not a right at all."[51]

It seems odd that one can have rights against other individuals to the enjoyment of one's property, but these rights evaporate when confronted by the government. Is this not precisely the kind of negation of property rights against which the Fifth Amendment was designed to protect? The judicial doctrine of the state's navigable servitude conveniently vitiates such rights, simply declaring them nonexistent as against the government.

The navigable servitude is a convenient doctrine for protecting the public treasury while encouraging public works. Indeed, recently several state courts have extended the doctrine even further to include under its sway tidal waters and marshlands. They want to prohibit dredging and to broaden the concept of the public interest in navigation to include fishing, swimming, boating, and recreation, and the right to have tidelands remain in their natural state. Some commentators look to the day when the navigable servitude or "public trust" doctrine can be extended by government to allow for a much wider range of uncompensated, police-power-type regulation. But more of that a bit later when we discuss the police power.[52]

What makes the navigable servitude doctrine particularly disturbing is that almost identical kinds of losses can be treated in diametrically opposite ways. One may receive either full compensation or absolutely none at all, depending on seemingly fortuitous factors, such as whether one's violated property falls along a "nonnavigable" or "navigable" river. In the latter case one will fail in an attempt at recovery; in the former case one will likely succeed. If we compare the following case with *Willow River Power* this anomalous situation will appear striking. Recall that in the preceding case, Willow River was denied compensation for losses sustained when a United States navigational improvement raised the water level on a navigable river. In *United States v. Kansas City Life Insurance Co.* (1950)[53] the loss appears not dissimilar in kind, yet the Court concluded that the property owner enjoyed a protected property right, and consequently, "just compensation" became the property owner's due. In this case, the federal government, while improving navigation upon the Mississippi River by installing a dam, raised the water level continually to its high-water mark. This resulted in the underflowing of Kansas City Life's land, which lay along the banks of a nonnavigable tributary of the Mississippi. The land, as a result, became waterlogged, which substantially depreciated its market value, and completely destroyed its value as agricultural land. Because the land happened to lie along a nonnavigable river, the Court did not have to perform its various logical gymnastics—no need to determine high-water marks, or to make fine distinctions on the question of consequential injury. The case was simply subsumed under the general rule that the destruction of privately owned land by flooding is a taking to the extent of that destruction. Thus, in the case of *Willow River Power* the government did not have to pay for raising the water level and injuring the plaintiff's land, while in the case of *Kansas City Life* such an increase in the water level triggered a governmental obligation to pay for what it had taken.

Some justices have noted the inconsistencies inherent in such outcomes. Unfortunately they would not strengthen the rights of property owners; rather, they desire a more exclusive rule that would further diminish the instances in which government would be required to compensate land-owners. Justice Douglas and three of his colleagues, for example, dissented from the majority's conclusion favoring compensation in *Kansas City Life*. Douglas argued that because an owner riparian to the Mississippi would not have a right to the unfettered flow of the Mississippi in its natural state, neither should an owner situated on a tributary to the Mississippi. Finding it incongruous that the owner abutting the Mississippi would be denied compensation while owners on tributaries could recover damages, Douglas concluded that in neither instance should governnment pay for con-sequential injuries. Now, what Justice Douglas's position gains in logical consistency, it then sacrifices in fairness. Given the murky state of the law, however, it was just a matter of time before someone articulated this posi-tion, which strengthens the government at the expense of the property owner. This position harkens back to the pre-*Pumpelly* days when con-sequential damages were treated as *damnum absque injuria*.

While the high court has not embraced Douglas's attempt at consistency, it has done nothing in the intervening years to clarify this confusing and contradictory area of the law. Often it looks as though rules are made after judges have intuited the "correct" response—either "taking" or "no tak-ing."[54] In a recent case dealing with the navigable servitude, the Court may have given a bit of pause to those who want to stretch the concept even farther. *Kaiser Aetna v. United States* (1979)[55] served to reaffirm that there is a limit to the navigable servitude doctrine imposed by the Fifth Amend-ment's takings clause even if the justices cannot define precisely where this limit lies. Kaiser Aetna, operating in Hawaii, had dredged out a two-foot-deep pond cut off from a bay by a strip of beach for the purposes of improving access to its private marina. The government then filed suit to determine two issues: whether the company by dredging had placed itself under the authority of the Corps of Engineers for approval of future im-provements, and whether the pond must be open for the public's use now that it had been rendered navigable. Justice Rehnquist concluded for the Court that while Kaiser placed its property under the regulatory power of the Corps of Engineers by its dredging, it did not follow that the govern-ment could demand that the public have access to the pond. He wrote: "This Court has never held that the navigational servitude creates a blanket exception to the Takings Clauses whenever Congress exercises its Com-merce Clause authority to promote navigation."[56] While adverting to one of the Court's favorite phrases—that there is no set formula for determin-ing when a taking has occurred, and each case must be determined on its own merits—Rehnquist displayed an appreciation of the arbitrariness of much adjudication in the area of riparian condemnation cases. He noted a "shifting back and forth of the Court in this area until the most recent decisions bear the sound of 'Old, unhappy, far off things, and battles long ago.'"[57] Thus, if the government wishes to convert Aetna's pond into a public aquatic park it can do so only by invoking the eminent domain power and paying just compensation. Three of the justices, Blackmun, Brennan, and Marshall, would have found the pond subject to the federal government's navigable servitude, thus denying compensation. The owners, according to the dissenters, acted at their own risk in dredging their pond.

Enough has been said regarding the government's navigable servitude to illustrate just how confusing *ad hoc* decision making can be. It results in no clearly delineated rules, and no firm guidelines for property owners about what uses of their property place them at risk. So arbitrary are the outcomes in these cases that they hardly approximate the rule of law.

Before moving along, I might mention another arena in which the consequential damages controversy has been waged, one in which, happily, *ad hoc* decision making has resulted in more protection for property owners. The leading case on airport noise is *United States v. Causby*,[58] which the Supreme Court decided in 1945. Justice Douglas delivered the opinion of the Court. The Causby's chicken farm was subjected to frequent low overflights of military aircraft, the noise and glare from which caused 150 chickens to die of fright, diminished the remaining chickens' productivity, and caused constant upset to the Causby family. The Causbys came to fear that they might be the victims of a plane crash, of which there had been several in the immediate vicinity. Their chicken business was completely destroyed as a result of the overflights, at least that was the finding of the court of claims. That court found that the United States had taken an easement over the property as of June 1, 1942, when the flights began. It awarded the Causbys compensation in the amount of $2,000. What Douglas and his fellow justices sought to determine was whether the government had taken the Causbys' property within the meaning of the Fifth Amendment. This was denied by the United States, which contended that because the federal government had asserted control over navigable airspace,[59] no physical invasion of the property of the landowners had occurred. The injuries suffered by the Causbys were merely consequential, and as such were *damnum absque injuria*.

Douglas's reasoning apparently turned upon the question of property definition. That is, did the Causbys have a property interest in the airspace immediately above their farm that had been detrimentally invaded by the flight of the military aircraft? Interestingly, Douglas summarily rejected the old common law *ad coelum* doctrine, i.e., that the owner of the land owns the airspace above it to the heavens.[60] Such dogmas have no place in the modern world for good, pragmatic reasons. They would render all over-flights prohibitively expensive if not impossible, as each owner of the sub-adjacent land could file suit for trespass. But where do the owner's rights end if the government by congressional act has declared the navigable airways to be public highways? The Court refused to decide that issue with any precision:

> The airplane is part of the modern environment of life, and the inconve-niences which it causes are normally not compensable under the Fifth Amendment. The airspace apart from the immediate reaches above the land is part of the public domain. *We need not determine at this time what those precise limits are.* Flights over private land are not a taking, unless they are so low and so frequent as to be a direct and immediate interference with the enjoyment and use of the land. [Emphasis added.][61]

But what is clear from Douglas's opinion is that if the owner is to enjoy the full use of his property, he must be considered to control the "immediate reaches of the enveloping atmosphere." As much as the owner can use and occupy, so much is his own, even if all the space is not occupied by build-ings. Douglas analogized the airplane flight intrusions upon the Causbys' enjoyment to a hypothetical situation in which the government might construct an elevated railway over their land. Even if none of the supports adhered to the land, the owners would still be ousted from an important element of their enjoyment of the land, and they would have to be compen-sated for that loss. Thus, the damages inflicted on the Causbys' land were not "merely consequential"; rather, they were "the product of a direct invasion of respondents' domain."[62] This novel device, then, of an air easement "taken" by the government allowed the Causbys to recover for their losses.[63] The Supreme Court remains satisfied with its ruling in *Causby*, for when a similar situation came before it again in 1962, it reached a similar conclusion: when airplane overflights are so disruptive as to virtually destroy an owner's enjoyment of his property, a taking in the constitutional sense has transpired, and the government must pay for the air easement it has taken.[64]

In conclusion, "just compensation," promised to property owners by the Fifth Amendment, has proven itself to be a complex notion. Surely, if the government condemns your property the just compensation language of-fers protection, but will you be made whole again? Certainly not if your particular piece of property held special meaning for you, or you sustained uncompensable business losses. And receipt of "fair market value" will seem of little comfort to you if you never wished to sell in the first place, and no true market bargain could have taken place.

As it turns out, the problems of an actual condemnee pale in comparison to those of the owners of property inadvertently infringed upon as the incidental by-product of a government public works. Over a certain range of injuries, these property owners can feel fairly certain that the courts will insist that governments compensate for their destructive actions: if one's land along a nonnavigable river has been flooded and rendered useless by a governmental improvement in furtherance of navigation; if one's land suffers peculiar damages resulting from direct airport overflights. But if one's situation strays much beyond the precise factual situation of an earlier case decided in favor of the landowner, the outcome is much more dubious. As we have seen, the question of whether a damage is "merely consequential" and hence irrecoverable, or whether, instead, it is a "taking," often turns upon distinctions that bear a tenuous relation to the reality of the injury or loss.

One should keep in mind that these are not the truly tough cases in this area of the law. These are the easy ones in which a definite physical invasion has been sustained either on, under, or over an owner's piece of property. Nevertheless, the decisions are often unpredictable. The truly tough cases arise over the issue of governmental regulation of property under the states' police power. The difficulty lies in the judicial attempt to determine when an uncompensated regulation under the police power is so invasive of property rights that its aim could be accomplished constitutionally only by the use of eminent domain. As one might infer from the previous discussion, matters get even more chaotic in these sorts of cases. Given the Court's adherence to *ad hoc* decision making and its avoidance of general rules or principles, this confusion seems unavoidable. When property owners would come forward to push courts to extend inverse condemnation to cases of governmental regulation, rather than just consequential injuries of a physical type, the confusion is magnified. All of this in due time, but let us now consider the third critical concept in the Fifth Amendment's taking clause: "public use."

Public Use. In the last section I dwelled upon the inconsistencies in the Supreme Court's interpretation of the "just compensation" and "property" elements of the Fifth Amendment's takings clause. We should not, however, lose sight of the fact that in regard to the interpretation of these elements, things have actually improved since the early nineteenth century. Consequential damages, for example, are now recoverable. But such benefits for property owners have not been replicated in the Court's interpretation of the "public use" proviso.

With one mighty obfuscation, Justice Douglas, in a decision that confused the law almost beyond redemption, dealt a devastating blow to the public use limitation upon what government can constitutionally take.

Prior to Douglas's decision in *Berman v. Parker* (1954),[65] *public use* had been interpreted as placing limits upon governmental confiscations. One of the most often cited limitations, adverted to in a long succession of rulings at every level, was the stricture that the state cannot use the eminent domain power to transfer property from one private individual to another. Yet in *Berman v. Parker* Douglas weakened this limitation. In *Berman* the Court decided that urban renewal, even with the sale of property for development by private contractors, constituted a public use, or in the Court's much looser reformulation of the Fifth Amendment, a "public purpose."

Even before *Berman v. Parker*, the public use constraint had not proven much of a barrier to governmental takings, or for that matter to takings by private businesses invested with the power of eminent domain. And there were numerous instances in various states in which eminent domain was permitted even for transfers between private individuals. Such activities were accepted because they had been going on since colonial times, or because they were perceived as serving some desirable public end in promoting the development of the country. Examples of transactions that transferred property from private individual A to private individual B include the colonial mill acts that carried over after the Revolution; the practice in certain states of granting eminent domain powers to landlocked owners to take land for access roads; and other uses including irrigation, drainage, reclamation of wetlands, mining operations, lumbering, and clearing a disputed title.[66]

The exceptions were the result more of the habits and accretions of history than of any consensus among early jurists that private takings in general were permissible. Indeed, there was a sense of the injustice involved in government transfers from individual A to individual B. This judicial distaste is most vividly displayed in a passage from Justice Chase's decision in *Calder v. Bull* decided in 1798: "A law that takes property from A and gives it to B: it is against all reason and justice, for a people to intrust a legislature with such powers; and therefore, it cannot be presumed that they have done it."[67] Against such transfers justices still imbued with natural law conceptions of property instinctively recoiled. The Supreme Court, however, displayed great deference to the determination by state courts that a particular use constituted a public use. It never invalidated a single such determination.[68] This deference, as we shall see, extended also to acts of Congress. The Court generally gave legislators wide scope in their determinations of public use.[69]

By the time the Supreme Court became actively involved in the public use issue, around the turn of the century, two different approaches had been developed by the state courts—one narrow and one broad. The narrow version tended to restrict governmental initiatives, limiting "public use" to "use by the public." This meant that, even when private companies had been delegated the power of eminent domain, their projects had to be open to the public, and the public was entitled to use the property by right. The broad approach, by contrast, equated the phrase *public use* with more nebulous terms such as *public advantage, public purpose, public benefit,* or *public welfare.* The latter version in effect transformed the eminent domain power by making it as extensive as the taxing or police powers. Though indecisive with regard to the two definitions in its early adjudiction, the Supreme Court has more recently opted for the broader, more permissive definition.[70] A parallel movement occurred in the state courts in the late 1930s, when federal housing subsides for states that comdemned slums were widely upheld, despite an initial false start when a federal court declared that the federal government could not take property for such purpose in its own name.[71]

What has happened in recent decades, in addition to the adoption of the broader view of public use as public advantage, is the Supreme Court's growing reluctance to interfere once Congress has determined that a taking is for a public use. Although such a determination in earlier years was not considered conclusive, and judicial review was, consequently, viewed as appropriate, the modern tendency has been to consider such questions virtually untouchable. The slight leeway left open by the earlier cases has been effectively closed in later cases. For example, in *United States v. Gettysburg Electric Railway Co.,*[72] the Supreme Court allowed that a congressional act authorizing condemnation for the preservation of the Gettysburg battlefield was an appropriation for a public use. Justice Peckham argued that "when the legislature has declared the use or purpose to be a public one, its judgment will be respected by the courts unless the use be palpably without reasonable foundation."[73] And he went on to express the Court's frequently expressed doctrine of deference to Congressional decisions:

> In examining an act of Congress it has been frequently said that every intendment is in favor of its constitutionality. Such act is presumed to be valid unless its invalidity is plain and apparent; no presumption of invalidity can be indulged in; it must be shown clearly and unmistakably. This rule has been stated and followed by this court from the foundation of the government.[74]

Thus, even though the Court here could focus upon no distinct constitutional provision that would grant the federal government the power to take property for monuments, it deduced such power from others, by judicial inference from the power to declare war and raise taxes. Even this loose standard of review for palpable unreasonableness would undergo further erosion.[75]

Justice Black in *United States ex rel. TVA v. Welch* (1946),[76] went a long way toward removing the Court from being the final arbiter over the question of public use. The Tennessee Valley Authority by act of Congress had been given the authority to condemn all property that it deemed "necessary for carrying out its purpose" of erecting the Fontana Dam project. In constructing the dam a reservoir had been created that swept away a highway that formed the only reasonable access to the plaintiffs' private property, which was sandwiched between the reservoir and a national park. Instead of constructing a new highway, which it deemed too expensive, the TVA decided to acquire the private land and add it to the national park. The six landowners complained that the TVA in taking their property had acted beyond the authority conferred upon it by Congress. The Court's majority, in deciding against the landowners, displayed the utmost deference to congressional and administrative authority. Justice Black wrote: "We think it is the function of Congress to decide what type of taking is for a public use and that the agency authorized to do the taking may do so to the full extent of its statutory authority."[77] He cited Justice Holmes's 1925 pronouncement that when Congress has spoken on the subject of public use, "its decision is entitled to deference until it is shown to involve an impossibility."[78] Exactly what Holmes meant by an "impossibility" is unclear. Yet what is clear from this declaration is that even the cursory standard of review for palpable unreasonableness found in *Gettysburg Electric Railway* had been jettisoned.

It was left for Justice Douglas finally to emasculate "public use" as a limitation upon governmental condemnation. In *Berman v. Parker*,[79] the Court was called upon to determine the constitutionality of a congressional act granting to the District of Columbia the power to acquire through condemnation tracts of land for redevelopment in blighted areas. Lands acquired could be leased or sold to private developers who were willing to make improvements consonant with a comprehensive general plan drawn up by the district's Redevelopment Land Agency. The appellants owned a department store in one of the blighted areas that itself was not in disrepair. They claimed that the condemnation of their property for urban redevelopment constituted a violation of due process and a takings under the Fifth Amendment. Particularly objectionable to them was the feature of the law that might permit their property to be transferred to another private party for that party's own private gain.

In a decision remarkable for its confusion of the central issues, Douglas and his colleagues concluded that the appellants' "innocuous and unoffending" property could be taken for the larger "public purpose" of remediating urban blight. Now, what should have been clear to Justice Douglas was that the case before him dealt with the federal government's power of eminent domain as exercised by delegation to an agency in the District of Columbia. The issues, then, were whether the use of this power as it affected the taking of an unoffending department store ran afoul of the Fifth Amenndment, and whether the act itself was constitutional. What Douglas discerned, instead, was a case dealing with the federal government's police powers over the District of Columbia. This confusion opened the floodgates for expanding the takings power of government. Why was this so? Because traditionally the limitation on the exercise of the police power, the power of the states to regulate property, has been something called the "public purpose." This broad phrase allows quite a wide range of state regulatory behavior—from minimum wage laws, maximum hour legislation, price fixing, to health and safety laws—so long as they serve some loosely defined notion of the public purpose. Now, *public purpose* had been considered a more expansive term than *public use*. What Douglas accomplished by his confusion of police power with eminent domain in *Berman v. Parker* was the application of the more permissive criterion of the police power's public purpose to eminent domain. Public use as a constraint on governmental seizures suffered a crippling blow as the result of Douglas's confusion.

To begin with, Douglas closed any loopholes in the legislative deference doctrine that may have remained from *Gettysburg Electric Railway*'s "impossibility" criterion:

> Subject to specific constitutional limitations, when the legislature has spoken, the public interest has been declared in terms well-nigh conclusive. In such cases the legislature, not the judiciary, is the main guardian of the public needs to be served by social legislation . . . this principle admits of no exception merely because the power of eminent domain is involved. The role of the judiciary in determining whether that power is being exercised for a public purpose is an extremely narrow one.[80]

If the legislature is "well-nigh" the final arbiter of "public needs," then what is the purpose of the Bill of Rights or the Constitution? The Court apparently lost sight of the purposes behind the Fifth Amendment's property clauses: to limit congressional seizures of property; to place conditions on those seizures that are necessary for a "public use," and to protect individual property rights.

As Douglas's opinion unfolds, protections for property rights diminish. In an enormously influential passage, quoted in numerous state and federal court decisions on both the limits of the eminent domain power and the police power, Douglas wrote:

> We do not sit to determine whether a particular housing project is or is not desirable. The concept of the public welfare is broad and inclusive. The values it represents are spiritual as well as physical, aesthetic as well as monetary. It is within the power of the legislature to determine that the community should be beautiful as well as healthy, spacious as well as clean, well-balanced as well as carefully patrolled . . . . If those who govern the District of Columbia decide that the Nation's Capital should be beautiful as well as sanitary, there is nothing in the Fifth Amendment that stands in the way.[81]

The effect of this passage has been to confuse police power criteria with eminent domain criteria.

In the 1980s several important cases have been decided, on both the state and federal level, that have served to weaken the "public use" constraint on takings even further. As we saw in chapter 1, in *Poletown Neighborhood Council v. City of Detroit*,[82] the Michigan court found constitutionally permissible the taking by the city of the neighborhood of Poletown to provide General Motors with land for the construction of a Cadillac plant. "Public use" was equated with the much broader "public purpose" standard. The California Supreme Court in 1982 decided a case, *City of Oakland v. Oakland Raiders*,[83] that extended eminent domain to novel limits, and also weakened "public use." Even more telling, is a case decided by the United States Supreme Court in 1984, *Hawaii Housing Authority v. Midkiff*,[84] which solidified this trend. These latter two cases merit close scrutiny.

When the Oakland Raiders football team had the temerity to desert its fans for the bright lights and larger stadium of Los Angeles, thereby diminishing Oakland's municipal treasury, the city fathers having exhausted all other remedies to retain the team, tried a novel ploy. Why not seize the team under Oakland's power of eminent domain? Rather than dismissing this tactic, the California Supreme Court permitted the city to pursue its case in the trial court. It reversed the Superior Court of Monterey County's summary judgment for the defendant, and remanded the case for trial of the issues on the merits.

Justice Richardson, writing for the majority, focused upon two principal issues: (1) Whether intangible property (here, a football franchise and all of the property rights attendant upon that ownership) can be taken under eminent domain, and (2) whether the public use constraint upon the condemnation power precludes an action of this type. The city contended that, yes indeed, what it sought to condemn is "property," and hence subject to established eminent domain law, and that the validity of its public use contention must be determined by a court after a full trial adducing all the relevant facts. The respondent Raiders argued, on the contrary, that eminent domain law does not permit the taking of "intangible property" unrelated to realty. Thus, the taking of their football franchise, a "network of intangible contractual rights," should be precluded. On the second point, the Raiders denied, as a matter of law, that the taking could be for a public use.

On the first question, after examining precedents of California, federal, and other jurisdictions, Justice Richardson concluded that intangible property is just as subject to confiscation as real or personal property. Franchises,[85] materialman's liens,[86] contracts, bus systems including routes and operating systems, and private utilities[87] have all been taken by various organs of government and upheld by courts. Furthermore, Richardson could discern no constitutional or statutory barrier to the taking of such intangible property. Thus, despite the court's inability to discover any precedent for the taking of a football franchise, it concluded that sufficient precedent existed for the taking of other intangible property. Therefore, it discerned no bar to this taking on this ground.

The public use issue resolved itself in a manner remarkable only to those ignorant of the evisceration of the public use constraint in recent years. After rehearsing the refrains that should be familiar to readers of chapters 1 and 2—that public use is a use that concerns the whole community or promotes the general interest, but it is "not essential that the entire community, or even any considerable portion thereof, shall directly enjoy or participate in an improvement"[88]—the court grudgingly acknowledged that no case anywhere has ever held that a municipality can acquire and operate a football team. Nevertheless, Justice Richardson and his colleagues found sufficient analogy in other recreational purposes pursued by governments and upheld by courts to conclude that the "operation of a sports franchise may well be an appropriate municipal function."[89] If government can acquire a baseball field in order to construct recreational facilities, can employ eminent domain to take land for a county fair or to build an opera house, or can take land for parking facilities at a stadium, why not this?

> If acquiring, erecting, owning and/or operating a sports stadium is a permissible municipal function, we discern no valid reason why owning and operating a sports franchise which fields a team to play in the stadium is not equally permissible.[90]

The ensuing passage in Justice Richardson's decision dramatically underscores my point that the public use constraint as currently understood is bankrupt. It is incapable of providing the check against unlimited takings for which it was originally intended. "A public use defies absolute definition," Richardson proceeds, quoting an earlier case, "for it changes with varying conditions of society . . . changing conceptions of the scope and functions of government."[91] The next paragraph is even more remarkable. Here the justices reveal that the judiciary's conception of government's proper functions has undergone a transformation, a transformation that triggers a great enlargement of eminent domain. The Constitution, as they conceive it, does not stand in the way of enshrining *their* particular conception of government. In the words of Justice Richardson:

> While it is readily apparent that the power of eminent domain formerly may have been exercised only to serve traditional and limited public purposes, such as the construction and maintenance of streets, highways and parks, these limitations seem merely to have corresponded to be accepted, but narrower view of appropriate governmental functions then prevailing. The established limitations were not imposed by either constitutional or statutory fiat. Times change.[92]

This viewpoint is disquieting, for what it implies is that once the ideas of judges change concerning the proper limits of government, constitutional provisions can be simply read into oblivion. If the plain words *public use* mean anything, they mean something other than private use. Simply because some of the public benefits from having a football business in its midst, this should no more entitle its representatives to seize that business than its enjoyment of Big Macs entitles its city fathers to confiscate Ronald MacDonald. These distressing implications of the court's reasoning did not escape one member of that body, and certainly a surprising choice for a defender of property rights, Chief Justice Rose Bird. In the closest any member of the court came to dissenting from the majority viewpoint, she filed an opinion characterized as a "concurrence and dissent." While concurring in the Court's decision to remand the case for determination on its merits, she nevertheless entertained serious reservations about the wisdom of the city's action and the possible future ramifications of any holding that an organ of government has the power to take an ongoing business to prevent it from leaving a locality.

What particularly troubled the chief justice was not only the novelty of the court's interpretation of eminent domain principles but the potentiality for abuse of such a boundless power as it propounded. If the city of Oakland were allowed to take the Oakland Raiders, then where could the line be drawn in the future?

> For example, if a rock concert impresario, after some years of producing concerts in a municipal stadium, decides to move his production to another city, may the city condemn his business, including his contracts with the rock stars, in order to keep the concerts at the stadium? If a small business that rents a store-front on land originally taken by the city for a redevelopment

project decides to move to another city in order to expand, may the city take
the business and force it to stay at its original location? May a city condemn
any business that decides to seek greener pastures elsewhere under the unlimited interpretation of eminent domain law that the majority appear to
approve?[93]

She also objected to the majority's reliance on inverse condemnation cases
to justify its contention that contracts can be taken by eminent domain.
Her point appears well taken. The inverse condemnation cases serve to
shore up property rights because they insist that when government takes
real property, it must compensate the owners for any ancillary losses—
such as those sustained through the business's inability to meet or profit
from its prior contracts. The situation differs dramatically in the instant
case, for the city sought directly to take the contracts. It is difficult to see
how the inverse condemnation cases can serve as precedent for this latter
type of behavior.

Given the California legislature's narrow definition of judicial review in
the determination of "public use," combined with the customary deference courts pay to legislative judgments, the chief justice, albeit reluctantly,
concluded that "there is no constitutional or statutory ground for barring
the City's action." A successful challenge to the city's taking would entail a
demonstration that either the city acted in "gross abuse of discretion" or in
an arbitrary, capricious fashion, totally lacking in evidentiary support. It is
not surprising, then, that the lower court, upon remand, concluded that,
yes indeed, the Raiders had to return to Oakland.

On May 30, 1984, the Supreme Court of the United States decided a case
that all but buried the public use restraint on government's power to take
private property. In *Hawaii Housing Authority v. Midkiff* a unanimous
Court condoned the taking of property by the state's housing authority
from large landowners to be resold to leaseholders under the provisions of
the Hawaii Land Reform Act of 1967. Justice O'Connor, writing the decision for her colleagues, concluded that nothing in the public use clause of
the Fifth Amendment, as made applicable to the states through the Fourteenth Amendment, barred such a transfer.

What is ominous about the Court's failure to discover a constitutional
impropriety in this eminent domain procedure is that the public use
proviso has been understood, from its inception, as a barrier to governmental transfers of property from one owner to another, unless a clear,
pressing public use can be discerned. But in this instance, the Hawaii
legislature used as a justification for the taking of property from one set of
owners to be resold to another merely a desire to reduce the concentration
of ownership in the state.

The Hawaii Land Reform Act of 1967 sought to address the problem of a perceived shortage of fee simple residential land in the islands with an attendant "artificial inflation of residential land values." The legislature viewed the land pattern as imposing "financially disadvantageous" terms, restricting the freedom of those who wished to enjoy the land fully, and favoring the few landowners over the many.[94] The solution reached was ambitious. Homeowners who currently leased their land could invoke the aid of the Hawaii Housing Authority to take the land by eminent domain and then repurchase it at "fair market value" from the authority. When challenged by a large landholding trust, this taking provision was found not violative of the public use restriction of the Fifth Amendment by the United States District Court for the District of Hawaii. The United States Court of Appeals for the Ninth Circuit found otherwise, with the two-judge majority concluding that, as one of them wrote, "in my view, the Hawaii statue accomplishes . . . [an] invalid result, for if it does not constitute a transfer for the private use of another, that term can have no meaning."[95]

The case eventually found its way to the Supreme Court. Justice O'Connor, writing for a unanimous court, began her analysis by rehearsing the Hawaii legislature's finding that, as a heritage from Hawaii's early monarchial days of feudal land tenure, an oligopolistic pattern of landownership persisted in the islands. While the state and the federal government owned 49 percent of Hawaii's land, another 47 percent was in the hands of a mere seventy-two private landowners. The eminent domain solution was adopted by the legislature, in preference to an alternative scheme that would have required landowners to sell to their lessees, because the landowners were leery of the federal tax consequences of outright sale. Indeed, the landowners maintained that these tax liabilities were the primary reason for their choice to lease instead of sell their land in the first place.

Berman v. Parker, not surprisingly, served as the starting point for O'Connor's analysis of whether the act violated the Fifth and Fourteenth Amendments by falling afoul of the public use requirement. Here, *Berman*'s police power-eminent domain confusion, which I previously discussed, came to full fruition. In finding that no transgression of the public use proviso was triggered by the act, the Court's decision relied heavily upon that confusion. Its decision quoted extensively from Douglas's remarks, particularly those equating an eminent domain case with "traditionally . . . a policy power" issue, and concluding that "once the object is within the authority of Congress, the right to realize it through the exercise of eminent domain is clear." Deference to legislative judgments is, à la *Berman*, also endorsed.

The critical passage in the Court's decision must be quoted in full; its language is elliptical, yet its intent is clearly discernible.

> The "public use" requirement is thus coterminous with the scope of a sovereign's police power.
>
> There is, of course, a role for courts to play in reviewing a legislature's judgment of what constitutes a public use, even when the eminent domain power is equated with the police power. But the Court in *Berman* made clear that it is "an extremely narrow" one.[96]

Now, that first sentence is perplexing. How can a limitation (i.e., the public use requirement) be coterminous with a state's power to regulate (i.e., the police power)? But the remainder of the passage makes the court's meaning unmistakable. What it now contends is that the eminent domain power is as broad as the police power: whatever legislatures can regulate they can also take. This makes explicit what is still only implied in *Berman*. Why is this so significant? Because if the police power is virtually unlimited in its purview (as, indeed, it has been since the Court abandoned substantive due process in the late 1930s), then so is eminent domain. This, in effect, reads the public use clause as a limitation on government takings, out of the Fifth Amendment. Following this reasoning, if a legislature determines that a public purpose is served by taking A's property and giving it to B, one would imagine that only the most blatant seizures, clothed in no public purpose language, would fail the Court's test. If the Court refuses to pierce the veil of an act's justificatory language and examine the substance of its public use claim, then the clear language of the Fifth Amendment means nothing. It is just such a strict scrutiny that the court of appeals was willing to undertake, and the Supreme Court was not. Their diametrically opposite conclusions, then, should come as no shock.

Appeals court Judge Alarcon's criticism of the district court's analysis is just as pertinent a challenge to the subsequent reasoning of the high court:

> To hold . . . that the public use limitation is subsumed under a "police power/ due process analysis" . . . would be to ignore the explicit language of the constitution and to disregard the fifth amendment protections granted to citizens of the states under the fourteenth amendment.[97]

By employing the much looser police power-due process test—under which an act need only be "rationally related to a conceivable public purpose"— the Supreme Court had no difficulty upholding the Hawaii Land Reform Act. If regulating oligopolies is a legitimate exercise of the police power, and if willing buyers are unable to buy lots at "fair prices," then the Hawaii legislature's solution is a "comprehensive and rational approach to identifying and correcting market failure."[98] Whether the scheme holds out any likelihood of achieving its stated goals, is not for the Court to decide, said

Justice O'Connor, repeating a refrain heard continuously since the late 1930s.

The reason that anyone other than lawyers should care about *Hawaii v. Midkiff* is that by effectively neutralizing the public use limitation on government takings the Court has opened the floodgates. Following this decision, would it be a legitimate exercise of eminent domain for a state to declare that it is a public purpose for tenants to own their apartments, and to condemn apartment houses and resell the units to their tenants? Why not, given suitable public purpose language in the act? Why not take a football franchise away from an owner who wants to move the team, and transfer the team to a new owner?

And why should landowners lease their land when doing so might subject them to a forced sale to their tenants? This question should have given the Court pause, as it did one member of the appeals court. But the Supreme Court has steadfastly refused, during the past fifty years, to examine the cogency of legislative schemes. Now, in *Hawaii v. Midkiff* the Court has extended its extremely loose standard of review of economic regulation under the due process clause to eminent domain proceedings. It has done so despite the explicit language of the Fifth Amendment: no taking without a public use. The modern Court has been leery of anything that might smack of the activist measures of the "Old" Court of the early part of this century, a Court that struck down many regulatory measures as violations of the due process clauses of the Fifth and Fourteenth Amendments. Even if one endorses such judicial quiescence on property rights issues, which I do not, the eminent domain cases are different from due process adjudication. This is precisely because the takings clause of the Fifth Amendment is explicit. It imposes limitations on takings, while the due process clause is much more nebulous, hence subject to judicial interpretation. The takings clause of the Fifth Amendment should not be so casually read out of the Constitution.

Will *Hawaii v. Midkiff* be another *Berman v. Parker* in the sense that the latter case has had such far-reaching effects in weakening constitutional protection for property rights? My expectation is that it probably will. An early harbinger comes from the California Supreme Court. In *Nash v. City of Santa Monica*, decided in October 1984, that court rejected the challenge to a rent control ordinance raised by a landlord. Nash objected to a portion of that ordinance that prohibits the removal of rental units from the market by demolition. He raised due process objections after the rent control board had denied him permission to demolish his building. His contention was that there must be a limit on the state's power to compel an individual to pursue a business against his will.

In rejecting Nash's contention, the court's majority opined that even if the rent control ordinance constrained the landlord's options—so that he could escape his landlordly obligations only by selling his property—he was no worse off than the landowners in *Hawaii v. Midkiff*. If it is permissible for a state to compel a sale of property from one private party to another, then what is wrong with constraining a landlord's options for the use of his property?

Just like *Berman, Hawaii v. Midkiff* seems to be spawning progeny in areas of the law beyond eminent domain, for this plaintiff raised a due process, not a takings, complaint. This does not bode well for the protection of property rights in the future.

The Police Power: Its Early Life and Peculiar Development

The police power of the states is an even more elusive governmental perquisite than the power of eminent domain. It is more expansive, less circumscribed by constraints upon its exercise, and its origin is pretty much taken for granted. Strictly speaking, the federal government, as a body holding derivative powers only from the consent of the states, does not possess the police power,[99] except where it holds original sovereignty— over the nation's capital, United States territories, and public lands. The waters have become somewhat muddied, however, because the national government possesses certain explicitly granted powers that enable it to legislate over some areas with police-power-type authority. These powers include the power to regulate interstate commerce, to make war, to tax, and to promote the general welfare.

The police power is most often defined as the power of a sovereign government, or in our case of the states, to legislate to protect the health, safety, morals and general welfare of its citizens. Until the turn of the century, police power was defined as affecting three public concerns— health, safety, and morals. Gradually it was expanded to include the catch-all component of general welfare. The addition of general welfare provided a broader basis for state intervention in the ordinary affairs of business life, such as setting hours of labor, rates of pay, maximum and minimum prices charged for goods and services, and licensing. Although such regulations could only loosely comply under the health, safety, and morals standard of the police power, they were more easily defensible under the vaguer criterion of general welfare.

I should also note that the police power as a device to regulate economic relations differs from legislation in criminal matters. The latter proscribes (in most cases) acts intrinsically vicious. The former enforces merely conventional restraints. Thus, the criminal law directs itself at behavior that is evil in itself (*malum in se*); the police power regulates behavior that is only wrong because government declares it to be so (*malum prohibitum*).[100]

The police power has a long history. Yet, like the eminent domain power, it has tended to be accepted by judges and theorists simply on the basis of precedent, without careful examination. In an early case, *Gibbons v. Ogden*,[101] Chief Justice Marshall wrote about the police power, giving it broad sweep. He assumed that such a power naturally inhered in the states, and could be exercised at their discretion, in the absence of conflict, as he discerned in this case, with a superior power of the federal government. Of "inspection laws," a considerable component of police power legislation, he contended:

> They form a portion of that immense mass of legislation, which embraces everything within the territory of a state, not surrendered to the general government; all of which can be most advantageously exercised by the states themselves. Inspection laws, quarantine laws, health laws of every description, as well as laws for regulating the internal commerce of a state, and those which respect turnpike-roads, ferries, etc., are component parts of this mass.[102]

Despite the sweeping scope Marshall envisioned for the police power, the court did delimit its operation when its exercise came into conflict with federal powers, specifically the power of Congress over interstate commerce, which includes navigation within each state.[103] Thus, the Court overthrew an act of New York granting to Robert Livingston and Robert Fulton exclusive navigational rights over all waters of the state for boats powered by fire or steam. The act was found to be repugnant to the commerce clause of the Constitution because it barred such vessels licensed by the United States from traversing waters within that state. One limit, then, to a state's police power is the supremacy of the federal government over a particular subject of regulation. But Marshall observed that over the states' unencumbered domain of police power regulation, the constitutionality of quarantine and health laws has never been denied.[104] From Marshall, then, one can impute two justificatory arguments for the police power that would point to its ancient lineage—governments have always passed such legislation; therefore, governments indubitably have such powers—and its general advantageousness.

Before the adoption of the Fourteenth Amendment, the Supreme Court had scant opportunity to adjudicate cases raising the issue of the limits upon the states' police powers. The few cases that did reach the Court fell within its jurisdiction either because of diversity of citizenship or because the plaintiff alleged that a state's regulation conflicted with a superior right of the United States, usually under the commerce clause. One such case, appealed on the latter grounds, was *Thurlow v. Commonwealth of Massachusetts*, which was decided along with two others from Rhode Island and New Hampshire raising the same issues. These are the *License Cases* (1847).[105] Massachusetts had passed a statute declaring that no one could sell wine in quantities less than twenty-eight gallons without being licensed, with licenses to be granted by county commissioners when they determined that such a grant would be in the public good. The Supreme Court held, in separate opinions written by its members, that the liquor licensing laws of all three states were not repugnant to any provisions of the Constitution, and particularly not inconsistent with the commerce clause. Chief Justice Taney, in his written opinion, could discover nothing in the Constitution to prevent the states from "regulating, restricting, or prohibiting" the liquor trade if they determined that such would be necessary to guard the health or morals of their people.[106] The chief justice, in terms that should be familiar to us from our previous discussion of the genesis of the power of eminent domain, discerned the origins of the police power in the very concept of sovereignty. Taney essentially equated the police power with the notion of sovereignty itself:

> But what are the police powers of a State? They are nothing more or less than powers of government inherent in every sovereignty to the extent of its dominions. And whether a State passes a quarantine law, or a law to punish offences, or to establish courts of justice, or requiring certain instruments to be recorded, or to regulate commerce within its own limits, in every case it exercises the same power; that is to say, the power of sovereignty, the power to govern men and things within the limits of its dominion. It is by virtue of this power that it legislates . . . And when the validity of a State law making regulations of commerce is drawn into question in a judicial tribunal, the authority to pass it cannot be made to depend upon the motive that may be supposed to have influenced the Legislature, nor can the Court inquire whether it was intended to guard the citizens of the State from pestilence or disease, or to make regulations of commerce for the interest and convenience of trade . . . . It is a question of power.[107]

Taney went much further than the Supreme Court would later be willing to go after the adoption of the Fourteenth Amendment in placing police power restrictions beyond the pale of federal judicial inspection. Even at the height of judicial scrutiny of legislative regulation of property, which would come some half-century later, motives of legislators in enacting regulations were considered immune from inspection. Still, Taney went much further than later justices would in barring judicial inquiry into the legislature's determination that a particular act furthered the health, safety, or convenience of the people. For Taney, sovereignty encompassed the raw, unreviewable power to legislate, and the judiciary must accept as conclusive legislative determinations as to desirability or necessity. Taney's vision of police power as equivalent to sovereignty, and hence untouchable by judicial review, was destined to fall out of favor once the Court interpreted the Fourteenth Amendment as a vehicle for inspecting state regulatory acts bearing on property rights. But Taney's viewpoint would live again, as the Court came in the late 1930s to reject the "Old" Court's (roughly 1890-1937) judicial activism in behalf of property rights. And Taney's view remains the dominant one to this day, but more of that in a moment when we come to examine the limits placed upon the police power by the due process clause. For now, what is significant is Chief Justice Taney's position, one apparently so self-evident that it required no elaborate proof, that the police power is coextensive with the very nature of sovereignty.

After the adoption of the Fourteenth Amendment and its eventual interpretation by the Supreme Court as a vehicle for inspecting state regulatory measures, the Court would have much greater opportunity to ruminate upon the origins of the police power. Consequently, its justifications would become more weighty. In *Munn v. Illinois* (1876),[108] Justice Waite pulled the police power rabbit out of the social compact hat.

> When one becomes a member of society he necessarily parts with some rights or privileges which, as an individual not affected by his relations to others, he might retain . . . . This [the social compact] does not confer power upon the whole people to control rights which are purely and exclusively private, . . . but it does authorize the establishment of laws requiring each citizen to so conduct himself, and so use his own property, as not unnecessarily to injure another. This is the very essence of government, and has found expression in the maxim *sic utere tuo ut alienum non laedas*. From this source comes the police powers, which, as was said by Mr. Chief Justice Taney in the License Cases, . . . "are nothing more or less than the powers of government inherent in every sovereignty" . . . . Under these powers the government regulates the conduct of citizens one towards another, and the manner in which each shall use his own property when such regulation becomes necessary for the public good.[109]

Here, we are given a more substantial argument for the police power. The *sic utere* maxim means "use your own property in such a manner as not to injure that of another."[110] All defenders of a natural right to private property have acknowledged such a restriction. It would be senseless to hold that A's absolute right to his property entailed his right to use it in such a way as to destroy B's unoffending property, for then B's absolute right to her property would be rendered exiguous. If A and B both possess rights of property because of some inherent human feature that all humans possess, then it would be contradictory to say that A's rights extend to the nullification of B's rights. Pragmatic[111] defenders of property rights also have adhered to the *sic utere* limitation, perceiving in it the principle by which government can assign rights to individuals in a manner that allows them to be compatibly exercised. On either a natural rights or a pragmatic account, then, government could have a role to play in policing private exercises of property rights to prevent injuries to other inherent property interests.[112]

Chief Justice Waite, in contrast to most of his colleagues, has at least given us the skeleton of an argument for the police power. By the social compact people agree to leave the state of nature in which they were free to engage in activities at their own discretion, subject to no master, and consent to join civil society. In the process they relinquish certain powers. They exchange an unbounded freedom to regulate their own affairs for security of person and property. Security now to be guaranteed and regulated by the democratic majority of all the compacting members or their duly appointed representatives. This regulatory power, transferred to government, is not without its limits, for to conceive of the contracting parties as ceding an unrestricted power would be absurd. Such a power would undermine the very purpose for which people joined civil society, the protection of their lives and property.

Justice Waite did not flesh out his argument in this detail. He did not need to because by simply adverting to the "social compact" he would have called to the contemporary reader's mind the contractarian, limited government arguments derived from John Locke that so influenced our founding fathers, and prevailed even unto the generation of their grandchildren. To proceed to infer from the social contract, as Justice Waite did, that government has the power to regulate individual acts that have spillover effects on others is not unreasonable. Given the assumption of the social compact as the legitimating mechanism for government, Justice Waite's position logically follows, but it seems to imply a greater level of judicial scrutiny of legislative regulation than Chief Justice Taney, for one, was willing to accept. Justice Waite explicitly acknowledged that there exists a private domain exempt from legislative intrusion. Interestingly, Justice Waite, speaking for the majority in *Munn*, upheld Illinois's setting of maximum prices charged for the storage of grain in warehouses, a result Taney would have undoubtedly approved.

Justice Waite's argument for the police power, at least after we have reconstructed it by establishing its proper context in the history of political thought, is certainly more substantial than anything we unearthed in defense of the eminent domain power. Yet, despite its clarity on the origins of the police power, it was unable to generate either agreement in its successor decisions or any precise guidelines as to the limit of the police power. Chief Justice Waite knew that those limits existed, for he denominated some rights as "exclusively private" and, hence, beyond the purview of governmental legislation, but he could not clearly define the private domain. His colleagues would be no more successful. One of the most frequently repeated phrases cropping up in police power cases is that the police power is "from its very nature, incapable of any exact definition or limitation."[113] Judges drew the inference from this claimed imprecision inherent in the police power that its limits would have to be defined atheoretically, that is, by a process of judicial inclusion and exclusion as they came to examine the facts of each case. "Governmental power must be flexible and adaptive. Exigencies arise," and the point where particular interests or principles balance, "cannot be determined by any general formulas in advance."[114]

One other justificatory utterance in behalf of the police power ought to be recognized before we move on, and that is the assertion that "all rights are held subject to the police power of the state."[115] This claim, which most often appears as an unadorned declaration, seems, probably unwittingly, to rely on a view of government quite alien to that held by John Locke or Chief Justice Waite. Rather, it assumes that government is the original grantor of rights, not simply their guarantor, as would be the case on a Lockean natural rights-social contract account.

A variant of this claim would emerge several decades later, now without any implication that the state was the actual creator of the rights held subject to the police power. As Justice Field wrote, and he was, according to popular wisdom, the purest of laissez-faire men:

> But the possession and enjoyment of all rights are subject to such reasonable conditions as may be deemed by the governing authority of the country essential to the safety, health, peace, good order, and morals of the community. Even liberty itself, the greatest of all rights is not an unrestricted license to act according to one's own will.[116]

Justice Field and his colleagues went on from this statement endorsing "reasonable regulation" to uphold a San Francisco ordinance requiring a license to sell liquor over the objections of a petitioner who sold liquor after he was denied a license.

With the exception of Chief Justice Waite's enunciation of the *sic utere* justification of the police power in *Munn v. Illinois*, one can discern scarcely anything that transcends the mundane in the Court's "justification" of the states' police powers. Most often when the justices felt the need for argumenation they resorted to historical precedent. These men genuinely believed in individual rights, which the government ought to protect, but they accepted too uncritically the position that a vaguely defined police power inhered in government. By failing to set out clear standards and justifications to limit the police power, the case law led, as if by an invisible hand, to decisions that eroded individual rights.

The Police Power and the Fourteenth Amendment

How has the Court attempted to limit the police power after the adoption of the Fourteenth Amendment? Let us see. The police power since the latter part of the nineteenth century has been hedged around in no precise way by principally three constitutional elements arising out of the Fourteenth Amendment: the due process clause, the equal protection clause, and the takings clause (as judicially read into the due process clause). Of the three, only the takings clause remains today as even a slightly effective barrier to police power regulation of private property. However, to set the record straight it will prove helpful to examine the judicial history of each of these conflicts—between police power and due process, police power and equal protection, and police power and takings—even though it is only the last issue that immediately concerns us. The reason that this wider investigation is necessary is that it very often was the case that plaintiffs would raise one of these clauses rather than another at any given time as they perceived the Court's likelihood of favorably receiving such a plea. Thus, it was often purely adventitious that a case was decided on due process rather than takings grounds.[117]

The first time the Supreme Court was called upon to decide whether provisions of the Fourteenth Amendment guaranteeing due process and equal protection to citizens of the states applied to property rights it balked. In 1872[118] owners of slaughterhouses objected to an act of the Louisiana legislature granting to a single corporation exclusive rights to operate a slaughterhouse in the city of New Orleans according to a prescribed fee scale. The plaintiffs objected to the legislation on the basis of both the Thirteenth and Fourteenth Amendments, citing the prohibition against involuntary servitude, the abridgment of privileges and immunities of United States citizens, the denial of equal protection of the laws, and the deprivation of property without due process of law. Justice Miller, speaking for the majority would have none of it. Upon his examination of the history of the two amendments, he found their application limited to securing liberty to formerly enslaved Blacks. Thus, the Thirteenth Amendment's stricture against involuntary servitude was found to apply only to the prohibition on slavery. The Fourteenth Amendment's due process clause did not apply to restrictions on butchers' exercise of their trade. Nor was the equal protection clause likely to be stretched beyond the protection of Blacks' rights to become a weapon against state regulatory measures.

Justice Miller, then, dispensed with the butchers' pleas and concluded that it was perfectly within the discretion of legislatures under their police power to determine the locations in which slaughtering may be conducted. Having found the objective of the act within the power of government, he went on to consider the means chosen—an exclusive grant accompanied by state mandated rates—and found them appropriate to the objective of removing slaughterhouses from densely populated districts. Nothing more was at work here, according to the majority of the Court, than a traditional police power exercise by a state, and they could find no barrier to such practices emanating from the two post-Civil War amendments.

As the Court came in the next few decades to hear a legion of cases objecting to police power regulations as violations of due process, its attitude changed. No longer would the due process clause be considered as exclusively applicable to the plight of manumitted slaves. It would be broadened to sweep widely over the regulatory powers of the states in respect to property rights. This repudiation of the narrow interpretation given to the Fourteenth Amendment in the *Slaughter-House Cases* is due in no small part to the dissenting opinion in that case written by Justice Field and joined by three of his brethren. Field lectured the majority that under the pretense of the police power states cannot encroach upon rights protected by the Constitution. The only police aspects he discovered in the act were those regulating the place of deportation for animals and a provision for inspection, and as for the rest he found only an exclusive grant of monopoly to a private corporation. While conceding that the Court had repeatedly upheld exclusive grants for such things as ferries, bridges, and turnpikes, because of their colonial lineage, he sought to distinguish these instances from monopoly privileges over one of the ordinary trades of life. If a grant such as the slaughterhouse one were permitted, Field anticipated that no line could be drawn against monopoly grants to any businesses, even those in the most mundane and populous objects of trade.

To buttress his economic arguments against monoplies—and indeed he quoted from Adam Smith to show how the Court's decision violated the right of free labor—Field had to demonstrate that the majority was wrong about the limitations of the Fourteenth Amendment. According to his rendition of the amendment, it was "intended to give particular effect to that declaration of 1776 of inalienable rights, rights which are the gift of the Creator, which the law does not confer, but only recognizes."[119] For Field, then, the "privileges and immunities" protection afforded by the amendment must be interpreted to include the right to pursue a lawful employment without being subjected to restraints that do not apply equally to all other persons. Field's position strays considerably from pure laissez-faire because (1) he was willing to bow to history and permit monopoly grants for such things as ferries, bridges, and turnpikes, and (2) he seemed to hold the general view that licensing or regulation of the terms upon which business is to be conducted if reasonable are permissible.[120] The property rights that Field sought to protect under the "privileges and immunities" barrier would soon be defended by the Court under the due process clause.

The Due Process Clause From the late 1890s to the middle of the 1930s, the Supreme Court used the due process clauses of the Fifth and Fourteenth Amendments to scrutinize police power regulations of property rights by federal, state, and local governments. This period has come to be known as the "substantive" or "economic" due process era of the "Old," supposedly laissez-faire, Court. I say "supposedly" because even during the ascendancy of economic due process, the Court did not indiscriminately rule against all police power restrictions on business. For every one of its famous decisions overturning legislation as violating due process—for the *Allgeyers, Lochners, Adairs,* and *Coppages*[121]—there were dozens of other cases, often virtually indistinguishable in factual detail from their more renowned mates, in which the Court upheld police power regulations. So even though in the famous, or more accurately stated *in*famous cases, the Court at times struck down regulations limiting the hours of labor of employees in bakeries, or establishing minimum wage laws for women, or state and federal laws banning yellow-dog contracts,[122] it also on other occasions upheld legislation limiting hours of labor, prohibiting various occupations either entirely or within certain geographical jurisdictions, enforcing occupational licensing restrictions, establishing working conditions within various industries, enacting wartime rent control ordinances, prohibiting the sale of adulterated drugs and food, and so on.[123]

What distinguished the "Old," substantive due process Court from its predecessors and successors was not its putative allegiance to laissez-faire but, instead, its willingness to review with a high standard of scrutiny legislative acts of a police power nature. Neither before nor since has the Court been willing to protect property rights if to do so it had to supplant so-called reasonable legislative judgments. But during the regnancy of substantive due process, the Court invoked a test for the legitimacy of police power regulations that occasionally, although not often, led to the invalidation of particular measures. This test appears in its purest form in *Lochner v. New York*, the case in which the Court invalidated a ten-hour limit on the workday of bakers, but it surfaces in other cases in slightly altered forms. In *Lochner* the Court stated that there are limits to the police power, and that were this not so, the Fourteenth Amendment would have no efficacy and the powers of the states would be unchecked. Writing for the majority, Justice Peckham went on to contend that in each case questioning the constitutionality of a police power measure, the question must be asked,

"Is this a fair, reasonable and appropriate exercise of the police power of the state, or is it unreasonable, unnecessary, and arbitrary interference with the right of the individual to his personal liberty or to enter into those contracts in relation to labor which may seem to him appropriate or necessary for the support of himself and his family."[124] Despite appearances to the contrary, Peckham did not intend his review to supplant legislative judgments but only to determine whether a statute fell within the legitimate purview of the police power. Necessarily, however, the line between the two was murky. Quite often decisions would proceed to scrutinize the economic sense or lack of it manifested by legislation. Indeed, when Justice Peckham elaborated his test for reasonableness, it did seem to require judicial judgment in respect to the cogency of the means chosen to solve a particular problem. In inquiring whether the ten-hour workday limitation for bakers was valid as a labor law, Peckham looked beyond the declaration in the statute that it was enacted to further the public health. This mere assertion, he contended, does not in itself make the act legitimate as a police power measure:

> The act must have a more direct relation, as a means to an end, and the end itself must be appropriate and legitimate, before an act can be held to be valid which interferes with the general right of an individual to be free in his person and in his power to contract in relation to his own labor.[125]

This means-end test called upon the Court to examine (1) the objective of a legislative act to determine whether the state has the constitutional power to enact such a piece of legislation, and (2) the appropriateness of the means chosen to serve that objective. A third standard of evaluation mentioned often in cases from this era is (3) that the means selected must be the least onerous alternative, so that if a perceived evil could be remedied by licensing or regulating, the Court would likely frown upon a statute that completely prohibited the activity. These tests were never applied rigorously, and their meaning remained ill defined. In *Lochner* what resulted was a finding that "no reasonable foundation for holding this to be necessary or appropriate as a health law" existed because bakers were neither incapacitated wards of the state nor practitioners of an unusually hazardous occupation.

Two heated dissents were appended to the *Lochner* decision, one written by Justice Harlan, joined by Justices White and Day, and the other written by Justice Oliver Wendell Holmes. Harlan's standard for reviewing police power acts would, by 1937, become the regnant view of the Court. When, he asked, can the Court declare such regulations to be in excess of legislative authority and, hence, void? He considered the answer indisputable:

"for, the rule is universal that a legislative enactment, Federal or state, is never to be disregarded or held invalid unless it be, beyond question, plainly and palpably in excess of legislative power."[126] All doubts about the validity of a statute ought to be resolved in favor of validity.

> If the end which the legislative seeks to accomplish be one to which its power extends, and if the means employed to that end, although not the wisest or best, are yet not plainly and palpably unauthorized by law, then the court cannot interfere. In other words when the validity of a statute is questioned, the burden of proof, so to speak, is upon those who assert it to be unconstitutional.[127]

Under these much more lenient criteria, Harlan arrived at a determination that the New York statute was legitimate. Its end was the public's health, and one could not say that there was no "real or substantial relation" between the means employed by the state and the end. Whether the act was wise or not was no concern of the Court's.

What Harlan's ultimately victorious test proposed was precisely what Peckham feared: legislative declarations of police power objectives would be taken at face value unless they were so preposterous as to defy credulity. By placing the burden of proof on challengers to demonstrate the unconstitutionality of police power acts, and by deciding all doubtful cases in favor of the suspect legislation, the Court would come to place a heavy burden on plaintiffs. Should the state have the benefit of the doubt when it limits individual rights by enacting minimum wage laws, licensing restrictions, maximum hours for labor, rent control, and prohibitions on industries? This question was answered very differently by the Court during the substantive due process era than it would be after the demise of that doctrine.

Justice Holmes would have gone further than Justice Harlan in acquiescence to legislative enactments. In a brief dissent that has become famous, Holmes would have dispensed with any firm criteria for testing police power legislation. For Holmes, it was sufficient that a majority had enacted its opinion into law. No further inquiry as to economic cogency, desirability, or constitutionality was necessssary.

> I think that the word "liberty" in the Fourteenth Amendment is perverted when it is held to prevent the natural outcome of a dominant opinion, unless it can be said that a rational and fair man necessarily would admit that the statute proposed would infringe fundamental principles as they have been understood by the tradition of our people and our law.[128]

This test, of a "rational and fair man" necessarily admitting that a statute infringed fundamental liberties, places an almost insuperable burden on challengers to police power enactments.

The fame of Holmes's dissent derives from his memorable barb against laissez-faire:

> The Fourteenth Amendment does not enact Mr. Herbert Spencer's Social Statics . . . a constitution is not intended to embody a particular economic theory, whether of paternalism and the organic relation of the citizen to the state or of laissez-faire.[129]

Holmes was simply wrong about our Constitution. The intellectual heritage of the founding fathers was decidedly individualistic. They feared the overweening grasp of the state as a danger to all rights of persons and property. They debated endlessly about the nature of republics and whether republics could remain bastions of freedom if extended over large territories. They labored to devise a limited government, limited by both its structure of built-in checks and balances, and by explicit constitutional prohibitions, such as those against *ex post facto* laws, impairing the obligation of contracts, bills of attainder, and so on. And they held a theory of the origins of government based on individual consent and rejected any paternalistic, organic government by divine right or ancient custom. The thought of our constitutional forebears, and equally of their anti-Federalist rivals, was imbued with the limited government, natural rights individualism of such thinkers as John Locke, Montesquieu, and Thomas Gordon. It is this patrimony that nurtured Justice Peckham's police power-due process test.

The Peckham test, being far from absolutist, led to a whole host of inconsistent decisions, and the swing votes on the Court from case to case accounted for even more confusing decision making. The substantive due process advocates held a middle ground. Some economic regulations were permitted; others exceeded the ill-defined bounds of the police power and were overturned. Thus, the advocates' position carried the germ of inconsistency within it. Finally, in 1937 the era of economic due process was vanquished. To see how their own inconsistencies served to defeat them, no better vehicle could be wished for than *Adkins v. Children's Hospital*. It would lead, almost inevitably, to its nemesis, *West Coast Hotel v. Parrish*, during the heady days of the New Deal.[130]

The *Adkins* decision disposed of two cases questioning the constitutionality of a 1918 act of Congress that fashioned a scheme for fixing minimum wages for women and children in all occupations within the District of Columbia.[131] The act's stated police power rationale was to provide for the good health and protect the morals of women and children. It declared unlawful all employments at below the set wage, punishable by fine and imprisonment. One plaintiff was a hospital that employed women at below the board-established wage; the other was a twenty-one-year-old woman formerly employed by a hotel who lost her job when the mandatory wage was set. She maintained that the wages previously paid to her by the Congress Hall Hotel were the best she could attain anywhere, and that she was deprived of her job as a result of the congressional act.

Justice Sutherland, writing for a divided court,[132] proceeded to examine whether the act authorized an unconstitutional interference with freedom of contract as guaranteed by the due process clause of the Fifth Amendment. Sutherland cited Marshall's doctrine "that every possible presumption is in favor of the validity of an act of Congress until overcome beyond rational doubt". Then he introduced the typical economic due process reservation: "But if, by clear and indubitable demonstration a statute be opposed to the Constitution, we have no choice but to say so."[133] He invoked, at great length, the *Lochner* decision, adopting the means-end test enunciated there. But by 1923 the Court's decisions on cases similar to *Lochner's* restrictions on the hours of labor had become clouded, even to the extent that Justice Taft, who dissented in *Adkins*, believed that one of them, *Bunting v. Oregon*,[134] had actually overruled *Lochner*.

Thus, Sutherland had a delicate task to perform in differentiating these cases from the standard of "reasonableness" and "necessity or appropriateness" set in *Lochner*. Sutherland, in contrast to Taft, concluded that subsequent cases were distinguishable and did not overturn *Lochner*.[135] These cases, in which the Court upheld various restrictions on hours of labor, could not serve as precedents for minimum wage legislation. Nor could such cases as those upholding rent control, or a ten-hour workday for women, which he similarly attempted to distinguish, serve as precedents. Given the "economic due process" justices' ambiguous position on police power regulations, it is no wonder that Sutherland had to tie himself in knots to condemn minimum wage legislation.

Thus, Sutherland was forced to posit a fundamental difference between statutes fixing the hours of labor (which sometimes makes them permissible if the occupation is inherently unhealthy or dangerous) and acts fixing wages, which he found invalid. The former, he argued, leave the heart of the wage contract untouched because once hours are restricted, employers and their workers are left free to rearrange the wage bargain. In contrast, minimum wage laws ignore the rights of one of the parties, the employer, and do not require of the employee any service equivalent to the fixed wage. The employer must pay it simply because the employee needs it. Hence, there is no equivalence between the value of the service rendered and the salary paid. If Sutherland was onto any distinction here, it was only one of degree, and not of a different kind. It does not seem sufficient to account for a judgment of validity in the one case and invalidity in the other.

Sutherland, in writing this opinion, was burdened by several decades of inconsistent rulings. Rather than overruling its prior decisions, the Court had instead attempted to make fine distinctions or ignore contrary decisions. He tried to make sense out of the chaotic record by declaring a general rule—freedom of contract—and then demarcating four categories of cases in which the Court had carved out exceptions. It might be helpful to examine his typology here because it does reveal some pattern to judicial behavior during the period when the Court was most protective of property rights. Sutherland began his endeavor by declaring:

> There is, of course, no such thing as absolute freedom of contract. It is subject to a great variety of restraints. But freedom of contract is, nevertheless, the general rule and restraint the exception; and the exercise of legislative authority to abridge it can be justified only by the existence of exceptional circumstances.[136]

"Exceptional circumstances" reminds one of a declaration by the nineteenth-century utilitarian, John Stuart Mill. He wrote, in the fifth book of his *Principles of Political Economy*, that noninterference or laissez-faire ought to be the general rule in regard to governmental intervention in the economy, but when he got finished enumerating all the "exceptions" hardly anything was left of the general rule. Sutherland was in a similar predicament.

In Sutherland's review of the "exceptional" cases, in which governmental regulations bearing upon the freedom of contract were upheld, he discovered four categories of cases. In the first, the fixing of rates for certain businesses was upheld because those businesses were considered by the court to have been "affected" or "impressed with a public interest." This category Sutherland easily dismissed as not applicable to the present case. Yet it may serve our purposes to tarry here for a moment because, once more, we will discover a chain of cases in which the Court first allowed for a little bit of regulation under "exceptional" circumstances, and then gradually opened the floodgates.

Traditionally, businesses "affected with a public interest" were only those, like ferries, bridges, canals, turnpikes, and common carriers, that had been regulated in colonial times. The railroads were eventually added. The idea was that certain businesses were so public by nature that an overriding public interest in their fair operation justified regulation. Attempts to define such businesses were necessarily vague. The distinction between these businesses and ordinary occupations was somewhat arbitrary and more the result of history than any unique quality they possessed. What criteria there were usually referred to the public nature of the business, the fact that it was open to all users almost by right, and that all comers tended to be charged the same price.

Chief Justice Waite, in *Munn v. Illinois*,[137] laid out the parameters of this category of businesses "affected with a public interest." He traced the distinction back to England's famed jurist, Lord Hale, in the seventeenth century. Lord Hale wrote that when property falls within this public domain, it "ceases to be *juris priviti* only." As Waite put it:

> When, therefore, one devoted his property to a use in which the public has an interest, he in effect, grants to the public an interest in that use and must, submit to be controlled by the public for the common good, to the extent of the interest he has thus created. He may withdraw his grant by discontinuing the use; but so long as he maintains the use, he must submit to the control.[138]

But in what business does the public not have an interest? Is the public interest greater in reasonable rates for cabs or trains than it is in the price of loaves of bread? The Court would wrestle with these kinds of dilemmas for decades.

In *Munn*, grain elevators were declared businesses "affected with a public interest" and, hence, subject to price regulation. As Waite reasoned, if common carriers are businesses "affected with a public interest," why not grain warehouses, which stand at "the gateway of commerce"? To those who might object that such legislative interferences were oppressive, Waite responded, appeal not to the Court but to the polls, for the legislature is the ultimate judge of what is reasonable regulation within its powers. His colleague Justice Field dissented, presaging a liberal construction of the due process clause (remember this was 1876, before Field's position would ascend in the substantive due process era). He warned that under the majority's ruling no business would be long safe from regulation because hardly a business exists in which the public has no interest. Then all property would be held "at the mercy of the majority of the legislature."[139]

And that was about how things turned out, except that the Court would become for a time during the substantive due process era more activist in exercising judgment over legislative determinations. During this era the Court would (1) uphold rate regulation over railroads,[140] (2) uphold insurance price fixing, even though the Court conceded that the insurance business was not clothed with a public trust, nor did the public have a right to demand its services,[141] (3) uphold rent control, under the theory that an ordinary business could become "clothed with a public interest" as a result of a temporary, wartime emergency,[142] and (4) eventually sounding the deathknell of economic due process, would uphold price fixing for mills, contending that "businesses affected with a public interest" was not a closed category.[143] Yet, the Court during the hegemony of due process would also strike down legislative schemes, declaring that those businesses subjected to regulation ought to be immune from interference because they were *not* businesses "affected with a public interest." Thus, the Court would invalidate statutes that (1) fixed wage rates in the meat packing industry,[144] (2) fixed prices at which theater tickets could be resold by scalpers,[145] (3) fixed gasoline prices,[146] and (4) called for the licensing of ice manufacturing.[147] The Court, then, had a rather malleable standard. Once again, even during the ascendancy of the substantive due process "Old" Court, the decision making was eclectic.

Let us bring to a close this rather lengthy disgression, and return to *Adkins* where Justice Sutherland enumerated those "exceptional" categories of cases in which freedom of contract can be abridged. So far, we have followed his typology through the first category—businesses "affected with a public interest," and thereby subject to government price fixing. He found this irrelevant to the minimum wage law he was considering in *Adkins*. Likewise, he discerned features of the next three categories that could be distinguished from *Adkins*: (2) those dealing with statutes relating to contracts for the performance of public works were obviously inapplicable; (3) those prescribing the character, method, or time of payment were merely designed to prevent fraud, and set no precedent for wage fixing; and (4) those fixing hours of labor were upheld only for dangerous industries and never for all businesses.

Sutherland was at his most vulnerable when he declared that all rights—contractual, liberty, and property—fall short of carrying absolute force. Rather, they are general rules only, subject to the vagaries of changing times and circumstances. When the Court in 1937 succeeded in vanquishing substantive due process, Sutherland's equivocations would be used against him, to devastating effect. Then he would attempt to withdraw them, but his recantation would come too late. Let us reproduce Sutherland's parting words in *Adkins*, because they illustrate how shaky were the stanchions upon which the defenders of property rights on the high Court stood.

> *The liberty of the individual to do as he pleases, even in innocent matters, is not absolute.* It must frequently yield to the common good, and the line beyond which the power of interference may not be pressed is neither definite nor unalterable, but may be made to move, within limits not well defined, *with changing need and circumstance.* But, nevertheless, there are limits to the power, and when these have been passed, it becomes the plain duty of the courts, in the proper exercise of their authority, to so declare. To sustain the individual freedom of action contemplated by the Constitution is not to strike down the common good, but to exalt it; for surely the good of society as a whole cannot be better served than by the preservation against arbitrary restraint of the liberties of its constituent members. [Emphasis added.][148]

Given all the exceptions to freedom of contract sanctioned in case after case by the Court, it is no wonder that the era of economic due process was doomed. Regulations were upheld that sanctioned rate fixing in laundries, antimonopoly laws, Sunday laws, usury laws, workers' compensation acts, zoning, state statutes restraining owners of land from leasing to Orientals, prohibition laws, legislation prohibiting option contracts on future sales of grain and prohibiting sales of stock on margin, and statutes preventing the operation of pool halls.[149]

The beginning of the shift away from the means-end test and the high degree of judicial scrutiny it applied to all legislative interferences with property rights came in 1934 in *Nebbia v. New York*. In a 5-4 decision the advocates of economic due process went down to defeat. The Court upheld a New York statute making it illegal to sell milk to consumers at below ten cents per quart and under nine cents to retailers. This depression-era act aimed at propping up the milk industry, in which producers' incomes were falling below the cost of production. Nebbia, caught in the act of selling for below the established price, contended that the milk industry, not being a business "affected with a public interest," a public utility, or a monopoly, nor dependent on public grants, could not be subjected to price fixing by the state. The Court determined otherwise. Even though the majority's decision adverted to the means-end due process test, it nevertheless found that "reasonableness" could fluctuate as a result of changing circumstances. As Justice Roberts phrased it for the majority, "A regulation valid for one sort of business, or in given circumstances, may be invalid for another sort, or for the same business under other circumstances, because the reasonableness of each regulation depends upon the relevant facts."[150] In the process of upholding the New York statute, the Court seemingly abandoned the standard of business "affected with a public interest," citing many cases in which the private character of businesses did not immunize them from price regulation, and setting a standard that would, apparently, render all businesses subject to such regulation at the discretion of legislators. Justice Roberts remarked, "The statement that one has dedicated his property to a public use is, therefore merely another way of saying that if one embarks in a business which public interests demands shall be regulated, he must know regulation will ensue."[151]

West Coast Hotel v. Parrish,[152] decided in 1937, would effectively bury judicial review of economic regulatory legislation. Elsie Parrish, a chambermaid working in the hotel, brought an action to recover damages for the difference between the wages paid to her and the higher minimum wage mandated by the state of Washington for women and children. The defendant hotel appealed to the Supreme Court from a judgment against it in the state Supreme Court, challenging the act as a violation of the due process clause of the Fourteenth Amendment. The hotel relied on the high court's previous decision in *Adkins v. Children's Hospital* invalidating a District of Columbia minimum wage act. Chief Justice Hughes, writing the Court's opinion to which four of his brethren assented, argued that a combination of factors necessitated reappraisal of *Adkins*. These factors included the challenge of the Washington Supreme Court upholding the state's minimum wage law, the close division in *Adkins* itself, the adoption by many states of similar provisions, and changing economic conditions.

Sutherland's artificial distinction in *Adkins* between maximum hours laws as valid and minimum wage laws as invalid would come back to haunt him, as would his concession that freedom of contract is not absolute and must bend to changing circumstances. As to the former, Justice Hughes dissolved the distinction, seeing no difference between the two types of regulation. If maximum hours acts were held permissible by the Court, why not minimum wage laws? Hughes's logic certainly surpassed Sutherland's, but he thereby acknowledged a much greater purview for legislative interventions in the economy. Sutherland's refusal to embrace an absolutist position on freedom of contract provided Hughes with ready ammunition, and he would use it both to erode contractual freedom and to dispense with the means-end test for violations of due process. Herewith, Justice Hughes's remarks:

> In each case the violation alleged by those attacking minimum wage regulation for women is deprivation of freedom of contract. . . . The Constitution does not speak of freedom of contract. It speaks of liberty and prohibits the deprivation of liberty without due process of law. In prohibiting that deprivation the Constitution does not recognize an absolute and uncontrollable liberty. Liberty in each of its phases has its history and connotation. But the liberty safeguarded is liberty in a social organization which requires the protection of law against the evils which menace the health, safety, morals and welfare of the people. *Liberty under the Constitution is thus necessarily subject to the restraints of due process*, and regulation which is reasonable in relation to its subject and is adopted in the interests of the community is due process. [Emphasis added.][153]

Now, Justice Hughes seems to have turned due process on its head, for during the heyday of economic due process, the clause was interpreted as a restraint on governmental interferences with liberty. Hughes transmuted due process into an authorization for governmental restraint provided that restraint satisfies the new, loose standard of "reasonableness." Under this criterion of "reasonableness," and "adopt[ion] in the community interest," Hughes had little difficulty in upholding the minimum wage statute. "What can be closer to the public interest than the health of women and their protection from unscrupulous and overreaching employers."[154] And if the protection of women is a legitimate end, who is to say that a minimum wage act is not a permissible means? Certainly not this Court, now unwilling to find anything "arbitrary or capricious" in the belief of legislatures that propping up wages will put more people to work and, thus, alleviate the "unparalleled demands for relief" engendered by the Great Depression. "Even if the wisdom of the policy be regarded as debatable and its effects uncertain, still the legislature is entitled to its judgment."[155]

The Court's majority placed great importance on altered economic circumstances in reaching its decision to overturn *Adkins*. And Sutherland, who laid the groundwork for the consideration of precisely such circumstantial factors by defending freedom of contract in relativistic terms, was left in the unenviable position of fighting a rearguard battle in dissent. Given his own refusal to embrace absolutism, repeated again in this dissent, what ground could Sutherland stand upon, except the protestations that he himself rendered feeble, that "the meaning of the Constitution does not change with the ebb and flow of economic events,"[156] and that the Court has no power to change the meaning of the Constitution, which can be altered only by amendment. Minimum wage laws, for the four dissenters, still retained their "essentially arbitrary" complexion; they were not "reasonable restraints."

What seems so troublesome about the "economic" or "substantive" due process era is that, in a way, its critics were right. The "Old" Court did exercise its judgments, its views on economics, its views about what was "reasonable" and what "unreasonable" in the field of governmental regulation of economic liberty and of property rights. And it weaved a tangled web of inconsistent rulings, which over time gained for the Court the appearance of arbitrariness. But while the "Old" Court was a fickle protector of property rights, the solution taken by its successors erred also, and to a greater degree, by embracing complete consistency, but now consistency in the name of legitimating all governmental restrictions on economic liberty. The due process clause, after *West Coast Hotel*, never again would be used as an effective bulwark against economic interventions by the state.[157] When the Court would refer to the bad old days of substantive due process, it would do so in scathing terms, warning itself to remain ever vigilant against a return of the ghost of *Lochner*. Even when the Court would come to invalidate an arbitrary zoning ordinance, in *Moore v. City of East Cleveland* (1977),[158] on the grounds that it violated liberty as protected by the due process clause, it would do so with the clear understanding that it was not returning to the egregious past of substantive due process.[159] The ordinance forbade Mrs. Moore from housing under her roof a son and grandson along with another grandson when one was a cousin of the other.

In our modern era, the high Court under the due process rubric exercises only what it calls mild review of regulations affecting property rights. This standard places the burden of proof of unconstitutionality upon the objector. It displays deference even in debatable instances to the constitutionality of legislative enactments and upholds regulatory measures if a "state of facts could exist that would justify such legislation."[160] Any act that seems "reasonable" or holds any "rational" relationship to the objectives sought is upheld. The only rights that the Court is willing to accord any greater protection under the due process clause of the Fourteenth Amendment as against state laws, are those specified in the Bill of Rights. These are viewed by the Court as "fundamental rights," and possible infringements on them are subject to a high degree of judicial scrutiny, employing means-end type criteria. Freedom of speech, press, and religion, the right to be free from cruel and unusual punishment, freedom of association, the right to vote, and the right to privacy (a judicial construct of Justice Douglas's), all fall within this favored category.[161] When legislation is challenged as abridging any of these "fundamental interests," the Court applies a standard of strict review. The burden of proof of constitutionality shifts to the state; and the state must demonstrate a "compelling state interest" in order to carry its burden.

Thus, the Court embraces a two-tier approach to the protection of liberties under the due process clause. When it comes to property rights almost anything will pass the loose test and light scrutiny, but when so-called fundamental interests are involved, a much more scrupulous, means-end test is applied and legislative interferences merit great suspicion.[162] Why liberty of the press deserves greater protection than the freedom to engage in a business or profession, to set one's own prices for one's product, or to take a job at a mutually agreed upon wage has not been well defended.[163] Is this dichotomy between personal freedoms and economic freedoms convincing? Should not events in the Eastern Bloc give us pause? There, states abolished property rights, and all proclamations to the effect that thought is free are hollow.

In the absence of convincing arguments for the dichotomy, perhaps it is fair to say that the Court has chosen to protect one set of rights in preference to another. This is not any different from the error charged against the "Old" Court, that is, supplanting legislative judgments by judicial preferences. But the dispute is misdirected, for the Court should serve as the ultimate guarantor of *all* constitutional rights of person and property against legislative measures that imperil them.

The Equal Protection Clause. The equal protection clause of the Fourteenth Amendment, too, has been judicially interpreted in such a way as to afford little protection to the ordinary property owner. As in the case of the due process clause, the burden of proof falls upon the plaintiff, not the government, to prove that a legislative classification discriminates against him or her. This presumption of validity, however, does not apply where a classification affects what the Court has come to view as fundamental rights. Thus, for challenged statutes affecting suspect racial categories, the right to travel, or vote, the Court exercises a high degree of scrutiny. The state, to carry its burden of proof, must demonstrate a state interest compelling enough to override the individual's "fundamental right."

Typical of the way in which the modern Court's interpretation of the equal protection clause operates so as virtually to exclude from protection economic liberty is the case of the *City of New Orleans v. Dukes* (1976).[164] Nancy Dukes operated a hot-dog pushcart in the French Quarter of New Orleans, a quaint area of the city frequented by tourists. The city passed an ordinance prohibiting all pushcarts within the district except for those that had been in operation for at least eight years. Dukes challenged this ordinance as a violation of the equal protection clause, adverting to the "grandfather clause" in the ordinance that permitted some vendors to escape the harshness of the order. The court disagreed. It found that the ordinance rationally furthered legitimate city purposes lying within the purview of the police power, specifically the purposes of preserving the appearance and customs of the district as valued by its residents and as a tourist attraction. The Court argued that the states, and by delegation cities, have traditionally been accorded wide latitude in the regulation of their local economic affairs under their police powers, and that in the exercise of these powers they may make rational distinctions with substantially less than mathematical exactitude. The Court therefore concluded that when local economic regulations are challenged solely on the grounds that they violate equal protection, the Court will consistently defer to legislative determination as to the desirability of a particular statutory discrimination.

Here, Dukes and her fellow vendors' livelihoods were at stake. The ordinance effectively put them out of business with the slight exception of the few who through longevity escaped the prohibition. Apparently for the modern Court, the right to engage freely in nonnuisance, noncriminal-type behavior will not be protected as a "fundamental right." Are citizens less free, say, when they were denied the right to vote in the South in the 1960s simply because they were Blacks, or when they are, as here, prohibited from exercising a benign occupation simply because certain politicians find it unaesthetic? Why should city councils hold a pretty nearly unchallengeable prerogative to prefer one set of business ventures (the restaurants housed in buildings) to another (the pushcart vendors)? The Court's narrow conception of the protection afforded by the equal protection clause gives free rein to such discriminatory regulations. Under the

Court's current standards, the outcome of this case would have been dramatically altered had the New Orleans ordinance prohibited all pushcarts in the district except those operated by Whites. Then, a Black challenging the prohibition as a violation of the equal protection clause would have been treated by the Supreme Court quite differently. Instead of the regulation's enjoying a presumption of validity, it would have been immediately subjected to strict review because it established a distinction based on a "suspect" racial classification. The Court would have quickly dispensed with any defense offered by the city to carry its burden of demonstrating an overriding, compelling state interest.

Property rights—the right to use, dispose of, and enjoy your land; the right to put your property to any peaceful use you choose; the right to engage in any nonviolent, nonfraudulent business venture; and the right to set your own prices for your products and to negotiate freely to purchase necessary factors of production, including labor—find little support in the modern Supreme Court's interpretation of either the due pocess or the equal protection clauses of the Fourteenth Amendment. Today the police power over economic or property rights finds its only somewhat effective challenge in another constitutional clause, that is, the Fifth Amendment's prohibition on federal taking of property without just compensation, and the Court's construction of that clause into the Fourteenth Amendment as a bar to similar excesses by the states. We shall turn now to a discussion of this check upon the police power.

Eminent Domain and the Police Power: Where to Draw the Line?

We have reached the heart of the contemporary takings controversy. Both courts and commentators have grappled with the problem of where to draw the line between legitimate, uncompensated regulation under the rubric of the police power and regulation that goes too far and is tantamount to a taking under eminent domain. To rephrase the dilemma in simpler terms: when does a regulation so trench on property rights that it constitutes a taking? What we are dealing with here are instances in which the state sees no need to further its ends via an explicit condemnation under its eminent domain power. Rather, for various reasons—to spare the state's treasury, or because it thinks such actions legitimately fall within its police powers—it decides to limit aspects of an owner's property rights. Several theories have been offered by judges in an attempt to differentiate constitutionally permissible regulations from those that fall afoul of the Fifth Amendment's takings clause. The results have been less than satisfactory. The legal commentators have fared no better in their attempts either to rationalize what the courts have done or to provide a new principle of differentiation. Before delving into the efforts of the latter, let us examine the various theories of the courts. I will focus particularly on the efforts of the Supreme Court, which took a leading role in setting the pattern for lower federal and state court decisions.

The Noxious Use Test. The earliest test devised in the modern era[165] by the Supreme Court to distinguish legitimate police power measures from their offending cousins was enunciated by Justice Harlan in 1887 in *Mugler v. Kansas.*[166] Harlan developed what has come to be called the "noxious use" or "harm test." This test flowed from the tort law of private nuisances, which itself had its origin in the notion that private property cannot be used in ways that injure the similar rights of enjoyment held by other owners. If A did use private property in such an invasive manner, B would have recourse to the courts for recovery for damages suffered. When extended by the courts to the domain of public law, police power regulations would be sustained if they attempted to prevent such incursions by prospectively limiting potentially intrusive behavior. But as we will discover from a brief examination of the cases exemplifying this noxious use principle, many activities proscribed by state legislation, and acquiesced in by the courts, were clearly not activities that would have been declared nuisances had a private party complained of their existence under the tort law.

In *Mugler*, a brewery owner objected to a Kansas ban on the manufacture and sale of liquor within the limits of the state. He claimed that his brewery, erected prior to the adoption of prohibition, was useless for any other purpose. Consequently, he argued that his property had sustained a loss of $7,500, the property having been worth $10,000 before the state forbade the manufacture of liquor and only $2,500 afterward. The statute, Mugler argued, should be held void under the Fourteenth Amendment.

Justice Harlan proceeded to analyze the case by paying the usual judicial deference to determinations by legislatures of the necessity behind an exercise of the police power. Yet he cautioned that there are limits beyond which legislatures may not rightfully go. The Court must serve as the final arbiter of the constitutionality of a challenged measure, still recognizing that "every possible presumption is to be indulged in favor of the validity of a statute."[167] And he continued:

> If, therefore, a statute purporting to have been enacted to protect the public health, the public morals, or the public safety, has no real or substantial relation to those objects, or is a palpable invasion of rights secured by the fundamental law, it is the duty of the courts to so adjudge, and thereby give effect to the Constitution.[168]

In this instance Harlan could uncover no such state duplicity, nor a deprivation of the citizens' constitutional rights. Instead, he found ample facts to justify the state's conclusion that prohibition was justified as a way of curtailing the dangers attendant upon the consumption of intoxicating liquors. As to the plaintiff's contentions that the act violated the Fourteenth Amendment by taking his property and trenching upon his due process rights, Harlan found such objections unconvincing. The Fourteenth Amendment's prohibition on the deprivation of property without due process of law, he reasoned, has never been regarded as incompatible with an equally vital principle, namely, the principle that "all property in this Country is held under the implied obligation that the owner's use of it shall not be injurious to the community."[169] This principle is vital for the peace and safety of society.

As to the charge that the state's prohibition edict amounted to a taking of Mugler's property, Harlan likewise found no merit in it. He differentiated the present case from one like *Pumpelly v. Green Bay Co.*, in which permanent flooding by the government effectively ousted the owner from possession of his land. For Harlan, *Pumpelly* clearly involved eminent domain, whereas *Mugler* concerned only the police power. A prohibition, Harlan concluded, that simply limits the use of property for purposes that a legislature declares injurious to the health, safety, or morals of the community, cannot constitute a "taking" of property, or an appropriation of property "for the public benefit." The important features of property ownership remain undisturbed. One can use and control the property for lawful means, and one can dispose of it unrestrained. Harlan found these factors to be of paramount importance. One is restricted only in the sense that one cannot use the property for certain specified purposes. These purposes are forbidden because they are adjudged "prejudicial to the public interests." To burden the state with the requirement that it must compensate owners prohibited from putting their property to a "noxious use" that would inflict "injury upon the community," would make no sense at all, for

> the exercise of the police power by the destruction of property which is itself a public nuisance . . . is very different from taking property for public use, or from depriving a person of his property without due process of law. In the one case, a nuisance only is abated; in the other, unoffending property is taken away from an innocent owner.[170]

Apparently, the features of the Kansas prohibition act that made it a police power measure rather than an unconstitutional taking were, for Harlan, (1) the fact that no physical invasion had been perpetrated by the government against the claimant's property, (2) that the property had not been appropriated by the state in a manner that would enhance the public benefit, (3) that the property use in question had become, by legislative determination, a public nuisance, so that the state merely acted to abate a nuisance not to confiscate innocent property, and finally (4) that the owner still enjoyed other incidents of property ownership, remaining free to put his property to any other permissible use. That was an unoffending business activity before Kansas acted, could then be made illegal, and the property subject to seizure and destruction upon any violation, Harlan found unexceptionable. The state's police power cannot be hemmed in by the state's prior acquiescence. Harlan concluded by declaring that he could discover nothing here inconsistent with liberty and property.

The noxious use test, particularly under the influence of Justice Harlan, would take an even more troubling turn, but the *Mugler* decision is troubling in its own right. A business previously legal, not a common law nuisance, and not conducted in a way that impaired others' rights was prohibited outright by legislative decree. The Court's noxious use test condoned this. But its decision gave a pretty open-ended sanction to future legislatures to declare previously innocent occupations suddenly "noxious public nuisances" and to demand their abatement. The very next year, employing the noxious use test from *Mugler*, Harlan and his colleagues on the high court upheld a Pennsylvania statute prohibiting the manufacture or sale of oleomargarine in the state.[171] Liquor is considered by many citizens as a danger to the health and safety, to say nothing of the morals, of society, but margarine?

Relying on the noxious use test enunciated in *Mugler*, the court could find nothing in the record to demonstrate that Pennsylvania acted unreasonably in banning from the market all products imitating butter. Sufficient necessity for the measure was found in the state's desire to protect the public from fraud, lest people be deceived by unscrupulous merchants passing margarine off as butter. The state must determine the apposite means, regulatory or prohibitory, for dealing with this danger to the public health, not the courts. Thus, the statute did not deprive the margarine manufacturers of property without just compensation. The Court's deference toward legislative interferences in the marketplace seems stretched to the limit in this case. The Pennsylvania act itself stated that it was an "act for the protection of dairymen," hence it was not exclusively an effort to eliminate fraud. Giving every possible presumption to the validity of legislative judgments unless disproven beyond a reasonable doubt, the Court could give little solace to the plaintiff. Relief from arguably "unwise" legislation must be sought in the legislature or at the ballot box, not in the courts.[172] Public opinion today would find the bans on liquor and margarine foolish, and property rights advocates would also find them defective. But their beliefs would derive from different sources. Conventional opinion would simply find it humorous that magarine could ever have been judged so threatening to the public health as to justify an outright exclusion from the marketplace. Yet the state's power to ban certain business activities as noxious or harmful would probably not be questioned. A property rights advocate, however, would condemn any wholesale prohibitions on noninvasive, nonfraudulent, noncoercive businesses as one of the worst kinds of governmental interferences with individual rights.

A third case decided on a noxious use standard puts the property rights advocate into a real quandary. What should courts do about cases in which the exercise by A of the right to use personally owned property and engage in an otherwise innocuous business has direct, adverse consequences for other surrounding property owners? The case that raises this dilemma, *Hadacheck v. Sebastian*,[173] differs from the two previous cases in that it does not deal with any generalized health or safety concerns to the public, but rather with A's use of his property directly affecting several Bs' enjoyment of theirs. In other words, the case is much closer to the private nuisance-type complaint that formed the original basis for police power regulation.

In *Hadacheck* the owner of a brickyard in a residential area of Los Angeles petitioned the Court after having been convicted of a misdemeanor for violating a city ordinance making it unlawful to operate a brickyard within the city. Hadacheck challenged the ordinance as a violation of his due process and equal protection rights under the Fourteenth Amendment. He contended that his property had been diminished in value from $800,000 before the prohibition to only $60,000 after, the property being suited only to the manufacture of bricks. Further, he argued that the brickyard, which was not a nuisance per se (that is, a nuisance as recognized by the common law), could not be prohibited by the city unless by its improper manner of operation it had become a nuisance in fact. The city could not use the police power arbitrarily or unreasonably to prohibit the business outright rather than simply calling for the abatement of any nuisance elements of its operation.

Justice McKenna, writing the opinion for the Court, remarked about the police power that it is one of the most essential powers of government and the least limitable. Although its exercise may fall harshly upon some individuals, the imperative nature of its exercise precludes any limitations upon it, except when exerted arbitrarily. The consideration that apparently swayed the Court against Hadacheck's position was the notion that if vested interests could hold against the police power, then cities would remain forever mired in outmoded patterns of development. Rather, McKenna and his colleagues believed: "There must be progress, and if in its march private interests are in the way they must yield to the good of the community."[174] In regard to the plaintiff's contention that his business was not a nuisance per se and, therefore, could not be banned under the police power, the Court cited a previous case, *Reinman v. Little Rock* (1915).[175] That decision upheld a prohibition on livery stables within the city. This demonstrated that the police power could be employed to ban offending businesses, so long as it was exerted neither arbitrarily nor with unjust discrimination. Thus, a business conducted properly can rise to the nature of a nuisance prohibitable under the city's police powers simply by being in the wrong place at the wrong time. It in effect becomes a noxious use, and the property owner must absorb the loss. Such the Court thought, was the price of progress.

For property rights advocates, the circumstances presented in *Hadacheck* constitute a genuinely tough case. Should such matters as A's use of his property interfering with B's enjoyment of hers be left strictly to the private law of nuisance, with B's seeking remedies for each offense by private suit to the courts? Or should the state have the power to prohibit such baneful uses of property under its presumed police power? If so, should this be a prospective ban, as in zoning, or only retrospective? Under the latter theory, a specific business, like Hadacheck's, would be prohibited if its continued existence were shown to represent a nuisance. Such perplexing questions will have to await a response until the final chapter, when we have discovered something more about the nature of property rights and the state. For now, it is something to keep in mind as we examine some of the cases subsequent to *Hadacheck* that dealt with similar facts. They reached compatible conclusions, although on a different theory for distinguishing police power from takings. Such cases, *Goldblatt v. Town of Hempstead* (1962) and *Consolidated Rock v. Los Angeles*, (1962)[176] would likewise reject the pleas of a prohibited business, not on a noxious use theory but, rather, on a criterion developed by Justice Oliver Wendell Holmes, a criterion developed sixty years ago yet still dominant in courts, federal and state, today. Holmes's theory called for *ad hoc*, case-by-case decision making and eschewed general principles.[177]

The Diminution in Value Test. Pennsylvania Coal Co. v. Mahon (1922)[178] gave Justice Holmes the opportunity to develop a theory that he had toyed with in earlier cases.[179] The theory embodied the notion that the police power and the power of eminent domain form a continuum. If the state goes too far in the exercise of its police power it commits an unconstitutional action tantamount to a taking. The facts of the case were these. The state of Pennsylvania, taking note of a widespread threat of subsidence in towns throughout the state as a result of the mining of coal, enacted the Kohler Act. This act annulled the original covenant in which the coal companies conveyed property to purchasers with the condition that the new owners would own the surface rights only. The sellers had retained the right to mine beneath the ground without liability for any damages sustained by the surface owners. The Kohler Act granted to the surface owners the right to seek an injunction against further extraction that might undermine their property. The plaintiff, the Pennsylvania Coal Company, advanced four arguments against the Kohler Act: (1) that the statute impaired the obligation of contract against the expressly stated prohibition in the Constitution; (2) that the statute took the company's property without due process of law; (3) that the statute, rather than being a bona fide exercise of the police power, was the work of an organized minority designed to confiscate the rights of producers and augment the property rights of a favored few; and (4) that if surface support were necessary for the public use in anthracite coal districts, it could constitutionally be acquired only through condemnation proceedings under eminent domain and the payment of just compensation.

Curiously, Justice Holmes chose not to focus directly upon the first complaint of impairing the obligation of contract.[180] Instead, he viewed the central issue as this: was the Kohler Act of such character as to fall within the purview of the police power? If so, did it so oppressively affect property owners as to go beyond the pale of legitimacy for police power measures?

The present case arose as a bill in equity brought by the Mahons to prevent the coal company from mining and causing their home to collapse. The Mahons owned a single-family house the subsurface rights of which had been contracted away. Justice Holmes began his analysis by asking whether the police power can be stretched so far as to destroy existing rights of property and contract. Holmes enumerated the continuum theory of the police and eminent domain powers in this way:

> Government hardly could go on if to some extent, values incident to property could not be diminished without paying for every such change in the general law. As long recognized, some values are enjoyed under an implied limitation and must yield to the police power. But obviously the implied limitation must have its limits or the contract and due process clauses are gone. One fact for consideration in determining such limits is the extent of the diminution. When it reaches a certain magnitude, in most if not all cases there must be an exercise of eminent domain and compensation to sustain the act. So the question depends on the particular facts. The greatest weight is given to the judgment of the legislature, but it always is open to interested parties to contend that the legislature has gone beyond its constitutional power.[181]

Holmes's explanation of how the "diminution in value" test should be applied is not clear. It is not surprising, therefore, that some commentators have extracted not only the "diminution in value test" but another one, a "balancing test" from his decision. Others have denied that this balancing theory, so popular among contemporary land-use advocates, can be imputed to Holmes's opinion.[182] As far as I can tell, it appears that balancing—that is, weighing public benefit against private loss—enters into Holmes's thinking only to answer the question of whether the Kohler Act is a legitimate police power measure under due process grounds. An important ingredient of the Court's substantive due process criteria was the consideration of whether a substantial enough public benefit existed to outweigh the loss to private liberty caused by a given measure. That appears to be what Holmes had in mind when he pointed to the fact that the instant case dealt with a single private house, and in ordinary private affairs the public interest does not warrant much in the way of state interference. While the extent of the taking of the private interest of the mining company was great, Holmes could discover little in the way of public damage, public nuisance, or public interest to weigh against this private loss. To put Holmes's conclusion in balancing test terms, a slight public benefit was extracted at a substantial private cost. Thus, it appears that on substantive due process grounds alone, this measure could have been invalidated, although Holmes nowhere explicitly draws this conclusion.

Instead, he proceeded to shift the ground back to a diminution in value test to assess the general validity of the Kohler Act where the right to mine had been contractually reserved. Here he reasoned that to make it commercially impracticable to mine coal had practically the same effect as if the government had appropriated the mine for itself or otherwise destroyed it. He warned:

> When this seemingly absolute protection [the Fifth Amendment's takings clause] is found to be qualified by the police power, the natural tendency of human nature is to extend the qualification more and more until at last private property disappears. But this cannot be accomplished in this way under the Constitution of the United States.[183]

Holmes continued by enumerating what he called a "general rule," even though on the next page he would deny that "general propositions" could be dispositive of such cases. Putting such inconsistencies aside, Holmes's "general rule" comes down to this: "while property may be regulated to a certain extent, if regulation goes too far it will be recognized as a taking." And then he proceeded to caution overzealous legislators that a "strong public desire to improve the public condition is not enough to warrant achieving the desire by a shorter act than the constitutional way of paying for the change."[184] But, again, this is a matter of "degree" and cannot be settled by general propositions. What Holmes probably intended by this rather confusing formulation was that no set formula can be established a priori to determine when a police power measure is so punitive as to amount to a taking. But probably, as in this case, where the property is rendered totally worthless by a regulatory measure, that measure would pass beyond the pale of constitutionality, and would amount to a taking. Whether less onerous acts that, say, diminished property values by 80 percent or 60 percent or 50 percent, similarly constituted a taking could not be determined arbitrarily beforehand but must await a judicial evaluation of the facts in each particular case.

All that can be said in the way of general rules is the formulation of the notion of a continuum between police power and eminent domain. An overweening exercise of the former would be tantamount to the latter; therefore, it would be unconstitutional because it would take property without the payment of just compensation. If legislators still wished to accomplish their aims, they would have to return to redraft the legislation and take the property by eminent domain. Whether Holmes intended all of this or not, this is how his so-called diminution in value test has been interpreted by the courts. They have embraced Holmes's atheoretical call for *ad hoc*, case-by-case decision making. Scarcely a case of this type goes by without a court's remarking that no set standards exist for discriminating legitimate police power regulations from unconstitutional takings.

Under this principle, the widest latitude has been provided for judges to mold the law to their own concepts of fairness or equity. Few property owners have benefited from the diminution in value standard; most have not fared nearly as well as the Pennsylvania Coal Company, which succeeded in having the Kohler Act overturned. In our own era, Holmes's parting admonition enjoys little favor: "So far as private persons or communities have seen fit to take the risk of acquiring only surface rights, we cannot see that the fact that their risk has become a danger warrants the giving of them greater rights than they bought."[185] Ironically, Holmes's methodology would in the future serve as a vehicle for the erosion of property rights without payment of just compensation. Courts, enamored of state land-use measures, would validate regulations limiting a landowner's rights over property to the extent that it could be used for little more than scenic vistas or land banks for state planners.[186]

Before examining how the diminution in value test has operated in the courts, Brandeis's dissent in *Pennsylvania Coal* ought to be mentioned because many environmentalists have found it appealing. Brandeis provides a rationale for expanding the police power and, consequently, constraining the takings clause as a hedge upon its exercise.[187] Brandeis would have given his approval to the Kohler Act. He saw in it nothing more remarkable than the prohibition of a use of land that in the course of time had come to constitute a noxious use under the familiar standard enumerated by the court in *Mugler* and *Powell v. Pennsylvania*. He argued that existing contracts cannot preclude the exercise by the state of the police power, and that courts ought to defer to legislatures. The state had not transferred to itself the property affected. A police power measure was not invalid simply because the act deprived an owner of the only profitable use to which the property could be put. Brandeis did little more than repeat familiar and heretofore accepted Supreme Court doctrine as regards the police power-takings distinction.

In reading Brandeis's dissent, one is struck by the realization that as ambiguous as Holmes's diminution in value test was from a property rights perspective, it still constituted a substantial improvement over what had preceded it. That leading contemporary commentators wish to return to Brandeis's position reveals the extent to which they value preserving open space and endangered species and devalue property rights. Under a Brandeisian standard it could be only a matter of time before police power enthusiasts conclude that using one's property for suburban tract housing constitutes a noxious use.

To see how Holmes's test operates, let us examine one case that reached the Supreme Court and another, similar case from California that the high Court declined to consider. *Goldblatt v. Town of Hempstead*[188] was decided by the Supreme Court in 1962 on generally Holmesian principles. The town of Hempstead passed an ordinance in 1959 that in effect prevented Goldblatt from continuing to make sand and gravel on his property. It prohibited excavation below the water table and imposed an affirmative duty to refill. The business had been ongoing since 1927, and had resulted in the excavation of a twenty-acre lake. Residential neighborhoods burgeoned around the site, and apparently the suburbanites found the pit aesthetically offensive. The town had tried several years before to terminate the business by zoning restrictions. This attempt was prevented by the courts on a prior suit by Goldblatt. Later, in 1959, the town brought an action to enjoin any further mining on the site, maintaining that the owner had not complied with the new ordinance. The trial court granted the injunction, which prevented further mining until the company complied with the ordinance and obtained a permit.

Goldblatt pleaded that the ordinance was unconstitutional. It was not a regulatory, police power measure affecting his business but, rather, a complete prohibition on its mining operations. The ordinance confiscated his property without compensation in derogation of the Fourteenth Amendment, and it took his property without due process of law. Additionally, he contended that the ordinance effectively deprived him of the favorable judgment received in his previous suit against the town's zoning restrictions, and that the ordinance operated as *ex post facto* legislation barred by the Constitution.

The Court decided otherwise. Conceding that the ordinance operated so as to completely prohibit a beneficial use—sand and gravel mining—to which the property had previously been devoted, the Court did not believe that this fact alone determined the question of constitutionality. If the ordinance otherwise passed muster as a legitimate police power exercise, the fact that it deprived the owner of the most beneficial use of his property does not render it unconstitutional. Adverting to Holmes's formulations from *Pennsylvania Coal v. Mahon*, the Court proceeded to caution that it was not ignoring the principle that government regulations if too onerous can amount to a taking. But, in good Holmesian fashion, it declared that "no set formula" exists to determine where regulation ends and taking begins.[189] A comparison of values before and after the regulation is a relevant but not conclusive consideration, for here the Court recalled that in *Hadacheck v. Sebastian* it had upheld an ordinance that decreased a property's value from $800,000 to $60,000. This decision, of course, was rendered on a pre-Holmesian standard of noxious use, a factor that went unremarked. In *Goldblatt* the Court discovered a way out of the whole problem of determining how far regulation can go before becoming a taking because the record failed to display evidence to show whether or to what extent the ordinance would diminish the value of the property.

Having dispensed with the heart of the issue on a diminution in value test, the Court then proceeded to examine whether the ordinance was a legitimate police power measure. Indulging in the usual presumption of constitutionality, and invoking the vague criterion of reasonableness to judge police power regulations,[190] the Court found nothing in the record to support a finding that the appellant, Goldblatt, had sustained his burden of demonstrating the unreasonableness of the measure. Because Goldblatt failed to susain his heavy burden, the measure stood as a valid police regulation, one enacted to insure the "public safety." Rather inexplicably, the Court concluded that it had upheld the prohibition even on the supposition that the depth limitation would confiscate the entire mining utility of the property, as maintained by Goldblatt. This decision vividly displays the inadequacy of the Court's doctrine that the burden of proof falls on the plaintiff to prove unconstitutionality, and that every benefit of the doubt will be given to the challenged legislation. Would it not have made more sense to say in this case that in the absence of proof of the necessity for the legislation, or a showing that a less burdensome alternative was impracticable (both important missing elements cited by the Court), the presumption should have been that the measure was unconstitutional? Should not such important property rights as the right to conduct a business be overcome only by the most pressing evidence that such business constitutes a public danger? In other words, should not the state have to demonstrate the overwhelming necessity for its action before courts acquiesce to the erosion of property rights?

Some of these curiosities in *Goldblatt* might have been resolved had the Court not denied *certiorari* to a California case, *Consolidated Rock v. Los Angeles*.[191] That case was virtually identical to *Goldblatt*, but it provided the evidence that the court found missing in *Goldblatt*, that is, evidence concerning the diminution in value of the affected property. Consolidated Rock Products Company, as lessee of 348 acres in Tujunga Wash within the city of Los Angeles, appealed to the California Supreme Court to overturn a trial court ruling denying it an injunction. The injunction had been sought to prevent the city from enforcing a zoning restriction preventing rock, sand, and gravel operations on the property. The trial judge, after an on-site examination of the affected parcel, had conceded that the property had great value if used for excavation of these resources, but "no appreciable economic value" for any other purposes. Its use for the two purposes permitted by the zoning plan—for agricultural or residential uses—was determined to be particularly "preposterous," given the land's susceptibility to continual flood hazard and soil erosion. The trial court also expressed reservations about the city's claim that the surrounding residential communities of Sunland and Tujanga, both havens for sufferers from respiratory ailments, would be unduly burdened by the inauguration of mining operations. Dust, noise, or danger to children were considered as potential hazards that could, however, be dealt with by the company to minimize any affronts to adjacent properties.

Despite these findings, the trial court entered judgment for the defendant, the city of Los Angeles. All the factors cited by the trial court were considered as matters upon which in their totality "reasonable minds might differ." Thus, upon applying the customary rule of judicial deference to legislative determinations, and the *Euclid* principle that zoning regulations must be upheld if they are fairly debatable, the trial court, and subsequently the California Supreme Court, upheld the zoning restriction as applied to this property. Despite the parcel's unsuitability for any of the permitted uses, and without mention of the diminution in value test, the California Supreme Court deflected a prime opportunity to clarify that all too ambiguous test. *Consolidated Rock* possessed the evidentiary material lacking in *Goldblatt*—evidence of the extent of the diminution in value caused by the zoning restriction—yet the Supreme Court of the United States would fail to avail itself of this opportunity to clarify its standards.

The Balancing Test. As mentioned previously in discussing *Pennsylvania Coal v. Mahon*, commentators and courts have extracted an additional test from Holmes's decision, one that focuses not so much on the diminution in value suffered by a landowner but rather, balances private loss against public benefit to test for an impermissible exercise of the police power amounting to a taking. Even though Holmes apparently rejected such a balancing test in *Pennsylvania Coal*, it, has its adherents. The Supreme Court, in *Penn Central Transportation Co. v. City of New York* (1978),[192] employed such a balancing criterion to uphold the city's ambitious, and in one respect innovative, historic preservation law. The New York City Landmarks Preservation Commission had refused to grant Penn Central permission to erect a fifty-three-story office building atop Grand Central Terminal because the terminal had been designated as a landmark under the city's historic preservation ordinance. The company then filed suit, alleging that the application of the landmarks preservation law to the company constituted a taking of its property without just compensation and an arbitrary deprivation of its property without due process.

The trial court granted injuctive relief; the New York Supreme Court Appellate Division reversed; and the New York Court of Appeals upheld that reversal. Finally, the case reached the United States Supreme Court. The New York preservation law's novel element is a provision whereby owners denied building rights on one piece of property, because it has been designated a landmark, can transfer the development rights that normally would have accrued to the property under the zoning law to an adjacent piece of property. The property to which the rights are transferred can then be developed to greater heights than would have been permitted under the zoning height restrictions. Such transferable development rights are much applauded by strict land-use advocates. They favor this device because it saves the public treasury and, thus, permits more regulation. Instead of the city's having to compensate owners for denial of permission to build, the city can distribute these development rights.

Justice Brennan wrote the decision of the Court in which he was joined by five of his colleagues. They found the question of the legitimacy of transferable development rights as a substitute for payment of just compensation in instances of a taking to be moot. In this case they could discern no takings. A balancing criterion seemed to play a central part in their determination that no taking had occurred, although the decision is too eclectic to say for certain which test was the decisive one. But Brennan's statement that land-use restrictions on real property may constitute a taking if not reasonably necessary to effectuate a substantial public purpose, or if they perpetrate an unduly harsh impact on an owner's use of property, does appear to express a balancing test. At least, the rest of the decision makes more sense if the rather disjointed arguments are interpreted in this balancing context.

Brennan took into account Penn Central's private loss in the balancing. He found this loss to be not terribly weighty because the company could

still profit from its current use of its property and the transferable development rights offered something in the way of offsetting any loss from the
denial of the use of preexisting air rights. He also considered the public
benefit to be derived from the preservation law, which was, as stated in the
measure, to preserve New York City as a tourist and business center while
benefiting its citizens by strengthening civic pride, education, pleasure, and
economic well-being. After rehearsing previous decisions on takings, zoning, and air rights, and after recalling the Court's customary standards for
deciding takings cases—that "no set formula" exists to determine when
government's failure to compensate would invalidate a regulatory measure;
that each case must, therefore, be determined on its "particular circumstances"; and that what this requires is "ad hoc, factual inquiries"—Brennan concluded that there was nothing in the New York preservation law as
applied to Penn Central that would render it a taking.[193] He declared:

> This is no more an appropriation of property by government for its own use
> than is a zoning law prohibiting, for "aesthetic" reasons, two or more adult
> theaters within a specified area, see Young v. American Mini Theatres . . ., or
> a safety regulation prohibiting excavations below a certain level. See Gold-
> blatt v. Hempstead.[194]

In one sense Brennan is absolutely right. If the Court finds the encroachments on property rights in these two cases permissible, why not approve
the present encroachment? But on a deeper level, perhaps something is
amiss in this whole tradition. These decisions tend to build upon one
another. In Brennan's statement we see a good example of this slippery
slope.

The Harm-Benefit Test. To complete this survey of takings tests, we will
next examine one of the newly emerging tests, a variant of the balancing
test, and one of which land-use enthusiasts have become enamored. This
test is expressed most conspicuously not in a U.S. Supreme Court case but,
rather, in a case decided by the Supreme Court of Wisconsin, *Just v. Marinette County.*[195] It is a "harm-benefit test." It dictates that when a regulatory act aims to *prevent a public harm,* no compensation need be given
to affected property owners to guarantee the act's constitutionality, but
when an act aims to *further a public benefit,* it would have to be accompanied by compensation to affected property owners to avoid a taking. The
Justs contended that a county shoreland zoning ordinance that prevented
them from filling in their marshlands and placed the property in a con-
servancy district was unconstitutional because it amounted to a taking of
their land without compensation. After paying deference to the Holmesian
diminution in value test, where a constructive taking is held to occur when

a police power measure restricts a landowner beyond what the landowner should bear, the court went on to elaborate its harm-benefit test. The court began with Professor Freund's definition of the powers of eminent domain and police—"It may be said that the state takes property by eminent domain because it is useful to the public, and under the police power because it is harmful."[196] The court concluded that the necessity for compensation arises under the police power only when restrictions are placed on property in order to create a public benefit, but not when employed to prevent a public harm. In this case, the court believed that an unambiguous instance of harm prevention motivated the restriction, citing the state's obligation to prevent further pollution of navigable streams under the public trust doctrine. Operating from the assumption that rivers in their natural state are unpolluted, it thought that Marinette County's regulation could be viewed only as preventing future harm to the environment, not as securing a public benefit.

The Wisconsin court in *Just* struck a mighty blow against the notion that ownership of private property carries with it the right to do with it as one wishes. No absolute or unlimited right exists to change the natural character of land, the court opined, so as to make it useful for some purpose to which it was unsuited in its pristine state. Consequently, the police power, reasonably employed, can serve to prevent harm to public rights by limiting the use of private property to its natural uses.[197] In rejecting cases from other jurisdictions that the Justs relied upon, cases that struck down similar regulations as takings,[198] the court contended that these other decisions laid too much stress upon an owner's right to change commercially valueless land when that change would do damage to public rights. The court struck at the very heart of the property rights conception—that what is mine may be used by me as I see fit provided only that I not use it in a manner that violates the like right of other owners. The court referred approvingly to a Jackson County Zoning Department motto that reads, "The land belongs to the people . . . a little of it to those dead . . . some to those living . . . but most of it belongs to those yet to be born."[199] It concluded that the shoreland ordinance simply "preserves nature, the environment, and natural resources as they were created and to which the people have a present right."[200]

Where did this so-called right of the people come from? Did they purchase it? No. Did God grant it to them? Undoubtedly, the Wisconsin Supreme Court would have felt unfashionable if it had made such a claim. Then how did this public right arise? The court remained silent on this point. What can "public" rights mean in this context? This looks suspiciously like a transfer of property rights from A to benefit some Bs, and without the payment of compensation. If the citizens of Marinette County want the Justs' property to remain in its pristine state, why should they not have to pay for that property?

The *Just* decision is troubling for more fundamental reasons, as is the harm-benefit test that the court employed. The court made several assumptions that are dubious: (1) that all property is residually "owned" by the community in the sense that the government can tell its nominal owners how that property may be used; (2) that any deviation from the natural state in which a nominal owner found the property may require governmental permission; (3) that natural is always good and always unpolluted, and that develoment, on the contrary, must always remain suspect; and (4) that public benefit can be readily distinguished from public harm. The conclusion of the court on the last point seems far less irrefutable than this court imagined. Is harm prevention all that occured in this case? If we take the contrary assumption concerning property rights to that embraced by the court, and argue that ownership entails the right to use and transmute property for future use, then what Marinette County did by its shoreland zoning restrictions was to enhance its resource base by appropriating a right incident to the Justs' ownership without paying for it. Only on a collectivist assumption (like point 1) about ownership can it be maintained that the county acted to prevent harm to the public's rights. On noncollectivist assumptions, if the County wished to preserve its supposed property rights in navigable waterways against pollution it would have either to request an injunction and demonstrate that harm would come to the waterway if the marsh were filled or to appeal to the tort law after the Justs had filled their swamp and demonstrate that its rights had been impaired. The harm, then, would have to be comparable to a harm recognized in the tort law, when harm occurs between two private owners. That is, it would have to be more serious than what would occur as a by-product of a landowner's right to use the land. The highly speculative, environmental harms that the court and the county perceived from development would, then, not suffice to stop the Justs from using and transforming their property. If the county wished to preserve the Justs' swamp in its natural state for environmental purposes, then the county would have had to pay for that right either by taking an easement or by taking the entire parcel under its eminent domain power.

The harm-benefit test seems more deleterious to property rights than any of the other standards—balancing, diminution in value, or noxious use—because it is so malleable. Judges sympathetic to environmentalist objectives find it the perfect tool, for whether some particular use of property is a harm or a benefit lies almost entirely in the eyes of the beholder. As dangerous as the other tests are, this new one is worse. It epitomizes the rule of men rather than the rule of law.

Efforts of the Commentators. The record of our courts in establishing a definitive criterion for discriminating legitimate police power measures from their overzealous, unconstitutional cousins has been disappointing, to say the least. To fill this breach, commentators have proffered alternative proposals in the law reviews, with little more success. Only a few of the most ambitious and notable attempts need be mentioned here. First, we will examine the efforts of three commentators who are the least sympathetic to property rights, then move on to a transitional group of experts who seek a middle ground to accommodate the police power to the need to protect certain portions of owners' rights, and finally, discuss a small group of commentators who are more concerned with safeguarding property rights.

1. Professor Joseph Sax has proposed not one but two resolutions to the taking by regulation dilemma. In his earlier effort, later rejected by Sax himself, he offered the following distinction, drawn from a conception of property as the value that each owner has left after the incompatibilities between his desired use of his position and others' desired uses of theirs has been resolved.[201]

> The rule proposed here is that when economic loss is incurred as a result of government enhancement of its resource position in its enterprise capacity, then compensation is constitutionally required; it is that result which is to be characterized as a taking. But losses, however severe, incurred as a consequence of government acting merely in its arbitral capacity are to be viewed as a noncompensable exercise of the police power.[202]

After examining the leading cases, Sax concluded that this rule—embodying the entreprenurial/mediator distinction—would leave most but not all of the decisions intact. The exceptions are the railroad grade crossing cases and *Central Eureka Mining* (in which the Supreme Court denied compensation when the government shut down the gold mines during World War II in order to free up workers for the war effort).[203]

Now, Sax's rule seems unsatisfactory because, as he applies the rule, it would leave *Goldblatt* and *Consolidated Rock* uncompensated, as simply cases in which government acted as a mediator. The only advantage of the rule would lie in its apparent condemnation of instances in which states employ zoning regulations to in effect transform private property into public nature preserves, e.g., the wetland cases.

Several years later, Sax returned to the fray with another proposal, one even more forgiving of governmental, uncompensated takings. Disowning his earlier contention that whenever government enhances its resource position it must compensate, he now viewed much of this activity as an exercise of the police power in vindication of "public rights" and, hence, noncompensable.[204] Undoubtedly, Sax's change of mind was attributable to his growing enthusiasm for governmental husbandry of the environment, an environment that in his view was suffering degradation as a result of our too-limited conception of "public rights."[205] His new formulation sought to remedy this putative fault. As an indicant of Sax's transformation, one need only point to his rejection of his earlier admonition that in wetland cases government, when it acts to enhance its resources by regulation, must compensate the affected owners.[206] Sax now wondered why the wetland owner, when seeking to alter the natural state of the property, should not be viewed as imposing restrictions upon others' use of the oceans.

Under Sax's later test, the duty to compensate would devolve upon government only when it restricted private uses of property that did not have spillover effects upon others. No taking, and no compensation, would occur when government acted in instances in which private uses were in conflict, and it merely regulated externalities. In the latter category would reside such activities as the following: (1) A's use of land that restricts B's options in using B's own land, (2) A's use of a common to which B has an equal right, e.g., dumping industrial pollutants in a stream, polluting the air, diminishing a visual prospect, and (3) A's use of A's own property that affects the health or well-being of other people, e.g., dumping of toxic substances, erecting a housing development in a remote area that requires expensive communal services. Sax contended that any activities falling within these three categories can be regulated without compensation by government, "however severe the economic loss on the property owner."[207]

Only by a stretch of the imagination could one conceive of very many examples of cases, excluding actual governmental takings of title or perpetration of consequential damages, in which the government would be required to compensate under this rule. Even the most innocuous of activities has some spillover effects, for no action occurs in a vacuum. Furthermore, to instruct government to act as a single property owner would in deciding between two conflicting property uses, that is, to act as an output maximizer, as Sax does, is to play fast and loose with property rights.[208] Sax, in addition, seems far too amenable to leaving these decisions in the hands of legislators on the assumption of the "rationality" of the legislative process.[209] Another problem with Sax's formulation is that his category of compensable regulations, narrow as it is, seems not even to qualify as legitimate police power actions, regardless of the question of compensability. If an action has no spillover effects, how can government regulate it at all? If the police power is supposed to protect the public health, safety, morals, and general welfare, it cannot reach purely self-regarding activities.

Harvard University law professor Frank Michelman in his article "Property, Utility, and Fairness"[210] attempted to resolve the takings issue by employing both utilitarian and Rawlsian fairness[211] criteria. By invoking utilitarian considerations, Michelman hoped to arrive at a solution that took efficiency into account; John Rawls's fairness criteria were employed to satisfy our ethical intuitions. Utilitarianism, with its concern for the maximization of satisfaction, would not dictate compensation in every case where expectations are disappointed, Michelman argued, for such a requirement would often nullify any advantage from an efficient project (that is, one that satisfied Pareto criteria—of advancing the good of someone while injuring no one, after the hypothetical payment of compensation to the losers). Rather, only those impositions that proved "critically demoralizing" would require compensation. To determine when to compensate, then, a utilitarian would examine three factors: efficiency gains, demoralization costs, and settlement costs. Whenever demoralization costs exceed settlement costs, compensation ought to be paid. But if either of these costs exceeds efficiency gains, the measure should be rejected as inefficient, and the question of compensation should never arise. The more a person suffers an injury distinct from that of the general public and easily quantifiable, the stronger the case for compensation becomes.

Next, Michelman invoked a quasi-Rawlsian standard of fairness to evaluate the compensation issue; a rule that as Michelman interprets it, would allow departures from full compensation if it can be shown that some other rule would work out best for each person. The disadvantaged claimant, on this account, ought to consider whether over the long run the entire system will tend to benefit people in the same circumstance:

> A decision not to compensate is not unfair as long as the disappointed claimant ought to be able to appreciate how such decisions might fit into a consistent practice which holds forth a lesser long-run risk to people like him than would any consistent practice which is naturally suggested by the opposite decision.[212]

Thus, Michelman's position does not diverge from the familiar judicial justification for police power measures: don't complain; rest assured that the benefits and burdens will even out over the long haul.

Michelman claimed that both the utilitarian and Rawlsian formulations would lead to pretty much the same answers in most cases; both rules turn upon the same factors: the disproportionateness of the harm a measure inflicts on an individual, and the likelihood that those harmed would be able to extract balancing concessions. Only to the extent that people are not as far-sighted as the Rawlsian fairness model assumes, would the two standards diverge, and the utilitarian rule would allow a greater likelihood of compensation to those demoralized individuals unwilling to wait a while for their equilibrating rewards. For judges who might be a bit overwhelmed by all this philosophizing, Michelman, in the end, distilled out the cash value of his principles. Compensation is due only when (1) a physical occupation occurs, or (2) an owner experiences the nearly total destruction of some previously crystallized value that did not originate under clearly speculative or hazardous conditions.

Michelman's formulations, although undoubtedly inventive, seem unsatisfactory on several counts. (1) Combining utilitarian and Rawlsian principles seems an unduly arduous route to traverse simply to reach the conclusion that owners should be compensated only when they are virtually wiped out by government regulations. (2) His utilitarian formulation would be unquantifiable, leaving those who seek to apply it with only hazy guidelines about trading off "settlement costs," "demoralization costs" and "efficiency gains." (3) Why should not a utilitarian demand that *actual* rather than *hypothetical* payments be made to losers in order to guarantee that a proposed government measure was truly efficient? If no compensation to victims were required, then it would be all too easy for governments to fudge on their cost/benefit analyses, and losses of utility might result. (4) In regard to the Rawlsian standard, why should actual losers concern themselves with prospective gainers when the losers suffer substantial financial losses today; does this not require a rather substantial transformation of human nature, a magnanimity and selflessness we do not often witness in adjudicatory proceedings? In the final analysis, Michelman's scheme would amount to even less protection for property owners than any of the currently employed judicial standards, and would be only slightly more amenable to plaintiffs' pleas than Sax's latter principle.

A more extreme position on the takings issue was propounded by Fred Bosselman, David Callies, and John Banta in *The Takings Issue: An Analysis of the Constitutional Limits of Land Use Control.*[213] The authors' explicit intention was to goad environmentalists into more regulatory activity by surmounting their fears of the Fifth Amendment's takings clause as a barrier. They proposed and then analyzed five strategies that could be employed by governmental land-use regulators to neutralize the compensation requirement. (1) They urged the demystification of the takings clause by firmly rejecting Holmes's "liberal construction" propounded in *Pennsylvania Coal v. Mahon.* Rather, they advocated a return to a "strict construction" of the clause. Compensation would be required only when government actually takes possession of the title to land. (2) The second strategy would revolve about the balancing test—that is, weighing the importance of the public purpose against the loss of value to each landowner. But it would rely on the gradual increase in weight given by courts to environmental purposes behind land-use regulation. Thus, the authors hope, an increasing knowledge of environmental damage would make many (if not all) public purposes weigh so heavily that they could "virtually never" be overbalanced by an individual owner's loss of property values. (3) Employing the British experience with legislative experimentation in land-use regulation, the third strategy called for the codification of legislative standards to define more precisely the boundary between regulation and taking. (4) Another ploy called not for legislative codification but, rather, for a more scrupulous attention to factual details and the drafting of regulations to resolve disputes over land-use restrictions. (5) The final proposal would circumvent the takings issue, instructing governments to use their acquisition powers, instead of their regulatory powers, whenever they seek to limit severely the development of land. Governments would acquire either the fee title, easements, or development rights, or institute a system of compensable regulation. However, given budgetary limitations, this last alternative—the one most congenial to the protection of property rights—appeared most dubious to the authors of *The Takings Issue*.[214]

Apparently, the strategy that held the greatest appeal to Bosselman and Company was the first. *Pennsylvania Coal v. Mahon*, they argued, should be overruled and the Court should declare "that a regulation of the use of land, if reasonably related to a valid public purpose, can never constitute a taking." This would place land-use regulation in the same category as other police power regulations, subject to the weakest possible test of constitutionality—that the regulation have a reasonable relation to a valid public purpose.[215] Brandeis's dissent in *Pennsylvania Coal v. Mahon* would, then reign victorious. The Supreme Court should declare "that when the protection of natural, cultural, or aesthetic resources or the assurance of orderly development are involved, a mere loss in land value will never be justification for invalidating the regulation of land use."[216] The old "physical invasion test," which dates back to the middle part of the nineteenth century and is the narrowest of all the tests, would be resuscitated. Compensation would be due only for title seizures, or invasions of the type perpetrated in *Pumpelly v. Green Bay* (where a dam flooded the plaintiff's land), and not at all for regulatory excesses.

Another strategy endorsed by the Bosselman team is that employed in the state of New Jersey in the early 1980s where, under the "public trust doctrine," the state has claimed a preexisting title to land bordering oceans, rivers, and marshes. This has wreaked havoc in New Jersey, for practically all landholdings from colonial times on have been put in jeopardy, with the state unable to deliver definitive maps showing to which land it claims title.

The Bosselman recommendation to repair to the anachronistic physical invasion test—anachronistic because it did not respond to the kinds of regulatory activities conducted by governments in our day—would, indubitably, present the courts with a less ambiguous standard than the conglomeration of tests they currently employ. However, it has one glaring liability. Property rights would stand virtually indefensible against a whole host of environmentally inspired land-use regulations. Even worse, almost any regulation, from whatever motivation, would be nearly unchallengeable.

2. Several commentators have attempted to hoe a middle course between guaranteeing some protection to property owners confronted by restrictive land-use regulations and the supposed need of government to control growth, regulate its direction, and decree its location. They endorse versions of a strategy adumbrated by Bosselman and his associates in their fifth recommendation, that is, a variety of regulation with compensation. As Bosselman correctly pointed out, courts have been reluctant to permit a middle ground between, on the one hand, declaring a regulation unconstitutional and granting an injunction against its application, or, on the other, holding it valid as it stands. A compromise between these extremes would allow an otherwise invalid regulatory measure to stand, provided that the owner is awarded such compensation as is necessary to prevent the regulation from failing constitutinal muster. This type of remedy has been advocated most conspicuously in the American Law Institute's Model Land Development Code and by John J. Costonis.[217]

Rejecting the extreme position taken by Bosselman, because it ignores questions of fairness to those property owners forced to contribute an inordinate amount to the commonweal, Costonis endorses what he calls the "accommodation power." Costonis does not go as far as the free-market advocates, whose position we will examine momentarily, whom he sees as embracing an "anachronistic model." He nevertheless gives greater cognizance to property rights claims than our previous group of police power enthusiasts. In borderline cases, like the wetlands cases in which virtually all development is prohibited, Costonis would allow regulation, but accompanied by payment. Compensation would be pegged not to the "highest-and-best-use" standard (or market value) normally employed in eminent domain cases but, instead, to a less demanding criterion of "reasonable beneficial use." Thus, if a regulation denied a property owner a reasonable beneficial use, it would have to be accompanied by the payment of compensation, enough compensation to raise the property owner to the reasonable beneficial use level. Costonis suggests that legislatures rather than courts should avail themselves of this "accommodation power," and that judges should not have the option of awarding compensation on their own authority. Thus, property owners would not have the option of compelling government to compensate for regulatory excesses.

Another middle-of-the-road solution that has surfaced in recent years is related to the Costonis regulation-with-compensation remedy. Donald Hagman[218] proposed a scheme whereby those landowners who benefit from regulation would be taxed and the funds recouped by government would go to compensate the regulatory losers. "Windfalls for wipeouts," as Hagman cleverly called his scheme, holds some attraction. It would ameliorate the condition of the victims of currently uncompensable regulation, yet its drawbacks seem to outweigh this advantage, for it would necessitate an even greater amount of governmental involvement in the marketplace. Governments would have to assess the amount, recipients, and duration of windfalls, seemingly an insuperable task, considering the sifting and unpredictable effects of regulations on land values. And the level of taxation would have to be fixed on an *ad hoc*, case-by-case basis for each parcel of affected property; again, a task requiring near omniscience and calling for subjective judgments likely to trigger numerous court challenges.

Another proposal, closely related in spirit to the previous two alternatives, would rely on a marketable privilege called a "transferable development rights" (TDRs), much as in the *Penn Central* case. Frank Schnidman and Costonis also endorse this alternative.[219] Property owners deprived of the right to erect buildings of substantial height within cities or of profitable density in a residential area, would receive TDRs. They could either transfer them to another zone (designated a transfer zone), where these privileges could be applied to allow greater height or density than the normal zoning would, or the TDRs could be sold in the marketplace to another builder.

Now, what appears objectionable about this scheme is that it carries zoning to its ultimate limit. Although it recognizes that zoning causes unearned windfalls and undeserved wipeouts, it then proceeds to argue not for the abolition of zoning but rather for the extension of governmental intervention. It says something like this: "We will take from all property owners an incident of ownership—the right to build in the airspace above one's property—and nationalize it without compensation. Then if someone wants to build, he or she will have to pay another one of the victims for that privilege." If a little government regulation is inequitable, as the authors concedes, why will more be better? Such a scheme gets government off the hook for regulatory excesses at virtually no cost. But the costs would be borne by someone. Would it not create an inefficient market in government privileges much like the selling of taxicab medallions in New York City?

3. A few commentators, more enamored of the free market than are their colleagues, have proposed solutions to the takings issue that would curtail police power excesses. Two of these legal theorists are Bernard Siegan and Robert Ellickson. In numerous books, including *Economic Liberties and the Constitution, Planning without Prices*, and *Land Use without Zoning*,[220] Professor Siegan has argued for the return to the substantive due

process criteria for adjudicating police power cases, for the replacement of zoning by free market mechanisms such as restrictive covenants, and for the circumscription of government's regulatory zeal. Siegan's work on zoning will be examined in greater detail later.

Ellickson, in his article "Alternatives to Zoning: Covenants, Nuisance Rules, and Fines as Land Use Controls,"[221] came close to embracing Siegan's purist position, yet he stepped back from a wholehearted embrace of the marketplace. Employing both efficiency and equity criteria to evaluate land-use regulations, he concluded that master planning and zoning are not the most felicitous vehicles for resolving conflicting land uses. Alternatively, he argued that conflicting land uses might best be left to market resolutions; either by one owner buying out a neighbor, or by covenants, leases, easements, or defeasible fees. Ellickson also proposed certain alterations in nuisance law that would encourage the internalization of the costs of spillover effects. Nuisance-type behavior short of that justifying the grant to a plaintiff of injunctive relief could be penalized by an award of damages to the injured party. Only in a relatively small number of cases of pervasive nuisances, in which the spillovers would be so diffuse as to defy any of the previously enumerated remedies, would government play a more incursive role. It could levy fines, or in extreme cases of indeterminate noxiousness, enact mandatory regulations.

The thrust of the free market advocates' case, then, is that the police power should be judiciously exercised by government. When it is utilized, landowners should be compensated for any restrictions on non-nuisance-type behavior. Although Ellickson considered his recommendations for the enhancement of the availability of the nuisance remedy a departure from strict laissez-faire, it is only a departure if laissez-faire is defined as "anything goes." Under a traditional definition of laissez-faire, which incorporates the notion that A's use of his property must not impair B's use of hers, Ellickson's proposals seem compatible with a free market rendition of property rights. Ellickson's principal deviation from laissez-faire occurs in his acknowledgement that community standards—e.g., in respect to building heights, setbacks, subdivision design—may be enforced by a nuisance board with the power to assess fines or prohibitions for cases of "pervasive nuisances."

This examination of judicial tests and commentators' proposed remedies has not been encouraging. Is this problem of distinguishing legitimate police power regulations over property from regulations that go too far insoluble? I think not, but I am skeptical of achieving such a solution by pursuing any of the currently favored paths. Siegan's and Ellickson's ideas point to a solution, but even here I think a workable solution will depend on a fundamental analysis of the justification and meaning of property rights. But first, we need to engage in a bit more investigation of our courts and their interpretations of the police power as a regulatory device over land. Zoning and more recent land-use legislation will be the focus of the next section. Again, we will traverse a rocky course.

Zoning and Land Use: What Can I Build and Where Can I Build It?

It is in the areas of traditional zoning and its newer cousins, regional or statewide land-use legislation, where the courts' inability to draw a line between legitimate regulation and invalid, because confiscatory, police power exactions has taken the greatest toll upon property owners. That cities, counties, or states should have the power to tell the owner of a property to what use it can be put is by no means self-evident. Perhaps because zoning is today so omnipresent we take it for granted. We assume, unquestioningly, that government inherently possesses such powers. But it was only in the late 1920s that the Supreme Court gave its official blessing to such regulations after many states had adopted enabling acts delegating to municipalities the right to draw up comprehensive plans to structure the use of land within their domains.[222] And it was only a mere twenty years earlier that the high Court recognized a right in local governments to control the heights of buildings.[223]

When the Court endorsed zoning in 1926, in *Village of Euclid v. Ambler Realty Co.*,[224] it did so at a time when the doctrine of substantive due process was still very much alive. Even more surprising is the fact that the Court's decision was written by Justice Sutherland, certainly one of the most enthusiastic supporters of that doctrine. This case, the first in which comprehensive zoning was ruled upon by the Supreme Court, might have been for all intents and purposes the last zoning case the Court heard, for the principles laid down in *Euclid* remain the regnant ones governing zoning to this day. In fact, it very nearly was the last zoning case the Court agreed to hear. Except for a scant few in the late 1920s the Court completely bowed out of zoning cases, returning to the fray only very gingerly and irresolutely in the middle-1970s. It remained principally to the state courts and to a lesser extent lower federal courts to handle all of the myriad cases that arose as zoning swept the country, leaving in its wake disgruntled property owners, its share of corruption, and windfall profits for some people fortunate enough to have good political connections.

Courts throughout the land have generally upheld zoning so long as it emanates from a comprehensive plan and allows owners some use of their land that could be construed as profitable. The courts have frowned upon blatant corruption, or "spot" zoning, which conspicuously burdens some property more than surrounding parcels, or down-zoning in anticipation of a future eminent domain proceeding. Even if a plaintiff triumphs in court, the remedy is likely to be the traditional one in cases of the invalidation of a police power measure; the offending portion of the ordinance is struck down, but the owner receives no compensation for the burden placed upon the property and for the losses sustained during the tenure of the offending ordinance. (Only recently, and in a few jurisdictions, have victorious owners successfully sought compensation under an inverse condemnation theory.) What irate property owners often learn subsequent to a victory in the courts, is that the city can come right back with a slightly altered zoning classification for their property and the expensive, frustrating, and time-consuming battle must be joined all over again. They are in much the same situation as Goldblatt was with his numerous, ultimately unsuccessful battles to keep his sand and gravel business functioning in the face of a barrage of zoning ploys by the town of Hempstead.

As we discovered with other police power measures, persons who challenge zoning regulations on property rights grounds—on a takings, due process, or more rarely, an equal protection theory—must bear a heavy burden of proof to convince the courts of the regulations' invalidity. The courts have agreed that zoning measures must stand if their constitutionality is fairly debatable. To see how the Supreme Court's attitude toward zoning developed, we have only to repair to an examination of *Euclid v. Ambler Realty*, a leading case if there ever was one.

Ambler Realty Company brought suit to challenge the village of Euclid's zoning ordinance as it affected Ambler's unimproved land. The company contended that the ordinance operated to reduce the value of the property, that it deprived the company of liberty and property without due process of law, and that it destroyed the value of the property without payment of compensation. The district court enjoined the village from enforcing its zoning ordinance, and the case reached the Supreme Court on an appeal lodged by the village. The appellant contended that the ordinance fell within the purview of its police power, which is wide enough to meet new conditions; that the Court ought to bow to its legislative determination of necessity unless unconstitutionality could be clearly demonstrated; and that the financial loss suffered by Ambler Realty should not suffice as the test of invalidity.

Justice Sutherland, writing for the Court, noted the claim of the realtor to have sustained a loss in value on the property from $10,000 to $2,500 per acre. He then framed two constitutional questions: Does the regulation violate a right of property under the guise of the police power? and, Is it unreasonable and confiscatory? Echoing the prior history of police power adjudication, he wrote: "The line which in this field separates the legitimate from the illegitimate assumption of power is not capable of precise delimitation. It varies with circumstances and conditions."[225] Analogizing zoning to the common law of nuisance and its *sic utere tuo ut alienum non laedas* principle (do not use your property so as to injure another), Sutherland proceeded to construct a phrase destined for frequent quotation: "A nuisance may be merely a right thing in the wrong place,—like a pig in the parlor instead of the barnyard. If the validity of the legislative classification for zoning purposes be fairly debatable, the legislative judgment must be allowed to control."[226] Finding no compelling reasons to demonstrate that the provisions of the ordinance were clearly arbitrary or unreasonable, especially in the face of studies by professional commissions supporting zoning, he found that the ordinance in its general scope and dominant features passed constitutional muster. The Court's decision left open the possibility that future challenges to specific portions of zoning ordinances might still be sympathetically considered.

In finding zoning to constitute a reasonable exercise of the police power, the *Euclid* Court was swayed by the desires of some property owners to protect their property values and the serenity of their residential neighborhoods. But, as the Court frequently reminds us, times change, and a power first beloved by suburban property owners has become—remember California—in some instances their nemesis. And they have little recourse. Since the Court's definitive pronouncement in *Euclid* approving zoning in general, property owners have had rather limited grounds of appeal in challenging such ordinances. They can take any one or more of the following tacks: (1) that the zoning scheme exceeds the authority vested in the municipality by the state; (2) that the ordinance includes no *general*, comprehensive plan, but rather embodies "spot" zoning; (3) that the ends sought by the offending measure exceed those justified under land-use regulation; (4) that the means employed are arbitrary and unreasonable; or (5) that the classifications made deprive the landowner of the equal protection of the laws.[227]

The four cases dealing with aspects of zoning that the Supreme Court decided in 1927 and 1928 shed some, but not much, light upon the boundaries of its legitimacy. In the first, *Zahn v. Board of Public Works*,[228] Sutherland, again writing for the Court, upheld a zoning measure dividing Los Angeles into five zones. The measure was upheld over the plea of a lot owner whose land was placed in a residential zone with the effect that it retained less value than it would have, had it been available for business development. Deferring to the conclusion of the city council that the public welfare would be promoted by the scheme, and discerning nothing clearly arbitrary or unreasonable about the measure, Sutherland again rehearsed the "settled rule" of the Court that it cannot substitute its judgment for that of a legislative body. Thus, the ordinance withstood challenge, being not violative of due process or equal protection either in its general scope or as applied to Zahn's property. Once again, in *Gorieb v. Fox*,[229] Sutherland and his brethren upheld an ordinance prescribing building lot setbacks on *Euclid*ean grounds. Here the regulation, in the Court's mind, gained its justification from the "great increase and concentration of population in urban communities and the vast changes in the extent and complexity of the problems of modern day life."[230]

The two challenged measures brought to the Court in 1928 failed to meet constitutional standards, for the Court discovered something in each that rendered it "arbitrary and unreasonable." *Nectow v. City of Cambridge*[231] dealt with a zoning ordinance similar to that previously upheld in *Euclid*. The plaintiff's land had been placed in a residential zone. He attacked the measure as depriving him of due process under the Fourteenth Amendment and requested an injunction mandating that the city pass upon his application to erect an otherwise lawful building on the property. Sutherland, again authoring the Court's opinion, referred to Nectow's loss of a contract for sale of the property in the amount of $63,000 after adoption of the zoning classification when the prospective purchaser refused to go through with the deal. Also relevant was the finding of a court-appointed master who determined that no practical use of the land could be made under its present residential designation, considering that adjoining pieces of land were used for industrial sites or railroading. The determination by the master that no substantial relation existed between the classification of this piece of property and the public health, safety, morals, or general welfare was considered determinative in this case. What Sutherland did here was to draw a line beyond which zoning regulations should not be upheld. He wrote:

> The governmental power to interfere by zoning regulation with the general rights of the landowner by restricting the character of his use, is not unlimited, and other questions aside, such restrictions cannot be imposed if it does not bear a substantial relation to the public health, safety, morals; or general welfare.[232]

Where zoning, then, unreasonably burdens a parcel of land without any substantial police power justification it should be invalidated. But the Supreme Court would not see fit to develop the niceties of this distinction because, almost instantly, it would bow out of all zoning cases. Its one last fling before its half-century of silence occurred in *Washington ex rel. Seattle Title Trust Co. v. Roberge*.[233] A zoning measure precluded a philanthropic house in a residential district from expanding without the written consent of two-thirds of its neighbors within 400 feet of the property. The neighbors balked, and so the philanthropy was denied a permit to enlarge its structure. The Court found the two-thirds consent provision violative of due process because of its "arbitrariness" and its imposition of "unnecessary and unreasonable" restrictions with no justification for them discernible in the police power. The Court could unearth nothing in the evidence to indicate that the structure would pose a nuisance or conflict with the general zoning plan.

After its long hiatus, the Court would return only gingerly to the zoning fray. It decided two rather peculiar cases that did not strike at the heart of the ordinary range of zoning disputes, a few cases with First Amendment implications, and a few others concerning "exclusionary" zoning. But it sidestepped (on procedural technicalities) the tough issues presented by the newer type of land-use cases that came before it.

In the first category of peculiar cases, I place *Village of Belle Terre v. Boraas* (1974),[234] which was tried on equal protection grounds. The Court upheld a zoning restriction that prohibited the occupation of a dwelling by more than two unrelated individuals. Under its cursory standard of review reserved for economic and social legislation (and the Court did not consider this regulation to touch a fundamental right or a suspect classification, thus eliminating the need for strict review), the Court upheld the measure as a valid land-use restriction. It rested its determination on the precedents set in *Euclid* and in the totally irrelevant eminent domain case of *Berman v. Parker* (over which we have previously puzzled). Three years after *Belle Terre* the Court, without reversing itself, and by a convoluted attempt at distinction, overturned on due process grounds an ordinance that prohibited the cohabitation of a grandmother with two grandchildren who were cousins. In *Moore v. City of East Cleveland* (1977)[235] the Court did feel that a fundamental right was involved—family living—and, therefore, invoked its strict standard of review. Despite the Court's best efforts, it is difficult to see why these two cases should have been decided in diametrically opposite ways; they both dealt with liberty and the right to use one's property as one wishes. These two seemingly contradictory decisions illustrate the divergent outcomes produced when the Court examines police power measures either on a loose standard of scrutiny (deferring to legislative judgments unless indisputably "unreasonable," as in *Belle Terre*), or instead on a standard of strict review (as in *Moore*). Under the strict standard the state must carry a heavy burden in order to prove that a "compelling state interest" should prevail over a fundamental right.[236]

Two other zoning cases fall within the second category because they examine zoning as it impinges upon First Amendment freedoms. The first, *Young v. American Mini Theatres* (1976),[237] upheld a Detroit zoning ordinance prohibiting the operation of any "adult" movie theater or bookstore within 1,000 feet of any two other such establishments or within 500 feet of a residential area. A divided Court, with two dissenters, rejected the theaters' contentions that the ordinance violated their First Amendment rights and deprived them of equal protection under the Fourteenth Amendment. Justice Stevens, for the majority, argued that "the mere fact that the commercial exploitation of material protected by the First Amendment is subject to zoning and other licensing requirements is not a sufficient reason for invalidating these ordinances."

In a more recent case, *Schad v. Borough of Mount Ephraim* (1981),[238] the Court seemed to distance itself from the decision reached in *American Mini Theatres*. Asked to review the conviction of the plaintiff for violating a zoning ordinance by introducing coin-operated booths for the viewing of live, nude entertainment, the Court held the ordinance invalid under the First and Fourteenth Amendments. Justice White, writing the opinion of the Court, found spurious the borough's attempt at justifying the ban on either the grounds that live entertainment conflicted with its desire to create a commercial area or that it would produce parking congestion and trash problems. Citing the Court's by now familiar distinction for the level of review required for zoning regulations when they affect only economic interests (cursory and deferential to legislatures) in contrast to that afforded when fundamental rights are threatened (strict and nondeferential), the Court classified this case in the latter category. But why does this case fall within the more protected "fundamental liberties'" category, if *American Mini Theatres* did not? Justice White attempted to answer that very question. It seems that the prior case was not controlling because it just dispersed adult theatres, rather than banning them from an entire borough as the present ordinance did. Given the classification of this case as affecting fundamental liberties, the court applied its standards for strict review, a means-end test: that the interests advanced by the borough be thoroughly examined; that the means chosen to further those ends be appropriate; and that the means chosen be the least intrusive. The borough failed this test. What is so perplexing about these two cases, and also the previous two, is that seemingly similar factual circumstances resulted in such dramatically different resolutions.

The next two cases address problems of "exclusionary" zoning raised by minorities or low-income groups. The whole concept of "exclusionary" zoning is, in a way, a redundancy, as all zoning aims at exclusion by protecting suburban property values through such devices as large minimum-lot requirements, setbacks, home size specifications, or bedroom minimums. Be that as it may, "exclusionary" zoning has come to mean something distinct from zoning itself. In the first of these recent cases, *Warth v. Seldin* (1975),[239] a closely divided Court held that various plaintiffs, who challenged a Penfield Zoning, Planning, and Town Board zoning ordinance that effectively excluded low- and moderate-income people from living in the town, lacked standing to bring the suit. These plaintiffs lived outside the boundaries of the town, and the majority of the court found that they did not meet the test to challenge "exclusionary" zoning. To satisfy that test they would have had to demonstrate with specific facts that the zoning ordinance harmed them and that they personally would benefit in a tangible way from the Court's intervention. Justice Brennan in his dissent found this reasoning fallacious. He saw a bitter irony in the fact that the very success of an "exclusionary" scheme could be turned into a barrier to a lawsuit seeking its invalidation.

A later decision, *Village of Arlington Heights v. Metropolitan Housing Development Corporation* (1977),[240] reached beyond the standing question to the merits of the case. But in the end the Court concluded that the respondents failed to carry their burden of proving that the village had entertained a racially discriminatory intent in denying rezoning to Metropolitan Housing for the construction of federally assisted, racially integrated, low- and moderate-income housing. MHDC and an individual minority member had filed suit requesting an injunction and declaratory relief. They alleged that the rezoning denial was racially discriminatory and, hence, violated the equal protection clause of the Fourteenth Amendment.[241] The Court found no evidence in the lower court proceedings to demonstrrate that a racially discriminatory intent had motivated the board's decision. Such evidence would require an examination of such elements as the historical background, disproportionate impact on certain groups, specific antecedent events, departures from normal procedures, or contemporary statements of decision makers.[242]

The final three cases that we will discuss deal with the newer, more controversial land-use legislation inspired by environmentalist concerns for preserving open space while also conserving the public treasury. The first two cases reached the Supreme Court after winding their ways through the California courts. *Agins v. City of Tiburon* (1980)[243] was, really, a nondecision. The Aginses filed a complaint against the city of Tiburon, a wealthy coastal enclave, seeking damages of $2 million under an inverse condemnation theory. They also sought a declaration that the zoning ordinance promulgated by the city was facially unconstitutional because it took their property without payment of just compensation. The zoning ordinance had been mandated by the state under the requirements of the California Coastal Plan. The plan required that coastal cities prepare a general plan governing land use and the provision for open space. Tiburon's plan impinged on the Aginses' own plans for their land. They had originally puchased their five-acre lot with a view of San Francisco Bay with the intent of developing it for residential use. The zoning ordinance frustrated their plans for intensive development by placing their property in a "Residential Planning Development and Open Space Zone" that limited development on such a plot to from one to five single-family residences, depending upon the design and the results of an environmental impact report. Having been apprised of this limitation, the Aginses, rather than filing an application to develop their land under the restrictions, instead filed a $2 million suit alleging that the ordinance completely deprived them of the value of their property. The city then undertook proceedings to condemn the Aginses' land under eminent domain. This attempt was eventually abandoned by the city, resulting in the plaintiffs again filing their $2 million suit.

The California Supreme Court did address the merits of the case. The majority of that court declared that the inverse condemnation remedy did not lie for damages caused by zoning ordinances. Injured parties must seek their remedies either in a declaratory judgment invalidating the offending ordinance or in a mandamus proceeding. The majority seemed especially sensitive to the need to preserve the public purse. This seemed to be a principal reason for denial of inverse condemnation as a remedy for possibly overzealous land-use regulations. "Policy considerations" persuaded them that inverse condemnation would be an inappropriate remedy, one that would usurp the legislative prerogative by forcing compensation. These "policy considerations" included the need to develop cities upon a rational plan, the necessity to preserve natural resources, and, in general, changing attitudes toward the regulation of land. For good measure, the California majority went on to deny the Aginses' right to declaratory relief also, claiming that no such remedy of invalidation was available simply for a decrease in the value of a property interest. Carrying the Holmesian diminution in value test to its logical limit, Justice Richardson declared:

> Accepting as we must the general proposition that whether a regulation is excessive in any particular situation involves questions of degree, turning on the individual facts of each case, we hold that a zoning ordinance may be unconstitutional and subject to invalidation *only when its effect is to deprive the landowner of substantially all reasonable use of his property.* The ordinance before us had no such effort.[244]

The Agins family fared no better before the Supreme Court. It completely ducked the constitutional issues, deciding not to decide. It declared that no concrete, judiciable controversy existed regarding the application of a zoning ordinance to the Aginses' property because they never applied for a permit to develop their property. Now, where does this decision leave the property owners? Must they present their preferred plan and have it rejected and then fight their case through the layers of California courts and eventually to the Supreme Court?

In the remainder of the decision, which has the status of dicta only, the Court indicated that if the Aginses brought their case to the high Court again, it would be quashed on its merits, for the Court could find nothing offensive about this zoning ordinance.

> In this case, the zoning ordinances substantially advance legitimate governmental goals. The State of California has determined that the development of local open-space plans will discourage the "premature and unnecessary conversion of open-space land to urban uses." The specific zoning regulations at issue are exercises of the city's police power to protect the residents of Tiburon from the ill-effects of urbanization. Such governmental purposes long have been recognized as legitimate.[245]

And what's more, the Aginses should applaud the zoning restrictions that ensnare them because all property owners will benefit from reciprocal restrictions under the police power. At least, such is the Court's view about how the police power functions. Remarkably, the unanimous Court concluded that the ordinance did not prevent the best use of the appellants' property, nor extinguish a fundamental attribute of ownership.

Thus, the Court seems just as enamored of the newer land-use devices as it was back in 1926 with the old-style zoning. While the Court in *Agins* completely dodged the question of the availability of inverse condemnation as a remedy for financial losses resulting from land-use regulation, at least four members of the Court (Brennan, Stewart, Marshall, Powell, and perhaps Rehnquist) indicated in a later case that they might not be unsympathetic to an inverse condemnation plea from a land-use restriction.

The case is *San Diego Gas & Electric Company v. City of San Diego* (1981).[246] San Diego Gas brought suit alleging a taking of its property without just compensation. It owned land that had been purchased for the purpose of constructing a nuclear power plant. The property at the time of the company's acquisition had been zoned mostly for industrial use and the rest for agricultural use. The city then rezoned parts of the property with the effect that the industrial portion shrunk, replaced by an open-space plan accompanied by a proposal that the city acquire the property for a park. California taxpayers seemed less enamored of environmental causes when they were requested to pay for them, and they proceeded to turn down a bond issue for the acquisition. The company then repaired to the courts, arguing that the rezoning as open space took 219 of its 412 acres without compensation, and seeking relief in inverse condemnation, invalidation, and mandamus. Again, the United States Supreme Court refused to decide the merits of the case. Justice Blackmun, writing the Court's opinion, dismissed the case for lack of a final judgment by the state court. He discerned some indication in the California Appeals Court's decision of a desire to have the trial court conduct further proceedings on remand.[247]

The four dissenters and Rehnquist, (who agreed with the dissenters on the merits of the case but concurred with the majority because he failed to find a final judgment) addressed the central issue of the case. Justice Brennan argued that as soon as private property is taken—whether by condemnation, occupancy, physical invasion, or regulation—the landowner has suffered a constitutional violation that should trigger a compensation requirement. He proposed a rule, novel for the Court, that would afford much enhanced protection to adversely affected property owners.

> The constitutional rule I propose requires that, once a court finds a police power regulation has effected a "taking," the government entity must pay just compensation for the period commencing on the date the regulation first effected the "taking," and ending on the date the government entity chooses to rescind or otherwise amend the regulation.[248]

Under Brennan's rule, the offending governmental agency would have the option of either formally condemning the property or continuing with the offending legislation but with the payment of just compensation to the property owner. Brennan closed by criticizing the California Supreme Court's reasoning in *Agins*. That court, Brennan believed, placed policy considerations of expense before constitutional rights; the former should never be permitted to abrogate the latter.

It is not at all clear where this leaves us. One of the dissenters, Justice Powell, has resigned from the Court and Justice Rehnquist said only that he agreed with much of Brennan's reasoning. What direction the Court will take on these matters were in no way resolved in a subsequent case, *Williamson County Regional Planning Commission vs. Hamilton Bank of Johnson City*,[249] in which the Court once again failed to reach the substance of the issue on the same technicality as in the two previous decisions. And beyond that, it is doubtful how often plaintiffs would be successful even under Brennan's undeniably improved rule. The courts remain much enamored of zoning and land-use legislation, and even under Brennan's rule they could simply refuse to find a taking in the first place, thereby rendering the rule moot. In other words, they can do what the California Supreme Court did in *Agins*. They could deny that the land-use restriction constituted a taking, and thereby eliminate the possibility of recovering damages under inverse condemnation. Despite this likely scenario, Brennan's rule would serve an important function. It would warn the lower courts that the Supreme Court will be much less likely to let property owners suffer substantial losses under the guise of police power regulation. And it would throw a curve to those law professors who urge municipalities to engage in the most sweeping types of land-use legislation in order to push the courts in an environmentalist direction. As things stand now municipalities risk very little by heeding this advice. The worst consequence they face is invalidation. If Brennan's rule were adopted, cities would have to think very carefully before engaging in regulatory behavior that flirted with the very reaches of constitutionality or beyond. If their attempts were invalidated they would have to pay in cash for their unconstitutional excesses.[250]

Conclusion

We have just traversed a legal quagmire, and we have discovered a few painful lessons. (1) That the power of eminent domain claimed by government has been too often simply taken for granted. It lacks a solid, theoretical defense by its supporters. (2) That the courts have been mercurial protectors of property rights. On the positive side they have extended the early interpretation of the takings clause to cover some consequential damages and physical invasions. On the negative side, they have permitted regulatory excesses checked only by a series of inefficacious tests for distinguishing police power from eminent domain. Meanwhile, the due process clause and the equal protective clause have dwindled almost beyond sight as props upon which to hang a defense of property rights. (3) That in increasingly important areas of regulatory zeal such as land-use legislation the courts have afforded little protection to property owners. They have provided much encouragement to those in government and in academia who view property as the collective preserve. In a nutshell, the courts have failed to champion rights of property that should be cherished by all free people. These rights are important not only for their tendency to preserve the edifice of other liberties but also for their own sake because property is the physical embodiment of human effort, creativity, and values.

Notes

1. Robert Heinlein, *Elsewhen* in ASSIGNMENT IN ETERNITY (New York: Signet, 1953).
2. Virtually all commentaries have remarked upon the confusion. See, for example, Arvo Van Alstyne, *Taking or Damaging by Police Power: The Search for Inverse Condemnation Criteria*, 44 S. CAL. L. REV. 1, 2 (1971); Dennis Binder, *Taking Versus Reasonable Regulation: A Reappraisal in Light of Regional Planning and Wetlands*, 25 U. FLA. L. REV. 1, 2 (1972).

3. See, for example, *Berman v. Parker*, 348 U.S. 26, 32 (1954), in which Justice Douglas, when called upon to determine whether the taking of a nonblighted building for urban renewal was a legitimate public use under the takings clause of the Fifth Amendment, declared that he was dealing with an instance of the police power because Congress exercises that state-like power over the District of Columbia.

4. This is a passage from Justice Patterson in *Vanhorne's Lessee v. Dorrance*, 2 U.S. 304, 310 (1795).

5. MAGNA CHARTA, ch. XXIX. (*Disseised* refers to a deprivation of a freehold, as when someone is forcibly ousted from possession of land.)

6. William B. Stoebuck, *A General Theory of Eminent Domain*, 47 WASH. L. REV. 553, 562-64 (1972). Stoebuck traces the earliest parliamentary act authorizing compensation back to the statutes of sewers of 1427, and later finds examples of the use of eminent domain with compensation in statutes dating from 1514 and 1539.

7. For more on English condemnation law, see Philip Nichols, THE LAW OF EMINENT DOMAIN, 3d ed. by Julius L. Sackman (New York: Mathew Bender, 1980) at § 1.21; Ernst Freund, THE POLICE POWER: PUBLIC POLICY AND CONSTITUTIONAL RIGHTS (Chicago: Callahan, 1904), 505; Stoebuck, *A General Theory of Eminent Domain*.

8. With the exception of the Colony of South Carolina, which rejected the need for compensation.

9. Nichols, EMINENT DOMAIN at § 1.22. Nichols lists seven colonies that promulgated such mill acts prior to the revolution: New Hampshire, Massachusetts, Rhode Island, Delaware, Maryland, Virginia, and North Carolina. Under the New England acts, he says, landowners damaged by such overflowage brought suit under the act, while in the southern states mill-owners sued out a writ of *ad quod damnum* (an ancient English writ that called upon an agent of the government to assess the likely damages before an act could be undertaken). For more on the mill acts, see Morton Horwitz, *The Transformation in the Conception of Property in American Law, 1790-1860*, 40 U. CHI. L. REV. 248, 251 (1973).

10. 91 U.S. 367 (1875). Prior to this direct acquisition by the federal government of land for a public building in Cincinnati, Ohio, federal officials condemned land only through the intermediary of the states. Justice Strong, writing for the majority of the Court, argued that:

> Such an authority [to acquire land in the states] is essential to its [the United States government's] independent existence and perpetuity. These cannot be preserved if the obstinacy of a private person, or of any other authority, can prevent the acquisition of the means or instruments by which alone governmental functions can be performed [at 371].

Congress had authorized the secretary of the treasury to acquire land in Cincinnati. Justice Strong discerned in the Fifth Amendment takings clause an implied assertion that in making just compensation property could be taken by the federal government (at 372-73). Such an implication required considerable ingenuity, given the universally acknowledged interpretation of the takings clause as being a restriction on governmental activity rather than a grant of power; and given the clear language of Article 1, Section 8, clause 17, which implies that federal takings can be accomplished only through the consent of the states' legislatures. As in most things constitutional, there is enough ambiguity to justify almost anything; witness the very next clause (18), the necessary and proper clause, which permits Congress to enact "all Laws which shall be necessary and proper for carrying into Execution the foregoing Powers." This, coupled with clause 7, granting Congress the authority to establish post offices and post roads, might provide enough ammunition for a creative mind to discern at least a very specific grant of eminent domain powers to the federal government. Nevertheless, no such power was ever explicitly granted to the federal government.

11. See J.A.C. Grant, *The "Higher Law" Background of the Law of Eminent Domain*, 6 WIS. L. REV. 67, 81 (1931).

12. See Forrest McDonald, *The Takings Issue: A Constitutional Perspective: Historical Background to 1791*, Conference on the Takings Issue, a Constitutional Perspective, sponsored by The Law and Liberty Project of the Institute for Humane Studies, and Liberty Fund, Inc., October 14-16, 1976, 49.

13. 1 ANNALS OF CONGRESS 451-52 (1789). For a discussion, see Bruce Ackerman, PRIVATE PROPERTY AND THE CONSTITUTION (New Haven: Yale University Press, 1977), 192 n. 10. Ackerman also notes that no commentators have discovered any American or English cases prior to 1789 that required compensation in the absence of legislative authorization (193 n. 13).

14. McDonald, *The Takings Issue* at 42, calculates that property of various kinds worth $100 million was taken from individuals during the Revolution, and without the payment of compensation. Such a figure is, he cautions, only a conservative estimation.

15. Hugo Grotius, DE JURE BELLI ET PACIS (1625), bk. VIII, ch. 14, § 7.

16. Samuel Pufendorf, DE OFFICIO HOMINES ET CIVIS, Tit. II, ch. 15, § 4. Similar refrains can be found in Vattel, LE DROIT DES GENS (1758), bk I, ch. 20, § 244; Bynkershoek, QUAESTIONEM JURIS PUBLICI LIBRI DUO (1737), 218; Burlamaqui, PRINCIPLES OF NATURAL AND POLITICAL LAW (1747), pt. III, ch. 5, § 25; Montesquieu, SPIRIT OF THE LAWS (1748), bk 26, ch. XV; Blackstone, COMMENTARIES, bk. I, ch. I, 135. Blackstone's formulation is worthy of note because he explicitly rejects the notion that private property should yield to the public good (in other words he rejects any post-Holmesian balancing test; but more of this shortly), and insists that nothing less than full compensation will suffice when the sovereign takes property.

> So great moreover is the regard of the law for private property, that it will not authorize the least violation of it; no, not even for the general good of the whole community. If a new road, for instance, were to be made through the grounds of a private person, it might perhaps be extensively beneficial to the public; but the law permits no man, or set of men, to do this without consent of the owner of the land. In vain may it be urged, that the good of the individual ought to yield to that of the community; for it would be dangerous to allow any private Man, or even any public tribunal, to be the judge of this common good, and to decide whether it be expedient or no. Besides, the public good is in nothing more essentially interested, than in the protection of every individual's private rights, as modelled by the municipal law. In this, and similar cases the legislature alone can, and indeed frequently does, interpose, and compel the individual to acquiesce. But how does it interpose and compel? Not by absolutely stripping the subject of his

property in an arbitrary manner; but by giving him a full indemnification and equivalent for the injury thereby sustained. The public is now considered as an individual, treating with an individual for an exchange. All that the legislature does is to oblige the owner to alienate his possessions for a reasonable price; and even this is an exertion of power, which the legislature indulges with caution, and which nothing but the legislature can perform.

17. Madison, it might be judicious to record for the sake of historical accuracy, as a coauthor of the FEDERALIST PAPERS, was an original opponent of the notion that the Constitution was defective because it lacked a Bill of Rights. But when such became the operative tool in placating the opposition, Madison complied. In his first draft of what would become the Fifth Amendment's taking clause, it appeared as part of a proposed Seventh Amendment, and the public use limitation was a bit stronger: "No person shall be . . . obliged to relinquish his property, where it may be necessary for public use, without a just compensation." ANNALS OF CONGRESS, 1st Congress, 1st sess. cols. 433-36; and see Stoebuck, *A General Theory of Eminent Domain* at 595.

18. John Locke, SECOND TREATISE OF GOVERNMENT, ed. Peter Laslett (New York: New American Library, 1960), § 135, pp. 402-3. And a bit later, Locke warns (§ 138, pp. 406-7):

> The *Supreme Power* cannot take from any Man any part of his *Property* without his own consent . . . . For a Man's *Property*, is not at all secure, though there be good and equitable Laws to set the bounds of it between him and his Fellow Subjects, if he who commands those Subjects, have Power to take from any private Man, what part he pleases of his *Property*, and use and dispose of it as he thinks good.

19. One could go on almost endlessly citing references, but a few should suffice to characterize the rest. First, the commentators: J.B. Thayer, *The Right of Eminent Domain*, MONTHLY LAW REPORTER, n.s. IX (1856) at 241,

> The Right of Eminent Domain may be defined as the right of taking private property for public purposes. It belongs to no private individual, but is one of the sovereign rights of the State. It attaches to the State as the right of property attaches to man; it is, so to speak, one of the natural rights of the State.

Certainly an innovation in natural rights theory, but one fears terribly difficult to prove!

And, Thomas M. Cooley, TREATISE ON THE CONSTITUTIONAL LIMITATIONS (Boston: Little, Brown, 1868), 524,

> All these rights [of eminent domain] rest upon a principle which in every sovereignty is essential to its existence and perpetuity, and which, so far as when called into action it excludes pre-existing private rights, is sometimes spoken of as based upon an implied reservation by the government when its citizens acquire property from it or under its protection.

And for more modern authorities: *Eminent Domain*, 29A CORPUS JURIS SECUNDUM 147, §§ 2, 3, pp. 162, 169-70,

> Eminent domain is an inherent and necessary attribute of sovereignty, existing independently of constitutional provisions and superior to all property rights . . . the individual's rights yielding to considerations of the common welfare.

The right of eminent domain is not conferred, but may be recognized, limited, or regulated, by constitutions. Constitutional provisions relating to the exercise of the right of eminent domain are but limitations on a power which would otherwise be absolute or without limit.

And for sheer assertiveness, Morris Cohen, *Property and Sovereignty*, 13 CORNELL L. Q. 8, 24 (1927),

But I think it is a sheer fallacy based on verbal illusion to think that the rights of the community against an individual owner are no better than the rights of a neighbor. Indeed, no one has in fact had the courage of this confusion to argue that the state has no right to deprive an individual of property to which he is so attached that he refuses any money for it. Though no neighbor has such a right the public interest often justly demands that a proprietor should part with his ancestral home to which he may be attached by all the roots of his being.

Nichols, THE LAW OF EMINENT DOMAIN, § 1.1

The power of eminent domain is inalienable, and being an essential attribute of sovereignty cannot be even partially bargained away. Without it, the state cannot be a state. The power is as enduring and indestructible as the state itself.

The cases reveal no greater depth of reasoning. In *West River Bridge v. Dix*, 47 U.S. 507, 531, 532 (1848), Justice Daniel wrote:

In every political sovereign community there inheres necessarily the right and the duty of guarding its own existence, and of protecting and promoting the interests and welfare of the community at large . . . . This power, denominated the *eminent domain* of the state, is, as its name imports, paramount to all private rights vested under the government, and these last are by necessary implication, held in subordination to this power, and must yield in every instance to its proper exercise . . . .

Under every established government, the tenure of property is derived mediately or immediately from the sovereign power of the political body. . . . It can rest on no other foundation, can have no other guarantee.

(Held that a bridge owned by an incorporated company holding a one-hundred year franchise from the state can be taken and condemned by the state; not an impairment of the "obligation of contracts" clause of Art. 1, § 10, of the federal Constitution. All contracts, then, are subject to eminent domain, the Court declared.)

In *Kohl v. United States*, 91 U.S. 367, 371-72 (1875), Justice Strong disagrees with J. Daniel on the tenure question but reaches the same end by alternate means:

No one doubts the existence in the state governments of the right of eminent domain—a right distinct from and paramount to the right of ultimate ownership. It grows out of the necessities of their being, not out of the tenure by which lands are held. It may be exercised, though the lands are not held by grant from the Government, either mediately or immediately, and independent of the consideration whether they would escheat to the Government in case of a failure of heirs. The right is the offspring of political necessity; and it is inseperable from sovereignty, unless denied to it by its fundamental law.

J. Strong then invokes the authorities to buttress his claims: Vattel, Byn-kershoek, Kent's COMMENTARIES, and Cooley. (Held that the eminent do-main power exists within the federal government.)

In *Searle v. Lake County School District*, 133 U.S. 553, 562 (1890), Chief Justice Fuller wrote:

> That right [eminent domain] is the offspring of political necessity, and is inseperable from sovereignty unless denied to it by its fundamental law.

In *United States v. Lynah*, 188 U.S. 445, 465 (1902), Justice Brewer asserted:

> All private property is held subject to the necessities of government. The right of eminent domain underlies all such rights of property.

Thus, a conspicuous line of argument advanced in these Supreme Court cases is that property, under whatever theory of tenure one might choose, must succumb to the superior power of the government's eminent domain. The reasoning is thin, but after all *everyone* knows the state has the power, so why waste one's efforts on proving the obvious.

20. By 1820 a majority of states did not have a constitutional provision requiring compensation, but statutes secured this purpose, except in South Carolina. By 1850 half of the states had a constitutional requirement; and by 1868 only five did not. In its absence, judges accomplished the same purpose by appealing to the natural law. Chancellor Kent's decision in *Gardner v. Village of Newburgh*, 2 Johns Ch. 162 (N.Y., 1816) is representative of the breed. After paying homage to the natural law authorities (Grotius, Pufendorf, Bynkershoek, and Blackstone) he concluded that "a provision for compensation is an indispen-sable attendant on the due and constitutional exercise of depriving an individ-ual of his property; and I am persuaded that the legislature never intended, by the act in question to violate or interfere with the great and sacred principle of private right." Thus, Kent granted equitable relief in the form of an injunction to a landowner who would be injured by the diversion of a stream of water from his property by the town's taking water from the stream on adjoining land. He found a defect in the legislature's compensating the owner upon whose land it would place the conduits, and not Gardner, whose enjoyment of the flow would be impaired. On states' adoption of a constitutional require-ment of compensation, see Grant, *The "Higher Law" Background*, 70; and Bernard Siegan, ECONOMIC LIBERTIES AND THE CONSTITUTION (Chicago: University of Chicago Press, 1980), 42.

21. E.g. where it could be demonstrated to a court's satisfaction that the taking was for a private not a public use, or the taking went beyond the legislative instructions, or the state took land way in excess of what was needed for the stated public improvement.

22. 7 Pet. 243, 247 (U.S. 1833). Marshall dismissed the case for lack of jurisdic-tion, arguing that the Fifth Amendment "must be understood as restraining the power of the general government, not as applicable to the states."

23. 6 How. 507 (U.S. 1848).

24. *Id.* at 532.

25. For an incisive analysis of the history of the prohibition of impairing contracts clause, see Siegan, ECONOMIC LIBERTIES AND THE CONSTITUTION, 5, 62-66. Siegan points to Marshall's defeat in *Ogden v. Saunders*, 25 U.S. 213 (1827) as the root of this partial nullification. In a case dealing with the validity of state bankruptcy laws, a closely divided Court confined the obliga-tions of contract clause only to laws affecting existing contracts. Future con-

tracts, then, could be regulated by the states, thus opening the floodgates to state control of economic activity. Marshall, if he had prevailed, would have applied the clause to the protection of freedom of contract in all its time-frames.

26. 166 U.S. 266 (1897).
27. The history of legislative and judicial treatment of the railroads is murky indeed. As both beneficiaries of governmental largess in the form of rights of way, delegation of eminent domain power, and tax-backed stock subscriptions, immunity from torts for damages caused by their ordinary operation and victims of state price regulation as "businesses affected with a public interest," the railroads were in an anomalous position. With grade crossing cases, to name just one example, where railroads had to construct safety grades or ‚grade separations to accommodate public streets, some courts allowed recovery for such costs, some did not, while others upheld 50-50 cost sharing. Several sources make admirable sense out of this choppy history. See Harry N. Scheiber, *The Road to Munn: Eminent Domain and the Concept of Public Purpose in the State Courts,* 5 PERSPECTIVES IN AMERICAN HISTORY 329, 387-93 (1971); Charles McCurdy, *The Concept of Confiscation in the Industrial Age: General Theory and Judicial Strategy,* Institute for Humane Studies, 1976, 38-53. McCurdy succinctly captures the contradictory posture of the railroads:

> Regulatory litigation [after the 1860s] put railroad attorneys in a difficult position. In consequential injury and municipal-bond cases they had argued for a narrow, interpretation of "takings" clauses; they also had contended that railroads were built by "agents of the State" for public purposes. In order to challenge maximum-rate statutes and other police regulations, however, corporate counsel was required to emphasize the private interests of railroad investors and, in the process, deny fifty years of railroad law that had been formulated, in most states, for their benefit.

Here we have an excellent example of an industry that fattened itself at the federal trough suddenly facing the obverse of state largess in the form of price regulation. If the state can dispense goodies, it can also take them away. McCurdy points out that the Supreme Court, eager to promote development, rejected the view of some state courts that the use of municipal bonds financed through the taxing power violated due process, because they went to private businesses (the railroads), eligible for a public subsidy. The high court, in two cases, rejected this argument: *Olcott v. Supervisors of Fond du Lac County,* 16 Wall 678 (U.S. 1873) and *Pine Grove Township v. Talcott,* 19 Wall 666 (U.S. 1874).

28. *Chicago Burlington* at 235. A noble sentiment Harlan retrieved from a prior case, *Davidson v. New Orleans,* 96 U.S. 97 (1877), where the Court held that the assessment of certain real estate by the city to pay for the drainage of swamps did not violate due process of law. Typical of the Court's unwillingness to define the parameters of basic constitutional clauses, and its preference, instead, for case-by-case adjudication (with all its tendencies to produce confusing and incompatible decisions), is the claim in *Davidson* that the Court cannot set down a definition for what is due process. Rather, the Court opted for a "gradual process of judicial inclusion and exclusion, as the cases presented for decision shall require" (at 104).

29. *Armstrong v. United States,* 364 U.S. 40 (1960).

30. *Long Island Water Supply Co. v. City of Brooklyn*, 166 U.S. 685 (1897); *Lynch v. United States*, 292 U.S. 571 (1934); *U.S. Trust Co. of New York v. New Jersey*, 431 U.S. 1 (1977).
31. *United States v. General Motors Corp.*, 323 U.S. 373, 377-78 (1945).
32. *Joslin Mfg. Co. v. City of Providence*, 262 U.S. 668 (1923); *Mitchell v. United States*, 267 U.S. 341 (1925); *United States v. General Motors Corp.*, 323 U.S. 373 (1945). In the latter case, where the U.S. government took temporary use of a specially equipped warehouse, it was held that the tenant on long-term lease was not entitled to recovery for loss of goodwill or injury to its business. Recovery, however, may include expenses attendent upon moving out, rental of storage space, and tearing out equipment, in this case of a temporary eviction. Other losses that the Court mentioned as noncompensable included future loss of profits, the expense of removing fixtures and personal property from the premises. Such losses were considered "consequential" and, hence, not recoverable, the Court reasoning that such losses would be the same as might ensue upon the sale of property to a private buyer. Again, one might suspect the logic here, because when business persons sell their buildings, or sublet on their leases, they have presumably factored in these ancillary costs and found the deals satisfactory despite such costs. No such assumption, of course, can be made where the government forcibly takes property or lease-holds over the owner's objection. Because the latter transaction is not voluntary, but coerced, no assumption can be made that those "consequential" losses are acceptable to the "seller," and, indeed, the opposite assumption is far more likely. Even the Court seemed somewhat unconfident about its own conclusion:

    No doubt all those elements would be considered by an owner in determining whether, and at what price, to sell. No doubt, therefore, if the owner is to be made whole for the loss consequent of the sovereign's seizure of his property, these elements should properly be considered. But the courts have generally held that they are not to be reckoned as part of the compensation for the fee taken by the Government. (379)

    Thus, the Court refused to depart from the rule derived from precedents, that compensation is required for the taking of a group of rights over physical things but not for business losses.
33. Although the modern trend, at least with some business losses and business moving expenses, is to provide legislative cures for these problems. And courts, more often, have been receptive to plaintiff's pleas. See *Almota Farmers v. United States*, 409 U.S. 470 (1973), in which the Supreme Court allowed that just compensation for the taking of a leasehold should include payment for improvements that had a useful life exceeding the remaining time on the lease and likelihood of lease renewal.
34. See *Almota Farmers v. United States.*
35. Thus, in *United States v. Reynolds*, 397 U.S. 14 (1970), the Court said that if lands condemned were within the original scope of a project, no enhancement value would be paid.
36. *United States v. Toronto, Hamilton and Buffalo Nav. Co.*, 338 U.S. 396 (1949).
37. See *United States v. Commodities Trading Corp.*, 339 U.S. 121 (1950). Here the company attempted to recoup just compensation for black pepper requisitioned by the War Department in 1944. The government claimed the OPA ceiling price of 6.3 cents per pound constituted such "just compensation,"

while the company claimed 22 cents. The Court of Claims struck an Aristo-
telian mean of 15 cents. Justice Black, speaking for the Supreme Court,
opined that the Court had never prescribed a "rigid rule" but one flexible
enough to accommodate varying circumstances. He isolated the following
consideration as a dominant one: "What compensation is 'just' both to an
owner whose property is taken and to the public that must pay the bill"
(123-24). Black concluded that the ceiling price ought to be taken as the
measure of "just compensation." If judicial awards should exceed ceiling
prices, he feared, people would withhold their goods during wartime until
requisitioned, thus defeating government's interest in shielding itself from
untoward price increases. The Court found it irrelevant that the company had
paid 12.7 cents for this same pepper. See also *United States v. Fuller*, 409 U.S.
488 (1973), which makes a similar hedge against "fair market value" as an
absolute standard. (Held that grazing rights under the Taylor Grazing Act did
not constitute an element requiring compensation when private property was
taken.) Another fudge factor practiced in some jurisdictions, and acceded to
by the Supreme Court (*United States v. Miller*, 317 U.S. 369 (1943)), is the
practice of setting-off any benefits to a landowner's remaining property from
the public improvement for which a portion of the property was taken, thus
lowering the award. Again, the Court repeated its noble sentiments—that "just
compensation" means the full and perfect equivalent in money of the property taken, so that the owner will be put in as good a position as the owner
would have occupied had the property not been taken.

38. In *Gardner v. Village of Newburgh*, Chancellor Kent granted an injunction to a
beneficiary of a stream's waters when the city tried to deflect the stream's
course on another's property. Justice Story, of the U.S. Supreme Court, would
have allowed compensation for consequential damages. He argued, in a dissenting opinion in *Charles River Bridge v. Warren Bridge*, 11 Pet. 420 (U.S.
1837), that such was required by higher law maxims of justice:

> If the public exigencies and interests require that the franchise of Charles
> River bridge should be taken away, or impaired, it may be lawfully done,
> upon making due compensation to the proprietors. And this franchise is
> property—is fixed determinate property. We have been told, indeed, that
> where the damage is merely consequential (as by the erection of a new
> bridge, it is said that it would be), the constitution does not entitle the party
> to compensation; and *Thurston v. Hancock*, 12 Mass. 220, and *Callendar v.
> Marsh* . . . are cited in support of the doctrine. With all possible respect for
> the opinions of others, I confess myself to be among those who never could
> comprehend the law of either of these cases, . . . Suppose a man is the owner
> of a mill, and the legislature authorizes a diversion of the water course which
> supplies it, whereby the mill is injured or ruined; are we to be told, that this
> is a consequential injury, and not within the scope of the constitution? If not
> within the scope of the constitution, it is, according to the fundamental
> principles of a free government, a violation of private rights, which cannot
> be taken away without compensation. The case of *Gardner v. Village of
> Newburgh* . . . would be a sufficient authority to sustain this reasoning; if it
> did not stand upon the eternal principles of justice, recognized by every
> government which is not a pure despotism [at 638].

Indeed, Justice Story's worst fears would be realized because almost the identical fact pattern as his hypothetical mill example, but now an electric generat-

ing plant, would be denied compensation for consequential damages when a state-constructed dam lowered the water table of a river. See *United States v. Willow River Co.*, 324 U.S. 499 (1945).

39. *Callendar v. Marsh*, 1 Pick. 417 (18 Mass., 1823). The Supreme Court, too, rejected consequential damages in a street-grading case: *Smith v. Corp. of Washington*, 20 How. 135 (U.S. 1857). For a discussion of this issue, see Harry Scheiber, *Private Property, "Takings", and the Rights of the Public in American Law, 1790-1860*, Conference on the Takings Issue, Institute for Humane Studies, 1976.

40. R. Kratovil and F. Harrison, Jr., *Eminent Domain—Policy and Concept*, 42 CALIF. L. REV. 596, 611-12 (1954).

41. 80 U.S. 166 (1871).

42. *Id.* at 181.

43. *Id.* at 177-78. In *Pumpelly* the Court was interpreting the constitutional provision relating to eminent domain in the Wisconsin Constitution, which mimicked that of the Fifth Amendment; it read, "the property of no person shall be taken for public use without just compensation therefor." The Court still maintained Marshall's position that the Fifth Amendment is a limitation upon the power of the federal government, and not the states. That doctrine would only fall some twenty-five years later.

44. *United States v. Lynah*, 188 U.S. 445 (1903).

45. William E. Burby, REAL PROPERTY (St. Paul, Minn.: West, 1965), 45-46.

46. 192 U.S. 217 (1904).

47. The government, in effect, was arguing that it enjoyed the same right as any riparian owner to prevent injury to its property, whatever consequences might befall proprietors lying downstream.

48. In many other cases after *Pumpelly* recovery was denied because the injuries sustained were found to be merely "consequential": *Transportation Co. v. Chicago*, 99 U.S. 635 (1878) (no compensation for obstruction of access to street or river when municipality constructs bridge or tunnel across navigable river); *Scranton v. Wheeler*, 179 U.S. 141 (1900) (no compensation where construction of a pier by Congress destroy abutter's access to navigable river). Gradually, it became well established that for such injuries as loss of access to a navigable river due to governmental improvements or loss of wharves and piers jutting out below high-water mark resulting from governmental actions to improve navigation, or for government wharves or other improvements built upon the bed of a navigable waterway or below the high-water mark, no compensation would be judicially allowed if such were not specified by legislatures or Congress. See *Barney v. Keokuk*, 94 U.S. 324 (1877); *Greenleaf-Johnson Lumber Co. v. Garrison*, 237 U.S. 251 (1915); *Willink v. United States*, 240 U.S. 572 (1916); *United States v. Sponenbarger*, 308 U.S. 256 (1939); *United States v. C.M. St. P & P R. Co.*, 312 U.S. 592 (1941); *United States v. Commodore Park*, 324 U.S. 386 (1945); *United States v. Virginia Elec. & Power Co.*, 365 U.S. 624 (1961).

49. 324 U.S. 499 (1945).

50. *Id.* at 502.

51. *Id.* at 510. Justice Roberts dissented in this case, declaring that the government should pay for the owner's loss of property rights.

52. Donald Large, *This Land Is Whose Land? Changing Concepts of Land as Property*, WIS. L. REV. 1041, 1070-73 (1973). He cites these cases: *Potomac*

Sand and Gravel Co. v. Governor, 266 Md. 358, 293 A. 2d 241 (1972) (upholding law banning dredging in tidal water and marshlands); *Marks v. Whitney* 6 Cal. 3d 251, 491 P. 2d 374 (1971) (neighbor succeeded in getting court to prevent owner from filling in his tidelands; held riparian landowner owns tidelands subject to a "public trust easement"). Joseph Sax, *The Public Trust Doctrine in Natural Resource Law: Effective Judicial Intervention*, 68 MICH. L. REV. 471 (1970), wants to expand greatly the public trust doctrine to allow for greater uncompensated regulation.

53. 339 U.S. 799 (1950). See also an earlier case reaching the same conclusion, *United States v. Cress*, 243 U.S. 316 (1917).

54. A particularly confusing decision is *United States v. Grand River Dam Authority*, 363 U.S. 229 (1960), where a state agency sued to recover compensation for losses sustained through incorporation of its dam by a U.S. government project. The authority wanted, in addition to compensation received for the condemnation of its trust, flowage rights, and relocation of transmission lines, compensation for the "taking" of its water power rights and franchise to develop electric power. Even though the franchise pertained to a nonnavigable tributary of the Arkansas River, the Court disallowed any recovery, in the process apparently confusing its own rules about the distinction between navigable and nonnavigable rivers, now claiming that the U.S. power of flood control extends to tributaries of navigable streams—which goes to show that even the Court cannot keep its own rules clearly in focus.

55. 100 S. Ct. 383 (1979). The case arose from the state of Hawaii.

56. *Id.* at 389.

57. *Id.* at 391.

58. 328 U.S. 256 (1946).

59. By the Air Commerce Act of 1926 and the Civil Aeronautics Act of 1938, the United States claimed for itself "complete and exclusive national sovereignty in the air space." Navigable air space is defined as airspace above the minimal safe altitudes of flight prescribed by the Civil Aeronautics Authority.

60. *Cajus est solum ejus est usque ad coleum.* Also, the owner was considered to possess downward to the center of the earth.

61. *United States v. Causby* at 266.

62. *Id.* at 265.

63. The decision actually reversed and remanded the case back to the court of claims on a technicality, i.e., that the lower court had not determined whether the air easement was temporary or permanent in nature, hence no decision could be reached as to the fairness of the $2,000 damages awarded by the court of claims to the plaintiffs.

64. *Griggs v. Allegheny County*, 369 U.S. 84 (1962).

65. 348 U.S. 26 (1954).

66. On private uses of eminent domain, see Stoebuck, *A General Theory of Eminent Domain* at 595-96; Nichols, EMINENT DOMAIN, § 7.62, from which this list is compiled. Nichols states (§ 7.61) that the taking of property for a factory from an unwilling, selfish owner, even if it would benefit the whole community would be inadmissible: "The public mind would instinctively revolt at any attempt to take such land by eminent domain." Yet, as we recall from chapter 1, that is precisely what was accomplished, with state court judicial acquiesence, in the Detroit instance of the taking of property for a Cadillac plant. Nichols cites a case that reached the contrary determination,

i.e., that such a taking is invalid: *Howard Mills Co. v. Schwarts Lumber & Coal Co.*, 77 Kan. 599, 95 P.559.

67. *Calder v. Bull*, 3 Dal. 386, 388 (1798).

68. Nichols, EMINENT DOMAIN, § 7.212. For example, in *Head v. Amoskeag Manufacturing Co.*, 113 U.S. 9 (1885), the high court upheld a state statute authorizing any person to erect a water mill and mill dam across a nonnavigable stream, upon payment to other owners along the stream for damages caused by overflowage. The plaintiff had argued that such a delegation of the eminent domain power violated due process under the Fourteenth Amendment because it took property for a private, not a public use. The Court reviewed the history of mill acts stretching back to colonial days, and then went on to duck the question of whether such delegations violated the public use limitation on eminent domain, preferring to rely on the state's legislative (police power) power to regulate the conflicting interests of riparian owners. Once again, the Court displayed a great interest in furthering development of the country, having noted the improvement of the mill acts over common law tradition, which would have barred the way to such construction projects. It seems from this decision that if compensation were forthcoming, the Court would be willing to overlook the niceties of public use restrictions.

Scheiber argues (*The Road to Munn* at 372-73) that judges up to the 1840s displayed great deference to legislatures in their determination that the delegations of eminent domain to corporations, such as the mill dams, was a public use, but that later in the nineteenth century resistance developed and judicial scrutiny became more apparent. Also, judges became less deferential to legislatures' determinations that a use by them of eminent domain was for a public use.

69. Its last invalidation on the grounds of failure to satisfy the public use proviso occurred in 1937; see *Thompson v. Consolidated Gas Util. Corp.*, 300 U.S. 55 (1937), where the Supreme Court affirmed a district court decree enjoining the enforcement of a gas proration order of the Railroad Commission of Texas. Arvo Van Alstyne, *Statutory Modification of Inverse Condemnation: The Scope of Legislative Power*, 19 STAN. L. REV. 727, 753 (1967).

70. See Comment, *The Public Use Limitation on Eminent Domain: An Advance Requiem*, 58 YALE L. J. 599, 609 (1949). The author attributes the shift from indecisiveness to the broader view to have been accomplished in a 1916 decision by Justice Holmes. See *Mt. Vernon-Woodberry Cotton Duck Co. v. Alabama Interstate Power Co.*, 240 U.S. 30 (1916). A later case, *Rindge Co. v. Los Angeles County*, 262 U.S. 700 (1923), further elucidated this point. Here a road was taken through a single private ranch. The Court decided that it was not necessary that an entire community, or a considerable portion, should directly use an improvement to constitute a public use. Furthermore, takings did not have to be limited to mere business necessity but may extend to matters of recreation, public health, and enjoyment. Takings could also be in anticipation of future needs, not merely present ones.

71. See Nichols, EMINENT DOMAIN, § 7.5156. Takings for federal housing under the Public Works Administration Act of 1933 were held by a circuit court not to constitute a legitimate use for which the government could exercise the power of eminent domain. To circumvent this decision, Congress enacted legislation that would subsidize the states in erecting public housing. And the legitimacy of takings for purposes of urban renewal has been well

established in the states since 1949. For more on public use, see Allison Dunham, *Griggs v. Allegheny County in Perspective: Thirty Years of Supreme Court Expropriation Law,* SUP. CT. REV. 63, 66-73 (1962). Dunham surveyed the eighty-nine Supreme Court cases on condemnation law from 1932 to 1962 and found only five cases challenging the public use component.

72. 160 U.S. 668 (1896).
73. *Id.* at 680.
74. *Id.*
75. But the Court would still insist that the ultimate decision regarding what constitutes a public use is a judicial question. See *Cincinnati v. Vester,* 281 U.S. 439, 446 (1930).

> It is well established that in considering the application of the Fourteenth Amendment to cases of expropriation of private property the question what is a public use is a judicial one. In deciding such a question, the Court has appropriate regard to the diversity of local conditions and considers with great respect legislative determinations and in particular the judgments of state courts as to the uses considered to be public in the light of local exigencies. But the question remains a judicial one which this court must decide in performing its duty of enforcing the provisions of the Federal Constitution.

Here the Court denied the city's "excess" takings because it went beyond statutory provisions.

76. 327 U.S. 546 (1946).
77. *Id.* 551-52.
78. *Id.* at 552. The Court attempted to distance itself from its earlier pronouncement in *Cincinnati v. Vester* that the question of public use is a judicial one, but its reasons for doing so were never clearly delineated. As with much judicial practice, if the Court does not wish to overrule itself or change a stated rule, and thus admit an error, it will satisfy itself by muddying the argument so much by drawing artificial distinctions, thus sorely trying people's patience. For Holmes earlier formulation, see *Old Dominion Co. v. United States,* 269 U.S. 55, 66 (1925).
79. 348 U.S. 26 (1954).
80. *Id.* at 32.
81. *Id.* at 33.
82. 304 N.W. 2d 455 (Mich.) (1981).
83. 183 Cal. Rptr. 673, 646 P. 2d 835 (1982).
84. 52 L.W. 4673 (1984).
85. *West River Bridge v. Dix,* 47 U.S. 507, 533 (1848); *Monongahela Nav. Co. v. United States,* 148 U.S. 312 (1893).
86. *Armstrong v. United States,* 364 U.S. 40 (1960).
87. *City of Oakland v. Oakland Raiders* at 677.
88. *Id.* at 679.
89. *Id.* at 681.
90. *Id.* at 680.
91. *Id.*
92. *Id.*
93. *Id.* at 683 (Bird, dissenting and concurring opinion).
94. Hawaii REV. STAT. §§ 516-83.
95. *Midkiff v. Tom,* 702 F. 2d 788, 805 (1983), Judge Poole's concurring opinion.

96. *Hawaii Housing Authority v. Midkiff*, 52 U.S.L.W. 4673 at 4676.
97. *Midkiff v. Tom* at 799.
98. *Hawaii v. Midkiff* at 4676. But is this a case of market failure? As Justice O'Connor herself earlier pointed out, landowners had been dissuaded from selling their land because of governmental policy, i.e., punitive federal tax liabilities. This hardly constitutes market failure; rather, it smacks of governmental failure.
99. For example, in an early case, *New York v. Miln*, 11 Pet. 102, 139 (U.S. 1837), Justice Barbour wrote: "That all those powers which relate to merely municipal legislation, or what may properly be called *internal police*, are not thus surrendered or restrained; and that, consequently, in relation to these, the authority of a state is complete, unqualified, and exclusive." The case dealt with the constitutionality of New York State's passenger laws, which placed upon the master of a ship the responsibility to report within twenty-four hours of arrival the names, ages, and last legal settlement of all persons aboard the ship. The master of the "Emily" here appealed from a fine levied against him for noncompliance. The Court held that the act was not a regulation of commerce (hence, it did not trench upon federal powers to regulate interstate commerce) but, rather, was a police regulation within the sovereign powers of the states. New York had such rights before the adoption of the Constitution, the Court reasoned, and it did not cede them to the federal government with the signing of that document. The Court was satisfied with the justification given by the state for the legislation: it was intended to prevent the influx of foreigners who might become paupers and a burden upon the state. In *Prigg v. Pennsylvania*, 41 U.S. 539 (1842), the Court again stated that the police power had not been conceded by the states to the United States; the instant case overturned a fugitive slave law enacted by the state of Pennsylvania. See also *Patterson v. Kentucky*, 97 U.S. 501 (1878); *L'Hote v. New Orleans*, 177 U.S. 587, 596 (1900); *Jacobson v. Massachusetts*, 197 U.S. 11, 25 (1905).
100. Freund, THE POLICE POWER, PUBLIC POLICY AND CONSTITUTIONAL RIGHTS, 21-22.
101. *Gibbons v. Ogden*, 9 Wheat 1 (U.S., 1824).
102. *Id.* at 203.
103. *Id.* at 197.
104. *Id.* at 205.
105. 5 How. 504 (U.S., 1847).
106. *Id.* at 576-77.
107. *Id.* at 583.
108. 94 U.S. 113 (1876).
109. *Id.* at 124-25. The *sic utere* justification for the police power would be adverted to in subsequent cases. See *Patterson v. Kentucky*, 97 U.S. 501 (1878), *Northwestern Fertilizing Co. v. Hyde Park*, 97 U.S. 659 (1878). Also, in an earlier case from Massachusetts, Chief Justice Lemuel Shaw advanced the same argument (*Commonwealth v. Tewksbury*, 11 Metcalf 55, 57 (Mass., 1846)): "All property is acquired and held under the tacit condition that it shall not be used so as to injure the equal rights of others, or to destroy or greatly impair the public rights and interest of the community; under the maxim of the common law, *sic utere tuo ut alienum non laedas.*"
110. BLACK'S LAW DICTIONARY, 5th ed., 1238.
111. By *pragmatic defenders of property rights*, I have in mind theorists who hold that property rights are not natural but, rather, are the creatures of govern-

ment. Utilitarians such as Jeremy Bentham, or social contractarians such as Jean Jacques Rousseau would be pragmatists.

112. We must hold our breath until the conclusion before we will be prepared to examine whether government may legitimately exercise this police power under the *sic utere* theory.

113. *Slaughter-House Cases*, 16 Wall. 36, 62 (U.S., 1872). See also *Northwestern Fertilizing Co. v. Hyde Park* (Strong dissent) at 680: "Nothing, I admit, is more indefinite than the extent or limits of what is called the police power"; *Lawton v. Steele*, 152 U.S. 133, 136 (1894), conceding a "large discretion" to legislatures in determining what measures fall under its police power; *Lochner v. New York*, 198 U.S. 45, 53 (1905): "There are, however, certain powers, existing in the sovereignty of each State in the Union, somewhat vaguely termed police powers, the exact description and limitation of which have not been attempted by courts. These powers, broadly stated, and without at present, any attempt at a more specific limitation, relate to the safety, health, morals and general welfare of the public"; *Eubank v. Richmond*, 226 U.S. 137, 143 (1912): "one of the least limitable of the powers of government."

114. *Eubank v. Richmond* at 143.

115. See *Boston Beer Co. v. State of Massachusetts*, 97 U.S. 25 (1877); the Court upheld a Massachusetts prohibition act under which the liquor of this company was seized. Starting with the claim that all rights are held subject to the police power of a state, the Court reasoned that if the public safety or morals requires the discontinuance of any business, the legislature may prohibit it despite whatever inconvenience private individuals or businesses might sustain.

116. *Crowley v. Christensen*, 137 U.S. 86, 89 (1890). See also *Lochner v. New York* (1905) at 53; the same formulation appeared ("Both property and liberty are held on such reasonable conditions as may be imposed by the governing power of the state . . ."), but the decision reached this time ran against the regulation. In *Lochner* the court struck down a New York statute limiting the hours of labor in bakeries to sixty hours per week.

117. Before adoption of the Fourteenth Amendment the commerce clause (Art. I, Sec. 8.3) played a more significant role as a check upon the states' police power. Because we have already discussed some of these cases in previous footnotes, and for the sake of brevity, no further discussion of this check will appear. The commerce clause served more as a territorial dispute between the states and the federal government about who should regulate rather than as a protection for individual property owners.

A recent case that found a police power regulation to constitute an unconstitutional burden on interstate commerce was *Pike v. Bruce Church, Inc.*, 397 U.S. 137 (1970). An order under the Arizona Fruit and Vegetable Standardization Act decreed that cantaloupe growers would have to pack their fruit in containers in Arizona before shipping them on to their California packing plants. This burdened the growers to the tune of $200,000. The Supreme Court held that the regulation unconstitutionally burdened interstate commerce.

The constitutional prohibition on the states' impairing the obligation of contracts (Art. I, Sec. 10.1) has proved an even weaker check against the police power because courts have repeatedly held that a contractual obligation can be superseded by a proper exercise of the police power. As Freund explained it

(THE POLICE POWER, PUBLIC POLICY AND CONSTITUTIONAL RIGHTS, 556):

> The principle is that a person cannot, by entering into a contract, impair the power which the state must have for the protection of peace, safety, health, and morals. If this were not so, an owner of property who apprehended that a police power regulation would be passed affecting his property would have it in his power to nullify its effect in advance, by making contracts inconsistent with its enforcement.

For a meticulous treatment of how the obligation of contract clause became so limited in its effect, see Bernard Siegan's discussion of *Ogden v. Saunders*, 25 U.S. 213 (1827) in his ECONOMIC LIBERTIES AND THE CONSTITUTION (Chicago: University of Chicago Press, 1980), pp. 62-66. A closely divided Court, with Chief Justice Marshall writing for the three dissenters, held that the New York state bankruptcy law did not violate the contract clause. A debtor released from his debts under the law pleaded that he no longer owed the money to his creditor. The bankruptcy law took effect prior to the transaction between the two parties. Had Marshall prevailed, the contract clause would have applied retrospectively as well as prospectively, thus providing much greater protection to the individual's freedom to contract.

118. *Slaughter-House Cases.*
119. *Id.* at 105.
120. But he would have no patience for governmental attempts at rate setting unless the business affected had been granted a special privilege from the government. See his dissent in *Munn v. Illinois*, 94 U.S. 113 (1876).
121. For a comprehensive treatment of the substantive due process era one could not do any better than Bernard Siegan's ECONOMIC LIBERTIES AND THE CONSTITUTION. The discussion that follows owes a large debt to this work. The four cases referred to are the most famous examples of instances in which the high Court overturned business regulations. See *Allgeyer v. Louisiana*, 165 U.S. 578 (1897) (in a unanimous decision the Court read liberty of contract into the due process clause); *Lochner v. New York*, 198 U.S. 45 (1905) (in a 5-4 decision the Court overturned portions of a New York statute limiting to sixty hours per week the labor of workers in bakeries); *Adair v. United States*, 208 U.S. 161 (1908) (struck down portions of a congressional act making it a misdemeanor to force employees to sign a contract not to become members of a labor union); *Coppage v. Kansas*, 236 U.S. 1 (1915) (followed *Adair* in striking down a similar Kansas statute).
122. In sequence: *Lochner; Adkins v. Children's Hospital*, 261 U.S. 525 (1923); *Coppage; Adair.*
123. But on numerous occasions (and these greatly outweigh in numbers the cases rejecting regulations) the Court upheld police power controls over business. The following is a partial listing. 1) Limitations on hours of labor: *Atkin v. Kansas*, 191 U.S. 207 (1903), upheld constitutionality of Kansas statute making it a crime for a government contractor to work employees more than eight hours. *Mueller v. Oregon*, 208 U.S. 412 (1908), upheld state act limiting hours of work for women. Also to the same effect: *Riley v. Massachusetts*, 232 U.S. 671 (1914), in factories; *Miller v. Wilson*, 236 U.S. 373 (1915), in hotels; *Bosley v. McLaughlin*, 236 U.S. 385 (1915), in hospitals. *Bunting v. Oregon*, 243 U.S. 426 (1917), sustained a law limiting the hours of work of men in major manufacturers to ten hours. 2) Various licensing provisions and out-

right prohibitions on businesses: *Fischer v. City of St. Louis*, 194 U.S. 361 (1904), city could ban within its limits cow stables that did not have a permit. *Murphy v. California*, 225 U.S. 623 (1912), upheld ordinance prohibiting billiard halls. *Reinman v. Little Rock*, 237 U.S. 171 (1915), upheld city ordinance banning a livery stable from the city. *Hebe Co. v. Shaw*, 248 U.S. 297 (1919), upheld state law forbidding sale of filled milk, i.e. a milk substitute made of condensed milk and coconut oil. *Everard's Breweries v. Day*, 265 U.S. 545 (1924), upheld federal statute forbidding sale of liquors, including those acquired before passage of act. *Graves v. Minnesota*, 272 U.S. 425 (1926), upheld regulation requiring a license and a diploma to practice dentistry. 3) Various regulations on the manner in which particular businesses could be carried out: *Plymouth Coal Co. v. Pennsylvania*, 232 U.S. 531 (1914), upheld regulation that in mining coal supporting pillars must be left. *Champlin Refining Co. v. Corporation Comm'n.*, 286 U.S. 210 (1932), upheld regulation prorating oil in common pool against charge it was a price-fixing scheme. *Gant v. Oklahoma City*, 289 U.S. 98 (1933), upheld ordinance prohibiting drilling for oil within city without posting a bond. 4) Rent control laws: *Block v. Hirsh*, 256 U.S. 135 (1920); *Marcus Brown Holding Co. v. Feldman*, 256 U.S. 170 (1921); *Edgar Levy Leasing v. Siegel*, 258 U.S. 242 (1922), as temporary wartime emergency legislation.

124. *Lochner v. New York*, at 56. Previously, Peckham acknowledged that, indeed, the states possess police powers, ill defined though they be, with the legitimate exercise of which the Fourteenth Amendment does not interfere. The right of contract, however, is protected by the due process clause of the Fourteenth Amendment, unless certain circumstances exist that limit this right. It is important to take notice of the fact that during this era the Court was not absolutist, for there are numerous statements in its decisions to the effect that liberty, rights, freedom of contract, etc. are not absolute but, rather, must accommodate conflicting interests and impinging circumstances.

125. *Id.* at 57-58.

126. *Id.* at 68 (Harlan dissent).

127. *Id.* at 68.

128. *Id.* at 76 (Holmes dissent).

129. *Id.* at 75.

130. *Adkins*; *West Coast Hotel Co. v. Parrish*, 300 U.S. 379 (1937).

131. The act established a board of three members composed of representatives from employers, employees, and the public. The board was instructed to hold public hearings, investigate prevailing wage rates, examine employees' hours, and set standards for minimum wages in various occupations.

132. Taft, Sanford, and Holmes dissented, and Brandeis took no part in the case.

133. *Adkins* at 544.

134. *Bunting v. Oregon*, 243 U.S. 426 (1917). This decision upheld a limit on the hours of work for men and women in mills, factories, and manufacturing establishments in Oregon.

135. *Adkins* at 554. Sutherland concluded that the Court upheld acts limiting the hours of labor only where it was shown that long hours of labor were detrimental to health.

136. *Id.* at 545.

137. *Munn v. Illinois*, 94 U.S. 113, 126 (1876). Recall that we previously discussed this case, referring to Chief Justice Waite's presentation of a contractarian theory of the origins of the police power.

138. *Id.* at 126.
139. *Id.* at 140 (Field dissent). Field would have limited this category of businesses "affected with a public interest" and, therefore, subject to regulation, to those businesses that enjoyed a grant from the government, e.g., ferries, private bridges, and so on.
140. *Chicago, Burlington and Quincy RR v. Iowa*, 94 U.S. 155 (1876).
141. *German Alliance Insurance v. Lewis*, 233 U.S. 389 (1914).
142. *Block v. Hirsch*, 256 U.S. 135 (1920).
143. *Nebbia v. New York*, 291 U.S. 502 (1934).
144. *Wolff Packing Co. v. Court of Industrial Relations*, 262 U.S. 522, 536 (1923). In this case the Court attempted to enumerate the features of a business that rendered it "affected with a public interest," and hence subject to price regulation. The business must (1) be under the authority of a public grant of privileges that either expressly or by implication impose an affirmative duty of rendering a public service as demanded by any member of the public, e.g., railroads, other common carriers, public utilities, or (2) be one of certain occupations regarded as exceptional by Parliament or during colonial times, e.g., keepers of inns, cabs, grist mills, or (3) not have been public at its inception but have risen to such status over time, and thus have become subject to regulation; its service has become indispensable, or its charges exorbitant or arbitrary (the *Munn v. Illinois* class of businesses, where the business has in effect granted the public an interest). Obviously, this third category presents an opportunity for expansion.
145. *Tyson & Bros. v. Banton*, 273 U.S. 418 (1927). Here Sutherland tried to maintain that the authority to regulate prices comes from a different branch of the police power than the powers to license or regulate, and that price fixing could not be exercised against ordinary businesses but only those "affected with a public interest." Holmes, in dissent, would have upheld price fixing of theater tickets, finding such phrases as businesses "affected with a public interest" to be merely "apologetic" niceties employed when the Court wished to uphold some regulations. Instead, he contended that "property rights may be taken for public purposes without compensation if you do not take too much" (at 445). He would have sanctioned much greater leeway for legislative judgments than the majority:

     I do not believe in such apologies. I think the proper course is to recognize that a state legislature can do whatever it sees fit to do unless it is restrained by some express prohibition in the Constitution of the United States or of the state, and that courts should be careful not to extend such prohibitions beyond their obvious meaning by reading into them conceptions of public policy that the particular court may happen to entertain [at 446].
146. *Williams v. Standard Oil*, 278 U.S. 235 (1929).
147. *New State Ice. Co. v. Liebman*, 285 U.S. 262 (1932). This decision seems to defy Sutherland's distinction in *Tyson Bros. v. Banton* between the different branches of the police power. Here the public-private distinction is employed to invalidate licensing, not the usual price fixing.
148. *Adkins* at 561.
149. This list is Justice Strong's from his dissent in *Tyson & Bros. v. Banton* at 452.
150. *Nebbia v. New York* at 525.
151. *Id.* at 534.
152. 300 U.S. 379 (1937).

153. *Id.* at 391.
154. *Id.* at 398.
155. *Id.* at 399.
156. *Id.* at 402 (Sutherland dissenting).
157. Siegan, ECONOMIC LIBERTIES AND THE CONSTITUTION, 6, states that since 1941 the Supreme Court has granted relief to only one business prohibited by government, and that ruling was shortly reversed in another case. He writes that "almost regardless of how unfair, inequitable, unreasonable, arbitrary, or capricious legislators may be in depriving people of their business interests, the federal courts will not invoke their powers to safeguard the aggrieved party." Siegan also states (at 17) that since 1937 and the demise of substantive due process, the Court has managed to avoid striking down any economic or social law on grounds it violated due process. However, *Moore v. City of East Cleveland*, 431 U.S. 494 (1977), which I will discuss in a moment, seems to belie this statement, but it is only one small and rather ambiguous exception because the Court had to elevate family life to a "fundamental liberty" before it could protect it, which standard would still exclude from rigorous scrutiny the run-of-the-mill type of economic regulation.
158. 431 U.S. 494 (1977).
159. *Id.* at 502. Powell wrote for the majority:

   Substantive due process has at times been a treacherous field for this Court. There *are* risks when the judicial branch gives enhanced protection to certain substantive liberties without the guidance of the more specific provisions of the Bill of Rights. The history of the *Lochner* era demonstrates, there is reason for concern lest the only limits to such judicial intervention become the predilections of those who happen at the time to be Members of this Court. That history counsels caution and restraint. But it does not counsel abandonment.

   Of course, Powell could set no definite guidelines for when such review would be legitimate; no limits could be set by drawing "arbitrary lines" (at 503). At least, the *Moore* decision displayed some willingness by the Court to rein in the more ludicrous excesses of government.
160. *Id.* at White's dissent, which reviewed the current standards for due process review.
161. Curiously, the takings clause of the Fifth Amendment, although most decidedly part of the Bill of Rights, is not accorded this high standard of review, but the right to privacy and the right to vote are, even though they are nowhere mentioned in the Bill of Rights.
162. This two-tier approach was presaged by a famous footnote of Justice Stone's decision in *United States v. Carolene Products Co.*, 304 U.S. 144, 152 and n. 4 (1938). The decision upheld the Filled Milk Act of 1923, which prohibited the addition of fats other than milkfat to milk sold in interstate commerce. Stone wrote:

   Even in the absence of such aids [declarations of legislative findings of facts justifying an act] the existence of facts supporting the legislative judgment is to be presumed, for regulatory legislation affecting ordinary commercial transactions is not to be pronounced unconstitutional unless in the light of the facts made known or generally assumed it is of such a character as to preclude the assumption that it rests upon some rational basis within the knowledge and experience of the legislator.[4]

[n.4] There may be narrower scope for operation of the presumption of constitutionality when legislation appears on its face to be within the specific prohibition of the Constitution, such as those of the first ten amendments, which are deemed equally specific when held to be embraced within the Fourteenth.

163. Siegan, ECONOMIC LIBERTIES AND THE CONSTITUTION, chs. 9 and 10, is, as usual, brilliant in exploding this false dichotomy, so I see no need to repeat his argument here.

164. 427 U.S. 297 (1976).

165. During the middle part of the nineteenth century, as we have previously discussed under the section dealing with eminent domain, the test employed was one of physical invasion. That is, if the state invaded one's land so as to effectively destroy one's title or a significant portion of one's rights over that land, such consequential damages would be recoverable under an inverse condemnation plea. But this test does not address the problem before us now, which deals not with effects of governmental improvements upon injured property owners but, rather, with the nonmaterial injuries, usually pecuniary, suffered by property owners as the result of governmental edicts as to how they can use their property. The physical invasion test, then, dealt with the easy cases, and was fairly quickly antiquated by governments' growing zeal for economic intervention. The physical invasion test still serves its narrow purpose (and not particularly well, as evidenced in the navigable servitude cases).

166. 123 U.S. 623 (1887).

167. *Id.* at 661.

168. *Id.*

169. *Id.* at 665.

170. *Id.* at 669.

171. *Powell v. Pennsylvania*, 127 U.S. 678 (1888).

172. Justice Field dissented from the conclusion of the majority, wondering how a healthy and nutritious article could be prohibited, and, indeed, prohibited without compensation. Field would have pierced the veil of police power rationale proffered by the state. He pointed to a New York case in which the state court did precisely that, perceiving in an act similar to Pennsylvania's only an attempt to protect the dairy industry from competition (*People v. Marx*, 99 N.Y. 377). If courts could not scrutinize the underlying motives of legislatures in enacting police measures, the most valued individual rights would be held captive to temporary majorities, Field wrote. An outright prohibition on the sale of an innocuous item Field could not abide, yet he was willing to allow the states less conclusive regulations of, for example, the conditions of sale and restraints on improper use.

173. *Hadacheck v. Sebastian, Chief of Police of the City of Los Angeles*, 239 U.S. 394 (1915).

174. *Id.* at 410.

175. 237 U.S. 171 (1915).

176. *Goldblatt v. Town of Hempstead, N.Y.*, 369 U.S. 590 (1962); *Consolidated Rock Products Co. v. Los Angeles*, 57 Cal. 2d 515, 370 P. 2d 342, 20 Cal. Rptr. 368, appeal dismissed, 371 U.S. 36 (1962).

177. It should be pointed out that even before Holmes's enthronement of *ad hoc* decision making, the Court handled takings claims in a rather cavalier manner, expressing no set principles for when the police power exceeded its

bounds, and on the whole deciding the overwhelming number of cases in favor of the challenged legislation. The unifying principle, to the extent there was one, was that the Court would defer to legislative judgment unless that judgment was clearly arbitrary or unreasonable, with a presumption of validity placed upon the legislation. In other words, pretty much the standard applied in other due process cases, although there was little regard shown for whether the challenged legislation was the least onerous that could have been enacted. For example:

1. *L'Hote v. New Orleans*, 177 U.S. 587 (1900). Court rejected property owner's claim that the establishment of a red-light district in effect took or damaged his property due to a diminution in its value. The Court denied that its function was to second-guess legislatures as to the wisdom or desirability of their acts. "If he [the property owner] suffers injury, it is either *damnum absque injuria*, or in the theory of the law, he is compensated for it by sharing in the general benefits which the regulations are intended and calculated to secure." (This latter ploy, by the way, is popular today among commentators and courts desirous of extending the purview of the police power, particularly in the area of land-use legislation.)

2. *California Reduction Co. v. Sanitary Reduction Works*, 199 U.S. 306 (1905). Upheld an exclusive franchise granted to garbage company to collect garbage against takings defense by homeowners and to other company sued by franchise. Court found a regulation for public health and not a taking.

3. *Gardner v. Michigan*, 199 U.S. 325 (1905). Upheld garbage regulation as not a taking.

4. *Chicago, B. & Q. Railway Co. v. Illinois*, 200 U.S. 561 (1906). Upheld as police power regulation a statute by which majority of owners in a drainage district could petition for public improvement. Railway challenged act because it was made to bear the cost of tearing down its bridge across a stream and erecting a new one with a bigger opening for drainage. The Court argued that compensation has never been a condition of the proper exercise of the police power aiming at the public welfare (at 592). The prohibition on taking without compensation was not considered to constitute a limitation on an appropriate exercise of the police power.

5. *Hudson Water Co. v. McCarter*, 209 U.S. 349 (1907). Held that a state may prohibit diversion of its waters. Here the Court stated that no set formula in advance can be established to differentiate private rights of property, which can be limited only by compensation under eminent domain, and the police power, which can limit such rights in the public interest. Prior cases can serve to illuminate which instances fall on which side of the line. (This foreshadowed the standard laid down in *Pennsylvania Coal Co. v. Mahon*.)

6. *Welch v. Swasey*, 214 U.S. 91 (1909). Employing a means-end, substantive due process standard, the Court upheld building-height restrictions against a takings challenge.

7. *Laurel Hill Cemetery v. San Francisco*, 216 U.S. 358 (1910). Upheld ban on cemeteries in city, again claiming no set standard for distinguishing eminent domain from police power.

8. *Hamilton v. Kentucky Distilleries & Warehouse Co.*, 251 U.S. 146 (1919). Upheld wartime prohibition on sale of liquor as not a taking when chal-

lenged by liquor owner possessing product prior to ban. War powers of Congress were legitimately exercised even if attended by deleterious effects to private parties akin to those resulting from an exercise of the state's police power. Also, *Jacob Ruppert, Inc., v. Caffey*, 251 U.S. 264 (1920). Where a ban was extended to nonintoxicating liquors and upheld against a takings challenge because Justice Brandeis saw no appropriation of private property by the government but only a lessening of value due to a permissible restriction.

9. *Walls v. Midland Carbon Co.*, 254 U.S. 300 (1920). Upheld state prohibition on the manufacture of carbon black unless the heat from natural gas consumed in the process was utilized. Against a takings challenge, the Court discovered only a legitimate exercise of the police power in the state's desire to protect the supply of natural gas by preventing waste.

10. *Lower Vein Coal v. Industrial Bd. of Indiana*, 255 U.S. 144 (1921). Upheld Workmen's Compensation Act against plea of takings.

11. *Alaska Fish Salting & By-Products v. Smith*, 255 U.S. 44 (1921). Upheld a licensing law even though it might destroy a business; in that eventuality, it would not be invalid or amount to a taking.

12. *Block v. Hirsch*, (1920). Upheld temporary wartime rent control under theory that property rights can be limited by police power if regulation does not go too far.

If the Court believed that a regulation was clearly unreasonable or arbitrary, it did invalidate such measures, as evidenced by *Wilcox v. Consolidated Gas Co. of New York*, 212 U.S. 19 (1909). Here the Court invalidated a gas rate regulation where it believed the act was plainly unreasonable and its enforcement would amount to a taking. The company would have been forced to operate at a loss. In the vast majority of cases, however, the Court met takings assaults upon police power acts with a remarkable lack of sympathy, sustaining them unless they were grossly without foundation. The standard employed in these cases, to the extent I can decipher any consistency between them, was that employed in other due process cases during this era of substantive due process.

178. 260 U.S. 393 (1922).

179. In *Laurel Hill Cemetery v. San Francisco*, 216 U.S. 358 (1910). The Court upheld a city ordinance banning cemeteries within its limits. Holmes, in reaching this decision acquiescing in legislative determinations, wrote:

> And yet again the extent to which legislation may modify and restrict the use of property consistently with the Constitution is not a question for pure abstract theory alone. Tradition and the habits of the community count for more than logic . . . The plaintiff must wait until there is a change of practice or at least an established consensus of civilized opinion before it can expect this court to overthrow the rules that the lawmakers and the court of his own state uphold [at 366].

Also, in *Block v. Hirsh*, 256 U.S. 135 (1920), the Court upheld a temporary, wartime rent control measure of the District of Columbia against the charge that it was a taking of property for a private, not public, use. Holmes thought that the relevant question was principally whether the statute went too far: "For just as there comes a point at which the police power ceases and leaves only that of eminent domain, it may be conceded that regulations of the present sort pressed to a certain height might amount to a taking without due process of law" [at 156].

180. Perhaps this oversight can be traced to the Court's often-repeated injunction that all contracts stand subject to future exercises of the police power and that property cannot be placed beyond the reach of that power by entering into a contractual obligation. The Court in this case was reminded of this doctrine in an *amicus curiae* brief submitted on behalf of the state of Pennsylvania.

181. *Pennsylvania Coal v. Mahon* at 413.

182. See Note, *Balancing Private Loss Against Public Gain to Test for a Violation of Due Process or a Taking without Just Compensation*, 54 WASH. L. REV. 315 (1979). The author argues that balancing public benefits against private loss is a sufficient standard to test for due process (e.g., so that a large public benefit would have to be shown to overbalance a small private loss; and an act would be invalidated if a trifling public gain engendered a substantial private loss) but not an apposite test for violations of the "takings clause." Furthermore, the author contends that Holmes used the balancing test in precisely this way in *Pennsylvania Coal*, where balancing was employed to test the measure's adherence to due process, and then a "diminution in value" test served to test whether a taking had occurred. He cites as evidence for his interpretation Holmes's statement that a large public benefit cannot justify denying compensation to injured property owners. For a contemporary advocacy of a balancing test for the takings issue, see Robert Kratovil and Frank J. Harrison, Jr., *Eminent Domain—Policy and Concept*, CALIF L. REV. 596 (1954); Comment, *Distinguishing Eminent Domain from Police Power and Tort*, 38 WASH. L. REV. 607 (1963); Zygmunt J. B. Plater, *The Takings Issue in a Natural Setting: Floodlines and the Police Power*, 52 TEX. L. REV. 201 (1974).

183. *Pennsylvania Coal v. Mahon* at 415.

184. *Id.* at 415, 416.

185. *Id.* at 416.

186. *Golden v. Planning Board of Ramapo*, 30 N.Y. 2d 359, 285 N.E. 2d 291 (1972). Upheld controlled-growth zoning involving up to an eighteen-year delay in development.

187. See Fred Bosselman, David Callies, and John Banta, THE TAKINGS ISSUE: AN ANALYSIS OF THE CONSTITUTIONAL LIMITS OF LAND USE CONTROL (Washington, D.C.: Council on Environmental Quality, 1973).

188. 369 U.S. 590 (1962). The case is not a perfect illustration of the application of the diminution-in-value test because evidence pertaining to loss of value was absent from the record, but the pickings are rather slim among Supreme Court decisions since the Court from the late 1920s to the mid-1970s abdicated its privilege to review land-use cases.

189. This Holmesian "no set formula" canard would be repeated in recent Supreme Court takings cases. See *Pennsylvania Transportation Co. v. City of New York*, 438 U.S. 104, 124 (1978); *Kaiser Aetna v. United States*, 444 U.S. 164, 100 S. Ct. 383, 390 (1979).

190. Curiously, the Court chose to flesh out "reasonableness" with criteria established in those bad old days of substantive due process, returning to *Lawton v. Steele*, 152 U.S. 133 (1894) in the process. That case enunciated a classic due process standard for testing a police power measure: that the interests of the public require such interference; that the means are reasonably related to the accomplishment of the purpose, and not unduly oppressive upon individuals.

191. *Consolidated Rock Products Co. v. Los Angeles*, 57 Cal. 2d 515, 370 P. 2d 342, 20 Cal. Rptr. 368, appeal dismissed, 371 U.S. 36 (1962).

192. 438 U.S. 104 (1978).
193. The Court here also flirted with a test devised by Joseph Sax, *Takings and the Police Power*, 74 YALE L. J. 36 (1964), in which he distinguished between police power measures that enhanced the entrepreneurial status of government and those that just mediated between the uses to which private parties put their property. In the former case, compensation would be required; in the latter, it would not. Justice Brennan, in distinguishing this case from *Causby* argued that here the city was not acting in its entrepreneurial capacity, and he referred to Sax elsewhere in his decision [at 124].
194. *Penn Central* at 135. For further discussion of this case, see Note, *Police Power and Compensable Takings—A Landmark Decision Clarifies the Rules: Penn Central Transportation Co. v. City of New York*, 11 CONN. L. REV. 273 (1979).
195. 201 N.W. 2d 761 (1972).
196. Freund, THE POLICE POWER, § 511, pp. 546-47.
197. *Just v. Marinette County* at 768.
198. *Dooley v. Town Planning & Zoning Commission of Town of Fairfield*, 197 A. 2d 770 (Conn., 1964); *Morris County Land Improvement Co. v. Township of Parsippany-Troy Hills*, 193 A. 2d 232 (N.J., 1963); *State v. Johnson*, 265 A. 2d 711 (Me., 1970); *MacGibbon v. Board of Appeals of Duxbury*, 255 N.E. 2d 347 (Mass., 1970).
199. *Just v. Marinette County* at 771 n. 6.
200. *Id.* at 771.
201. Sax, *Takings and the Police Power* at 61.
202. *Id.* at 63.
203. *United States v. Central Eureka Mining Co.*, 357 U.S. 155 (1958).
204. Joseph Sax, *Takings, Private Property and Public Rights*, 81 YALE L. J. 57, 58 n. 5 (1971).
205. *Id.* at 58.
206. Compare Sax's discussion of *Morris County Land Improvement Co. v. Township of Parsippany-Troy Hills*, 40 N.J. 539, 193 A. 2d 232 (1963), *Id.* at 66 n. 22 with his earlier discussion in *Takings and the Police Power* at 72-73.
207. Sax, *Takings, Private Property and Public Rights* at 70.
208. *Id.* at 80: "As a rule of thumb, it may be said that the proper decision as to competing property uses which involve spillover effects is that which a single owner would make if he were responsible for the entire network of resources affected, and if the distribution of gains and losses among the parcels of his total holding were a matter of indifference to him."
209. *Id.* at 79.
210. Frank Michelman, *Property, Utility, and Fairness: Comments on the Ethical Foundations of Just Compensation Law*, 80 HARV. L. REV. 1165 (1967).
211. Michelman employs Rawls's criteria for justice expounded in his early articles, but they are essentially congruent with his later theory expounded in his THEORY OF JUSTICE (Cambridge: Harvard University Press, 1971). Rawls's theory of justice embodies two principles, with the first taking precedence over the second: (1) that all people should enjoy a like amount of basic liberties, and (2) that equality ought to be the rule except where deviations can be justified by their tendency to promote the well-being of the least-well-off member of society. Michelman, by the way, takes considerable liberties with Rawls's two principles.

212. Michelman, *Property, Utility, and Fairness* at 1223.
213. Bosselman et al., THE TAKINGS ISSUE. For an analysis of this work, see Robert L. Bish, *The Takings Issue: Is the Fifth Amendment a Myth*, paper prepared for the CATO Environmental Symposium, Center for Political Economy and Natural Resources, Montana State University, December 1980.
214. *Id.* at 236-37.
215. *Id.* at 238.
216. *Id.* at 253.
217. John J. Costonis, *Fair Compensation and the Accommodation Power: Antidotes for the Taking Impasse in Land Use Controversies*, 75 COLUM. L. REV. 1021 (1975). See also Michael M. Berger, *To Regulate, or Not to Regulate—Is That the Question? Reflections on the Supposed Dilemma Between Environmental Protection and Private Property Rights*, 8 LOY. L.A. L. REV. 253 (1975).
218. Donald Hagman and D. Misczynski, eds., WINDFALLS FOR WIPEOUTS: LAND VALUE CAPTURE AND COMPENSATION (Washington, D.C.: Planners Press 1978). For critical evaluations of Hagman's proposal, see Dennis R. Honaback, *Windfalls, Wipeouts, and Nuisance Law: Strict Liability with or without Restricted Damages*, 19 URB. L. ANN. 3 (1980); Richard O. Brooks, *The Evaluation of Compensable Regulations: A Return to Beuscher's Defense of Invalidation*, 19 URB. L. ANN. 27 (1980).
219. Frank Schnidman, *Transferable Development Rights: An Idea in Search of Implementation*, 11 LAND & WATER L. REV. 339 (1976); John J. Costonis, *The Chicago Plan: Incentive Zoning and the Preservation of Urban Landmarks*, 85 HARV. L. REV. 574 (1972); John J. Costonis, *The Disparity Issue: A Context for the Grand Central Terminal Decision*, 91 HARV. L. REV. 402 (1977). See also Norman Marcus, *Air Rights Transfers in New York City*, 36 L. & CONTEMP. PROB. 372 (1971); Paul E. Wilson and H.J. Winkler, *The Response of State Legislation to Historic Preservation*, 36 LAW AND CONTEMPORARY PROBLEMS 329 (1971); *Penn Central Transportation Co. v. City of New York*, 438 U.S. 104 (1978).
220. Bernard Siegan, LAND USE WITHOUT ZONING (Lexington, Mass.: Lexington Books, 1972) and PLANNING WITHOUT PRICES (Lexington, Mass.: Lexington Books, 1977).
221. Robert Ellickson, *Alternatives to Zoning; Covenants, Nuisance Rules, and Fines as Land Use Controls*, 40 U. CHI. L. RV. 681 (1973).
222. While Herbert Hoover served as secretary of commerce, the department in 1924 promulgated a model Standard State Zoning Enabling Act that by 1925 had been adopted by nineteen states. Subdivision regulations, master plans, and local planning commissions soon became accepted phenomena across the land. Zoning was a German import.
223. *Welch v. Swasey*, 214 U.S. 91 (1909).
224. 272 U.S. 365 (1926).
225. *Euclid v. Ambler* at 387.
226. *Id.* at 388.
227. Nichols, EMINENT DOMAIN, at sec. 1.42, except for the second point, which he does not include.
228. 274 U.S. 325 (1927).
229. 274 U.S. 603 (1927).

230. *Id.* at 608. In reaching its decision, the Court echoed its formulation from *Euclid* that because it could not find the ordinance clearly arbitrary and unreasonable, having no substantial relation to the public health, safety, morals, or general welfare, it should be held valid.
231. 277 U.S. 183 (1928).
232. *Id.* at 188.
233. 278 U.S. 116 (1928).
234. 416 U.S. 1 (1974).
235. *Moore v. City of East Cleveland*, 431 U.S. 494 (1977) (previously discussed in this chapter).
236. These cases vividly illustrate the obscurantism of much Supreme Court deliberation. *Belle Terre*, for example, explicitly relies upon *Euclid* and *Berman v. Parker*, while *Moore* declares them to be irrelevant.
237. 427 U.S. 50 (1976).
238. 101 S. Ct. 2176 (1981).
239. 422 U.S. 490 (1975).
240. 429 U.S. 252 (1977).
241. A violation of the Fair Housing Act was also alleged, and the case was eventually remanded for consideration of this statutory complaint.
242. The majority cited *Washington v. Davis*, 426 U.S. 229 (1976) to show that proof of racially discriminatory intent is necessary, and that disproportionate impact, while not irrelevant, is not the sole criterion of an invidious racial discrimination.
243. 100 S. Ct. 2138 (1980).
244. *Agins v. City of Tiburon*, 598 P. 2d 25, 31 (Calif., 1979).
245. 100 S. Ct. 2138, 2141-42 (1980).
246. 101 S. Ct. 1287 (1981).
247. This gets a bit complicated, but the California Supreme Court had itself sent the case back to the appeals court on grounds of its decision in *Agins* denying inverse condemnation as a remedy. Also, the company had abandoned its original plan for a nuclear plant after an earthhquake fault was discovered. Instead, it wished to create a 150-acre industrial park. The company claimed that the city had a policy of denying permits on open-space land. The city, in turn, maintained that the company never requested a permit and that the city, as a charter city, could have granted such a permit on land designated for open-space use. The company sought $6,150,000 in inverse condemnation, and the trial court had granted it $3 million. The court of appeals in California had decided that inverse condemnation was not an appropriate remedy.
248. *San Diego Gas & Electric* at 1307 (Brennan dissent). This dissent has been cited in a few recent court decisions: *Burrows v. City of Keene*, 432 A. 2d 15 (N.H., 1981); *Hernandez v. City of Lafayette*, 643 F. 2d 1188 (5th Cir., 1981), *cert. denied* 50 U.S.L.W. 3570 (no. 81-605) (Jan. 18, 1982); see THE REPORT OF THE PRESIDENT'S COMMISSION ON HOUSING at 202.
249. 53 LW4969 (1985).
250. For the sake of completeness, I might refer the reader who wants a fuller picture of recent Supreme Court decisions on land use to the following cases: *City of Eastlake v. Forest City Enterprises, Inc.*, 426 U.S. 668 (1976), upholding a zoning provision requiring a 55 percent vote of the public for the granting of a variance against a due process challenge; *New Motor Vehicle Bd. of*

California v. Orrin W. Foy Co., 439 U.S. 96 (1978), holding that states may through a general ordinance restrict the commercial use of property and the geographical location of commercial enterprises; *Lake County Estates, Inc. v. Tahoe Regional Planning Agency*, 440 U.S. 391 (1979), held that the TRPA is not immune from liability for a takings claim, and cannot be protected from a suit under the Eleventh Amendment.

3

The Right to Private Property: Does It Exist? Where Does It Come From? Is Absolutism Defensible?

The Problem

> There is nothing which so generally strikes the imagination and engages the affections of mankind, as the right of property; or that sole and despotic dominion which one man claims and exercises over the external things of the world in total exclusion of the right of any other individual in the universe.[1]

Lamentably for the defender of property rights, Blackstone's absolutist declaration of a "sole and despotic dominion" fails to illuminate those tough cases in the law where the use by one person, A, of his property impinges upon the enjoyment by B of his property. It is precisely these conflicts that the private law of nuisance and the public law emanating from the state's exercise of its police power attempt to resolve. Courts have been notoriously irresolute and inconsistent in their attempts to set constitutional bounds to the police power. This judicial vacillation is intelligible, given the failure of jurists and philosophers to develop a sound theoretical underpinning for property rights.

How, to give just one example, can a fact pattern such as that exhibited in the much-debated case of *Miller v. Schoene* (1928)[2] be satisfactorily resolved without at least an implicit recognition of an underlying theory of property rights? A Virginia statute empowered the state entomologist to order the plaintiffs to cut down a large number of ornamental red cedar trees that the plaintiffs valued at $5,000 to $7,000. The trees harbored a highly communicable plant disease known as cedar rust, which, while benign in the host cedar trees, posed a destructive hazard to apple trees within a two-mile radius traversed by diseased spores. Cedar rust could be controlled and the apple trees protected only by destroying all infected cedar trees within two miles of apple orchards. The Cedar Rust Act, falling under the rubric of the police power required no compensation for the aggrieved owners of the ornamental trees. Despite the seemingly compelling arguments articulated in the brief for the plaintiff, that it is contrary to American principles of government to permit the taking or destruction of one man's property to enhance the prosperity of another, and that it is absurd to penalize one form of valuable property to protect another from the effects of a disease for which they are mutually responsible, the court decided otherwise.

Justice Stone, speaking for the majority of the Supreme Court, anchored his argument upholding the act as a legitimate exercise of the police power not on an examination of the rights involved—of apple orchard owners and red cedar tree owners—but rather on the economics of the situation. The apple orchards constituted a multimillion-dollar investment, were a principal agricultural enterprise in the state, and employed many Virginians; the red cedars were largely ornamental, with minimal value as lumber and no substantial commercial value. Either by acting or forbearing to act on the threat to the orchards the state ineluctably would have had to make a choice between competing interests.

> When forced to such a choice the state does not exceed its constitutional powers by deciding upon the destruction of one class of property in order to save another which, in the judgment of the legislator, is of greater value to the public. It will not do to say that the case is merely one of a conflict of two private interests and that the misfortune of apple growers may not be shifted to cedar owners by ordering the destruction of their property; for it is obvious that there may be, and that here there is, a preponderant public concern in the preservation of the one interest over the other. . . . And where the public interest is involved preferment of that interest over the property interests of the individual, to the extent even of its destruction, is one of the distinguishing characteristics of every exercise of the police power which affects property.[3]

Implicit in Justice Stone's analysis are several hidden assumptions: that there exists an identifiable entity called the "public interest," the content of which at any given time is discernible by legislators; that individuals possess mere "property interests" rather than the more indestructible "property rights," and these interests may be sacrificed to the greater good of the public's interest; that the state is properly in the business of balancing various private interests and denominating one among them as coincidental with the public interest; and, therefore, that the state may sacrifice one private interest to another private interest once the latter has been shrouded in the guise of the "public interest."

Whether Justice Stone and his colleagues realized it or not, their seemingly simple analysis on an economic, cost-benefit criterion really depends upon a whole set of assumptions about the nature of man, his relationship to other men and to the state, to say nothing about a theory of the proper limits of governmental intervention in the marketplace. Clearly, the Court's decision derived from a loosely held utilitarian conception of the nature of property and function of the state. For utilitarians, Jeremy Bentham being the most conspicuous example, the law itself and all property rights are merely the creation of the state. Therefore, a utilitarian would readily appraise the facts in *Miller* in precisely the manner accomplished by the Court, i.e. that the happiness of society, meaning the aggregate of all individual utilities, would be maximized by sacrificing the interest of the owners of that commodity with the least utility to society (the red cedars) to the greater interest of preserving the utility embodied in the apple orchards.

However, it is far from clear that utilitarianism ought to be either the preferred theory of justice in respect to property rights, or the apposite theory for determining the proper functions of the state. As this case illustrates, a utilitarian judicial disposition justifies its advocates in sacrificing the good of some individuals to that of others because utilitarians must attempt to quantify something as abstruse and subjective as the "public interest." What should give us additional concern about the decision in *Miller* is the Court's reliance on two earlier police power cases that gave short shrift to property rights. In *Mugler v. Kansas* (1887),[4] the Supreme Court upheld a state law prohibiting the manufacture of liquor within the boundaries of Kansas, denying that the statute constituted a taking of Mugler's property in his brewery or a violation of his due process rights. *Hadacheck v. Sebastian* (1915)[5] provided the Court with another opportunity to champion the police power at the expense of a property owner divested of his business without compensation by a city ordinance. The city of Los Angeles enacted an ordinance prohibiting the production of bricks within a section of the city, thereby rendering Hadacheck's operation virtually worthless. The proximity of surrounding residential neighborhoods was the justification given for the ban. The plaintiff's operation was the only brickyard in the designated area. Despite the fact that the city's ban was aimed at a single business, the Court failed to detect any "arbitrariness" or "unjust discrimination" that would render suspect the exercise of the police power in this case. The plaintiff's contentions that his Fourteenth Amendment due process and equal protection rights had been traduced did not prove persuasive.

As the history of eminent domain and police power adjudication (which we examined in the last chapter) demonstrates, there is something very troubling about pragmatic, case-by-case, *ad hoc* decision making. Property rights are treated in inconsistent ways, and whether one receives compensation for one's losses often turns on distinctions that are impossible for the ordinary citizen to comprehend. Judges with the best of intentions have had to grapple with precedents that would defy Solomon to untangle. It is understandable why judges have failed to extricate themselves from this morass. Pragmatic decision making, inspired by utilitarian moral philosophy, has simply not worked. Virtually everyone admits that this area of the law is in a chaotic state. The time seems right to address the fundamental cause of this unfortunate state of affairs. Perhaps an alternative tradition to *ad hoc*, utilitarian decision making might hold out some hope for resolving this "muddle." The tradition I have in mind is not alien to our American constitutional heritage, for it is that of natural rights. I will argue that natural rights provides a consistent theory of property rights, and that a theory of property rights is essential for extricating ourselves from this impasse.

Natural rights theory exerted its greatest influence in the seventeenth and eighteenth centuries, and informed the thinking of the fomenters of the American Revolution and the founders of our nation. Admittedly, natural rights as the underpinning for a legal theory of property rights suffered a near-fatal beating, from which it is just now beginning to recover, at the hands of Jeremy Bentham, who castigated it as nothing more substantial than "nonsense on stilts." One would be churlish, indeed, to refuse to acknowledge a substantial element of legitimacy to Bentham's charges,[6] for the advocates of natural rights did fail to provide a logical, internally consistent, deductive defense of these rights. Bentham certainly had his point.

The ensuing discussion will be devoted to an attempt to supply the natural rights theory of property with such a deductive defense. I hope this defense will be persuasive to those like Bentham who are highly skeptical of "metaphysical rights." Before this constructive argument unfolds, it will be instructive to examine, first, what is meant by the claim that "A owns X," and, second what kinds of alternative defenses have been proffered by various rights theorists. It will be helpful also to examine the theories of property rights presented by utilitarians and by the more recent school of "wealth maximizers."

Undoubtedly, even the most rigorous (and one hopes, logically unassailable) defense of a right to property will not convince all persons, particularly those antithetical to the notion that individuals ought to control private domains to the exclusion of all others. However, a natural rights argument remains appealing to some thinkers because it claims universality, both of time and place. Eschewing all varieties of "relativity-of-knowledge" arguments that deny ultimate truth to any values, natural rights erects a moral fortress around the individual, providing protection against governmental assaults upon life and liberty. Others, however, find such a position tainted for precisely these same reasons. Because these theorists deny the existence of immutable truths and values, and they wish, in the name of equality, positive freedom, or justice, to agument the power of the state, natural rights arguments appear particulary irrelevant. The most a natural rights argument can aspire to is locigal rigor. Whether egalitarians, collectivists, or utilitarians find this argument persuasive or not, I do hope that they find something useful in it that might point the way out of our current legal bog. I suspect that this natural rights defense would lack persuasiveness to a Proudhon or a Marx, particularly Marx, who would dismiss it as mere "bourgeois logic."

"Property is theft," declared the socialist Proudhon,[7] thus capturing in one pungent phrase the prevalent, modern view that private possession lies under a cloud of moral suspicion. Is it not a tainted, oppressive, and inegalitarian encumbrance to be eradicated at the earliest possible opportunity? Karl Marx certainly thought as much. Property, particularly in the means of production, took on an ever more sinister complexion as socialist thought progressed. In Marx's system, economic forces determined the course of history, and consequently the way property was owned in a particular society became crucial. By controlling as their personal capital the machines upon which laborers toiled in order to eke out a meager existence, the capitalists extracted a surplus value from the sweat of the laboring class, thus robbing it of a considerable portion of what it had produced. The exploitation of the laborers engendered by the capitalist system does not end with this illicit profit but, rather, extends to the alienation of the working man from both his product and his nature *qua* man. The capitalists' monopoly of property in the means of production enables that class virtually to enslave the proletariat. Just as the bourgeois government serves as the protector of the property of its favored class, so the other institutions of society, the church, and the arts, conspire to cement the ideology of the propertied class. The control of property, then, is crucial in Marx, for by that exclusive possession some men come to control all power centers within society and, consequently, their fellow men. Property is theft, but more importantly, property is slavery.

A property system grounded on a natural rights moral foundation can aspire only to demonstrate to the Marxist that the owners of resources, the capitalists, in no way exploit laborers. Rather, laborers are paid the equivalent of their contribution at the margin, a manner of compensation likewise enjoyed by all other factors of production. Profit, rather than being the vehicle of the capitalist's exploitation of wage slaves, becomes justifiable once the natural rights position unfolds its moral defense of original acquisition. But to expect more, for example a refutation of the young Marx's romantic imprecations against capitalism—that is, that it engenders the alienation of the worker from his product and from his nature—is to expect too much.

Other persistent objections to a property rights system will be surmounted more readily by a natural rights defense. In the eighteenth century men such as Thomas Spence and Tom Paine formulated classic objections to individual appropriation of land and natural resources, arguments destined to be echoed in the nineteenth century by the American Henry George, and the Frenchman P.J. Proudhon.[8] These eighteenth century thinkers contended that the earth ought to remain the common heritage of mankind precisely because it is not a product of man's labor. In other words, they conceded, to John Locke his argument that labor could transform a previously unowned thing into a personal possession, but they balked at the further claim that labor could create a property in that thing in perpetuity and to the exclusion of all others. As a further blow to Locke, the socialists carried his argument to what he would have undoubtedly considered illegitimate lengths. If all men have a natural right to the fruits of their labor, as Locke believed, then why, the socialists inquired, is this right not violated when all things to be labored upon belong already to others? Are subsequent laborers not disadvantaged because they merely receive a wage rather than title to the land upon which they expend their energies? If this objection proved valid, it would, of course, thoroughly undermine Locke's entire theory. Rather than acquisition through labor serving as a universally applicable principle, it would appear transistory only. Once all land were acquired, the principle would become contradictory. Or, perhaps, not even at such a distant point, but only at the instant the first man labors upon the property of another solely for remuneration. Fortunately, Locke can be rescued from this apparent contradiction.

It is not just socialists and Marxists who today share a profound skepticism about private property. If liberals are absolutists about any political value it is certainly not property. Even their rightly cherished First Amendment freedoms of speech, press, and assembly must be held subject to the balancing of competing interests, as the Holmesian example of shouting fire in a crowded theater illustrates. Modern liberalism, in contrast to liberalism's heritage in the writings of John Locke, Adam Smith, and Thomas Jefferson, holds that civil rights can be separated from property rights. For modern liberals like John Dewey, property rights are relatively unimportant. A democractic society can flourish by protecting civil rights while not unduly concerning itself with property rights.

Property, for the modern liberal, is a creation of the state. Individuals do not have rights to property independent of the state, as Locke had thought. Walter Lippmann succinctly captured this view as he castigated the Blackstonian "despotic theory" of property:

No civilized society has long tolerated the despotic theory of private property. This conception of property is alien to the central truths of Christendom, which have always held that property is not absolute but is a system of rights and duties that are determined by society.

Private property is, in fact, the creation of the law of the land. . . . It is a primitive, naive, and false view of private property to urge that it is not subject to the laws which express the national purpose and the national conscience.[9]

Richard Powell, in an article entitled "The Relationship Between Property Rights and Civil Rights," clearly states this modern liberal notion of property as the vehicle by which the state regulates competing liberties. Freedom for one, he argues, entails restriction upon others. I must be restricted so you can enjoy your freedom; reciprocally, you must be restricted so that I can exercise my freedom. Consequently, it is the task of the state to equalize these freedoms and restrictions over time to readjust constantly the *balance*. "Property rights, at any moment of time, represent the current wisdom as to how this balance is best served."[10] The temper of the judicial realists (those who ascribe the origins of all law to the behavior of judges rather than to any higher-law conception of inherent rights) is captured in Powell's epigram: "It has been well said that property rights are not protected by the courts, *but* what the courts protect these constitute property rights."[11] And how are judges to settle disputes concerning the existence, or nonexistence of a property right? Unsurprisingly, the test is one of consistency with the "public welfare."[12]

Why should this statist proclivity seem unsettling to even the most contented liberal? Precisely because the progression from courts slighting property rights in the service of the general welfare to governments abrogating all property rights in the name of social justice seems to be such a slippery slope. Judges, or indeed legislators, less benign than heretofore, or more radically collectivist, could discover full solace for an aggressive program of nationalization in Powell's epigram. No intrinsic limits can be drawn once it is conceded that all property is held at the sufferance of the state. And, indeed, how can liberty preserve its secure anchor once that private preserve, that sanctuary called private property, has been undermined by government? As Roscoe Pound so eloquently discerned,

The chief danger to property has not been from the covetous neighbor nor from the habitual thief. It has been from the acquisitive and confiscatory activities of rulers. The Will to power, the temptation to exercise power simply because one has it, has led rulers to arbitrary interferences with liberty of the person. Covetousness has led them to arbitrary seizure of property. Both have joined to bring about arbitrary interferences with the liberty of using property. It is significant that the current of thought which is giving up the idea of property is also giving up the idea of liberty. As the two grew up together they are a common subject of attack by those who conceive the one must go with the fall of the other. King Demos has shown the same tendencies that called for constitutional checks upon King Rex.[13]

A good example of the slippery-slope problem can be seen in the arguments of Morris Udall, one of the architect's of the unsuccessful attempt to enact land-use legislation at the national level in the early 1970s. If local land regulation in the form of zoning failed, then why not enact federal legislation? Udall embraced a view of land as a "national resource." He argued that leaving land-use decisions to the "unrestricted forces of the market" has led to irreversible loss of agricultural land, estuaries, wetlands, and open space, and the wasteful consumption of energy. What is needed, consequently, is a national program to collectivize the decision-making process.

Udall was fully aware of some of the problems that local governments had experienced in managing land. He wrote: "Unfortunately, the politics of zoning has often left special interests with the upper hand."[14] But instead of abandoning intervention, he proceeded to argue for its extension. Federal regulation could succeed where local regulation had failed. Preservation and development decisions should be left to "citizen participation and representation of all interests"—that is, to politicians—"rather than to the vagaries of the market."[15]

Udall's plan was undoubtedly well intentioned. It was directed at curing some of the problems with local land regulation. However, his faith in regulation seemed undiminished by past failures. In fact, these failures inspired him to campaign for even more extensive regulation at a higher level of government. The slippery slope is real, and it is alarming. What scintilla of liberty might be left to the citizen if one's decisions concerning where to build a house, a school for one's children, a plant for one's newspaper, or a press for one's publishing house can be acted upon only at the sufferance of politicians? The mention of private schools and presses should serve to underscore the connection, inextricable I would argue, between property and liberty. Modern liberals just might find something appealing about a natural rights position on property that provides such a firm foundation for liberty. Udall's conception of ownership as "stewardship" deserves to be rejected:

[A] great deal of future land use regulation will depend on a continuance of the shift in attitude about "ownership" of land toward acceptance of the idea of "stewardship" and on a recognition that development rights are not inherent in the ownership of land but are severable and can be transferred.[16]

Liberals should find this view suspect because if it undermines property rights, it also undermines liberty rights.

Property Theories and Property Defenses

It is the purpose of the following discussion to examine three questions. (1) What does it mean to claim that "Alpha owns X," or alternatively, that "X is the property of Alpha?" (2) What are the necessary components of a complete theory of property rights? (3) And what kinds of theories have been advanced by political philosophers, and what defects or redeeming qualities are exhibited in these efforts? Only after these questions have been examined, can one hope to offer a property defense that is both an improvement over its predecessors and useful for resolving quarrels over the legitimacy of the police power and eminent domain.

The typical legal theorist takes great pains to debunk the commonsensical view of property as the relationship between a person, Alpha, and the piece of property, X, that Alpha owns. There is, however, an important insight that this supposedly naive view captures that is neglected by repairing to "lawyer's talk." Morris Cohen, in his influential article "Property and Sovereignty," expressed this cleavage between ordinary language and the concept of property as entertained by lawyers:

> A property right is not to be identified with the fact of physical possession. Whatever technical definition of property we may prefer, we must recognize that a property right is a relation not between an owner and a thing, but between the owner and other individuals in reference to things.[17]

One may wonder why this distinction seems so critical that lawyers so often reiterate it.[18] A careful examination of Cohen's argument reveals the answer. He precedes this quoted passage with an emphatic statement that in the world of nature there are no property rights. Most lawyers received their training from advocates of the legal-realist view of the law. Legal realists believe that the law is whatever judges say it is. This view contrasts with the older legal naturalist position, which held that judges discover the law, and that this higher law exists independently of their wishes. Most of our early jurists were legal naturalists. One of the things they discovered in the natural law was that men have property rights prior to the existence of governments. Most modern lawyers, as good legal realists, want to insure that the designation of property rights is solely the province of the state, that is, in large part, of the lawyers. Rights, rather than constituting a moral presumption that transcends, precedes, and endures beyond the existence of any one state, are changeable, discretionary, and subject to political control.

Surely, there is some cogency to "lawyer's talk" about property. The layman's idea of property as the thing that man owns is, undoubtedly, simplistic. Certainly, rights enter into the picture. When "Alpha owns X" he has certain rights over X.[19] Perhaps it would prove felicitous to elevate the layman's view in order to incorporate the notion of rights. Then we would not abandon the ordinary person's insight that "Alpha owns X" is fundamentally a relationship between a person and a thing, and only derivatively between Alpha and the rest of mankind and their laws. This relation of ownership between Alpha and X entails certain negative duties placed upon all others. These duties can either be enforced by the laws of a state when breached or left to self-defense, as in that much maligned "state of nature" so beloved by political theorists of the eighteenth century. The advantage of this formulation is that it does not beg the question by building the suppositions of the legal realists into the very definition of property.

If we wish to analyze the meaning of the claim "Alpha owns X," it might prove useful to examine the proposition in a simple setting, without government, and limited to a small universe of actors. Let us imagine a world inhabited by three people, Alpha, Beta, and Gamma, in which there exist three desirable goods, X, Y, and Z. Alpha owns X; Beta owns Y; and Gamma owns Z. In the absence of any government,[20] what does the claim "Alpha owns X" mean? The following propositions formalize layman's view of the connection between Alpha and X when he uses the terms *ownership* or *property*.

If Alpha owns X, then:
1. Alpha can *possess, use* (e.g. transform, destroy, waste), and *transfer* (through voluntary exchange, gift, bequest) X at Alpha's discretion.[21]
2. Alpha must not use X or permit others to use X in ways that inflict injury upon (cause harm to) Beta and Gamma, or Y and Z.
3. If X harms Beta, Gamma, Y or Z,[22] Alpha is responsible for the damages and must pay full compensation.
4. Beta and Gamma do not own X,[23] and consequently they cannot possess, use, or transfer X without Alpha's consent.
5. If X is harmed by Beta (or by Beta's use of Y) or by Gamma (or by Gamma's use of Z), Alpha is entitled to compensation equivalent to the damage caused. That is, Alpha is entitled to be made whole again.
6. It is wrong for Beta or Gamma to take X away from Alpha against Alpha's will.[24] If X is taken by Beta or Gamma without Alpha's consent, Alpha has the right to recover X, or if X has been destroyed, to receive its equivalent (in money or goods).

The initial three propositions concern Alpha's privileges and responsibilities that ownership of X entails. The remaining three deal with the negative duties owed by Beta and Gamma to Alpha in Alpha's use and enjoyment of X. Now, if we extend our universe to include all valuable things and all individuals, nothing essentially changes. The picture simply becomes more cluttered. The likelihood of harms to X increases dramatically, particularly from what the economists term "spillover effects" or "externalities," e.g. air pollution, water contamination, noisome odors, annoying noises. The extent to which various degrees of these irritants constitute harms, and the extent to which ownership of X entails freedom from annoying and hazardous interferences, I can attempt to answer only after I formulate a property rights defense.

First it will prove helpful to examine the attempts by political theorists and economists to defend property rights. A complete theory of property rights ought to be internally consistent,[25] and deduced from an indubitable proposition or set of propositions. Furthermore, it should provide separate theories to explain how one comes to acquire property legitimately, what constitutes a proper use of that property, how one can transfer title to what one owns to another person, and what means one may employ to recoup one's property if it is taken, lost, or damaged.[26] In other words, we are seeking a logically unassailable theory that is composed of several discrete elements—theories of acquisition, legitimate use, transfer, and rectification.[27] A variety of offerings exist in the literature to explain all or part of these four elements. For example, concerning original acquisition (certainly the most troublesome hurdle to be surmounted by any theory that presumes to defend private property), arguments from first occupation, labor entitlement, divine ordination, historical accident, might makes right, or simply unmitigated force have been offered. Natural rights theories have competed with theories based upon social utility. Natural rights defenses of property emerged earlier in modern political thought, and so I will examine them first. An evaluation of utility as the justification of property along with its latest wrinkle, wealth maximization, will follow.

In the seventeenth century three works appeared by theoreticians who embraced the notion of a law of nature. Such a law is of universal application, trancends all bounds of time and place, and derives its content and force not from the caprice of man but from his God-given reason. No human convention, no matter the number who might concur nor the augustness of their reputations, could contravene this natural law. Indeed, in the work of the most radical of the three, John Locke's *Second Treatise of Government*, no government could claim its citizens' allegiance should it transgress the most sacred of all men's natural law privileges, the natural right to property. By *property* Locke included life, liberty, and estates. But let us first pause for a brief examination of Hugo Grotius's *De Jure Belli ac Pacis* (1625) and Samuel Pufendorf's *De Jure Naturae et Gentium* (1672), for Locke's argument was in many significant respects both a response to and an improvement upon theirs.

"God gave to mankind in general," Grotius intoned, in phrases destined to be echoed by his illustrious successors in the natural law tradition, Pufendorf, Locke, and Blackstone, "dominion over all the creatures of the earth, from the first creation of the world; a grant which was renewed upon the restoration of the world after the deluge."[28] Mankind, as joint inheritors of one "general patrimony," held all things of this earth as their "common stock."

Grotius next posed the question of how man moved from this common right to the goods of the earth to private ownership. Whereas Locke would seek his answer in the realm of logical deduction, Grotius, as did Pufendorf and later Blackstone, would find theirs in an historical rule synthesized from philosophers, poets, and the Bible. In the primitive state of innocence, Grotius wrote, man exercised a general right to seize for his own use or consumption whatever he needed, and it became unjust to deprive anyone of what he had once captured. Cicero's example of a theater seat as common property, yet the particular possession for a time of him who occupies it, would be rehearsed over and over again by natural law devotees. Such a state of affairs depended for its continuation upon a great simplicity of manners and goodwill, sentiments easily eroded as inventions undercut this idealic existence. A race of giants, strong and violent men, followed, only to be eradicated by the deluge and an era of sensuality and intoxication that culminated in the Tower of Babel and the dispersion of mankind. As the number of men increased, flocks became the property of individuals and pasture land remained in common. Finally, this too had to be divided.

> When the inhabitants of the earth began to acquire a taste for more delicate fare than the spontaneous productions of the ground, and to look for more commodious habitations than caves, or the hollow of trees, and to long for more elegant clothing than the skins of wild beasts, industry became necessary to supply those wants, and each individual began to apply his attention to some particular art. The distance of places too, into which men were dispersed, prevented them from carrying the fruits of the earth to a common stock, *and in the next place, the WANT of just principle and equitable kindness would destroy that equality which ought to subsist both in the labor of producing and consuming the necessaries of life.* [Emphasis added.][29]

It is worth our notice that Locke will completely drop this moralistic condemnation. It carries with it a prejudice that taints property ownership, implying as it does that if man were any better he would be worthy of a higher state, namely communism. Biblical and Greek myths of the fall and of a golden age corrupted by man's selfishness are baggage from the past prudently jettisoned by Locke.

How, then, did property move from communal ownership to the private preserve of individuals? Remember that Grotius, in contrast to Locke, is searching for an historical rather than a philosophical account of this occurrence. It could not have happened by a simple act of the mind, because a man could never know what others intended to appropriate unless he were given an outward sign. "Property therefore must have been established either by express agreement, as by division, or by tacit consent, as by occupancy." Grotius is often elusive and imprecise. What he seems to mean is that before anyone held anything by right, that is by the consent of others, he may have occupied various lands. It would have seemed natural to grant each man a right to that which he had occupied. Thus, private property hinges upon two factors—consent and first occupancy—with the former seemingly a higher-order principle than the latter. It seems that in theory at least, those who first consented to property could have chosen some principle of distribution other than the one Grotius suggests. But Grotius clearly prefers, to each that which he has occupied. All acquisitions that occur after the agreement to divide the land come out of that which is still left in common, under the principle of first occupancy.

Grotius's theistic background enters in, once again, when he allows for a reversion to the primitive right of all to use the common in cases of extreme necessity when all recourse to the magistrates or entreaties to owners have proven bootless. Thus, there is a residual right possessed by all, when suffering extreme duress, to claim portions of that which others hold as their private property. Grotius invented a reservation, supposedly written into the original agreement that established private property, in favor of this "primitive right of nature." Property, then, is not absolute. It is hedged in by duties to others and rights that the indigent can claim for succor. It is not a theft to take what is necessary to preserve your life; and the stock of every individual must be shared if the provisions for a voyage fall short. But one is bound, in more prosperous times, to pay restitution.[30] Grotius entertained other limitations upon property: men have a right to innocent use of the property of others when that use constitutes no hardship to the owner (e.g. free passage through a country); all men have a right to purchase the necessities of life at a reasonable price except when the owners need the goods for their own consumption; and where sovereignty has once been established, all land "would afterward be considered as holding by the laws of the country," and all rights to property must give way to the superior sanction of the law.[31]

In Locke's writings, private property is a natural right, but for his predecessor, Grotius, property in its first invention is a creation of human will. Once established, however, it becomes a breach of the law of nature for one man to seize the property of another. In this significant respect, Locke departs from the other natural law theorists. He holds a modern view of natural rights, where rights mean entitlements to things that men hold by virtue of their nature, combined with their acts. Grotius still held to a classical notion of natural rights as meaning simply something that is right or good by its conformity to reason, a use of the term embraced by Aristotle.[32] Thus, for Grotius, what is naturally right consists of two categories of propositions: principally, those things that are right independently of man's will, and derivatively, those things that become right because of the way man exercises his will. The case of property falls into the latter classification. Property is initially a creation of human will, but once established, it carries with it the force of natural right. Then it becomes wrong by the law of nature for one man to seize what another has once acquired. The formulation is reminiscent of that advanced by St. Thomas Aquinas.

Grotius's justification of property is problematic on several counts. To begin with, it is definitely not a defense of unlimited, individual dominion. It leaves substantial scope for claims by both the indigent and, even more expansively, by the sovereign. Indeed, Grotius went so far as to declare that "the sovereign has a greater right over the property of his subjects, where the public good is concerned, than the owners themselves have. And when the exigencies of the state require a supply, every man is more obliged to contribute towards it, than to satisfy his creditors."[33] And Pufendorf, Grotius's disciple, extended the argument in support of the right of indigents to seize necessities to include a positive duty upon the property owner enjoying a surplus to come to the aid of those in desperate straits.[34] Both theorists conceded that the *need* of some people places claims upon the property of others to the extent that the original community of property and its "natural equity" reemerges. All property is held, then, under a cloud. One's title and free use is good against all comers only to the extent that others subsist at a level that frees them from registering claims ("rights") of necessity against one's property.

Another problematic element in Grotius's argument is that it begins with common ownership of the goods of the earth among all mankind. Beginning a defense of private property by hypothesizing a pristine state of commonality is to undermine the proof at its inception. Locke struggled against the identical obstacle. It weakened both the appeal and the logical cogency of his position. Pufendorf, interestingly, appended a new wrinkle onto the common ownership phrase, one that Locke unfortunately did not adopt. Pufendorf distinguished between negative and positive community:

> The term community is taken either *negatively* or *positively*. In the former use things are said to be common, according as they are considered before the interposition of any human act, as a result of which they are held to belong in a special way to this man rather than that. In the same sense such things are said to be nobody's, more in a negative than a positive sense; that is, that they are not assigned to a particular person, not that they cannot be assigned to a particular person.[35]

In contrast, *positive community* means that things belong to several designated individuals in the same manner: they enjoy a common use. It is in the negative sense, of something that nobody owns, that Pufendorf speaks of common ownership in the state of nature. The argument would be improved appreciably if the notion of "common ownership" were jettisoned. It would be more felicitous to say merely that the goods of the earth were originally unowned.

Even more damaging than these two problems of positive and negative duties, and common ownership is the claim by Grotius and Pufendorf that property rights depend upon a human compact, that they are not an ineluctable outgrowth of the natural law. It was precisely this point that Locke took such great pains to dispel. He tried to demonstrate that private property could legitimately derive from common ownership without the mechanism of a compact. The danger of hinging property upon human consent appears most conspicuously if we follow Pufendorf's argument to its logical limit. The grant by which God allowed man to use the products of the earth for sustenance, Pufendorf concluded, does not provide the immediate cause of dominion, "but that dominion presupposes absolutely an act of man and an agreement, whether tacit or express." While God gave man an indefinite right to use the earth, its products and creatures, the manner and extent of that use were left entirely to human judgment: "Whether, in other words, they would confine it [property] within certain limits, or within none at all, and whether they wanted every man to have a right to everything, or only to a certain and fixed part of things,"[36] was entirely left to human discretion. Furthermore, all human conventions concerning property, provided they are neither self-contradictory nor destructive of society, are approved by the law of nature.

What undoubtedly prompted Locke to abandon this contention that all private property derives from human assent was the tenuousness of such a position. It placed all claims to dominion and, thus, to the exclusion of others from one's domain, upon nothing more solid than the whims of our progenitors. Also, a private property system would in no way be preferable, morally, to one grounded upon community of property or presumably, feudalism, or even slavery. All systems would reflect the dead hand of the past, mere accident and arbitrary caprice from the perspective of modernity. What if we follow Pufendorf's argument to limits that he would find regrettable? If current property distributions depend upon the assent of individuals dead for millenia, why can we not simply alter these patterns by a new compact? That is, if the principle of consent was the applicable one for the original establishment of property eons ago, why is it not applicable today? Obviously, none of us has consented to the current order of ownership. Why should we not have our say? Why should we defer to decisions of those long in their graves and certainly no more entitled to make them than we? Such implications, in addition to being revolutionary, are obviously, impossible to implement. Given the premise of equality that Pufendorf endorses, no group of individuals should ever be entitled to bind their successors. Would new compacts have to be negotiated along with the arrival of every new infant? No wonder Locke sought a buttress for property in something more solid than human will.

As if these faults were not serious enough, the property defense of the early natural law theorists is subject to an even more ominous fault. If men initially acquire their holdings by first occupancy or seizure, how does one delimit these claims? What we have, here, apparently is a serious boundary problem. (Locke would attempt to solve the problem by abandoning first occupancy in favor of the "mixing-one's-labor" principle, accompanied by the proviso that "enough and as good" be left for others). If one lays initial, or presumptive, claims to property by occupying what is unowned, what constitutes the outward sign of such an occupancy? Is it sufficient to whisper, "Yonder thing is mine," or must one declare to the world or inform every man that "this thing is mine"? Can one claim all of America for oneself if one happens to be the first arrival?[37]

The only possible resolution to these boundary problems within the Grotius-Pufendorf system is to repair to the compact for the establishment of property. Here, presumably, overblown claims can be whittled down by common consent. But, as we have previously demonstrated, this stratagem is far from unproblematic.

The boundary problem is even more extensive than previously indicated. Movable and landed property do not constitute the only possible objects of human acquisition. What about fluids (the oceans, major rivers) the air, the minerals beneath the earth, and so on? Both theorists simply deny that such fungible things can become a man's property. The reason is that they cannot be circumscribed within stationary bounds.[38] Surely the problem cannot be resolved in such a straightforward fashion. If one can come to own a portion of land by clearing a path or, more ambitiously, building a road, why can one not claim a sea-lane by being the first to sail upon that route? Why can't a man form a quadrant of the sea by carefully conserving the fish, providing food, or seeding the sea with new species of fish? The technological problems would be different, and probably more complex, but this complexity need not abrogate the principle of appropriation, at least not without a more persuasive rationale.[39]

John Locke's Attempt to Defend a Natural Right to Property

Viewed historically, Locke's theory of property was nothing if not revolutionary. It was a direct, if nowhere expressly stated, repudiation of the English land tenure system imposed upon the Anglo-Saxons by King William after the Norman Conquest of 1066. Given Locke's heated diatribe against the divine right of kings doctrine in his *First Treatise*, it should not be surprising that he rejected the feudal mode of land ownership, tied as it inextricably was to the claims of kingly preeminence. The victorious William, with but scant regard for the niceties of any philosophical theory of individual property rights, declared by force majeure all land in England forfeited to the crown. To his loyal men-in-arms, he distributed these rich spoils of war, but on the condition that various servitudes would be owed to the king. Thus the king's vassals were merely owners of various interests, or estates in land, while the king retained dominion over all the lands of the realm.

The final remnants of this feudal indenture lapsed only in 1660, a scant few decades before Locke penned his *Second Treatise*, when the Tenures Abolition Act nullified the last incidents of military tenure.[40] Despite the demise of these oppressive obligations that ran with the land, the common law pertaining to property remains to this day imbued with concepts adhering from the moribund tenurial system. The Continental civil law notion of land as held in absolute ownership or dominion by its possessor remains far removed from the Anglo-American separation of land and estates in land,[41] the latter generating such divided tenures as life estates, remainders, and reversions.

> The effect of all the encompassing tenurial system was that from its inception the common law recognized that ultimate title to all land resided solely in the king (the State). . . . The conception of absolute ownership with unlimited rights over a thing which could be exclusively enjoyed in the civil law sense of dominion did not, and does not, exist.[42]

Locke, the debunker of kingly divine prowess, skillfully manipulated biblical quotations to deny Robert Filmer's assertion that God expressly granted dominion over men to present kings through descent from Adam. Likewise, Locke cast aspersions, at least by implication, upon William's pretension to hold dominion over all real property in his realm. It is not the province of the state mercurially to grant lands to the king's favorites.

Rather, men come to government already in possession of lands by right far loftier than kingly discretion: by natural right.

Have we not discovered here the inception of a dispute that will take on a slightly altered guise in the nineteenth and twentieth centuries? Locke's natural-rights-based origin of private property first confronted the statist divine right of kings theory of the origin of property in the seventeenth century. In the next two centuries the natural rights theory was destined to fight a rearguard battle against a utilitarian theory of the beginnings of property, simply another albeit milder variant of the statist case. Just as the earlier statist heirs of King William argued that all property is a grant from the king as holder of ultimate dominion over all lands, the utilitarians would claim that all property rights are the creatures of the state. As such they are subject to alteration and even abrogation as circumstances, utility, and the opinions of the sovereign change. To both theories and to the inherited tradition of the common law, Lockean natural rights stands in substantial opposition.

Locke's defense of a natural right to property surpasses in logical inge-nuity that of his forebears Grotius and Pufendorf, yet in formulating his deduction as a counterpoint to theirs, he retained some rather inopportune features of their arguments. Banished from Locke's defense was the notion that a compact among men was required to validate private property, but communality of original possession in the state of nature and its correlative duties of altruism towards one's fellows still remained. This latter obliga-tion is expressed in a more muted fashion in the *Second Treatise* (as a duty upon everyone to preserve the rest of mankind when rendering such assis-tance does not jeopardize one's own preservation)[43] than in the *First Treatise*. There Locke echoes the sentiments of his natural law pre-decessors, thus preserving a seemingly insuperable barrier to any claims of absolute dominion over the land:

> God the Lord and Father of all, has given no one of us children such a Property, in his peculiar portion of the things of this World, but that he has given his needy Brother a Right to the Surplusage of his Goods; so that it cannot justly be denied him, when his pressing Wants call for it. . . . As *Justice* gives every Man a Title to the product of his honest Industry, and the fair acquisitions of his Ancestors descended to him, so *charity* gives every Man a Title to so much out of another's Plenty as will keep him from extreme want, where he has no means to subsist otherwise.[44]

This claim of "charity," theistic in origin, will reemerge, in the guise of the "enough-and-as-good-left-for-others" proviso, to cast a long shadow upon Locke's justification of individual property.

The problem that Locke sets for himself is a seemingly insoluble one. Can one demonstrate how men being by the law of nature all equal and independent and also the property of God, came to own separate portions of what God had so plainly granted to men in common?[45] Whether one consults natural reason or revelation it is apparent that God "has given the Earth to the Children of Men, given it to mankind in common."[46] Thus, Locke reflects, it seems to some observers an impossibility that such commonality can ever be transmuted into private property. "But I shall endeavor to show, how Men might come to have a *property* in several parts of that which Gad gave to Mankind in common, and that without any express Compact of all the Commoners."[47]

Property, then, accrues to individuals before the inception of government, while men still reside in the state of nature, and without the assent of any others. How is this transformation of communal property into private property accomplished without violating anyone's rights, and without depriving anyone of a God-given patrimony? Perhaps, it will prove felicitous to set out Locke's argument in as deductive a fashion as possible; herewith, Locke's proof of a natural right to individual property:

1. God gave the earth to mankind in common. (§25)[48]
2. God gave men reason to enable them to make use of the earth and all things therein. (§26) Including, one might add, all the inferior creatures which God made for the use of man. (§6) But before any of these goods of the earth can serve the needs of any particular man, there must be a means of appropriation, so that what food nourishes A can not henceforth be claimed as rightfully his by B. (§26)[49]
3. Although land and the inferior creatures are common to all men, yet every man has a property in his own person. (§27) Nobody else has a right to one's person.
4. Since every man owns himself, it follows that the "Labour of his Body, and the Works of his Hands" properly belong to him. (§27)
5. Whatever a man removes from the "State that Nature hath provided, and left it in, he hath mixed his *Labour* with, and joined to it something that is his own, and thereby makes it his *Property*." By mixing one's labor with something formed in nature one has annexed something to it that, thereby, excludes the common right of other men. (§27)

> Proviso I—By mixing one's labor with something out of the state of nature one acquires unquestionable property in it "at least where there is enough, and as good left in common for others." (§27)

By mixing one's labor with a thing and coming to own it exclusively, one has committed no robbery of what belongs to all in common, thus one's appropriation does not require the consent of all mankind. To claim otherwise, Locke argues, would be absurd, for then men would have starved to death despite the plenty God had lavished upon them. Here Locke undoubtedly claims too much; it is not that men would have starved without having a moral right to appropriate, for surely men would have eaten anyway, but that they would not have had a *right* to eat.

> Proviso II—God gave us all things to enjoy. The same law of nature that gives us property also sets bounds to that property. Therefore, spoilage and destruction are prohibited. "As much as anyone can make use of to any advantage of life before it spoils," belongs to the laborer, but whatever exceeds that limit belongs to others. (§31)

Thus, men are entitled to those fruits of the earth that they have mixed their labor with, provided that enough and as good remains for others, and that one does not sit idly by while such goods are destroyed or spoil.

6. One acquires property in land, as with movables, by mixing one's labor with it. "*As much land* as a Man Tills, Plants, Improves, Cultivates, and can use the Product of, so much is his *Property.*" (§32)

As was the case previously in regard to movables, appropriation does not hinge upon the consent of others, but it is limited by the same two provisions: that enough and as good remain in common for the like appropriation of others, and that spoilage must not occur. Indeed, Locke maintains that one's right to land extends not beyond what one can use, so that one does not possess a right to waste. In fact, the earth upon which a crop wasted might henceforth become the possession of any other man.

Far from constituting a theft upon the common, individual appropriation and use constitutes a benefaction upon the rest of mankind. The man who encloses ten acres of land and produces sustenance from it, rather than from one hundred acres left in their natural state, bestows a gift of ninety acres upon the rest of mankind.[50] Upon further reflection, the superfluity bestowed upon mankind appears even greater, until Locke hazards the opinion that usually ninety-nine hundredths of the value of any consumable good results from labor rather than nature. No wonder, then, that property in one's labor should entail ownership of the thing, rather than labor simply oozing out upon a thing.[51]

> Nor is it so strange, as perhaps before consideration it may appear, that the *Property of labour*, should be able to over-balance the Community of Land. For 'tis *Labour* indeed that *puts the difference of value* on everything . . . that the improvement of *labour makes* the far greater part of the value. (§40)

Locke has grasped something of immense significance here, but he has not fully exploited his insight. Look, he says, if man's labor creates ninety-nine hundredths or nine-tenths of the value of movable goods or land, should not those goods belong to their creators? But does this not leave the possessor still a thief, if only to the extent of one point in ten or one point in one hundred? Surely it does. Yet, we ought not be stymied. An argument can be made that man's labor (or, rather, his ingenuity) creates not just the preponderant portion of the value of any commodity but the *entire* value. This will be my argument, not Locke's, although it certainly would bolster Locke's contention that appropriation from the common constitutes no robbery.

As regards the enough-and-as-good proviso, Locke believes that abundance rather than scarcity describes the proportionality between men and available land. Had it not been for the introduction of money, and the entitlement to superabundance that such a vehicle legitimates, there would be land enough in the world for double its inhabitants.

7. Extended possessions—that is, those that exceed one's immediate consumption needs—can be validated by two means, i.e., by bartering away the excess for necessities, or by exchanging one's superfluities for gold or diamonds, durable goods that will not spoil. Thus, what surpasses the bounds of just property is the waste of useful things, and largeness does not ipso facto violate the boundary conditions. (§46-47)

Now, by the invention of money, something lasting that will not spoil, men unlocked the key to entitlements to larger possessions. For the useful but perishable supports of life, men agreed to exchange barren gold and silver. In contrast to the truly useful goods of the earth, such as food and clothing, money garners its value only from the consent of men. This agreement to the use of money occurs while men still reside within the bounds of the state of nature, and without a formal compact. Men simply put a value upon gold and silver and agree to exchange it for truly valuable commodities. The agreement, then, is merely a tacit one.

The invention of money entails not only the legitimation of large property holdings but also one further entitlement—to unequal possessions.

8. Men are entitled to their individual possessions acquired through labor and exchange, no matter that others may have title to less or more.

Industry is more the attribute of some men than others. Thus, possessions were likely to be somewhat unequal even before the introduction of money, and this would only become accentuated after the use of money provided the inventive with the opportunity to further enlarge their estates. After all, God gave the earth to the "use of the Industrious and Rational."

Thus, from communal property, and then possessions limited by spoilage and enough-and-as-good constraints, Locke purportedly established individual property rights to estates of whatever size, no matter how unequal they might be. The various steps in Locke's deduction merit careful scrutiny, for defenders of property rights of the natural rights school have never supplanted Locke's proof, usually offering variations upon Locke's theme.

Obviously, Locke has conceded too much to the adversaries of private property; opening your hand by delivering up your cards to the opponent is never a winning strategy. If admitting God into the argument involves one in such a patently weak strategy, then God ought to be summarily banished. God, vanquished from the property defense, would take along the fatal admission that the earth originally belonged to mankind in common. Such adjuncts of the commonality assumption as the enough-and-as-good proviso, the spoilage proviso, the claims of other men to one's superfluities before the invention of money, and the *deus ex machina* of the invention of money itself would likewise be jettisoned, as mere excess baggage. If we separate Locke's property defense from its historical context as a rebuttal to earlier natural law theorists, the mention of common ownership becomes completely extraneous. Observing Occam's razor, one could simply say that in the beginning the earth was unowned. One still would need to show how individuals came to have a right to distinct portions of the earth, but one would not have to lumber over supererogatory hurdles.

Step (3) presents another problematic component—that every man has a property in his own person. This remains merely an assertion, never proven. Does each man own himself because the law of nature, reason, teaches us that we are all equal and independent? Or because we are all the property of God? Or because we are all creatures of the same nature, thus barring any enforced, nonvoluntary subordination? One suspects that Locke had in mind some combination of these positions as justification for the self-ownership proposition, yet no explicit argument was ever forthcoming. Perhaps, he believed that such a claim was so self-evident that no argument was necessary. Unfortunately for Locke, others have not been so perspicacious, seeing instead in his claim mere tautology or vacuity.[52]

Even for Locke, this property in one's person is not absolute. Locke maintains that a man as the creation of God, cannot destroy himself by committing suicide, nor can he sell himself into slavery, thereby putting his very life at the mercy of another. In fact, all men have a duty, above all other duties, to preserve themselves. They cannot capriciously jeopardize the Lord's property in them. Thus, what Locke has propounded is an unsatisfactory theory of self-ownership in which men have both title to the use-value of their persons and the right to exclude others from using them, but not the ultimate rights of disposing of themselves completely to other men nor destroying themselves. These two latter rights belong only to God. Thus, man's ownership of himself is a right good against all other men, but it is not absolute. God retains certain incidents of ownership over each of us. Locke, then, not only fails to supply an argument for man's ownership of himself but also partially negates this asserted ownership by reserving certain rights in us to God.[53]

One modern defender of private property, economist, social critic, and anarchist Murray Rothbard, attempts to fill the Lockean lacuna by providing an argument for self-ownership. Rothbard's defense of what he takes to be the premier natural right, the right to property, rests upon a foundation of natural law. His conception of natural law begins with the insight that in a world comprising a vast number of diverse entities, each entity has its distinct and specific properties. Just as copper and iron possess particular characteristics that can be investigated and identified by man's reason, so man himself manifest a peculiar nature. By studying man's nature, the world in which he finds himself, and the modes of interaction between the two, certain necessary features of man's relationship to his fellows will emerge. Lacking the automatic instincts much in evidence in the behavior of plants and lower animals, each person on his own must learn about the world, use his mind to select his values, discover cause and effect, and act purposively to advance his life.

> Since men can think, feel, evaluate, and act only as individuals, it becomes vitally necessary for each man's survival and prosperity that he be free to learn, choose, develop his faculties and act upon his knowledge and values. ... [This is the] necessary path of human nature; to interfere with and cripple this process by using violence goes profoundly against what is necessary by man's nature for his life and prosperity.[54]

To interfere violently with another person's cognitive, volitional, or activating faculties is to engage in a profoundly "antihuman" act that "violates the natural law of man's needs."

The self-ownership axiom constitutes the linchpin of Rothbard's natural rights defense. If man's survival depends upon his ability to think, learn, value, and choose, then the right to self-ownership is paramount because it gives man the *right* to perform these life-sustaining activities. Of course, such reflections are merely dicta without a proof that men do indeed possess such a right to self-ownership. Rothbard attempts to construct such a proof negatively rather than positively, that is, by process of elimination, by excluding all other logical possibilities. If we consider the consequences of denying a right to self-ownership there are only two possible alternatives: either (1) a certain class of people, A, have a right to own another class, B, or (2) everyone has a right to own an equal, quotal share of everyone else. Now, alternative (1) implies that class A deserves rights attendant upon being human while class B remains subhuman with no rights. But this state of affairs would be patently contradictory, Rothbard contends, because the members of class B are just as human as the members of class A. Furthermore, such a dehumanization of class B would allow class A to live parasitically off the labor of its putative inferior, thus transgressing the basic economic requirements of life as implied by the law of nature, namely, production and exchange. This latter argument does not carry the force of the former, and appears to be nothing more than polemics. As regards the former, the refutation of an elitism of rights, while undoubtedly appealing, is reached all too facilely. It is precisely the claim of all tyrants, slaveholders, and redistributionists that they possess some faculty of merit, desert, need, or whatever that sets them apart and above the rights attendant upon being merely human. The argument cries out for a more detailed refutation of all of these claims as either unfounded or irrelevant.

Rothbard's refutation, as it stands, is an indicant, and a valuable one, of an argument, but it does not refute elitist rights, that is, the claim that being human is not the sole criterion of having rights, and that additional attributes are requisite before one has full property rights. Such an elitist view of rights, which would deny rights to class B, obviously contradicts Rothbard's view of natural law. Under the natural law all men possess the same nature and are, therefore, equal in the characteristics that matter the most from a moral point of view. But given a different view of either natural law or man's nature, the attribution of rights to classes of individuals would be very different. For example, Aristotle argued that some men, principally non-Greeks, were slaves by nature, and deserved their servitude. Nietzsche thought that some men, the supermen, were entitled to exercise their vitality by perpetrating almost any form of villainy upon the lesser forms of humanity. It is incumbent upon Rothbard to demonstrate that he has isolated the morally relevant features of human nature, and that this commonality, rather than any difference among men, should trigger the same rights for everyone.

The second logical possibility, that each person would have a right to own an equal quotal share of everyone else, rests upon an absurdity, Rothbard argues. It implies that while one is entitled to own a part of everyone else, one is not entitled to own oneself. Whatever entitles us to own shares in other humans, in other words, ought to entitle us to own ourselves. Paradoxes flow inexorably from such a position. No one could take any action (or rather to put it more precisely, have a right to take any action) without the prior approval of everyone else. A morality that leads to the destruction of mankind does seem fatally flawed. But, in actuality, this second alternative would collapse into the first. Because collective and unanimous control over each person's actions is inconceivable (e.g. all would have to vote on how each would vote, and on and on, leading to a *reductio ad absurdum*), power would rapidly devolve upon a ruling class.

One other logical possibility remains but it eludes Rothbard, who, one surmises, would find it equally absurd. What about this logical possibility—that nobody owns himself nor anyone else? But this is nothing more than a counsel of despair, an admission of failure, a confession that no morality, no moral code is possible. Men would act—gather fruit, beat up their neighbors, rape, pillage, and steal—with impunity. No one could remonstrate with the "aggressor," because no one would have a right to be free from "aggression." There would be no right and no wrong, and one could not distinguish between the aggressor and the victim.

Such a contemplation of a world without self-ownership and, hence bereft of morality, underscores the centrality of some conception of the ownership of persons to a moral system. Without a claim either of self-ownership or ownership of some by others, morality is inconceivable. The burden of proof should fall upon those who claim that there is some feature that distinguishes some men from others and entitles the better to rights they deny to the inferior. Rothbard's position, depending as it does upon an argument from properties common to all men, remains appealing, despite its incompleteness.

Now, let us rejoin Locke's argument and focus upon steps (5) through (8). It is apparent that in this portion of his argument, Locke attempts to surmount the boundary difficulties engendered by the theory of first occupancy as propounded by Grotius and Pufendorf. Leaving to one side the extraneous peculiarities introduced into Locke's proof by the spoilage and enough-and-as-good provisos, we will focus upon the labor theory of legitimacy. Is this any less problematical than the theory it replaced? Certainly not, for if one extends beyond the prosaic agricultural model Locke employs the same puzzles reemerge. Let us imagine a man who constructs a fence around 10,000 acres. Does he thereby acquire ownership of all that acreage, or merely of the thin band of land underlying the fence? By swimming in the ocean does one gain ownership of the passage, the seabed underneath, or the water displaced? If one sinks a well into a previously untapped underground pool of oil, does one then own the oil, the portion of the pool underneath one's surface land, or the entire pool no matter how large its extent?

Can Locke's simplistic criterion of entitlement—of mixing one's labor with an unowned thing—be salvaged in these tough cases? Lawrence Becker, in his book *Property Rights: Philosophic Foundations,*[55] suggests one possible remedy. He would reformulate Locke's mixing-one's-labor criterion of entitlement to read, people are entitled to hold as property whatever they produce by their own initiative, intelligence, or industry. These activities, loosely denominated labor, are purposive. This fact suggests a solution, namely, that the extent of land (or anything else) with which one's labor "mixes" for the purpose of acquisition would be defined by the purpose for which one labors. Becker wishes to distinguish such purposive labor-mixing from mere intent, declaration, occupation, play, or accidental improvement. Presumably, what he means is that some activity must be conducted in furtherance of one's purpose. This really does not get us very far. Indeed, it simply reprises Pufendorf's attempted delineation of the first-occupancy principle when he declared that the intention of the actor must be taken into account. What if one manages to be the first interplanetary sojourner on Uranus, and scientific speculation has it that the outer planets are loaded with diamonds? Does one acquire all those precious gems simply by entering one mine and declaring one's purpose to include complete ownership of all the diamonds reposing inside that entire planet?

Immanuel Kant, in a rather muddled presentation of an argument for a natural right to property, hints at another possible resolution of the boundary problem. He suggests that the right of taking possession of unowned things extends just as far as the person who wills to appropriate it can defend it.[56] Cultivation of the soil, Locke's criterion, is not necessary. It is a mere accident that would entitle the cultivator to possession only if the cultivator already owned the land (the substance) itself.[57] For Kant, unlike Locke, one comes to own virginal land prior to movables. Kant says that it is a postulate of Practical Reason "that every one is invested with the faculty of having as his own any external object upon which he has exerted his will," provided that it was not the prior possession of any other person.[58] Practically, one gains original acquisition by the following moves: (1) by prehension or seizure of an object that belongs to no one, by taking physical possession; (2) by a declaration of such possession, and by exercising one's free will in excluding others from using it; or (3) by appropriation in the sense of an idea of a legislative, common will, by which all are obliged to respect my act of will in appropriating the object.[59]

Kant's theory suffers from a Rousseauistic aberration, apparently. Once men join together to establish a juridical state, the sovereign becomes the proprietor and distributor of all land. This seemingly nullifies the force of original title from the state of nature. Thus, for Kant, all ownership in the state of nature is potential only; in fact, he states this explicitly.[60] Such an admission mortally wounds a natural rights defense of property, for property would be held only at the behest and sufferance of society. Indeed, Kant goes so far as to suggest that what the sovereign grants he can abrogate should shifting winds of public opinion dictate, provided only that indemnification be paid, e.g. in the case of church lands or the lands of the nobility.[61]

As a resolution to the boundary problem, Kant's suggestion is flawed. Limiting the extent of ownership by something as purely accidental and contingent as one's brute ability to defend one's claim seems hardly satisfying. And one would think, that force ought to be irrelevant from a moral point of view. If I have carried out Kant's three criteria for claiming original acquisition of a thing, why should my claim be any the less compelling because I happen to be a weakling, a cripple, or a pacifist? (What's more, given Kant's "categorical imperative," which directs that one act toward others in such a way that the maxim upon which one acts can be universalized, such a resort to force appears doubly irrelevant, if not contradictory. And the categorical imperative is the heart of Kant's moral system). Kant, then, provides little assistance in resolving Locke's boundary problem, which remains unsolved.

One further problem in Locke, among many still outstanding, deserves passing recognition. By the introduction of money into the property defense at steps (7) and (8), Locke intends to accomplish several things at once. These include transcending the spoilage proviso, and possibly the enough-and-as-good proviso (but this intention is far less clear), and justifying large and unequal estates. Locke maintains that by tacitly agreeing to the use of money men have implicitly agreed to inequality of possessions. But could this assent not be withdrawn once men were made cognizant of this supposedly necessary result of the use of gold and silver? Could they not shrink in horror from such a commitment? What then would become of Locke's property defense, when he could justify nothing more than the most limited and primitive type of possession? But notice what has transpired. For the hapless Locke, now, a critical portion of his property defense hinges upon nothing more solid than the consent of mankind, precisely the defect he was attempting to correct in the arguments of Grotius and Pufendorf. Recall that these two thinkers relied upon a compact among men to sanction the move from communal to private property. With ample justification, Locke found this reliance too unreliable. Lamentably, his own argument, at the critical juncture, fell victim to this same dependency upon the changing fashions of human whim.

Thus, a defense of property rights, grounded upon a natural rights formulation, has not heretofore been successful.[62] The most conspicuous ailments to which it has succumbed include the lack of a compelling defense of the self-ownership postulate, boundary problems left unanswered by the various principles of original acquisition, and the annoying tendency for a purportedly inexorable logical defense to hinge upon something as fanciful as human consent. Perhaps an attempt to break free from the structures of the Lockean paradigm will provide an avenue of escape from these conundrums. But first let us examine the efforts of the utilitarians in formulating a defense of private property.

Have the Utilitarians and Wealth Maximizers Succeeded Where the Natural Rights Theorists Failed?

Jeremy Bentham, that ingenious thinker, captured the antitheistic, antinatural law temper of his time. He formulated the archetypal defense of a utilitarian ethics and politics by refining a position but inchoately expressed in the works of Hume, Helvétius, and Beccaria, With Hume, Bentham shared an abhorrence of all morality derived a priori, and of all pretensions to universal, inexorable natural laws, and to all political arguments derived from the hypothesis of a state of nature and a social contract. Like Helvétius, Bentham adopted a moral system entirely founded upon human pains and pleasures. What is good, right, and just henceforth would be equivalent to what produces the greatest surplus of pleasure over pain. And the social maxim would become the greatest happiness for the greatest number. More rigidly consistent than Hume, Bentham abhorred any talk of natural laws or natural rights, fearlessly renouncing the older liberal tradition.

If one examines the notion of property held by contemporary lawyers, it becomes abundantly evident who was the victor and who the vanquished in this controversy between the natural law tradition and its utilitarian adversary. Today the conventional view of property simply echos that famous epigram of Bentham's: "Property and law were born together, and would die together. Before the laws property did not exist; take away the laws, and property will be no more."[63] The words of Justice Jackson in *United States v. Willow River Power Company* succinctly capture the modern view, with its pedigree in Benthamite utilitarianism: "Only those economic advantages are 'rights' which have the law back of them . . . whether it is a property right is really the question to be answered."[64] In other words, it is the function of courts—that is, the state—to determine what property rights individuals possess, rather than merely to safeguard rights that individuals have independent of state action. Perhaps Richard Powell expressed this view most clearly when he said that "property rights are not protected by the courts, but what the courts protect, these constitute property rights."[65]

For Bentham, the relation that comprises property is not material but rather metaphysical. It cannot be expressed exclusively by a physical proximity between the agent and the object, for one can own things continents away. In what, then, does property consist? "The idea of property consists in an established expectation," of being able to reap an advantage from the thing possessed, and this expectation "can only be the work of the law."[66] Were it not for the law, no enjoyment could be expected with certainty; for the savage, all possession is "miserable and precarious." As it was the work of the legislator that created the expectation that is property, so it is the task of the legislator to prevent derangements.

Of the four subordinate ends to be aimed at by the legislator in pursuit of the supreme end of maximizing the happiness of society—subsistence, security, equality, and abundance—security must take precedence, as the basis of all the others. Given this hierarchy of ends, Bentham argues that in all societies, irrespective of the mode of property distribution, the legislator ought to act in support of the existing property system. Whether the cultivator of the land is a proprietor, tenant, or slave does not matter.[67] Even if the amount of happiness produced by these systems dramatically diverges, the directive to the legislators is identical: preserve the status quo.

It is perfectly conceivable that a utilitarian more radical and more preoccupied with the immediate maximization of utility might heartily dissent from this tolerance of any system simply because it exists. Indeed, John Stuart Mill, Bentham's philosophical heir, proselytized for land nationalization. But Bentham took the long view. Aim directly at equality, and disaster will follow, thought Bentham, who still recalled the French Reign of Terror. Preserve security, and greater equality will eventually develop.

What this demonstrates, is that one can embrace either a radical or a conservative utilitarianism on the property question. If all property is the creature of the state—and both radicals and conservatives embrace this proposition—then one's strategy in any given situation would depend entirely upon one's "felicific calculus." If Bentham's calculator indicated that in the long run gradualism would maximize utility, rather than counseling the manumission of all the serfs of Russia immediately, the institution should be left to perish spontaneously as its usefulness waned. The more radical J.S. Mill's calculating machine might weigh the disutility of servitude as so onerous that the corresponding pleasure generated by its eradication would outweigh any pain to the slaveholders. Thus he would counsel immediate abolition. Utilitarianism, dependent as its formula is upon the calculator's estimation of other people's utilities, can justify immediate nationalization or denationalization, the abolition of slavery or its toleration, and so on. Given the impossibility of estimating an individual's utilities, and also comparing them with those of others, utilitarianism becomes indeterminate. Every legislator or social theorist who does the calculations is likely to come up with a different solution to maximizing the happiness of society. Property, then, cannot find a sound defense based upon such a foundation.

If it lies within the power of the legislator to determine what property rights citizens possess, then, logically, it must lie equally within the legislator's prowess to abrogate those rights, or extend them, or create new rights that weaken the old ones. Charles Reich, in an earlier incarnation as a staid Yale professor of law, before the *Greening of America*, constructed an elaborate defense of property based upon the utilitarian contention that property is the creation of law. The "new property" embodies what is the principal defect of utilitarianism, its fickleness. Reich brilliantly documents the corruption, elitism, and immorality of the bureaucratic state in its regulatory discretion and dispensation of government largess. He then proceeds to elucidate the necessary connection between liberty and property. "Property," he writes, "performs the function of maintaining independence, dignity, and pluralism in society by creating zones within which the majority has to yield to the owner. . . . in the final analysis the Bill of Rights depends upon the existence of private property."[68] But, then, (strangely) the solution to governmental encroachment upon individual liberty through the "New Feudalism" of the "public interest state," lies not in curtailing government largess—welfare payments, subsidies to industry, trade barriers, and the like—but, rather, in an extension of the concept of property to include all of these bounties. Reich wants to make professional licenses, food stamps, and welfare into property rights. In this way he thinks liberty can be protected. No one could be divested of newly won entitlements except by due process of law and some fault on the part of the individual. Because all property was originally the grant, or largess, of government, Reich argues, why not grant the same to those who live as the dependents of the state?

Reich goes so far as to suggest that a new property should be created in unemployment compensation, public assistance, and old age insurance—a veritable Homestead Act for the dependent. Have we not witnessed here a *reductio ad absurdum* of the utilitarian position? Property is necessary to safeguard liberty. Therefore grant property in other people's property to those people whose claims for benefits justify the very bureaucratic state that threatens liberty.

In recent years an interesting attempt has been made, by Ronald Coase, Harold Demsetz, and Richard Posner most prominently, to propound an "economic theory of property rights." Led primarily by legal theorists imbued with the free market economic views of the Chicago school, they have attempted to apply economic analysis to the law. Economic analysis, they contend, can uncover the underlying principles by which judges have in actuality adjudicated property rights disputes in the common law. More importantly, such analysis can show judges how they ought to decide such instances of conflicting rights in the future. In its earlier version, the theory appeared markedly utilitarian. That is, the objective of the judicial process was to minimize the more serious harm in cases of conflicting uses of property, where A's use of his property and B's use of his proved incompatible. It was left to Posner, in two important articles,[69] to provide a novel philosophical underpinning for the "economic analysis of law." By jettisoning and discrediting its assumed utilitarian underpinning, and replacing it with another normative standard—wealth maximization—he tried to free economic legalism from some of the anomalies associated with utilitarianism. What is common, however, to both utilitarianism and wealth maximization is the attempt to justify the possession of private property instrumentally. Private property is justifiable because it produces desirable outcomes for society or individuals. Like utilitarianism, wealth maximization rejects the notion that there are a priori rights inhering in persons.

Now, this instrumentalism can be seen most clearly in a seminal article, "Toward a Theory of Property Rights," written by Demsetz.[70] In the world of Robinson Crusoe, he argues, property rights would be absolutely irrelevant. However, in a world populated by many individuals, property rights become useful. They are "an instrument of society" by which it facilitates an individual's formation of expectations in dealing with his fellows. Property rights, in other words, specify how persons may be benefited and harmed, and thus who must pay whom to modify disagreeable actions. The primary function of private property becomes that of guiding incentives to achieve a greater "internalization of externalities." In this way individuals are made to bear the costs and benefits of their own activities and to absorb the costs of inflicting spillover effects upon others.

This process of designating property rights is far from static. It encompasses a fluid and ever-changing attempt to define new property rights in order to accommodate new cost-benefit possibilities. Demsetz propounds his central thesis: property rights develop to internalize externalities when the gains of internalization outweigh the cost of internalization. And he offers as an example the case of the abolition of the commons among American Indians with the advent of the fur trade. In this case the externality of overhunting led to the introduction of private property.

For Demsetz and his colleagues, then, private property is justified teleologically and historically by its good *economic* effects at a particular point in time. Private ownership appeals to the economist on several scores: (1) it attempts to maximize present value by factoring in alternative futures and their benefits and costs, and then selecting the course that maximizes the present value of the resource, and (2) it takes into account factors of supply and demand after the owner's death, as the owner constantly acts as the broker for his property, thus speaking for the good of future generations. Communal ownership, on the other hand, lies impugned on these grounds and others: (1) it ignores the good of future generations by the absence of anyone whose role it might be to act as agent for those who are yet to be born; (2) it leads to overuse of the resource because agreements to restrict use require a high cost of reaching an initial compact and high policing costs (or, in the jargon of the economists, high "transaction costs"); and (3) it results in great externalities as the full costs of an individual's activities upon the common are not borne directly by him.

While the designation of private property rights alleviates the externality problem, by concentrating the costs and benefits upon individuals, providing them with an incentive to employ their resources more efficiently, it does not provide a complete solution. If I consider constructing a dam on my property, I still do not factor into my cost-benefit analysis the effects of lowering the water level on my riparian neighbor's land. Economic defenders of property rights, hence, see a not inconsiderable role for the state in handling these cases of externalities. By redefining property rights, or by more inventive schemes, such as selling rights to pollute, or taxing polluters so that "optimum" levels of pollution are achieved, the state has an important role to play. Here, again, their approach differs radically from that of the modern natural rights theorists. The latter would condemn both schemes, and in addition deny that property rights should be redefined by the state merely to reduce harms or maximize benefits without regard to the intrinsic rights of individuals. As an example of this divergence, let us imagine that smoke polluters are prohibited from belching smoke into the air, a privilege they heretofore exercised with impunity. The economists of private property might argue that the polluters ought to be compensated for a change in the law that redefined away their existing property right that had permitted them to disgorge a "diseconomy."[71] In marked disagreement, the natural rights advocate would deny that polluting other people's property or air could ever constitute a "right." Hence, the polluters would be entitled to no compensation for being forced to desist from their harmful behavior. The economist of property, then, favors property because it promotes the efficient allocation and use of resources, while the natural rights philosopher endorses property because it promotes justice.

The divergence of the two schools is even more apparent when one examines the contribution of Ronald Coase in his "The Problem of Social Cost."[72] This is the most widely respected and influential piece embodying the Chicago school's approach to property rights. Coase develops a theory that should tell us how property rights ought to be distributed by courts in cases where there is a conflict between A's use of his property and B's use of his. Coase's deviation from the standard rights-based analysis of an externality situation is immediately evident. He contends that the problem is not simply one of A inflicting harm on innocent B, but rather one of reciprocal harms. For example, Coase argues that if factory A emits noxious fumes that penetrate airspace over B's house and sicken B, factory A has harmed B. But for B to attempt to stop A from polluting would constitute a harm to A. The problem for the legal system, on Coase's account, is to avoid the more serious harm.

Unfortunately, this argument plays havoc with commonsensical notions of causation. Let us imagine that Alphonso, enraged at a particularly revealing costume worn by belly dancer Daphne, avails himself of a nearby machete and decapitates the unfortunate woman. Has Alphonso harmed Daphne? Certainly. Has Daphne harmed Alphonso? Certainly not, if ordinary notions of harm, aggression, and causation hold any weight. But Coase would argue otherwise. After all, were it not for the proximity of Daphne's head to the machete, Alphonso would have swung with impunity, causing no harm, so her being there may be interpreted as the cause of his commission of the murder. Furthermore, any attempt on her part to prevent the decapitation would be understood as causing harm to Alphonso. Such a result makes Coase's view of reciprocal harms suspect. His theory renders otiose not only the concept of cause and effect but also that of personal responsibility, which underlies the common law tradition both of the criminal and tort law.[73]

Without devolving into extraneous details that extend the argument beyond our needs, Coase's main point is that from a social point of view the composition of output for the economy will be the same whether or not individuals who create diseconomies bear the liability for those damages. In the absence of transaction costs, it is irrelevant whether a farmer growing crops has the right to be free from damage caused by the wandering cattle of a neighbor, or the cattle owner has the right to be free from paying damages for the harm inflicted by his cattle. The two parties will bargain together to reallocate the original distribution of property rights anyway, and the mix of cattle and crops arrived at will be identical no matter how rights are originally assigned. But if we examine the individual pattern of distribution rather than the aggregative, it matters greatly to the cattle owner and the farmer which one of them acquires the original right. It makes all the difference in the world whether I, as the rancher, *have to pay* for the right to let my cattle wander freely and inflict damages, or whether I *receive payment* to desist from my cattle-grazing practices. Coase, and Posner after him, would not gainsay this point; however, they would view it as irrelevant to their position because what they are concerned about is the aggregate picture, that is, with maximizing wealth for society and not with the distribution of goods among individuals.[74] It is ironic that a view that sincerely intends to be supportive of individualism and property rights, is actually collectivist, and just as aggregative as utilitarianism. There is an even more serious problem with Coase's position. If maximization of production is the objective of the law in cases of conflicting harm, why stop there? Why should we wait for an actual conflict? Why should not the law seek to redistribute and even confiscate private holdings whenever overall production would benefit thereby?

Once transaction costs are factored in—the costs of reaching and policing bargains—the Coasian picture changes. It becomes increasingly difficult, particularly when the number of parties is large, as it would be in typical pollution cases, for the affected individuals to bargain for rights. Then, Coase says, the original assignment of rights becomes highly significant, because it will in all likelihood remain the final distribution of rights. Thus, it is important for judges initially to assign rights, when transaction costs are positive, to that party who would buy them if transaction costs were zero. Coase examines a hypothetical case. If a train emitted sparks that destroyed a farmer's crops, and the value of the product produced both by all trains and the marginal train were greater than the value of the crop produced by adjacent farmers, a judge should assign the right to spew sparks without incurring liability to train owners. They would buy the right if transaction costs were absent. Again, in contrast to the natural rights position, all rights are up for grabs. The only relevant factor is minimizing harms conceived now as equivalent to costs to society. The hapless farmer whose crops sustain uncompensated damages would gain little solace from the knowledge that his suffering was justified by the minimization of loss to society! Why should the farmer find satisfaction here when by the nonaggressive, noninvasive cultivation of crops that are unfortunately inflammable, he subjects himself to total loss?

According to Coase, the economic problem in cases of harmful effects, and by implication the problem as jurists ought to conceive it once enlightened by economists, "is how to maximize the value of production."[75] Now, this is precisely the point at which Posner attempts to construct a normative principle for the economic analysis of property rights with his concept of wealth maximization. (In 1981 Posner was appointed to the Seventh Circuit Court of Appeals in Chicago where he has performed prodigious labors and greatly advanced the cause of economic analysis in the law.) After having been impugned by his critics as nothing more than a utilitarian, Posner formulated a refutation of utilitarianism. He sought to replace utilitarianism's happiness-maximization value with wealth maximization. He hoped this would avoid some of the more flagrant deficiencies committed by the traditional utility maximizers.

Posner examines utilitarianism[76] and finds it wanting, in the process rehearsing some familiar objections to the doctrine, such as the following. (1) The boundary problems that are endemic to the view. Does one include animals in the universe of creatures to be made happy? And what about foreigners and the unborn? (2) Does one maximize average or total happiness? (3) How does one measure subjective values objectively, or calculate the effect of any given ruling upon total happiness? (4) And what about the "utility monster"—how does one weigh the happiness of the thief or the unproductive, those who achieve happiness by depriving others of theirs? Finally, Posner rejects utilitarianism because of the "peril of instrumentalism" perceived in it. Rights for the utilitarian are merely instrumental goods, subservient to the final good of happiness and hostage to it.

Using "wealth maximization" as the maximand, in place of happiness, Posner hopes will avoid the pitfalls to which utilitarianism succumbed. But what is wealth maximization? Posner embraces a definition of his own position advanced by one of his critics, Ronald Dworkin: Wealth maximization "is achieved when goods and other resources are in the hands of those who value them most, and someone values a good more if and only if he is both willing and able to pay more in money (or in the equivalent of money) to have it."[77] What matters for wealth maximization is ability to pay. Mere desire for a good entitles one to nothing. While in utilitarianism such an idle desire might provide a claim to a good, in wealth maximization the only thing that counts is begin able to pay more for it than other competitors are willing or able to, and more for it than the value the owner places upon it. Thus, in a system of wealth maximization, resources are *efficiently* allocated when there is no reallocation that would increase the wealth of society; that is, when no one values a good (and has the money to purchase it) more than the person who holds it.

This definition of wealth maximization appears problematic from the outset. Wealth maximization, as Posner defines it, can never be achieved. Can one imagine—with the myriad of goods in existence, shifting desires and needs, and a numerous and constantly changing cast of characters as some are born and others die—a situation of complete and utter stasis in which no movements were possible, in which all goods were in the hands of those who valued them most? Such a state of affairs is inconceivable. The natural rights position does not suffer from such a problem, for it is perfectly conceivable that a situation could exist in which people compossibly exercise their rights while violating no one else's rights. Utilitarianism, too, seemingly avoids this dilemma because it is satisfied if society strives to maximize the sum total (or the average?) of utility, and is satisfied by the process itself.

Furthermore, Posner appears to have succumbed to an illusion in his definition of wealth maximization, the illusion that the money value placed upon a good by an individual represents the "real" value of the good, and thus by A's placing a higher monetary value on a good than X, Y, and Z do, A has maximized the wealth of society by acquiring that good. An example will serve to illustrate the illusory nature of Posner's wealth maximization. If X owns a sand dune that no one heretofore was willing to purchase for more than $10, and then a sand fetishist comes along and offers $10,000 for it, has society's wealth been maximized? A utilitarian would argue that *individual* utility has been increased, and since for the utilitarian happiness is nothing more than the sum total of the happiness of individuals, society's utility would be maximized. X would have $10,000 which X values more than the sand dune or the exchange would not have taken place, and the sand fetishist has the sand dune, which maximizes the fetishist's utility or the fetishist would not have exchanged. But what about wealth, has it been increased? Before the exchange at time T_1, society had a sand dune and $10,000 (which really meant society had a sand dune, and little pieces of paper). After the exchange at time T_2, society has a sand dune and $10,000. The total of society's goods—its wealth—has not been augmented in the slightest; merely, the goods have changed hands. To argue otherwise is to make a whole series of unsubstantiated assumptions: (1) that those who are willing and *able* to pay more for a good will put it to a greater productive use that will benefit society; (2) that goods are somehow more valuable to society when in the hands of the rich who can outbid the poor for them, even though the poor person might need the goods more, or make greater productive use of them; (3) that it makes a difference in real terms to the wealth of society whether a loaf of bread costs one dollar or, due to inflation, fifty dollars.

The waters become even murkier when Posner instructs his critics that the principle of wealth maximization is equivalent to a variant of the Pareto-efficiency standard. Now, Posner rejects two variants of the Pareto formula, that of Pareto-optimality and Pareto-superiority in favor of a third, Kaldor-Hicks efficiency. In contrast to the latter, the two former demand that there be no losers in a process of free exchange or government reallocation of rights. Jules Coleman succinctly defines these two principles:

> Resources are allocated in a Pareto-optimal fashion if and only if any further reallocation of them can enhance the welfare of one person only at the expense of another. An allocation of resources is Pareto-superior to an alternative allocation if and only if no one is made worse off by the distribution and at least one person is improved. These two conceptions of efficiency are analytically related in that a Pareto-optimal distribution has no distributions Pareto-superior to it.[78]

Posner embraces the Kaldor-Hicks variant of the Pareto criteria that does not demand that all losers be compensated. A reallocation of resources is Kaldor-Hicks efficient if it enables the gainers to compensate the losers, whether or not they actually do so.[79]

To see how Kaldor-Hicks or wealth maximization would handle a judicial dispute over property rights, let us examine an example hotly disputed by Posner and Ronald Dworkin. Derek's home is reduced in value by $2,000 as a result of noise emanating from Amartya's airline. Posner writes: "Derek sues the airline alleging a nuisance. The evidence developed at trial shows that it would cost the airline $3000 to eliminate the noise and thereby restore Derek's home to its previous value, and on these facts the court holds that there is no nuisance."[80] This illustrates, argues Posner, how a system of wealth maximization would operate in the common law system. Alternatively, Posner would say that if the loss in value for the house were $10,000 there would be a nuisance.

Obviously, the problem with wealth maximization in its Kaldor-Hicks guise is that it, again, looks to aggregative phenomena, namely, redistribution of goods or rights to those who are most productive, or can use them better, while allowing gross, uncompensated injuries to fall on the unlucky losers. Economists don't deal in justice but efficiency,[81] and thus Kaldor-Hicks holds no brief for the losers.

But Posner thinks he has discovered a strategy that will satisfy the notions of justice we ordinarily hold. He attempts to fuse wealth maximization with what he terms a "Kantian" concern for individual autonomy. If one could imagine that individuals had consented to uncompensated losses, then individual autonomy would not succumb to Kaldor-Hicks, uncompensated moves. Posner proceeds to argue that people can be understood to have consented to wealth-maximizing institutions by accepting ex ante compensation. Many involuntary, uncompensated losses, he contends, that occur in the market or in institutions that take the place of the market where it operates inefficiently, are fully compensated ex ante and hence these losses are consensual.[82] As an example, Posner cites the difference between strict liability and negligence in automobile insurance, maintaining that if negligence were in fact a cheaper system, all individuals could be conceived as having consented to it even though some people who suffer injuries will not get ex post compensation (e.g. where no one was at fault in the accident) that they would have under strict liability. This argument, Posner says, resembles that of the welfare economists who defend Kaldor-Hicks as satisfying the Pareto-superiority criterion provided that, in the long run, individuals will benefit from similar public policies even though they remain losers under a present policy. As a further example, Posner introduces the losses suffered by a homeowner when a major plant moves away from the city, thereby depressing the property value of the home. Under the notion of ex ante compensation, the probability of the plant's moving was discounted in the original purchase price of the house.

Now, this argument of ex ante compensation is really vacuous because it can be extended to justify almost any kind of oppressive loss. Imagine that

California decrees, going even beyond the California Coastal Act, that no further development will be permitted within one thousand feet of the coast, and that no compensation will be paid. Even though Posner rejects such "takings" and, indeed, would like to limit the scope of even eminent domain with compensation,[83] his "ex ante compensation" concept can justify such an activity by simply alleging that the initial price of the property discounted for the probability of such a loss, so property owners deserve no ex post compensation and have actually consented to their loss ex ante. Obviously, such a notion of consent can justify almost any expropriation. It appears that the concepts of individual autonomy and consent have become vacuous. If someone murders me, have I consented to my death by participating in a system in which all people are not permanently constrained or manacled so that they could not engage in aggressive behavior, a system that is wealth maximizing?[84] Thus, Kaldor-Hicks, or wealth maximization appears indefensible on the grounds that Posner chooses to justify it, i.e., individual autonomy and consent.

Any complete moral system should inform us about how initial entitlements ought to be distributed. Posner claims that wealth maximization can generate a set of rights to liberty and property much more inviolable than those justified by utilitarianism. Economic liberty, keeping of promises, telling the truth, altruism, rights, and corrective justice can all purportedly emerge from the ethical principle of wealth maximization, placing the "Calvinist" virtues on a new foundation. That this attempt to derive morality from economic principles fails[85] can be seen most conspicuously in Posner's attempt to employ the principle of wealth maximization to derive an initial distribution of rights to goods. He says that rights ought to be assigned in a manner that will maximize wealth. But what of the original position (and Posner explicitly adverts to John Rawls), how should such valuable rights as the right to human bodies and labor be distributed? If transaction costs were zero, it would be a matter of indifference where an exclusive right was initially vested; the market would reallocate the right to the person who valued it most through a series of voluntary exchanges. If transaction costs are positive, a realistic assumption, then rights should initially go to those who are likely to value them the most. Workers ought to get the right to sell their labor, all persons should have a right to life, and women the right to choose their sexual partners.[86] If A is granted freedom in the first place, A will not have to enter into a transaction with B to buy freedom. Freedom is more efficient than slavery; therefore, individuals should be given ownership of themselves in the original position because they would purchase this right if they could from whoever had it.

Anthony Kronman and Ronald Dworkin[87] have succeeded in demolishing this claim to extract basic rights from wealth maximization. How can one tell that Alfred values his own body and labor more than Bernard does, when valuing under the principle of wealth maximization can be signaled only by willingness and *ability* to pay? If no one is entitled to anything in the beginning, how can anyone ante up anything of value with which to purchase title to his or her person? One cannot. Some principle other than wealth maximization must be employed, however surreptitiously, in order to escape this dilemma. Any cogency that Posner's position has derives from a subtle, and on his own grounds, illegitimate employment of adhesions from the natural rights position. For example, in enumerating the implications of the wealth maximization principle, Posner states that it implies, first, "an initial distribution of individual rights (to life, liberty, and labor) to their 'natural owners.'"[88] Obviously, this concept of "natural owners" is one innocently borrowed from Posner's adversaries. It is difficult to see how a system of wealth maximization could ever emerge from the original position without importing some alien principle governing initial entitlements. Thus, Posner's theory fails our first criterion for a defense of property: that it assign exclusive rights to individuals initially; that it provide a theory of original acquisition.

Utilitarianism and wealth maximization have both failed to provide a defense for private property that is internally consistent. Both systems are collectivist; utilitarianisms seeks to maximize society's happiness, and wealth maximization aims at "maximizing society's wealth." Rights that individuals possess, whether they be rights to life, liberty, or property, are held in both theories subject to overriding claims by society, society being the ultimate grantor and guarantor of such rights. All rights must succumb upon demand to either the utility- or wealth-maximizing objectives of society. Posner's wealth maximization, like utilitarianism, proved incapable of generating personal or property rights that were anything more than instrumental values. Posner has fallen victim to precisely the fault that he discerned in utilitarianism, namely the insecurity and instrumentality of rights.

In the case of the wealth-maximization, economic-analysis-of-law school, I note this failure with a good measure of regret. Demsetz, Coase, and Posner sincerely wish both to render property rights more secure and to bring some principle to the law that will make it more rational. These are worthy objectives. This makes the apparent weaknesses in their foundational principle—wealth maximization—an occasion for rethinking the usefulness of continuing to pursue these two objectives through essentially utilitarian means. If we wish to construct a theory that will provide principles for rationalizing the law, particularly the law on takings, perhaps we need to look in another direction. Case-by-case, *ad hoc* decision making has been a failure. Utilitarianism and its latest wrinkle, wealth maximization, are flawed and cannot lead us out of the muddle. What do we have to lose by exploring a new strategy?

Can a Natural Right to Property Be Defended?

We have seen that utilitarian theories of property cannot help us out of the morass of current decisional law on eminent domain and police power. Let us return to natural rights theory. Locke's deduction of a right to property certainly suffered from lapses in logic, and the self-ownership axiom remained unproven. Yet the allure of such an approach persists. If it were successful, it would enfold individuals within a protective layer of rights, immune from the depredations of any overzealous government. Individuals with their attachments to property would be logically prior to the state, the protector of their rights, and their "fiduciary," to use Locke's term, rather than their overlord.

Stage 1

How might one go about the process of deducing a right to property? As adumbrated earlier, a complete theory must be logically unassailable and provide within its bounds four elements: a theory of original acquisition, legitimate use, transfer, and rectification. I propose to proceed by first examining the necessary conditions for man's life, that is, for the survival of any hypothetical or "ideal type" man, and second, exploring the limitations upon these conditions of human survival imposed by the earthly environment man inhabits.

Why should one begin the process of justifying a moral order by investigating its propensity to maximize the chances of survival of an "ideal" man? The survival of the individual actor, or agent, is the minimal condition without which the pursuit of all other goals, desires, needs are impossible. This criterion of existence is the necessary requirement for anything else that makes life desirable. Thus, for each individual, pursuing the strategy that will maximize chances of survival—that is, make it the least contingent, the least dependent upon forces beyond his control, and the least reliant upon the actions of other individuals—will provide a foundation from which he can proceed to choose other values and objectives.

One may wonder why it is necessary to justify a moral order at all. If morality, right and wrong, were excluded from people's conceptual framework, people would still act, they would still appropriate goods. But they would not possess any *right* to those necessities, and others could, for example, devour parts of their bodies with impunity. Albert could not chastise Roger for munching on Albert's toes by declaring that he, Albert, had a right to exclude others from partaking of his body against his will, and that it was therefore wrong for Roger to dine on his appendages. Such an amoral state of affairs, where the survival of each depends on might and fortune, the shabbiest of contingencies, would be wholly unacceptable if our strategy is to maximize the survival chances of each hypothetical person. Survivalism necessitates the justification of a moral order. Some actions must be wrong, that is countersurvival when examined from a long-range perspective, and generalized for an entire population (à la Kant's categorical imperative), while others are right. Men must have rights to exclude others from performing wrong, or countersurvivalist activities.

Now, if each hypothetical person must value his or her survival, does that entail that the person must value the survival of all other persons? There is certainly nothing necessary about such a valuation, but out of pure self-interest it would be prudent to reflect that, given the fact we are all creatures of the same species, every other person must likewise seek his or her own survival. There is nothing in the argument for survivalism that differentiates one actor from another at this stage of the argument.

Our hypothetical man, Alpha I, needs the same rudimentary requirements to sustain his life as would any other man. Alpha I, thus, can stand for all men in their primitive, necessitous state. He is undifferentiated man. The conditions of his continued existence include the following: food, air, water, shelter, and clothing (in most climates), a spot of earth to stand upon, and perhaps a weapon to fend off beasts. None of these necessities are provided gratis by the environment, nothing comes automatically. There are no guarantees. Perhaps, if men were sustained externally by great godlike machines, with no effort required on their parts, no morality would be necessary. But we do not typically exist as coma victims, sustained by the magnanimous intervention of external forces beyond our control. If man did not act, did not choose to act as agents, he would die. Labor and effort, even in the crudest sense of exerting oneself in the act of breathing, or stooping to pick up a fallen apple, are the price men pay for their continued existence. This labor exaction is really a requirement imposed by a combination of our own necessitous nature and the earthly environment, which proved so abstemious and ungenerous as to refuse to provide a *deus ex machina* to fill our every need.

Earthly conditions, then, place limitatins upon man's survival. In the earth's natural, unimproved state, there do not exist goods in sufficient abundance and location to fulfill man's needs, given any but the most meager assemblage of population in a given locale. Weather, natural calamities, and unreconstructed predators threaten imminent disaster. The fact that Alpha I is not alone in the world presents additional challenges and potential depredations. Given these conditions, and the fact that men are not immortal, there are no guarantees for survival.

Man must act or labor, I have previously argued, in order to attain the rudiments necessary for his survival. This action, then, is purposive, that is, it is not simply behavior or reaction to stimuli, as in an amoeba or a plant reacting to light. Purposive activity aims at an end, and in this case the end is the agent's own survival. As Alpha I extends his arm to pluck a mango from a tree, his immediate purpose is to satisfy his hunger; his ultimate purpose is to sustain his life. What, we might inquire, are the conditions of purposive activity? The motility of the agent, obviously, is the paramount requirement: that Alpha I be free to move about; that he be free from constraints upon his physical person; that he be not bound down, enclosed, manacled, or stymied by the overweening force of other individuals. This motility condition is the same for all humans. A must move in order to survive; B must move in order to survive, . . . N must move in order to survive.

But in addition to this motility requirement, man must also be able to act upon material things, to touch, pick up, mold, transform matter. Here it is difficult to avoid Locke's felicitous, though not uncontroversial, metaphor of mixing one's labor with earth's natural endowments. Idle flailing about simply will not do. In such a fashion sufficient air might be acquired, but as for the rest of the goods necessary for man's survival, all depend upon an agent's acting upon matter.

What we have established thus far is that in order for Alpha I to survive, he must be able to move and to act upon matter. But does he have a *moral right* to engage in these two activities? That is, does he have a motility right and a property right? Or reciprocally, does anyone else have the right to inhibit his free movement or his interaction and acquisition (by assimilation to his body) of the material accoutrements of survival? Can one conceive of a reason for denying these two rights to Alpha I? In Rothbardian fashion, let us examine the possibilities. (1) Alpha I has no rights to motility and acquisition of matter, and neither does anyone else; (2) Alpha I has no rights, but some or all others do have rights; and (3) Alpha I has rights and so does everyone else. The first alternative is clearly unacceptable for the reasons expressed earlier, i.e., that a world bereft of morality is a world in which the survival of anyone is rendered as radically contingent, fleeting, and precarious as it could possibly be. Such an amoral universe is also logically absurd. Survivalism necessitates morality and rights, for without them purposive activity, aiming at the survival of the agent, is rendered as precarious and uncertain of fulfillment as possible. To deny rights to all is to augment the necessitous nature of man and the abstemiousness of nature with an additional hurdle—namely, that whatever effort Alpha I exerts to remedy his deficiencies can be canceled out by the whim and power of his fellows. Long-range planning for Alpha I's survival would constitute an act of folly on his part when everyone could exercise equal claim to the products of his labor and to his very body. And the claimant's demand would not be any better than anyone else's. Such a state of affairs, rather than maximizing survival, would maximize the chance of an early and swift death for Alpha I and all of his kind.

The second scenario, in which Alpha has no rights but some or all others do have rights, falls victim to logical absurdity—Alpha I was constructed in such a way as to stand for all mankind in their primitive necessities. It is logically inconsistent to claim rights for all or some of mankind with the exception of Alpha I, unless it can be shown that they have such rights in virtue of some characteristic that the unfortunate Alpha I does not share. But by our original assumptions about Alpha I, such an allegation would be impossible. All persons are identical in the features from which motility and interactive rights are derived.

Which leaves us with the third choice, that Alpha I has these rights and so does every other person. It should be noted that the case for motility and interactive-acquisitive rights has been defended not merely negatively, by process of elimination, as Rothbard argued for self-ownership. Rather, I have shown that survival is necessary for the pursuit of all other goods by purposive agents, that morality is necessary for survival, and that rights are necessary for morality. Thus, rights to what traditionally is called freedom, and interaction with and acquisition of matter (for now, on the most minimal level) have been deduced from three elements: (1) the conditions of man's survival, (2) earthly factors that impinge upon man's survival, and (3) man's capacity of choice as a purposive agent.

Stage 2

One environmental condition, previously mentioned, deserves further scrutiny. Alpha I is not alone. There exist other men who have a similar self-interest in survival, similar needs, and identical earthly imposed limitations. Grazing on the fruits of the earth will prove insufficient to sustain such an abundance of human lives; therefore, production becomes a necessity. And so, also, does the erection of boundaries. Why? Production requires long-range planning, and effort, for which an expectation of enjoyment is usually the primary inspiration. If there were no guarantees, and hence poor prospects that what one produced would serve to secure one's survival, life would be Hobbesian, "nasty, brutish, and short." In sum, it is not a plan whereby the prospects for the long-term survival of particular individuals (or all) could be reasonably expected.

If there were no mine and thine extending beyond what one has immediately assimilated to one's body (recall that such a right of interaction-acquisition has been established by the previous stage of the argument), there still might exist some production and appropriation. But it would remain haphazard, precarious, furtive, insecure—certainly not the characteristics likely to maximize the chances of survival. Indeed, your crop may be eaten by strangers with moral impunity.

More positively, what makes the notion of boundaries intuitively appealing is that people already come prepackaged (encapsulated) in containers called bodies. Our bodies, in a sense, provide the limiting conditions of a "natural" boundary. After all, we are not porous, immaterial waifs. Our bodies are not greatly expansible; we do not extrude our substance to fill the available empty space. We are rather neatly confined, like apples in their individual skins. To push the argument beyond intuition, the first boundary—to be protected by a right to exclude others—should be limited to the body of Alpha I and to the bodies of all other individuals. If the survival of agents is what matters, as indeed it must or else all further discussion is moot (because whether any people survived or not would be radically contingent), then these agents must have a right to exclude others from penetrating, or violating their integrity as entities. To deny this right of Alpha I to exclude others from intruding upon his person against his will, is to deny Alpha I's right to exist. And if Alpha I has no right to exist, neither does any other person, since Alpha I's characteristics are the same as everyone else's.

What about boundaries more extensive than the body, can they be justified? How should goods other than human bodies be distributed? Here, a Rothbardian procedure will assist in the examination of the possible strategies for boundary drawing. First, let us examine communism, the common ownership of all matter. This, obviously, would contradict our previously established right to motility. Practically, you could undertake movements into communally owned matter. After all, who could watch you and keep you immobile at all times, who would watch that person, etc., etc. What is significant, however, is that you would have no *right* to engage in even the most innocuous motion that invaded community property unless the community decided that such activity were permissible. But in order to take such a vote, there would have had to be a prior vote to decide how each person should vote and on and on to an infinite regress—simply because you could never reach a point where anyone had an ultimate right to inhabit the space he was in or to raise his hand (thus further intruding on community space) in order to vote.

In addition to the logical inconsistency of the communal ownership boundary, it is equally flawed on survivalist grounds—for such a system renders the survival of any Alpha I fatally precarious. His long term survival would depend upon the sufferance of a majority of others, or a dominant clique, or, more likely, a dictator.

Another alternative would be that one or a few people own matter. Again, on survivalist criterion, such a system is flawed because it does not provide the optimum chance for survival. Unless one were fortunate enough to be the sole possessor of property or a member of the elite of owners, one's survival would be held hostage to the whims and questionable generosity of the property-owning nobility.

What is even more dubious about any such pattern of distribution is that it implies the existence of some *deus ex machina* who, at the very beginning before anything was appropriated, handed out portions to some people and not to others. Barring the contrivance of this pseudo-God, there is no attribute by which some individuals are entitled by right to everything, permanently preventing others from acquisition. Again, the reason for this is that all individuals, by our argument, share in the attributes that entitle them to extend their boundaries to include portions of the earth. If some have a right to do it, all must.

We are left, then, with this alternative: each person has a right to pursue boundary-extending activities as a purposive human agent in order to optimize the chances for survival. Success is not guaranteed. Each must insure personal survival as best he or she can. Will this maximize the chances of survival for all persons, including those least advantaged? Whether one is least advantaged as a result of personal afflictions, being born in a disadvantaged generation (say there is another Ice Age) or lack of industriousness, such a system will allow for such activities as renting the use of others' property on the basis of one's future productivity, laboring for wages, saving for the future purchase of resources, and charity. Self-protected enclaves from which the propertyless would be excluded would not characterize the whole earth, because property in land and other goods is desirable and valuable principally for its profitable use. People would realize that the exclusion of others from trade or hire would nullify the profitable use of property. A situation in which the propertyless would have no right to inhabit a "spot of earth," one of the conditions of Alpha I's survival, would not arise.

A general right to pursue portions of the earth has found its justification, but it remains to be seen how Alpha I comes to acquire a right to a particular piece of matter (earth, natural resources, sea, air, or whatever). First of all, let us dispel the notion, popularized by John Stuart Mill and Henry George, that there is something peculiar about land that renders it unfit for ownership even though private property in movables is defensible. Things are useful, and hence have a value placed upon them, because they serve human needs and desires. A plot of land, a pig, and a chunk of gold are all useless, in human terms, until someone has perceived a use for them. Value means some quality that a thing has that enables it to meet some human need. If this same good comes to be valued by others, it acquires a market value (exchange value, or price). Land, then, is no different from any other commodity. In all cases, the value of a thing is not intrinsic to it; rather, it derives from human preferences. And whether one examines movables or landed property, the usefulness of the thing for human ends is the creation of the individual who acted purposively upon it; he is the true creator of its value. Thus, an argument justifying individual ownership of the products of one's labor, initiative, or foresight will equally substantiate property in land and natural resources.[89]

This notion of value as wholly a human invention provides the key to that justification. All value is the artifact of some purposive activity on the part of a particular individual. What I am arguing goes one step beyond Locke, who contended, alternately, that nine-tenths or ninety-nine hundredths of the value of any commodity was the handywork of man rather than nature. *I maintain that 100 percent of the value of a good is the work of human creativity.*[90] Under the forbidding deserts of Saudi Arabia precious oil lay useless and, therefore, valueless for millennia, until finally men perceived a use for it, unleashing untold new wealth and comforts upon mankind. The same with uranium, plutonium, and other precious elements, until only recently thought useless. Until some man discovered the utility of such natural elements to satisfy human purposes, purposes that might not have occurred yet to other men, all of these things were so much worthless debris. This creative process applies equally to what we now consider mundane utilities; their creation was once extraordinary, the result of transmuting the useless into the useful. Think of such ordinary products as telephones, cars, airplanes, rockets, computers, calculators, all the products of the past hundred years of human inventiveness.

It is not only the consummate genius, the first inventor of a new product or process, who is a true creator. Everyone who first takes something, unowned by others, useless, and puts it to human purposes, thereby creates use value. The shepherd who tames previously wild animals, the farmer who clears trees and rocks from a virgin field, the man who fills a marsh to furnish buildable land, all are creators of value.

To avoid confusion about terminology, let me try to clarify my position a bit more. Talk about value by economists, particularly in the nineteenth century, was incredibly muddled. Smith, Ricardo, and Marx all held a labor theory of value. There was much confusion in Smith and Ricardo particularly between use value (that is, the utility of a thing) and market value (or price). They took labor to be the determinant of *market* value. Of course, Marx drew radical conclusions from this theory, namely, that labor creates surplus value that the capitalist extracts from the laborer. What I am arguing here really has nothing to do with a labor theory of value in the sense it was used by classical economists or Marx. I am not talking about market value (or price) and how it is determined on a free market. However, if I were, I certainly would endorse not the labor theory of value but, rather, the modern theory of demand-determined prices based on consumer preferences. The marginal-utility theory of market value remedies the well-known faults of the labor theory of value. Rather, it is a philosophical point that I am making: that man's ingenuity, his mind creates all useful things, all things useful for the satisfaction of human wants and needs.

One other point needs to be clarified. By saying that to human ingenuity can be attributed 100 percent of an artifact's value, I do not mean to dismiss the contribution of nature. Obviously, if no "earthly stuff" existed, man could create no products. Indeed, there would be no earth nor mankind. And different kinds of "earthly stuff" have different properties. Some "stuff" can be transformed into food, others into clothing, others into energy, and so on. The contribution of nature is indispensable; it can neither be dismissed nor denigrated. My argument does not intend to do either. What I am contending, rather, is that value—as a purely human concept—is wholly created by human ingenuity and endeavor. Labor, properly directed by man's mind, creates value. (By adding the caveat "properly directed," I mean to indicate that if Roger picks up a hunk of coal and labors ten hours upon it with the intention of transforming it into food, he has created no value.)

Should those individuals who create value out of natural "stuff," that is, from a human perspective, out of something useless, thereby acquire a moral right to that thing (or process) in perpetuity? Most people would concede that if someone could create something out of nothing, *de novo*, maybe a pure act of the will, that someone would be entitled to keep it. After all, but for the act of mental gymnastics, no widget would exist for anyone else or society to claim. But by the preceding argument, it has been shown that all the value of any object, placed in the exchange market or held by anyone for personal use, has been created out of "natural stuff" that in its original state was of no use to anyone. From a moral perspective, this is not really any different from creating a widget out of thin air.

But this is merely an intuitive argument, and not especially compelling to someone who might deny that anyone is entitled to the exclusive ownership of anything, even something generated *de novo*. Strategies for justifying original ownership by the creators of that which they have created could take the following forms. (1) The creators are entitled to their artifacts because they have acted as benefactors of mankind; and there is certainly a hint of this strategy in Locke. (2) If there is no positive duty placed upon people to provide uncompensated benefits to others, then should not individuals be recompensed for the effort or pain expended in producing useful articles? (3) Who else could have a better claim to a thing produced by Alpha I than Alpha himself? If *prima facie* Beta I has no better claim, being of the same nature as Alpha I and not the source of the good, X, made by Alpha I, then no other individual could have a better claim than Alpha I to X. Is it not absurd to contend that Alpha I is entitled to the products of everyone else's labor but not to what he himself has produced? And that Beta I, Gamma I, etc. are entitled to all the products of others but not to what each has produced? What possible line of argument could justify such a conclusion, when all Alpha I's, Beta I's, etc. have precisely the same characteristics? The final possibility, that no one should permanently own anything has been previously dismissed as inconsistent with the immediate end of survival because it would render the survival of each person radically contingent. (4) Alpha I is entitled to X because he deserves to receive as his own property that which he produced by his own merit. (5) A utilitarian strategy is also conceivable in which one might argue that if Alpha I were not vested with his creations, all incentive to production and invention would be undermined.

While all of these strategies hold their separate allure, a solid justification for conceding property to those individuals who create specific goods can be deduced from our survivalist objective or value. The survival of each individual depends on his ability to carry out purposive action. If the end results of this purposive action are removed from the agent's control, and employed by others to satisfy their needs or desires, then the survival of Alpha I, the agent, is put in jeopardy. But for the action of Alpha I, no good X would exist to satisfy any human's needs or desires. To deny Alpha I's ownership—meaning the right to exclude others from taking X without Alpha I's consent—would be tantamount to granting to others, with precisely Alpha I's attributes, the right to live parasitically off Alpha I's efforts. But no such right could ever be defensible.

Let us examine more closely the denial of the proposition "that the person who creates X ought to own X." It would have to take the following form:

Alpha I produced X but is not entitled to X.
Alpha I did not produce Y and Z but is entitled to them.
Beta I produced Y but is not entitled to Y.
Beta I did not produce X and Z but is entitled to them.
Gamma I produced Z but is not entitled to Z.
Gamma I did not produce X and Y but is entitled to them.

The implications of these propositions are countersurvivalist in the extreme. If Alpha I, Beta I, and Gamma I wished to operationalize this "moral" schema, they would have joint and hence conflicting rights to X, Y, and Z; each thing would have two claimants (and potentially billions of claimants, as we extend the universe of people to reflect the real world). Hence, there would exist no exclusive claims to the use of any good. The survival of each person would be contingent upon his raw, physical prowess in removing adversaries, with their equally legitimate claims, from possession of each good necessary for his survival. What is even worse for the survival of each person, is that if he desires to act as a moral agent under this schema, his survival depends entirely upon the productive activities of others, contingencies entirely beyond his control. If others are lazy and unproductive, Alpha I has nothing to claim a right to. If he himself decides to refuse to produce, Beta I and Gamma I have nothing to claim as theirs by right. All will die. Thus, on a survivalist criterion, those who create a particular good through purposive action should be entitled to own that good. But for Alpha I, X would not exist as a value to serve human purposes.

Proudhon's, Grotius's, and Locke's defenses of property rights, for varying reasons, all fell victim to boundary problems. That is, their theories were undermined, or rendered inconsistent, because they could not adequately delimit the extent of each individual's legitimate claim to property. Can this new theory rectify the boundary problem in the natural rights tradition? By the first stage of our defense of property rights, the right to motility and to interaction with matter have been established, and by the second stage, a permanent right to that which one has created for one's survival has been established. One wonders, then, whether mere survival of the organism man, and the limited necessities required for that survival, sets the outward limit upon individual acquisition? One thinks not, and consequently a third stage of the argument presents itself.

Recall that Alpha I is an individual who represents the basic attributes and needs of all men for simple survival. Like a newborn infant, Alpha I and his kind are all potentiality, manifesting the same raw needs, desires, and conditions of life as all other men. Purely unindividuated, Alpha I's need air, water, food, shelter, a place to stand, etc., but beyond that they have not extended. Certainly, Alpha I is incomplete. Men have physical and mental attributes, desires for living their lives, values, hopes, and dreams that elude the primitive Alpha I.

Hypothetical man, Alpha II, is a more complete reflection of man, yet he too is not completely differentiated. He is not any particular man, but he possesses categories of attributes possessed by all men. Alpha II, then is a more adequate "ideal type." He possesses desires, wishes, and hopes beyond mere survival, for he wishes to live what Aristotle called the good life, and not simply mere life. His physical structure, mental capacities, view of the good, and values serve to differentiate Alpha II from his fellow human beings. But for the sake of our argument we need not specify the unique content of any of these attributes, values, or desires. All we need to know is that individuals do differ along these parameters.

Alpha II, like his truncated predecessor Alpha I, is capable of purposive activity if he chooses to exert himself. Given that all men have objectives that extend beyond mere survival, should they be entitled to property in those of their creations that satisfy desires extending beyond their basic survival needs? To deny ownership in superfluities would entail the establishment of a moral grab bag in which all creations beyond pure necessities would fall prey to rights claims by everyone in existence except their creator. This anarchy of rights, with all individuals having a legitimate right to each superfluity produced by Alpha II, would lead to a war of all against all. The exclusivity principle—for each article X there should be only one legitimate owner at any given time— would be massively violated. In the end, such a state of affairs would threaten survival. After all, who is to judge which are goods necessary for survival, and which are luxuries. Such a task would entail the existence of a godlike omniscience, or else the moral system would hinge upon caprice and, most likely, erroneous, *ad hoc* decisions by greedy individuals. It appears, then, that the objective of survival would be undermined by a denial of exclusive rights to individuals of everything that they have produced. No artificial barrier can be constructed to differentiate necessities from luxuries without undermining the entire system that seeks to ensure the survival of individuals as purposive agents.

Thus, in theory, anyway, the boundary problem has been resolved. Each individual has a perpetual property right in that which he or she has created, that is, in the values produced. Your right, then, is to the object or process itself, and not to the market value or price, which is nothing more than the appraisal in the minds of others, at the margin, of the value to them of your good. The preference orders of others are beyond your control, and form no part of your entitlement. If, for example, my neighbor erects a house on his land in the configuration of an elephant and proceeds to paint it with pink, blue, and purple stripes, and the market value of my house plummets, I have no recourse; no right of mine has been violated. "Aesthetic blights" are nonstarters in a theory of rights. I, as the affected homeowner, have no right to be recompensed by the elephant-house owner for the fall in value of my home as evaluated by potential buyers.

How well can the theory handle boundary questions in the tough cases? Is Alpha II entitled to Alpha Centuri's inhabitable planet if he discovers it, and is the first human to reach it? Barring the existence of other sentient, purposive agents that fit the same "ideal type" as Alpha II who are already inhabiting the planet, Alpha II would have a right to the planet as its discoverer, that is, as the person who brought it within the human orbit of value. The issue becomes a bit muddied if Alpha II reached the planet only moments ahead of other explorers, all of whom were aware of its existence and possibilities. Could Alpha II exclude all ensuing claimants by declaring his ownership of the planet, outright? If all parties were aware of Alpha II's prior arrival and claim, they would have no right to intrude upon Alpha II's planet. However, should three separate explorers set up base camps on the planet, each unaware of the priority or lack of it of the others, it would make more sense to conclude that each was entitled to that portion of the planet each had used or transformed, that each had acted purposively upon. But this hypothetical is, undoubtedly, a "lifeboat" case, and any theory tends to get rather messy in such extreme, hypothetical cases. Besides, is it so preposterous that Alpha II could claim ownership of planet X, when one recalls Columbus's claim of the New World for Spain?

Claims of property in rivers or oceans would stand on the same grounds as those to less fungible entities. If Alpha II sinks derricks in mid-ocean for the purpose of exploring for subterranean oil deposits, he has gained title to whatever oil he discovers, and the right to exclude all others from his platform and whatever immediate area of the ocean is required to secure and exploit his find. Farming portions of the ocean to cultivate fish should, likewise, entitle the owner to the right to exclude others from the increased harvest, increased by his own efforts.

Certainly, in all of these instances there is a question of the public recognition of these rights, rights that exist independently of acknowledgment by other people but yet depend for their observance upon awareness by other people. If some central clearinghouse for claims existed, it would certainly facilitate such public expressions of intent in regard to particular portions of matter. It is quite conceivable that the explorer of Alpha Centuri's planet had purely scientific objectives in mind, and gaining perpetual property in the planet formed no part of his purpose. Similarly, the person who judiciously plans his fishing in sectors of the ocean so that his catch in future years will not be depleted might intend to exclude other fishermen, but would be utterly indifferent to the passage of ships through his domain. A certain element of human convention does creep into this designation of private domains over fluid substances. This occurs simply because it is far less obvious what the relevant "purposive activity" is in dealing with oceans than with arable land. The theory, however, remains the same, no matter the nature of the particular matter involved. If Alpha II gains property rights over one hundred acres by transforming it into a form productive of values such as corn, cattle, and wheat, then Beta II should, likewise, own a portion of the sea by fishing in it on a continual basis, throwing back the young catch, and perhaps fighting off predators. And Beta II's claim should hold good against the person who wishes to use that portion of the sea for other purposes, whether they be sailing or oil drifting, just as Alpha II can exclude from his farm an intruder who wishes to erect a steel mill on his land. An aggressive act of trespass would be involved in both instances. Of course, Alpha II or Beta II might think it a matter of perfect indifference whether people crossed their land or sailed upon their portion of the ocean, and might not think it worth their trouble to enforce their rights, but they would have them nonetheless. Thus, anyone wishing to drill for oil under the fisherman's portion of the sea would have to purchase that right from him, just as subsurface mining rights are now purchased from landowners.

This defense of a right to property has proceeded from the conditions of man's survival on earth, and the consequent deduction of rights to motility, to interaction with matter, and then to property in that which one has transformed into something valuable to humans through purposive activity. The final stage of the argument demonstrated that the extent of a person's property is limited only by his purposive activity, and not by any artificial distinction between necessities and luxuries. Now, skeptics may still wonder why, if survival of the individual is the end to be sought, we should not aim at it directly by offering guarantees. To reemphasiize a point made earlier, there are no guarantees in life, and no one to do the guaranteeing. Without purposive action by some individuals, there is nothing available gratis to sustain anyone's life. Without human endeavor all life would cease. For those unfortunate enough to suffer from disabilities that render their pursuit of life-sustaining activities impossible or extremely difficult, again, there are no guarantees. The best hope for such people lies in the magnanimity of those who are so productive that they generate more value than they need for their own survival and enjoyment.

Why, some may inquire, should individuals respect the boundaries of private property carved out by others? This reciprocity is required out of logical consistency. If my right to my backyard depends on my being an Alpha II, then so does your right to your fertilizer. We are all creatures of the same nature, and rights were deduced from those attributes that make us human. To deny your claim to your fertilizer would entail a denial of the very grounds upon which I claim my backyard.

Another objection might arise over the following kind of circumstance. Imagine that Robert is starving and can survive only if he steals Tom's excess package of Twinkies. Let us place them on a desert island to make the case slightly more plausible. If survival is Robert's motivation, does he thereby have a legitimate claim upon Tom's superfluous Twinkies? Such a precept, if generalized, would undermine all property rights. As Kant would have it, such a principle could not be universalized into a categorical

imperative. If everyone acted upon this principle, there would be no security of property, survival would be rendered precarious, and we would be
back in the Hobbesian jungle.

One of the criticisms often leveled against Locke is that labor as the
source of original acquisition could not function as the legitimating principle once everything had been appropriated. Our theory does not fall victim
to such a charge. Leaving aside the unlikelihood of a situation in which
everything had been previously appropriated by man, there is an entire
universe out there, to say nothing of deserts and oceans on earth. How
would future generations fare under my scheme? Those who have nothing
to sell but their brains or physical capacities would voluntarily contract
with the owners of property to labor for wages. This would not violate the
principle that one is entitled to the value that one has created, for the
laborer has consented to receive the equivalent of the excess (or marginal)
utility he or she creates. Who is to judge the precise equation between the
goods produced and the money paid? Obviously, the two contracting parties will each make that evaluation, with both having made themselves
aware of the market for that service. Barring compulsion on the part of
either party, the bargain struck, however it might appear from the perspec
tive of some third party, is irreproachable on the principles previously
expounded. If property upon which one wishes to act purposively already
belongs to another person, one's only recourse lies in reaching a bargain
with the owner. All else would constitute theft. This argument deflects the
charge by the socialists that Locke's use of the labor-as-entitlement principle undermines capitalism because laborers are deprived of what they have
produced.

A complete theory of property rights should include, in addition to a
theory of original acquisition, theories of legitimate transfer and rectification for injustices. Justifying original acquisition, obviously, is the greatest
hurdle. Once that has been surmounted, the transfer of property through
voluntary transactions—exchange or bequest—is unproblematical. If person A owns thing X, then A can disown X by exchanging it for something
else, or simply disavowing X, or giving X gratis to anyone else. This transfer by voluntary consent applies equally to commodities, land, or raw labor
power.

Rectification—the return of X to A when X has been removed from A
without A's consent—is theoretically untroublesome but practically a bit
dicey. A ought to get X back, in all justice, but if titles to things become lost
through the ages, or the original genealogy of a plot of land becomes
interrupted by an illegitimate act of conquest or theft, rectification can
become problematic in actuality. If Adam had owned X by having created
it as a value, and he passed it on to his heirs, and then in the tenth

inheritance Arthur comes along and takes it by force, what do you do by way of rectification ten generations after the illegitimate theft when the heir of Adam claims X? And Arthur's heir holds X as his property in blissful ignorance of Arthur's impropriety? Prudence might suggest some generational statute of limitations on rectification. Certainly Adam the tenth should get X back, and so too Adam the eleventh who was willed X by his father, and even Adam the twelfth. But to go much beyond that, say, to the tenth descendent of the original victim, seems to defy any reasonable standard based on tying property to human purposive activity. The case for Adam's heirs would, indubitably, be strengthened if each generation after the theft had registered objections to the expropriation and demanded the return of X. All of this transcends the realm of idle speculation, when one reflects upon the recent claims of Indian tribes to the state of Maine, and to portions of the most exclusive real estate in Massachusetts.

Miller v. Schoene served as the opening salvo of this chapter. Now that our defense of a right to private property has been completed, we might return to our apple growers and ornamental cedar tree owners to see how that dispute might be resolved on natural rights principles. First of all, the legislation that permitted state agents to order the destruction of all cedar trees suspected of harboring cedar rust disease would be highly suspect, as would all exercise by the state of sweeping police powers. The reason such legislative fiat is objectionable lies in the fact that it must be fashioned in such all-encompassing terms, with such limited options for alternative abatement, and with scant proof of actual damages in particular instances. The preferable course, from a natural rights perspective would involve individuals' appealing directly to a court for a remedy, thus necessitating proof of actual or potential damage, and examination of alternative remedies less extreme than outright destruction. Yet, having proven that cedar trees harbor a disease that germinates in that source and subsequently attacks apple trees, the owner of the apple trees would be entitled to an injunction or recompense for the damage suffered. In other words, the apple orchard owner has the right to use and enjoy the property free from harms inflicted by others. There is no difference, in theory, between someone who aggressively acts to harm the apple trees by trespassing on the owner's property and hacking at the trees with an axe and the person who harms the apple orchard by passively permitting germs nurtured by his or her cedar trees to pass over the boundary line into the apple orchard and kill the trees. (It should be pointed out that I make no reference here to the actual state of the law but, rather, to how the case ought to be resolved on purely theoretical grounds of natural rights. In fact, under the common law a nuisance generally would not be found in a case where something occurred naturally on A's land that harmed B. See, eg., *Giles v. Walker*, 24

Q.B.D. 656, 1890). The natural rights solution may reach the same decision in this case (if we leave aside the question of the state's police power and assume it is a private litigation between two property owners) as the Supreme Court did operating on utilitarian or wealth maximization principles. But that is mere coincidence. Presumably, the Court (and utilitarians and wealth maximizers) would have decided the case differently if cedar rust trees had great economic value in the state and apple trees were of but nugatory value. From a natural rights perspective, such quantitative calculations are irrelevant. The only relevant considerations, from a rights viewpoint, are who has a right to what, and who aggresses against that rightfully owned thing.

Notes

1. William Blackstone, COMMENTARIES, 2:2 (1766).
2. *Miller v. Schoene*, 276 U.S. 272 (1928). See James M. Buchanan, *Politics, Property, and the Law: An Alternative Interpretation of Miller et al. v. Schoene*, 15 J. LAW & ECON. 439 (1972); Warren J. Samuels, *Interrelations Between Legal and Economic Processes*, 14 J. LAW & ECON. 435 (1971).
3. *Id.* at 279-80.
4. *Mugler v. Kansas*, 123 U.S. 623 (1887).
5. *Hadacheck v. Sebastian, Chief of Police of the City of Los Angeles*, 239 U.S. 394 (1915).
6. Jeremy Bentham, ANARCHIAL FALLACIES, 2 COLLECTED WORKS, ed. Bowring.
7. P. J. Proudhon, WHAT IS PROPERTY? AN INQUIRY INTO THE PRINCIPLE OF RIGHT AND OF GOVERNMENT (1840) (New York: Dover Publications, 1970).
8. Thomas Spence, THE REAL RIGHTS OF MAN (1775); Thomas Paine, AGRARIAN JUSTICE (1796); Proudhon, WHAT IS PROPERTY? (1840); Henry George, PROGRESS AND POVERTY (1879).
9. Walter Lippmann, NEWSWEEK, September 16, 1963, 21, as cited in Richard Powell, *The Relationship Between Property Rights and Civil Rights*, 15 HASTINGS L.J. 135, 139 (1963).
10. Powell, *The Relationship Between Property Rights and Civil Rights* at 140. See also Francis S. Philbrick, *Changing Conceptions of Property in Law*, 86 UNIV. OF PA. L. REV. 691, 729-32 (1938). Philbrick articulates what he calls a "modernized philosophy of property" in which the first tenet must be that property is justified solely by utilitarian considerations; that social interests must control our choices concerning property rights; and that individual interests ought to be of concern only insofar as they advance the general interest.
11. *Id.* at 140 n. 19.
12. *Id.* at 149.
13. Roscoe Pound, *The Law of Property and Recent Juristic Thought*, 25 A.B.A. J. 993, 995 (1939).
14. Morris Udall, *Land Use: Why We Need Federal Legislation*, In NO LAND IS AN ISLAND (San Francisco: Institute for Contemporary Studies, 1975), 59.

15. See also Morris Cohen, *Property and Sovereignty*, 13 CORNELL L.Q. 8, 26 (1927): "I wish however to urge that if the large property owner is viewed, as he ought to be, as a wielder of power over the lives of his fellow citizens, the law should not hesitate to develop a doctrine as to his *positive duties in the public interest*" (emphasis added); and John Snare, *The Concept of Property*, 9 AMERICAN PHILOSOPHICAL QUARTERLY, 200, 203 (1972): "But against Locke it should be noted that we needn't assimilate all rights to property rights nor must we suppose that property rights are so absolute that they can only be abridged by consent. We might consider property rights as merely *prima facie* rights which can be overriden by other moral concerns e.g., the *public welfare*" (emphasis added).

16. Udall, *Land Use* at 71.

17. Cohen, *Property and Sovereignty* at 12.

18. See also *United States v. General Motors Corp.*, 323 U.S. 373, 377-78 (1945): "'Property' is not used in the 'vulgar' and untechnical sense of the physical thing with respect to which the citizen exercises rights recognized by law. [Instead it] denote[s] the group of rights inhering in the citizen's relation to the physical thing, as the right to possess, use, and dispose of it." And see Neil Hecht, *From Seisin to Sit-in: Evolving Property Concepts*, 44 B.U.L. REV. 435, 439 (1964): "By way of clarification, the legal term 'property' does not refer to a thing (*res*) but to a concept. Property is a legal relation among people, or groups, in relation to a thing. The term 'private property,' therefore, refers to those interests or claims possessed by private parties and recognized and protected by law."

Robert Kratovil and Frank J. Harrison, *Eminent Domain—Policy and Concept*, 42 CALIF. L. REV. 596, 602 (1954): "The word 'property' may be used to describe either of two separate and distinct relationships: that which exists between the owner and other individuals with respect to the object owned or that which exists between the owner and the government with respect to such object."

W. Hohfeld, FUNDAMENTAL LEGAL CONCEPTIONS (Cook ed., 1919), 28, in which the author refers to the ambiguity of the word *property* as denoting either the physical thing or the legal interests pertaining to the thing.

19. *Cf:* Philbrick, *Changing Conceptions of Property in Law* at 691.

20. Extending the analysis to a complete universe of actors presents no novel elements. It is simply easier to discuss three actors in a model rather than three or four billion. Factoring the state in, however, does present new theoretical difficulties, the resolution of which must remain the task of the next chapter.

21. See Lawrence Becker, PROPERTY RIGHTS: PHILOSOPHICAL FOUNDATIONS (London: Routledge & Kegan Paul, 1977), 18-19. Pound, *The Law of Property and Recent Juristic Thought* at 997, where Pound notes that in the civil law tradition property involved six rights: the right of possessing, of excluding others, of enjoying the fruits or profits, of destroying or injuring, of using, and the right of disposition. Blackstone, COMMENTARIES at I:134, "The third absolute right, inherent in every Englishman, is that of property: which consists in the free use, enjoyment, and disposal of all his acquisitions, without any control or diminution, save only by the laws of the land." Snare, *The Concept of Property*, in which the author develops a set of rules for what "A owns P" means, which includes rules setting out a right to use, to exclude, to transfer, to punish, to receive a recompense for damages; and liability for

damages P inflicts on others. Cal Civ. Code § 654 (West, 1970): "The ownership of a thing is the right of one or more persons to possess and use it to the exclusion of others. In this code, the thing of which there may be ownership is called property." E. Furubotn and J. Pejovich, *Property Rights and Economic Theory: A Survey of the Recent Literature,* 10 J. OF ECONOMIC LITERATURE 1137, 1139-40 (1972). "The right of ownership in an asset, whether by a private party or the state, is understood to consist of the right to use it, to change its form and substance, and to transfer *all rights* in the asset thing, e.g. sale, or *some rights* through, e.g. rental."

22. This notion is captured in the law by the Latin phrase *sic utere tuo ut alienum non laedas* (use your own [property] so as not to harm another's).

23. On the question of exclusivity of title, see James Grunebaum, *Property Rules and Property Rights,* 61 PACIFIC PHILOSOPHICAL QUARTERLY 422, 423-24 (1980). Grunebaum points out that a system of property rules must be consistent (giving a clear criterion of title so that one cannot both own and not own the same thing at the same time); determinate (making it possible in principle to determine without ambiguity whether a person owns a given thing or not); and complete (insuring that if something is ownable according to a set of property rules, then it must be possible for someone to own it).

24. Unless Beta or Gamma are attempting a bit of self-help in the state of nature under proposition (3); in which case, they would be acting legitimately in seeking recompense for harm X caused them or their property. Alpha would be acting illegitimately by refusing to pay recompense for the harm he or his property caused. Beta and Gamma would be acting within their rights. Similarly, if Alpha stole Y or Z, their owners would be entitled to seek reparations from even a recalcitrant Alpha.

25. For example, Grunebaum in *Property Rules and Property Rights* at 425 argues that Marx's formulation "to each according to his need" fails the test of determinacy (and hence is an inconsistent principle) because for any indivisible X there may be several claimants who each "need" it.

26. Compare Hecht, *From Seisin to Sit-in* at 441, in which the author includes three components of property rights: acquisition, use, disposition, with Grunebaum, *Property Rules and Property Rights* at 422, where he says that all systems of property rules exhibit two essential functions: to assign rights to individuals or groups of individuals; and to prescribe mechanisms for acquisition, transfer, and alienation of these rights.

27. To borrow a term from Robert Nozick, ANARCHY, STATE, AND UTOPIA (New York: Basic Books, 1974).

28. Hugo Grotius, THE RIGHTS OF WAR AND PEACE (A. C. Campbell translation, DE JURE BELLI AC PACIS) (1901), bk. II, ch. II, § II.

29. *Id.*

30. Pufendorf embraces the basic argument but departs from the conclusion that restitution is in order. Employing Grotius's argument to its logical limit, he contends that if the indigent, necessitous person has a right to the goods of his fellows, then he owes them nothing; he has simply claimed what is legitimately his. Pufendorf, DE JURE NATURAE ET GENTIUM LIBRI OCTO (Clarendon, 1934), II: 304. But things of great value should be restored out of simple gratitude.

31. Grotius, DE JURE BELLI AC PACIS, bk. II, ch. III, § I.

32. *Id.* bk. I, Ch. I, § VI: "Natural right is the dictate of right reason, shewing the moral turpitude, or moral necessity, of any act from its agreement or disagree-

ment with a rational nature, and consequently that such an act is either forbidden or commended by God, the author of nature."

33. *Id.* bk. I, ch. I, § VI.

34. Pufendorf, DE JURE NATURAE ET GENTIUM, bk. II, ch. VI, § 6, 304-5.

35. *Id.* bk. IV, ch. IV, § 2, 532. See also Blackstone, COMMENTARIES, II: 8, in which Blackstone discussses how property becomes vested in individuals as their exclusive right "which before belonged generally to everybody, but particularly to nobody."

36. Pufendorf, DE JURE NATURAE ET GENTIUM, bk. IV, ch. IV, § 4, 536.

37. Pufendorf, suffering from both the benefits and drawbacks of an encyclopedic mind, exhibits shreds of various arguments, none of them reconciled, that might provide a hint to resolving boundary disputes. For example, he writes "that a *child* and an insane person cannot acquire dominion over a thing originally. . . . The reason is that to acquire dominion in this way *there is requisite, intention,* on the part of one acquiring it, that he wishes to have this thing in future as his own, and that he understands at the same time, that this act of his may beget that right in him. But this is beyond the power of such persons" (DE JURE NATURAE ET GENTIUM, bk. IV, ch. IV, 15, 556).

Later, he says that a man occupies land when he undertakes to cultivate it, or marks out its boundaries. Additionally, it is understood that he will not embrace more than what one family can probably defend (bk. IV, ch. 6, § 3, 570). Then a bit later, he takes another shot at it when he says that taking possession of a thing means "joining of body to body immediately or through a proper instrument"; one acquires movables by laying on of hands, and land by feet. Pufendorf confronts us with a superabundance of riches: at least five different principles. But of this he was certain, that "merely to have seen a thing, or to know its location, is not held to be sufficient to establish possession: (bk. IV, ch. V, § 8, 576).

38. Grotius, DE JURE BELLI AC PACIS (bk. II, ch. II, § 3); Pufendorf DE JURE NATURAE ET GENTIUM, bk. IV, ch. V, § 2, 558.

39. Additional objections to the argument from first occupancy are raised in Becker's PROPERTY RIGHTS, 26-30: (1) that it cannot operate where things are already owned, thus it is solely a mode of original acquisition, and (2) that it can justify no more than a liberty to occupy, not a right to keep.

40. See Roberts, *The Demise of Property Law,* 57 CORNELL L. REV. 1, 4 (1971), in which he cites the Tenures Abolition Act, 12 Car. II., 11-24, 1 Eng. Rev. Stat. 725 (1660).

41. For an interesting discussion of the difference between property law pertaining to ownership in civil law countries and estates under the common law, see Merryman, *Ownership and Estate (Variations on a Theme by Lawson),* 48 TUL. L. REV. 916 (1974); and also Hecht, *From Seisin to Sit-in.*

42. Hecht, *From Seisin to Sit-in* at 446-47.

43. John Locke, *The Second Treatise of Government,* in John Locke, TWO TREATISES OF GOVERNMENT, ed. Peter Laslett, (New York: New American Library, 1960), § 6, 311.

44. *Id., First Treatise,* § 42, 205.

45. Locke was not being flippant in his use of the notion common property, nor was he employing it in the negative sense of something unowned, as did Pufendorf and Blackstone. If one consults his frequent adversions to the term in the *First Treatise,* this point becomes readily apparent. In § 29 he writes that whatever

God gave by the words of his grant to Adam in Gen. 1:28, "it was not to *Adam* in particular, exclusive of all men: whatever *Dominion* he had thereby, it was not a *Private Dominion*, But a dominion in common with the rest of Mankind." And again, at section 32, Locke employs biblical references to show that God granted a community of property to Noah and his sons.

46. Locke, *Second Treatise*, § 25, 327.
47. *Id.*
48. All section citations refer to Locke's *Second Treatise*.
49. Locke puts this aptly when he writes: "The Fruit, or Venison, which nourishes the wild *Indian* who knows no Inclosure, and is still a Tenant in common, must be his, and so his, i.e. a part of him, that another can no longer have any right to it, before it can do him any good for the support of his life" (§ 26).
50. *Id.* at § 37, 336.
51. One supposes that this would be Locke's response to Nozick's query in ANARCHY, STATE, AND UTOPIA, where he wonders why labor is not lost upon a thing, rather than one's acquiring thereby ownership of the thing.
52. See J. P. Day, *Locke on Property*, 16 PHILOSOPHICAL QUARTERLY 207 (1966), who argues that the property in one's own person claim is tautologous, for it is no more meaningful than the statement that "this dog owns this dog."
53. See Jeffrey Paul and Ellen Frankel Paul, *Locke's Usufructuary Theory of Self-Ownership*, 61 PACIFIC PHILOSOPHICAL QUARTERLY 384 (1980).
54. Murray Rothbard, FOR A NEW LIBERTY: THE LIBERTARIAN MANIFESTO (New York: Collier Books, 1978), p. 28.
55. Becker, PROPERTY RIGHTS, 33-40.
56. Immanuel Kant, THE PHILOSOPHY OF LAW, AN EXPOSITION OF THE FUNDAMENTAL PRINCIPLES OF JURISPRUDENCE AS THE SCIENCE OF RIGHT (Clifton, N.J.: Augustus V. Kelley, 1974), 91.
57. *Id.* at 92.
58. *Id.* at 79.
59. *Id.* at 82.
60. *Id.* at 78.
61. *Id.* at 184.
62. See Samuel C. Wheeler III, *Natural Property Rights as Body Rights*, 14 NOUS 171 (1980). Wheeler attempts another neo-Lockean defense of property rights in which ownership of external things is rather ingeniously assimilated into rights over one's own body. He makes the claim "that there is no line between what's part of the body of a person and what is his property . . . . Your property is your body." Our right to move and use our bodies is essential to our right to exist as agents. "If we have a right to exist, then we have a right not to have our agenthood terminated." Now, there remains one portentous lacuna in Wheeler's argument, for he utterly fails to tell us why we have a right to exist. Without justifying this first presumption, his entire argument remains ungrounded.
63. Jeremy Bentham, THEORY OF LEGISLATION (Oxford: Oxford University Press, 1914), 146-47.
64. *United States v. Willow River Power Co.*, 324 U.S. 499, 502-3 (1945).
65. Powell, *The Relationship Between Property Rights and Civil Rights*, 140 n. 19 (1963). See also Charles Reich, *The New Property*, 73 YALE L. J. 733, 739 (1964): "Property is the creation of law. A man who has property has certain legal rights with respect to an item of wealth. Property represents a relationship

between wealth and its 'owner.'" And Philbrick, *Changing Conceptions of Property in Law* at 729-32, in which the author develops a "modernized philosophy of law," the first tenet of which must be that "property is the creature and dependent of law." Property as the creature of law can be justified only on utilitarian grounds; thus, individual interests in property are justifiable only so long as they cohere with the general interest. Grunebaum, in *Property Rules and Property Rights* at 422, claims to demonstrate that property rights are assigned purely by social rules. And Hecht, *From Seisin to Sit-In* at 439, notes that "the term 'private property,' therefore, refers to those interests or claims possessed by private parties and recognized and protected by law."

66. Bentham, *THEORY OF LEGISLATION*, 112.

67. *Id.* at 119.

68. Reich, *The New Property* at 772.

69. Richard A. Posner, *Utilitarianism, Economics, and Legal Theory*, 8 J. OF LEGAL STUD. 103 (1979); and *The Ethical and Political Basis of the Efficiency Norm in Common Law Adjudication*, 8 HOFSTRA L. REV. 487 (1980). See also *The Value of Wealth: A Comment on Dworkin and Kronman*, 9 J. OF LEGAL STUD. 243 (1980).

70. Harold Demsetz, *Toward a Theory of Property Rights*, 57 AMERICAN ECONOMIC REVIEW 347 (1967); reprinted in THE ECONOMICS OF PROPERTY RIGHTS, ed. E. Furubotn and J. Pejovich.

71. In point of fact, two economists in an article summarizing the work of the economists of property rights argue for precisely this point: See Furubotn and Pejovich, *Property Rights and Economic Theory*, 1143.

72. Ronald Coase, *The Problem of Social Cost*, 3 J. LAW & ECON. 1 (1960).

73. For an insightful refutation of Coase on the causality issue see Richard Epstein, *Nuisance Law: Corrective Justice and its Utilitarian Constraints*, 8 J. OF LEGAL STUD. 49, 59 (1979).

74. Posner makes this point explicitly; see "*Wealth Maximization*" at 251.

75. Coase, *The Problem of Social Cost* at 15.

76. Posner's critique of utilitarianism may be found in two places: *Utilitarianism, Economics, and Legal Theory* at 111-19, and *The Value of Wealth* at 251.

77. Posner, *The Value of Wealth* at 243. See Ronald Dworkin, *Is Wealth a Value?* 9 J. OF LEGAL STUD. 191 (1980).

78. Jules L. Coleman, *Efficiency, Utility, and Wealth Maximization*, 8 HOFSTRA L. REV. 509, 512-13 (1980).

79. *Id.* at 513; Coleman defines it more rigorously: "one state of affairs (E¹) is Kaldor-Hicks efficient to another (E) if and only if those whose welfare increases in the move from E to E¹ could fully compensate those whose welfare diminishes with a net gain in welfare. Under Kaldor-Hicks, compensation to losers is not in fact paid."

80. Posner, *The Value of Wealth* at 245.

81. I am indebted to Aaron Director for pointing this out to me with great persistence and energy.

82. Posner, *The Ethical and Political Basis of the Efficiency Norm* at 492.

83. Richard Posner, ECONOMIC ANALYSIS OF LAW (Boston: Little, Brown, 1972), pp. 22-23.

84. See Coleman, *Efficiency, Utility, and Wealth Maximization* at 535-38 for a refined assault on Posner's notion of ex ante consent. He denies that victims, by accepting the lower cost of entry into a negligence liability system, have con-

sented to their losses; just as by their accepting ex post compensation for a loss, the victims cannot be said to have consented to the injury. See also Ronald Dworkin, *Why Efficiency*, 8 HOFSTRA L. REV. 563, 576-77 (1980), where Dworkin criticizes ex ante consent, and at 583-84, where he argues that Posner's relaxed version of Paretianism is simply utilitarianism.

85. Posner, *Utilitarianism, Economics, and Legal Theory* at 139.
86. *Id.* at 125, and Posner, *The Ethical and Political Basis of the Efficiency Norm* at 500-502.
87. Anthony Kronman, *Wealth Maximization as a Normative Principle*, J. OF LEGAL STUDIES 227, 240-41 (1980); Dworkin, *Is Wealth a Value?* 207-8.
88. Posner, *Utilitarianism, Economics, and Legal Theory* at 127.
89. Henry George and others have tried to separate ownership of movables from ownership of land. They claim that the former is legitimate, the latter is not. The fact that one does not create land by acting upon the earth (as one creates a chair by assembling its parts) is what distinguishes, in the critics' view, the two kinds of entities. But this is an irrelevant objection for two reasons: (1) because the chair also requires natural components that people did not make, as do all things made by people, and (2) because to argue that a market value for land arises from the demand of the community, as George does, and therefore the community has a right to appropriate this value, is ultimately to destroy the basis of *all* property. This consequence would necessarily follow because the market value of any and all goods arises from the demand of consumers. Hence, there is no difference between land ownership and any other kind of ownership. If ownership of movables is legitimate, so is ownership of land. Or else both kinds of ownership are illegitimate. Thus, there can be, logically, no middle ground.
90. Israel Kirzner, *Entrepreneurship, Entitlement, and Economic Justice*, in READING NOZICK, ed. Jeffrey Paul (Totowa, N.J.: Rowman & Littlefield, 1981), 383. Kirzner adumbrates a "creationist" justification for property rights that is similar to the one I have advanced. However, his theory has some unfortunate implications, namely, that a person A could come to own what person B already owns if A perceives a new use for that object. I have tried to avoid this destabilizing result. On the whole, though, Kirzner's position and my own are very close in that we both argue that human creativity imparts value to natural things that, but for this creativity, would be valueless for human use.

4

Conclusion: Resolving the Constitutional Muddle

Given the conspicuous lack of success of both the courts and the commentators in resolving the eminent domain-police power muddle, and the attendant confusion and, often, injustice suffered by hapless property owners, is it not time that a different approach to the problem be attempted? The hallowed notion of the "rule of law," not of men, that underpins our legal system lies in tatters, at least in this arena of the law; it cries out for resuscitation. When a property owner is assured of payment in the case when government takes a sliver of his property for a road widening, yet receives no compensation at all when told, via the exercise of the police power of the state or municipality, that he must forever keep his wetland in its pristine, underdeveloped state, something has gone drastically amiss.

Building upon the defense of property rights advanced in the previous chapter, we will now attempt a rather radical—radical in the sense of going to the root—investigation of the governmental powers of eminent domain and police. Our previous investigations, from chapter 2, demonstrated a remarkable lack of philosophical acuity among early defenders of these two powers. Jurists who did consider their origins took them simply to be inherent powers of sovereignty, alleging that government would be inconceivable without them. But is this assertion so indubitable that nothing beyond its mere utterance is required to assure our assent? Hardly. For, as a simple thought experiment if nothing more, one can easily conceive of a government, functional and powerful enough, bereft of the right to take property, and shorn of at least a goodly portion of the police power as currently conceived. Concededly, this government of our imagining would be far different from the Leviathan we know today. Particularly, such a state would have no power to confiscate your property whether it intends to use it for its own public works, or instead, to resell it to General Motors for a Cadillac plant; no power to zone away the value of your land, or alternatively, to hand you huge, undeserved, unearned windfalls; no power to tell you whether you can develop your land and how it can be developed, à

247

la the California Coastal Commission; and no power to promulgate usury laws, minimum wage legislation, maximum hour acts, or laws compelling plant owners to negotiate with labor unions. Shorn of these arguably tangential, excessive, and illegitimate functions, perhaps this state of our fantasy would have other appealing characteristics. What might these be? Well, if the state did not have to fritter away its energies telling people how to live *their* lives and how to dispose of *their* property, might it not be a more capable executioner of its principal duties? As Adam Smith well understood, protecting the society against foreign aggression, insuring the safety of individuals against the predation of their unsavory neighbors, and providing an expeditious and fair court system to settle personal disputes, punish criminals, and enforce contracts are quite enough to keep any government fully occupied.[1]

In our attempt to resolve the eminent domain-police power muddle and to salvage the rule of law, the following strategy will be employed: (1) we shall examine the state, its origins, nature, and proper functions, an examination that will build upon the defense of property rights presented in the last chapter; (2) upon this theoretical scaffolding we will proceed to scrutinize the police and eminent domain powers to determine which if any elements of these assertedly "inherent" powers of government are legitimate, and then we will see how a hypothetical, ideal government might operate if deprived of substantial elements of these powers; and finally (3) we will descend back into the cave and take a look at the real world, that is, the United States government, and see how our land use and takings policies might be revised with the objective of bringing them into greater conformity with the state as conceived in ideal theory.

The State: Its Derivation and Limits

How might one generate a government from our defense of property rights? By property rights, I of course intend to include rights of life and liberty, for my deduction, let us recall, did include arguments in defense of the free movement of individuals, and the sanctity of their bodies. Now, the traditional way of justifying a state, of which modern rights theorists have remained much enamored, is by the invention of a handy vehicle—the social contract. David Hume, the eighteenth-century Scottish philosopher, was one of the first critics in what would become a long line, to heap scorn upon this notion. He derided it as a mere fiction, and a potentially destabilizing one at that. Having placed individual consent on a pedestal, could it not someday descend to challenge the activities of any particular government, thereby eroding people's allegiance to their rulers? Governments were founded, Hume the hard-nosed realist admonished Locke and his brethren, rather by force from within, fraud, or conquest, and seldom if ever by a peacefully agreed upon contract. Despite those taunts, contract theory still has its staunch defenders. But now the contract is usually conceived of as a hypothetical not an actual one.

Another possible defense of government from a natural rights perspective—one that unlike Locke's does not depend upon a social contract—has been offered recently by Harvard University philosopher Robert Nozick. In his book *Anarchy, State, and Utopia,* Nozick argues against the natural rights anarchists; he contends that a minimal state could emerge from an anarcho-libertarian environment without violating anyone's rights.[2] Basically, he gives an historical account. He traces a possible path of evolution from an anarchistic market system in which personal protection is offered by free enterprise protection agencies (much beloved by anarcho-libertarians). Nozick envisions a consolidation process taking place by which one leading protection agency will emerge. It then compensates clients of other agencies whose risky procedures the dominant agency prohibits. Through this process the dominant agency would be transformed into a minimal state. And no one's rights have been violated in the process, Nozick contends. This historical, evolutionary, and also hypothetical account may avoid certain of the problems endemic to a Lockean social contractarian viewpoint. But maybe it is a work of enormous inventiveness for naught. Perhaps, instead, a simpler theory might be generated, one that like the Lockean and Nozickian theories attempts to answer the questions, When is the state legitimate? And when do its citizens act wrongly if they attempt to overthrow it? Before attempting to derive such a theory, let us pause for a moment. Beyond Hume's flippant rebuttals to Locke's contractarianism, can we discern any fundamental inconsistencies in a theory that grounds government on a natural rights foundation, but by way of a unanimous consent social contract?

What can we make, then, of a theory that combines both a theory of consent (whether actual, as in Locke, or hypothetical, as in Herbert Spencer,[3] the nineteenth-century liberal social thinker) and one of natural rights to determine the extent of government's legitimacy? Both Locke's and Spencer's arguments take the following form: (1) people have, by nature, the natural rights of life, liberty, and property, for the protection of which governments may be established; (2) a government may be legitimately established by the unanimous consent of its future citizens, and that government's authority has just such bounds as they choose to impose, with the proviso that people cannot (Locke) or will not (Spencer) consent to absolute, arbitrary rule; and (3) when government exceeds its legitimate function—i.e., protecting natural rights—then it acts as an aggressor and may be legitimately resisted by its citizens.

Is this account of governmental legitimacy internally consistent? The answer is clearly no. If people have natural rights, then the consent of individuals to government is purely extraneous to the question of legitimacy and contradictory to a natural rights position. It is contradictory to assert, I will argue, that a rights-protecting state needs some sanction other than its performance as a rights protector to render it legitimate.

What Locke and Spencer have done by arguing that consent, whether hypothetical or actual, is the legitimator of government, is to pose an alternative theory to natural rights. They have not realized this. If consent is the vehicle of legitimacy, then it is perfectly conceivable that individuals could voluntarily consent to a government that systematically violated natural rights. What individuals will choose is unpredictable. It is merely an act of faith on Locke's and Spencer's part to suppose that universal consent will yield the rights-protecting minimal state that they desire. Even the device of a hypothetical contract is a tenuous gambit, for it is quite evident that a Rawlsian[4] would derive a redistributive state from such a contract.

Thus, point (2), that government authority is derived from individual consent, and point (1), that governments are legitimate only when they uphold natural rights, are not compatible. To say that individuals by consent establish and set the limits to governmental action, and then to assert that there is some other ethical principle—natural rights—by which laws are to be judged, is to conflate two entirely different theories.

Finally, point (3) appears to direct citizens to break laws, with moral impunity, that are not consistent with natural rights. The effect of such an injunction might be that individuals may break laws unanimously agreed upon by the contractees (or by a majority), as long as they think their natural rights are being abrogated. Obviously, Spencer and Locke cannot have it both ways. Either natural rights provide the ethical sanction for government, or individual consent does. By attempting to combine the two theories, the contractarians have succeeded only in promulgating a theory that can lead to contradictory evaluations in specific cases: government X acts legitimately because it was established by universal consent, and government X acts illegitimately because its actions violate natural rights.

Locke and Spencer were able to contain these two elements in their theory because they believed that individuals would voluntarily and universally consent only to the non-rights-violating minimal state. But to make such an assumption is, quite simply, to engage in an act of faith. It is far more consistent to follow the position taken by James Buchanan and Gordon Tullock. They are willing to accept any government that emerges from an act of unanimous consent as legitimate even if it might establish a rights-violating state.[5] If such a concession is made, as a consistent contractarian would be compelled to admit, then it becomes apparent that one must either be a contractarian on the question of the origins of governmental legitimacy or a natural rights proponent.

We have discovered from the previous discussion that the attempt to combine natural rights and social contract theory fails. What I propose to accomplish in the ensuing argument is to demonstrate that a consistent theory of governmental legitimacy can be formulated on a natural rights moral underpinning alone, without recourse to any element of consent theory. My property rights defense of the previous chapter will lead, then, rather felicitously to a theory of governmental legitimacy.

The theory that I propose is an entirely ahistorical theory. It examines the constitutional framework, laws, acts of enforcement, and method of adjudication of a given government over a designated period. It asks only the following question: Is government X acting to preserve and protect the natural rights of its subjects? If the answer is unequivocally (very unlikely in the real world) or predominantly in the affirmative, then it is a legitimate government, Thus, its citizens would be acting in contravention of natural rights if they attempted to overthrow it. If the answer is unequivocally or predominantly in the negative, then it is illegitimate and may be overthrown with moral impunity and when the time seems opportune. I have refrained from using the conventional terminology—i.e., that when government X is legitimate, its citizens are obligated to obey it—because of the statist connotations of such phraseology. It is not that citizen A owes allegiance to legitimate state X, but that legitimate state X owes citizen A the protection of A's rights. The only thing citizen A must do is refrain from violating the rights of citizens B, C, D . . . etc. Citizen A owes the government nothing. Its function is simply, in Locke's formulation, to give a univocal and universal interpretation to the natural law, that is, the law that designates exactly which categories of entities and territory qualify as property, what constitutes a violation of an individual's right to life, and which actions of one person limit the liberty of another.

I shall designate this theory of governmental legitimacy the time-frame theory, the injunctions of which are the following:

1. Examine government X at time frame t_1-t_2, or t_2-t_3 . . . or t_{n-1}-t_n.
2. Determine whether the government's constitutional structure (written or tradition), body of laws, and method of enforcement and adjudication are consistent with and protective of the natural rights of the individuals who live under its jurisdiction.
3. If, on balance, the government is acting in a non-rights-violating manner (if it is not systematically violating rights by conscripting, taxing, depriving people of their property, or not protecting the lives or property of individuals, and furthermore, if violations of rights occur as

mere accidents, nonsystematically, and are justly compensated), then it is legitimate.

4. Such a government, which systematically violates no one's rights, and protects the rights of all subjects from force, fraud, and violence ought not to be acted against. Anyone who overthrows such a government would be acting in an immoral fashion, acting to endanger the sanctity and security of the natural rights of fellow citizens.

What this theory alleges, then, is that Nozickian theorizing along historical lines is extraneous to the determination of the legitimacy of any particular government. Under the time-frame theory, a government is legitimate only if it is a non-rights-violating government and guarantees the rights of its citizens from invasion by other individuals or states. In other words, it must be a minimal state, limited in its functions to internal and external defense, promulgating the natural law, and establishing a judicial system with a final arbiter of disputes. Hence, it makes no difference to the question of legitimacy how such a government came to power, whether by violence, conquest, fraud, tradition, election, laws of succession, or whatever.

What about the cases in which a government has come to power through such unsavory rights-violating acts as mass slaughter or the forcible expropriation of people's property? Would such a state be legitimate under the time-frame theory if it were now, in t_1-t_2, non-rights violating? The answer would be yes, it is legitimate. But what about the individuals who now occupy positions of power in this government and who were massive violators of the natural rights of individuals prior to their acquisition of power? The Nozickian entitlement theory—that is, a theory based on property rights that contends that only property acquired either by original acquisition, voluntary transfer, or rectification is legitimately possessed—would apply to them as individuals, not as current officials of a government. The charges would be that they attained the property of individuals A, B, C, D by illegitimate means (not by either first occupancy, purchase, transfer, bequest, or inheritance from the legitimate titleholder), and they deprived individuals E, F, G, H of their lives. The present minimal state would try and punish them as rights violators. If it failed to do so, it would lose its status as a legitimate state.

Can this theory successfully handle such extreme cases as the following examples? A government came to power through extensive rights violations, and now all property is in the hands of or under the direct control of a dictator, and yet it is a strictly non-rights-violating government in t_1-t_2. Would it be a legitimate government? Well, we might say it is illegitimate because the government goes beyond the minimal state in being an owner of property and an intervener in the economic realm, which ought to be strictly separate from government. But what about the case where the dictator as a private individual owned all the wealth in the country and everyone else was forced to do his bidding in order to remain alive? In this instance, the government is not exercising any illegitimate economic function and the dictator is not using the power of the state to coerce anyone because the government owns no property and simply defends the property rights of citizen dictator under the minimal state. The answer to the question of legitimacy would be precisely this: the government is legitimate because it upholds rights and is a minimal state. However, the dictator who gained his wealth by violating property rights before he acquired political power is a criminal under the property "entitlement theory." He holds no legitimate title to the property he forcibly confiscated. Thus, the original titleholders could bring their cases before the judiciary of the dictator's minimal state. If their claims were honored and their property restored, an unlikely occurrence, then the government would retain its legitimacy. If, as is far more likely, the dictator's judges dismissed the legitimate claims of the titleholders, then they would be acting in a rights-violating manner and the government would no longer be legitimate. In Locke's felicitous phrase, one could then legitimately make an "appeal to heaven."

The previous example helps clarify the way in which the time-frame theory handles the question of governmental legitimacy: the theory applies to already existing governments, it is oriented toward the present, and it is an ahistorical principle. Thus, it stands in contrast to a theory of justice with respect to property claims that is oriented toward the past and is historical.

What course can the individual pursue against a government that is a gross violator of rights under the time-frame theory? If a government is a massive transgressor against individual rights, then obviously there is no immorality involved in acts that violate laws that are themselves rights-violating. And, in more extreme cases of gross and systematic incursions by government on individual rights, revolutionary measures would be justified, i.e., a revolution that would seek to establish a minimal state. Whether one obeys the edicts of such an "outlaw" government is simply a prudential, not a moral, question to be decided on pragmatic grounds: Will my resistance be successful; am I sacrificing myself and my own self-interest without even a remote chance of securing the minimal state; is my chance of successful resistance worth to me the likely penalty if I fail; is the time ripe; is it likely that the present government will be replaced by one even worse than the present one, rather than the minimal state I seek? And so on.

Is this theory unduly destabilizing and destructive of existing governments, as David Hume and Jeremy Bentham feared from all a priori, natural rights theories? The answer is yes and no. Yes, in theory it undercuts any supposed "moral obligation" to obey the edicts of many existing governments, and some of the rights-violating laws of even the best governments. But probably no, on prudential grounds. In all but the most grievous cases of governmental oppression, people will bear quite a lot from government without resorting to arms, as Locke foresaw.[6] And as the proliferation and apparent permanence of contemporary totalitarian states indicate, where rights transgressions are the most egregious and systematic, the opportunities for—and indeed the inclination toward—resistance are the most restricted. Rather than being destructive of all governments, the time-frame theory provides a much needed antidote to the twentieth-century fascination with the overweening, rights-violating bureaucratic state.

This minimal state we have just constructed would be scrupulously limited in its functions, limited to the protection of individuals against force and fraud perpetrated by their fellow citizens, the preservation of the society against external aggressors, and the provision of a fair and expeditious court system. Protecting individual rights—the triad of life, liberty, and property rights—constitutes the rationale for men suffering the existence of such an odd bird as a state. If it exceeds its proper bounds, it becomes itself an aggressor, and indeed a self-interested partisan. It is very difficult to see why it would be in the interest of any prudent person to tolerate such a headstrong, powerful enemy.

This discussion has not been a mere digression. Indeed, how can one assess the validity of the powers of police and eminent domain unless one has first answered these deeper theoretical questions?

Eminent Domain and Police Power: Ideal World

Eminent Domain

The position taken on the proper functions of government in the previous section is harmonious with views expressed by our earliest jurists and, thus, should not be viewed as quite such a radical departure from our American heritage. It does, however, go a bit further than most of them would have gone. But, as Justice Story's refrain in *Wilkinson v. Leland* (1829) indicates, judges at the inception of our nation realized the importance of property rights in a free society.

> That government can scarcely be deemed to be free, where the rights of property are left solely dependent upon the will of a legislative body, without any restraint. The fundamental maxims of a free government seem to require, that the rights of personal liberty and private property should be sacred. At least, no court of justice in the country would be justified in assum-

ing that the power to violate and disregard them—a power so repugnant to the common principles of justice and civil liberty—lurked under any general grant of legislative authority, or ought to be implied from any general expressions of the will of the people. The people ought not to be presumed to part with rights so vital to their security and well-being without very strong and direct expressions of such an intention.[7]

From the defense of private property previously developed and the theory of the legitimate functions of the state derived from that defense, we can now reach some conclusions about the supposedly inherent state powers of eminent domain and police. The power of eminent domain, the power of the state to seize property against the will of its rightful owner, whether accompanied by the payment of compensation or not is wholly unjustifiable. It is only upon utilitarian or pragmatic grounds, and not upon a property rights system as defended here, that eminent domain could conceivably be justified. But, and this is terribly important, pragmatic considerations of efficiency and the like cannot touch fundamental rights. That is, the right to property stands on higher moral ground than considerations of efficiency. An innocent person's life ought not be sacrificed by government even if by taking that life other more numerous deaths could be prevented—let us say, we hang an innocent person for a heinous crime as an example to deter potential criminals.[8] Similarly, property ought not be confiscated from an owner even if that seizure will accommodate a new state office building, a more convenient post office, or a noncircuitous highway. Indeed, by making this juxtaposition it should become apparent that if the case of the innocent person tells so decisively against efficiency considerations, the case is even stronger against property seizures. How can preventing crooked highways ever rise to such moral significance as to override anyone's fundamental right to property?

If Alpha II has no right to seize Beta's II's property in a state of nature, then government has no such right. Governments are merely the guarantors of preexisting rights. No pragmatic considerations could ever justify a government in violating someone's property rights, short of the extreme exigencies of war when government in protecting persons and property may have to march its armies through someone's land. Then, certainly, compensation must be paid to those bearing more than their fair share of the burdens of war. I can discern no theoretical justification for the power of eminent domain in peacetime. If government must construct military barracks, courts, and a few office buildings to carry out its limited functions, then it should purchase the land necessary for these installations on the open market just like any other private buyer.[9] Anything else would violate individuals' rights to private property.

A few words may be in order concerning crooked roads and other inefficiencies that might result from a prohibition on governmental seizures. For one thing, past excesses such as grants of eminent domain powers to private corporations—e.g. the railroads—have a nasty habit of coming back to haunt us. Congress in the early 1980s was confronted with a thorny dilemma as a direct result of its past largess to the railroads. Plans for the construction of coal slurry pipelines which entrepreneurs were perfectly willing to finance, and which would have provided lower-cost fuel to the eastern states and an outlet for exporting surplus coal production, ran afoul of the railroads. Unwilling to face the competition from a new, and probably cheaper, form of transport, the railroads simply refused to permit the pipelines to cross their rights-of-way. In an attempt to circumvent the recalcitrant railroads, the pipeline companies repaired to Congress, arguing that they should be granted powers of eminent domain, the same powers exercised to such great profit by the railroads in the last century.

Now, in a government strictly limited, as our ideal type government certainly is, this thorny congressional dilemma ought never to arise. In the first place, such a government would never have had the power of eminent domain, and hence could not have delegated it to, of all things, a private corporation. The railroads, then, would have had to buy land from willing sellers, and perhaps their tracks would be slightly more circuitous today. Likewise, the prospective slurry pipeline companies of today would have to pursue their ambitions on the real estate market. This hands-off policy by government has some attractive features: (1) members of Congress would no longer be in the business of trading off efficiency with justice (in the form of property rights); (2) past congressional decisions that, no doubt, seemed efficient and sensible at the time would no longer return to haunt future Congresses; (3) private businesses would not be able to avail themselves of a favorite line of argument: "You granted the No-Good-Nick Company a special privilege years ago, now give us the same." As to how this coal slurry pipeline-railroad contest ought to be resolved in our messy real world, more of that in good time.

Those enamored of efficiency arguments may yet remain unconvinced. Even some natural rights devotees might look askance upon the denial of eminent domain power to governments if it would wreak havoc upon society. Let us consider, then, the truly tough case, that in which government must amass contiguous parcels of property in order to construct some necessary public building. To accomplish this purpose, lots must be acquired that are currently in the hands of many different owners. In a study published in 1976 in the *Journal of Political Economy*, economist Patricia Munch attempted to resolve precisely this tough case.[10] She probed the heretofore unexamined assumption, made by proponents of eminent domain in the economic literature, that the use of eminent domain provides a comparative advantage over the free market in assembling contiguous parcels of land held by different owners. In other words, she assessed the assumption that governmental use of eminent domain is a more efficient tool than the market for amassing large parcels because it minimizes costs. She compared prices paid for land acquired for three large projects by the Chicago Department of Urban Renewal with prices paid for comparable parcels of land sold on the free market. Munch concluded that the advantage alleged for eminent domain could not be demonstrated. Rather, she discovered proof for an alternative hypothesis about how eminent domain proceedings operate on the purchase prices of land: "low-valued properties receive less than market value and high-valued properties receive more than market value."[11] Munch concluded:

> This study of urban renewal in Chicago suggests that ED [eminent domain] does not ensure that fair market value is paid in an assembly. . . .

> The full-cost calculus of the relative efficiency of ED and the free market in handling assemblies cannot be made without data on comparable market assemblies and on transaction costs, including labor inputs and foregone income on land due to delay in transferring it to a higher-valued use. *Both components of transaction costs are likely to be higher under ED. Thus, both theoretical considerations and the evidence available leave unproved the case for the superior efficiency of ED.* [Emphasis added.][12]

What the Munch study suggests is that the efficiency arguments in favor of eminent domain are dubious. Therefore, if moral considerations so strongly indicate that eminent domain is an impermissible power of government, and efficiency arguments in its favor are less than convincing, is it not sensible that the moral position should win out?

Police Power

What about the other presumed power of the state, the police power? If it were strictly a *police* power—one that operated to prevent crimes and punish criminals—it would be noncontroversial, falling squarely within government's proper domain. But as a hugely expansible excuse for a host of governmental interventions its legitimacy is highly suspect. As that power has been expanded in this century to allow economic regulation for the open-ended "general welfare," it clearly oversteps its proper bounds. Likewise, regulations aiming at protecting the "public morals" exceed government's proper functions. The enforcement of morals forms no part of government's legitimate purpose unless, of course, it is strictly limited to the prevention of criminal acts against nonconsenting persons (such as rape). When it is used to shut down adult bookstores and X-rated theaters, and to isolate red light districts it overreaches.

The police power has been stretched leagues beyond its legitimate boundaries. It is used to justify such governmental tampering with the market as minimum wage and maximum hour laws, workers' compensation acts, zoning, usury laws, and so on. The two other traditional justifications of the police power are "public health" and "public safety." Here, in an ideal system, government might play a very narrow role. For instance, it would be unexceptionable if local government were to pass an ordinance prohibiting the manufacture of bombs in the basement of residences or outlawing the storage of dynamite in the attics of nursing homes. Such brazen behavior obviously endangers lives. Just as in the criminal law there are the law of attempts and the law of conspiracy,[13] which allow government to act to prevent a crime before it has been committed, so it seems reasonable to permit government to act to proscribe behavior that endangers lives by its reckless disregard for the physical well-being of others. Quarantine laws, on the same theory, are just barely acceptable. In general, then, property owners should be left to pursue private remedies for the protection of their property in the courts: in nuisance law for recovery of damages, and via declaratory relief. Only to a very limited extent should government engage in police power regulations when the danger is both proximate and potentially life threatening.

But what about a case such as *Hadacheck v. Sebastian*, which we discussed in chapter 2? Should the state, under the guise of this restricted police power, get involved in banning brickyards from residential areas, that is, in mediating a dispute about apparently incompatible property uses? This is clearly a dispute between individual property owners that should be settled under the tort law and not by legislatures. Nuisance law, ideally, should give fair warning to property owners, by establishing unambiguous rules in early cases, that potentially annoying uses of property should be buffered in some way: by protective barriers, or the purchase of excess land. Laws should be passed protecting other property owners only from genuinely dangerous activities.

To those appalled by such radicalism, let us explore some free market remedies that would most likely replace the regulatory framework our states now enforce. Building codes and fire codes could presumably be replaced quite easily by privately enforced codes drafted by insurance companies. Few developers would construct hazardous firetraps if they knew beforehand that they could not acquire insurance for their buildings.

But what about that most sacred of all land-use cows, *Euclid*ian zoning? Are we to suffer in silence the egregious outrage of a slaughterhouse locating next door to our suburban retreat in Shaker Heights, Beverly Hills, or

Boca Raton? Surely a theory must be defective if it carries with it such distasteful consequences! Before we chuck theory to the winds, let us repair to a study concluded in the early 1970s by law professor Bernard Siegan, then a practicing attorney in the field of real estate law. His investigative piece, "Non-Zoning in Houston," sought to explore some of the presumptions usually made by zoning's defenders.[14] He set out to compare land-use patterns in Houston, the only U.S. city with a population in excess of a quarter of a million that does not practice zoning, with those exhibited by a traditional, *Euclid*ian zoned city, specifically, Chicago. In short, he discovered that the nightmarish images conjured up by supporters of zoning—of chemical plants encroaching on residential neighborhoods, of incompatible uses contending for the soul of a neighborhood, of residential property values depreciated by the appearance of gas stations or apartments in their midst—proved largely apocryphal. Rather, Siegan concluded:

> Economic forces tend to make for a separation of uses even without zoning. Business uses will tend to locate in certain areas, residential in others, and industrial in still others. Apartments, however, may be built in almost any area except within an industrial one. There is also a tendency for further separation within a category; light industrial uses do not want to adjoin heavy industrial uses, and vice versa. Different kinds of business uses require different locations. Expensive homes will separate from less expensive ones, townhouses, duplexes, etc. . . . [15]

In instances in which the market alone did not secure separation of incompatible uses, property owners seeking to maximize their returns pursued another legal course—they entered into restrictive covenants. Such devices, which run with the land either for a limited period (typically twenty-five years) or indefinitely, limit the uses to which purchasers of property can put their land. While restrictive covenants still bear a stigma from their use in the past as mechanisms for preserving the racial homogeneity of white neighborhoods, their feasibility as a land use device was demonstrated in Houston. Enforceable in the courts, and adaptable to changing circumstances—if they are not enforced by owner plaintiffs they simply lapse over a period of years—they offer a free market alternative to citywide zoning.

As for the claim of zoning adherents that residential property values would decline in the absence of regulations, Siegan could discern no difference in the appreciation of homes in Houston versus those in zoned cities, based on FHA figures. Additionally, zoned cities incur costs, both in money and in political corruption, that combine to make zoning even less attractive. Changes tend to be made more in response to the pressure exerted by special interest groups, and less in conformity to the recommendations of professional planners. Zoning itself is a costly activity, draining limited governmental resources. Also, zoning impedes innovation and restricts the supply of land for some kinds of uses. Other critics of zoning have pointed to the influence peddling, favortism, and nepotism that is bred into the zoning process. Siegan, in closing, found it curious that despite the strength of the arguments of zoning's critics, its advocates have not been moved to study the Houston alternative. "Instead, they advocate additional government controls over the use and development of property. The dogma persists that if zoning does not work, it is desirable to try more of it. Given the history of zoning, the new efforts will lead in their turn to even more controls."[16]

What Siegan's study suggests, minimally, is that zoning's usefulness has been greatly exaggerated. For those homeowners unfortunate enough to wake up one morning and discover a noisome brewery adjoining their backyard, one of two responses would be forthcoming from advocates of my ideal government: (1) It is just too darn bad that the homeowner was not foresightful enough to purchase a home in a development suitably protected by restrictive covenants; or (2) recourse lies in nuisance law, for no one has a right to use owned property in such a way as to adversely affect other people's enjoyment of theirs, *sic utere tuo ut alienum non laedas.*

It should go almost without saying, that for our minimal government of ideal theory, if *Euclid*ian local zoning is impermissible, so is regional, statewide, or national land-use legislation. Is it not rather refreshing, then, that Siegan's work strongly suggests that what is erroneous in theory is also unnecessary in practice?

Ideal Theory: Summation

This ideal government stands opposed to powers heretofore considered by most commentators as inherent attributes of government. Far from being inconceivable without eminent domain, government is quite imaginable shorn of its power to confiscate property. Indeed, as we have seen, at least one reputable scholar has argued that even the pragmatic rationale for eminent domain appears suspect.

The police power, too, seems a lot less sacrosanct. Government does have a legitimate role to play in protecting the public health and safety, narrowly conceived, yet it has no business meddling with "morality" or the "general welfare." Thus, zoning ought to be abandoned. Free market devices—such as restrictive covenants, nuisance law, private professional codes for building and fire standards—could more justly and expeditiously replace the heavy hand of government regulation.

Eminent Domain and Police Power: Real World

Eminent Domain

The Fifth Amendment to the federal Constitution (and virtually all state constitutions) in a backhanded sort of way acquiesced to the government's power of eminent domain. The Fifth Amendment does place stipulations upon its exercise—that "just compensation" be paid to dispossessed owners, and that the "taking" be for a "public use." Both of these limitations need to be refurbished. The "public-use" stricture should be resuscitated, and *Berman v. Parker* and *Hawaii v. Midkiff*,[17] which so eviscerated "public use," must be repudiated. Instead of paying deference to legislative judgments in the determination of public use, courts should independently evaluate the necessity for the taking. They should consider whether the taking was the least onerous course possible for effecting the public improvement, and whether the planned use was indeed a public one or a private one under the mere pretense of a public use. Takings for urban renewal, as in *Berman v. Parker*, should fail these tests, and fail miserably. What I am suggesting is that the question of public use be made ultimately a judicial question, as it is currently, but with no deference to legislative judgments and no presumption in favor of the constitutionality of a challenged taking.[18] Then the burden would be on the government to prove that taking the Oakland Raiders, Poletown, or rental land in Hawaii is a public use. It would be a difficult burden to carry.

"Just compensation" should undergo a further expansion to include recompense for a whole range of losses now usually disallowed, including payment of legal fees, assessment costs, loss of business goodwill, and the like. The fact should be squarely faced by legislatures, and if not legislatures, then by courts, that the analogy between takings and a private sale is false. Therefore owners should not be forced to bear the ancillary costs attendant upon a forced sale, as they would a voluntary sale. Also, courts ought to be more hospitable to recovery for consequential damages. They should allow relief for a wider range of tangential damages, and display a high degree of skepticism toward such government excuses for denying recovery as the navigable servitude and public trust doctrines.

One more qualification should be placed on eminent domain, either by state constitutional changes, legislative renunciation, or judicial denial. The delegation of eminent domain to private corporations and public utilities should be eliminated. In these instances of delegation to private companies the frequently expressed judicial disdain for taking property from A to give to B seems grievously transgressed. *In sum, eminent domain should be but sparingly used by all agencies of government. Legislatures and municipalities should restrain their appetites. If they do not, courts should rein them in or constitutions should be altered to mandate such limitations.*

Now, how should the slurry pipeline-railroad controversy be dealt with in the real world? Given that the railroads profited from grants of eminent domain powers in the past, and given the efficiency arguments in favor of the slurry pipelines, one might conclude that an exception to our foregoing argument ought to be made in favor of the pipeline companies. But would this not simply perpetuate bad precedent, and necessitate a potentially long string of exceptions in the future? Let us suppose that fifty years from now a novel technology comes along and the slurry pipeline owners attempt to thwart its construction in much the same way that the railroads are acting to curtail pipeline competition today. Should these innovative companies, then, be granted a right to take property? A preferred solution—one that will terminate this type of excess once and for all—is to simply deny the pleas of the pipeline companies. No solution is perfect, particularly when the history of the problem is clouded by past mistakes such as the original privileges and largess afforded to the railroads. The nasty situation confronting us now, with its choice of unsatisfying solutions, provides one of the best illustrations of the point that private corporations should never be granted extraordinary perquisites by government. Such Congressional acts of favoritism have a propensity to come back years later to haunt us.

Police Power

As for the ever more enveloping police power, it must be checked. Economic regulation and land-use restrictions ought, once again, to receive vigorous judicial scrutiny. Here I can do no better than to applaud the efforts of Professor Bernard Siegan in his revisionist work *Economic Liberties and the Constitution*.[19] Rather than reviling the "Old," *Lochner* Court's substantive due process heritage, as the legal tradition has for the last half-century, he seeks to revive it. According to Siegan, all police power regulations should receive judicial scrutiny under a strict standard. Such a standard would embody both a means-end test (that the means be appropriate ones to achieve a constitutionally permissible end) and a rule of least restrictiveness (that the means chosen be the least restrictive of individual and property rights). Our immediate interest here is less ambitious than Siegan's. We are concerned only with a portion of the police power, namely, the portion that impinges upon real property. In our real world, how can we more effectively limit police power excesses?

I am not overly optimistic about the likelihood of state or federal legislative bodies voluntarily restraining their regulatory passions. One does not have to be a diehard cynic, or a public choice theorist, to recognize that legislators will expand their empires if they think such actions will go unchecked. Burdensome regulations, which cripple private initiative while violating people's rights, serve to enhance the status of legislators and regulatory agencies. If formerly Jones could build an outhouse in his backyard without asking leave of any other person, and now he must plead for building permits from the Sepulveda Planning Commission, and regional and state Coastal Commissions, then the members of those bodies have POWER. It is an observable human characteristic that people, at least some people, delight in exercising power over the lives of others. One would be naive to suppose that individuals once possessed of such power would very often willingly surrender it unless forced to by some countervailing force. Such a counterforce might be exercised by an enraged citizenry, rebelling against the crushing burden of regulation. In fact, such an upsurge has been apparent in recent years, as businesspeople and workers alike sustained losses—of profit and employment—due to the regulatory Leviathan. Yet, this upsurge needs an internal governmental representative in order to have any expectation of fostering any but cosmetic changes from legislators. The most likely candidate for a countervailing internal force for the protection of property rights is the courts. This may seem like the slenderest of threads but the minds of judges can be persuaded by rational arguments, and if not these present judges, then we can hope for more felicitous appointments in the future. If judges remain fixed in their ways, then perhaps some constitutional revisions might be in order.

To begin, first, with the remedy of constitutional change. It is not inconceivable that state constitutions could be modified to discourage "over-legislation"[20] by government. A mandate that regulations that significantly deflate property values must be accompanied by payment of compensation would go a long way toward remedying the problem. Much as in the 1870s when state after state modified their takings provisions to allow compensation when property was "taken or damaged" rather than just "taken," a further extension of protection for property owners is now vitally necessary. The earlier movement occurred because an increasing number of property owners felt victimized when public improvements caused damage to their property and courts denied recovery because they termed such damages merely consequential and, therefore, *damnum absque injuria.* Today a similar accumulation of aggrieved property owners is arising as more and more disillusioned souls fall victim to such regulatory excesses as the California Coastal Act, no-growth policies, and open-space designations.

A movement of sufficient numbers to effect change on the federal level does not exist at this moment, but if enough states signaled a change in attitude, the federal courts would likely accomplish the same purpose through judicial construction. This is, in fact, what occurred in the 1870s when the Supreme Court allowed for recovery of certain damages formerly considered merely consequential.

After the adoption by half the states of "or damaged" clauses, the situation in regard to consequential damages improved considerably. If states modified their takings clauses once again to read something like this, *nor shall private property be taken, damaged, or appreciably diminished in value, without payment of full compensation for losses sustained*, several beneficial effects should result. Principal among these would be the reluctance of governments to engage in adventuresome regulatory schemes. They would have to compensate fully all owners sustaining direct and appreciable damages. Thus, less regulation would occur, and when it did, it would be better-assessed regulation. Cost-benefit analysis would become imperative as legislatures were forced to face the consequences of their actions. While from a rights perspective this solution is far from ideal, at least it would turn things around and point goverment in the right direction. Zoning, for example, would become egregiously expensive and should suffer a much-deserved demise. Additionally, plaintiffs would be able to avail themselves of inverse condemnation as a way to challenge regulatory excesses. This remedy would allow them to receive compensation for injuries of a monetary nature suffered as a result of land-use regulations.

Failing such constitutional changes, or in conjunction with them, the courts could embrace several doctrinal innovations that would help rein in regulatory excesses of the police power variety. Lamentably, it seems rather unlikely that the courts would adopt the view of that power expressed in our ideal model, i.e., that it should be strictly confined to pressing instances of protecting the public health and safety. As an alternative, then, for delimiting the police power, it might be advisable for courts to reexamine their rule that the burden of proof must fall upon plaintiffs to prove beyond reasonable doubt that a challenged act is unconstitutional. This burden, logically, ought to reside with the state once the plaintiff has presented a *prima facie* case. The presumption of validity adhering to police power measures, too, ought to be seriously reevaluated. Just as is now the rule in cases challenging laws on "equal protection," or "due process grounds," when states trench upon "fundamental rights," states should have to demonstrate that a compelling state interest overrides individuals' economic liberties. As Jeremy Bentham pointed out, all legislation is an infringement on liberty.[21] Therefore, a logical conclusion from this observation is that all legislation should bear a heavy burden of proving its constitutionality when questioned by plaintiffs who allege that it unnecessarily burdens their protected rights, whether civil or property. Courts, even in the bygone era of substantive due process have paid entirely too much deference to legislative judgments in regard to the necessity for police power regulations.

Other students of the police power have independently reached similar conclusions,[22] but even more remarkably the President's Commission on Housing in its final report called for revisions in the zoning law that relied, in part, on the same strategy. The commission was established by the Reagan administration to study the accelerating housing crisis. Decent, affordable housing has in the 1970s and 1980s eluded an ever-growing portion of the middle class. One of the most refreshing conclusions of the commission's report was its recommendation that zoning be curtailed if not eliminated throughout the country. The commission endorsed a three-pronged strategy:[23]

1. It called upon state and local legislatures to enact legislation providing that no zoning regulations denying or limiting the development of housing should be considered valid unless they were necessary to achieve a *vital and pressing governmental interest.*
2. In litigation, also, the legislatures should shift the judicial burden of proof, so that the governmental body seeking to maintain or impose the zoning regulation would bear the burden of proving its compliance with a "vital-and-pressing-governmental-interest" standard.
3. On the federal level (and as an alternative to the legislative route to change), the commission called upon the president to instruct the attorney general to evaluate this proposed "vital-and-pressing-governmental-interest" standard for judicially determining the validity of zoning regulations. The attorney general, if convinced of its viability, should seek an appropriate test case for challenging the present *Euclid* standard. The commission, in addition, requested that the attorney general evaluate the monetary remedy for wrongful zoning endorsed by Justice Brennan in his influential dissent in *San Diego Gas and Electric Co.*

This study represents a remarkable shift in public attitude. Only ten years ago President Nixon appointed a task force chaired by Laurance Rockefeller that endorsed a plan for national land-use legislation.[24] President Reagan's commission took a diametrically opposite approach. It called for "a program of land-use deregulation" and denounced the exclusionary and inflationary impact of land-use restrictions.

With the adoption of any one or more of these strategies—constitutional change, legislative curtailments, or judicial adoption of a shifted burden of proof—the takings issue should dissolve of its own weight. With the police power reined in by the compensation requirement (either by constitutional amendment or judicial remedy), the presumption of validity removed from legislative enactments, and a shift of the burden of proof, police power excesses would be too costly and embarassing to legislatures. Uncompensated takings of the flagrant type represented by Sea Ranch or the wetlands cases should be eliminated under these new rules.

Real World: Summation

Police power and eminent domain should be recognized for the distinct powers they truly are. They are not, as under the Holmesian standard they appeared to be, two poles of a continuum. In our real world, we ought to limit eminent domain to a narrow range of strictly public uses: highways, post offices, government buildings, courthouses, and the like. And the police power ought to be confined to essential regulations to protect the public health and safety. If it is used more expansively, injured owners should receive compensation. The two powers must be kept theoretically distinct. Confusing decisions of the *Berman v. Parker* variety should be avoided.

While it is somewhat suspect to endorse heightened levels of judicial activism, an important distinction needs to be made. In recent times we have seen activist judges in effect usurp legislative or executive functions by themselves managing schools, mental hospitals, and prisons. The arguments against these actions are well known. However, one arena in which the courts ought to exercise a high level of involvement has been virtually neglected for the last half-century. Activism in the name of protecting property rights is a perfectly legitimate, and indeed vital court function. Who, if not the courts, can stand as the final bulwark against government's propensity to seek the public good at the expense of trenching upon property rights? Courts should view themselves less as the partner of coequal branches of government, and more as the guardian of individual rights, property rights as well as civil rights. The courts have done a fine job in protecting the latter but not the former. Only then will property owners— that is, most of us—rest easy that they will not soon be numbered among the Justs, the Sea Ranch lot owners, the Tellico Valley farmers, or the Poletown homeowners. Of what use is a court system that refuses to enforce the plain intent of the Constitution to prevent such injustices?

Notes

1. Admittedly, Adam Smith did envisage and defend a fourth function of government, that of providing essential public works, works that would be socially useful yet not remunerative enough to entice a private entrepreneur to provide. This attribute of government I do not care to defend. But it should be said in

defense of Smith that most of what he envisioned under this rubric were such fairly innocuous services as streets, canals, harbors, fortifications for the protection of commerce and trade, embassies. Others were not nearly so benign, e.g., state provision of education, and maintenance of the church. Embassies aside, it is not clear why Smith's system of natural liberty breaks down in these instances. Smith failed to see precisely how strong his own argument for invisible-hand solutions is. If consumers desire such services, why will the market not provide them, given the ingenuity of individuals desirous only of their own advantage? And if the market does not provide certain of these services, is it not because consumers are not willing to pay for them at their cost? And then, why should government intervene to tell consumers that they must pay for these "public goods"—via compulsory taxation—and thereby sacrifice other goods that they value more highly? For Smith's position on public goods and the legitimate functions of government, see AN INQUIRY INTO THE NATURE AND CAUSES OF THE WEALTH OF NATIONS, ed. R. H. Campbell and A. S. Skinner, The Glasgow Edition of the Works and Correspondence of Adam Smith (Oxford: Clarendon Press, 1976), (bk. IV. ix. 50-51), 687.

2. Robert Nozick, ANARCHY, STATE, AND UTOPIA (New York: Basic Books, 1974), Part I. Anarcho-libertarianism is an extreme variant of the libertarian position. It accords such great autonomy to individuals that it can see no legitimate role for the state at all. Libertarians who are not anarchists do concede some functions to the state. These functions, however, are so limited that a libertarian government is usually referred to as a "minimal state." Such a state provides only police, national defense, and judicial services. Within libertarian circles there has been a continuing debate between the minimal staters and the anarchists, with Robert Nozick defending the former and Murray Rothbard the latter. Others of less prominence have also actively participated in the debate.

3. See Herbert Spencer, *The Great Political Superstition*, THE MAN VERSUS THE STATE (Caldwell, Idaho: Caxton Printers, 1940).

4. John Rawls, A THEORY OF JUSTICE (Cambridge: Harvard University Press, 1971). Rawls argued that if one imagines a situation in which individuals are placed behind a "veil of ignorance," and they do not know anything about themselves that would serve to differentiate them from any other person, then they would choose a quasi-egalitarian system of justice. Justice, on Rawls' account, would consist of (1) all persons enjoying a like amount of civil liberties, and (2) economic benefits being distributed equally unless an unequal distribution would benefit the least-well-off people in the society.

5. James Buchanan and Gordon Tullock, THE CALCULUS OF CONSENT (Ann Arbor: University of Michigan Press, 1962). At least, this position has the virtue of consistency, and is not caught in the Lockean-Spencerian bind.

6. John Locke, TWO TREATISES OF GOVERNMENT, ed. Peter Laslett (New York: New American Library, 1960) II, ch. XIX.

7. 2 Pet. 627 (U.S. 1829). See also *Vanhorne's Lessee v. Dorrance*, 2 U.S. 304, 310 (1795) (Justice Patterson):

> From these passages it is evident, that the right of acquiring and possessing property and having it protected, is one of the natural, inherent, and inalienable rights of man. Men have a sense of property, property is necessary to their subsistence, and correspondent to their natural wants and desires; its security was one of the objects that induced men to unite in society. No man could become a member of a community, in which he could not enjoy the

fruits of his honest labor and industry. The preservation of property, then, is a primary object of the social compact. . . .

8. This is a familiar counterexample to utilitarianism, illustrating that on the principle of maximizing collective happiness society might commit rather heinous outrages against individuals.

9. Economists no doubt would be troubled by efficiency concerns attending this solution. They would worry about holdouts demanding exorbitant sums for their property, transaction costs, and so on. I would argue that these problems are no different for government than for any large developer. Either government pays the price, negotiates downward, or abandons the project and tries again somewhere else.

10. Patricia Munch, *An Economic Analysis of Eminent Domain*, 84 JOURNAL OF POLITICAL ECONOMY 473 (1976).

11. *Id.* at 488.

12. *Id.* at 495.

13. This analogy is meant to be more suggestive than exact, for the law of attempts requires some act, although ultimately unsuccessful, indicating the intention on the part of the perpetrator to commit the crime. All I intend to indicate is that some prospective prohibitions may be warranted.

14. Bernard Siegan, *Non-zoning in Houston*, 13 JOURNAL OF LAW & ECO-NOMICS 71 (1970); and LAND USE WITHOUT ZONING (Lexington, Mass.: Lexington Books, 1972), ch. 2.

15. Siegan, *Non-zoning in Houston* at 142.

16. *Id.* at 143.

17. 348 U.S. 26 (1954); 52 LW 4673 (1984).

18. This is not so outlandish, and although it deviates from the acceptable practice in federal and most state jurisdictions, five states embody such a procedure in their constitutions: Arizona (Article II, Section 17); Colorado (Art. II, Sec. 15); Mississippi (Art. III, Section 17); Missouri (Art. I, Sec. 28); Washington (Art. I, Sec. 16). See Philip Nichols, THE LAW OF EMINENT DOMAIN, 3d ed. by Julius L. Sackman (New York: Matthew Bender, 1980) at Sec. 7.4.

19. Bernard Siegan, ECONOMIC LIBERTIES AND THE CONSTITUTION (Chicago: University of Chicago Press, 1980).

20. The term is a particularly apt one, borrowed from Herbert Spencer, *Over-Legislation*, THE MAN VERSUS THE STATE.

21. Jeremy Bentham, THEORY OF LEGISLATION (London: Kegan Paul, 1904), ch. 3; and ANARCHIAL FALLACIES, in THE WORKS OF JEREMY BENTHAM (Edinburgh: William Tait, 1839), Part 8. This is not strictly true, but true enough for our purposes. If one distinguishes between liberty and license, as Locke does but Bentham does not, such legislative acts as the criminal law do not infringe liberty.

22. Roger Pilon, *Property Rights and a Free Society*, in RESOLVING THE HOUS-ING CRISIS, ed. M. Bruce Johnson (San Francisco: Pacific Institute for Public Policy Research; Cambridge, Mass.: Ballinger, 1982).

23. THE REPORT OF THE PRESIDENT'S COMMISSION ON HOUSING. April 29, 1982, William F. McKenna, 200-201. The sagacity of the recommendations on regulatory policy are due in large part to one of the commission's members who served as the chairman of the Regulations Committee, Professor Bernard Siegan. The commission also called for a single permit-granting procedure to eliminate costly and time-consuming waste, thus, striking a blow at

California-type systems (p. 208). The report notes that the supreme courts of both Pennsylvania and New Jersey have shifted the presumption of validity and the burden of proof from the property owner to the municipality in cases pertaining to exclusionary zoning (p. 200).

24. William K. Reily, ed., THE USE OF LAND: A CITIZEN'S POLICY GUIDE TO URBAN GROWTH, A Task Force Report Sponsored by The Rockefeller Brothers Fund (New York: Thomas Y. Crowell, 1973). Citizens' Advisory Committee on Environmental Quality; established by presidential order.

Index of Legal Cases

General Index